FOR REFERENCE

Do Not Take From This Room

Arab Filmmakers
of the
Middle East

Arab Filmmakers of the Middle East

A Dictionary

ROY ARMES

Indiana University Press • *Bloomington and Indianapolis*

This book is a publication of

Indiana University Press
601 North Morton Street
Bloomington, Indiana 47404-3797 USA

www.iupress.indiana.edu

Telephone orders   800-842-6796
Fax orders   812-855-7931
Orders by e-mail   iuporder@indiana.edu

MANUFACTURED IN THE
UNITED STATES OF AMERICA

Library of Congress Cataloging-
in-Publication Data

Armes, Roy.
  Arab filmmakers of the Middle East :
a dictionary / Roy Armes.
    p. cm.
  English and French.
  Includes bibliographical references and indexes.
  ISBN 978-0-253-35518-8 (cloth : alk. paper)
1. Motion picture producers and directors—
Arab countries—Biography—Dictionaries.
2. Motion picture producers and directors—
Arab countries—Credits. 3. Motion picture
industry—Arab countries. I. Title.
  PN1993.5.A65A76 2010
  791.4302'320923927—dc22
  [B]
                                    2010007348

 1   2   3   4   5   15   14   13   12   11   10

FOR ANNIE

But we suffer from an incurable disease called hope. Hope for liberation and independence. Hope for a normal life where we shall be neither heroes nor victims. Hope to see our children go to school without danger. Hope for a pregnant woman to give birth to a living baby, in a hospital, and not to a dead child in front of a military control post. Hope that our poets will see the beauty of the colour red in roses, rather than in blood. Hope that this land will recover its original name: land of hope and peace. Thank you for carrying with us this banner of hope.

MAHMOUD DARWISH

CONTENTS

ACKNOWLEDGMENTS

Like its predecessor, the *Dictionary of African Filmmakers* (Indiana University Press, 2008), this listing is essentially a work of synthesis. In compiling it, I have drawn on the full range of material listed in the bibliography at the end of this volume. The principal published sources on which I have drawn, which demand special mention and which all contain more information on specific films and filmmakers than can be contained here, are, in order of publication: Hassan Abû Ghanima, "Trente films palestiniens" and "Filmographies," in Guy Hennebelle and Khémais Khayati, eds., *La Palestine et le cinéma* (Paris: E.100, 1977); Claude-Michel Cluny, *Dictionnaire des nouveaux cinémas arabes* (Paris: Sindbad, 1978); Shakir Nouri, "Répertoire chronologique des longs-métrages irakiens (1945–1985)," in *À la recherche du cinéma irakien, 1945–1985* (Paris: Éditions L'Harmattan, 1986); Ibrahim al-Ariss, Mouny Berrah, Claude Michel Cluny, Jacques Lévy, and Yves Thoraval, "Dictionnaire de 80 cinéastes," in Mouny Berrah, Jacques Lévy, and Claude Michel Cluny, eds., *Les cinémas arabes* (Paris: Éditions Cerf and Institut du Monde Arabe, 1987); Alberto Elena, *El Cine del tercer mundo: Diccionario de realizadores* (Madrid: Ediciones Turfan, 1993); Andrea Morini, Erfan Rashid, Anna Di Martino, and Adriano Aprà, *Il cinema dei paesi arabi* (Venice: Marsilio Editori, 1993); Hady Zaccak, "Filmographies," in *Le cinéma libanais: itinéraire d'un cinéma vers l'inconnu (1929–1996)* (Beirut: Dar el-Machreq, 1997); Sergio Di Giorgi and Joan Rundo, "1970–1998: Filmografia essenziale," in *Una Terra promessa dal cinema: Appunti sul nuovo cinema palestinese* (Palermo: Edizioni della Battaglia and La Luna nel Pozzo, 1998); Rebecca Hillauer, *Encyclopedia of Arab Women Filmmakers* (Cairo: American University in Cairo Press, 2005); Hamid Dabashi, "A Selected Filmography of Palestinian Cinema (1927–2004)," in *Dreams of a Nation: On Palestinian Cinema* (London: Verso, 2006); Rasha Salti, "Filmmakers' Biographies," in *Insights into Syrian Cinema: Essays and Conversations with Contemporary Filmmakers* (New York: Rattapallax Press / Arte East, 2006); and Nurith Gertz and George Khleifi, "Filmography," in *Palestinian Cinema: Landscape, Trauma and Memory* (Edinburgh: Edinburgh University Press, 2008).

Equally indispensable have been *CinémArabe* (Paris, 1976–1979), *International Film Guide* (London, 1964–2006, 2008–2010), *Images Nord-Sud* (Paris, from 1988), and the catalogues and web pages of various film festivals: the *Arab Film Festival* (Los Angeles, annually from 1987); the *Biennale des cinémas arabes* (Paris, biennally 1992–2006); the *London Palestine Film Festival* (2005–2006, 2008–2009); the festival *Jeunesse du cinéma arabe*, the *Festival du film arabe*, the *Deuxième Festival du film arabe*, the *Troisième Festival du film arabe*, *La semaine du cinéma arabe* (all Paris, 1983–1987); the *Festival: images du monde arabe* (Paris, 1993); *Il cinema dei paesi arabi*, Quarta edizione / *Arab Film Festival* (Naples, 1997); the *Dubai International Film Festival* (from 2004); the *Jordanian Short Film Festival*; the *ArteEast Touring Program—Lens on Syria* (United States, 2006); the *Middle East International Film Festival* (Abu Dhabi, from 2007); the *Emirates Film Competition* (annually from 2001), and the Dreams of a Nation website (on Palestinian cinema, New York).

Statistics concerning national size, population, and gross domestic product (GDP) are taken from seven *World Factfiles* published as daily supplements to the *Guardian* in 2009.

Individuals to whom I owe a very real and specific debt for information and encouragement (beyond the call of duty) are numerous. I owe a huge debt to Martine Leroy, for access to her data base on Middle Eastern films. I have also received stimulus, encouragement, and help from Rasha Salti, Haim Bresheeth, Lina Khatib, Maysoon Pachachi, Hazim Bitar, Abdalla Mohammed Bastaki, Hana El Hirsi, Ros Shotter, and Jaffar Mahajar. I am also endebted to the staff of Indiana University Press, especially Dee Mortensen, June Silay, and copyeditor Sarah Brown.

Moreover, I am deeply grateful to the Leverhulme Trust for awarding me the second Leverhulme Emeritus Fellowship, which has allowed me to finance both this dictionary and its predecessor, the *Dictionary of African Filmmakers*.

Though I have made every effort to check the information given, errors and omissions are inevitable in a work of this nature, and I would welcome contact from any readers who can help correct the mistakes and fill the gaps.

NOTE ON LAYOUT

This dictionary concentrates primarily on the makers of fictional feature films and feature-length documentaries, whose works are listed in the "Feature-Film Chronologies" and cross-referenced in the "Index of Feature-Film Titles." But because filmmaking in this area is so fragmented, I have also included in the listing of Arab filmmakers in part 1 over 900 short and documentary filmmakers from the Arab Middle East. Their names are listed at the end of the relevant feature film chronology, but their work is not indexed. The Arab Middle East has not developed the kind of overwhelming output of fictional features on video, characteristic of Anglophone Africa (especially Nigeria, where many thousands of feature-length videos have been produced and distributed since the 1980s), so I have been able to include work shot on video (principally Beta SP and more recently HD), as well as 35mm and 16mm film productions. Reference is also made to the increasing quantity of documentary material produced by the various Arab satellite television companies and intended principally for broadcasting. Al Jazeera English, for example, has of late provided both funding and considerable editorial freedom for documentary filmmakers from the wider Arab world. It is interesting too to note that, despite the technological developments and new promotional strategies which are likely to lead to a totally different media situation in the coming decade, the bulk of fictional feature films made in the Arab Middle East, like those in Africa, continue to be shot and distributed for initial exhibition purposes on 35mm film. The catalogues of the twentieth, twenty-first, and twenty-second editions of the JCC (Journées Cinématographiques de Carthage, Tunis, 2004, 2006, and 2008) show the continued strength and importance of conventional 35mm filmmaking across Africa and the Arab world, as well as the growing number of works, even by established filmmakers, which are digitally produced and reflect television formats: such as 52-minute documentaries and fictional works in a miniseries pattern of three 26-minute episodes.

In general, I have included in my chronological listings of fictional features all those works which are treated as such by the organizers of Arab and international film festivals, even if the works in question do not, strictly speaking, fulfill the conventional length requirements of a feature film. With regard to documentary production (now almost entirely in some digital format or other), I have excluded from the feature listings all works in the conventional 52-minute television format, though such works are referred to, of course, in the individual filmmaker entries.

As far as the treatment of specific filmmakers is concerned, I have tried to be as flexible and inclusive as possible, and I have again adopted the very liberal definitions used by festivals such as the JCC in Tunis or the Arab Film Festival (AFF) in Los Angeles as to what constitutes an "Arab filmmaker" and an "Arab film." I have therefore included the work of Arab filmmakers born or living in exile, who reflect in their work on the problems of living as emigrants, whether in Europe, Canada, or the United States, while excluding—as far as possible—European and North American filmmakers with no direct birth links to the Middle East. In a situation where so many filmmakers live and work across national boundaries, even within the

Middle East, I have followed the filmmakers' own ways of defining themselves and chosen to group them according to their own or their parents' nationality, rather than by their place of birth, work, or residence. The result, at the moment of going to press, is a list of over 550 feature-length works made by around 250 feature filmmakers, whose efforts are backed up by those of some 900 short and documentary filmmakers, many of them students graduating from one of the numerous audio-visual training courses in the area.

This dictionary offers broadly the same kind of information as that contained in its predecessor, the *Dictionary of African Filmmakers*. The work begins with an introduction, which sets out to place the filmmaking in its historical context. In an area like the Middle East, which has been constantly torn by war and internal strife, it seemed to me crucial to spell out this contextual situation, because it has had so profound an influence on the work of all feature filmmakers and has also led to the production of a mass of committed documentary filmmaking.

Part 1 comprises an alphabetical listing of all the Arab filmmakers from the Middle East whom I have been able to locate. The names of those who have completed at least one fictional or documentary feature-length film shot on 35mm, 16mm film, or in some video format are distinguished by being set in capital letters. Because of the nature of film production in the Middle East, particularly in, and in relation to, Palestine, the listing of filmmakers includes documentary and short film directors. Here too I have relaxed—as the filmmakers themselves do—any distinction between film and video productions. Foreign, usually Egyptian, makers of feature films are distinguished by an asterisk (*) in the alphabetical filmmakers and chronological listings (parts 1 and 2). Where available for an individual filmmaker, date and place of birth, training, and/or professional experience, and an indication of any

other creative activity are given, together with a listing of short and feature-length films. Film entries in these director listings include mention of date, length, and format, where this information is available.

Part 2 deals in alphabetical order with the countries to which the feature filmmakers are conventionally aligned. Because of the minimal amount of feature filmmaking that has occurred to date in the seven states of the Gulf, these are grouped together at the end (though there are huge differences between Yemen and its royal or princely neighbors). Each chronology of national feature-film output is preceded by a list of feature filmmakers, followed by a similar listing of relevant short and documentary filmmakers, and supplemented by a selection of bibliographical references. The dates of films given here can be no more than approximate, since I have used a wide variety of sources, some employing production dates and others using release dates. In any case, there may be a wide gap between a film's foreign festival screening and its eventual release at home (particularly if there are censorship problems), and a number of films have, for whatever reason, obtained no local commercial release at all.

Part 3 is an index of feature-film titles in both English and French. In each case, the director's name, the film's date, and the country of origin are given. The Arabic transcriptions of the film titles are very simplified forms, derived from a variety of national sources and intended merely to identify and differentiate films, which, in many cases, do not have formal English or French titles. These transcriptions are not indexed.

The bibliography lists books on relevant aspects of world cinema and book-length studies of Arab filmmaking within the Middle East, as well as a selection of books relating to the political development of the various countries and areas of the Middle East.

ACRONYMS

ABC	Australian Broadcasting Corporation
AFC	Amman Filmmakers Collective (Jordan)
AFF	Arab Film Festival (Los Angeles)
ALBA	Académie Libanaise des Beaux Arts (Beirut)
CLCF	Conservatoire Libre du Cinéma Français (Paris)
CNC	Centre National du Cinéma (Lebanon)
	Centre National de Cinématographie (Paris)
DEA	Diplôme d'Études Approfondies (France)
DIFF	Dubai International Film Festival (UAE)
EHESS	École des Hautes Études en Sciences Sociales (Paris)
ESAV	École Supérieure d'Audiovisuel (Toulouse)
ESEC	École Supérieure des Études Cinématographiques (Paris)
ESRA	École Supérieure de Réalisation Audiovisuelle (Paris)
FAMU	Filmov Akademie Múzickych Umení (Film and Television Faculty of the Academy of Performing Arts) (Czechoslovakia)
FEMIS	Fondation Européenne des Métiers de l'Image et du Son (Paris)
FLN	Front de Libération Nationale (Algeria)
GDP	gross domestic product
IDHEC	Institut des Hautes Études Cinématographiques (Paris)
IESAV	Institut d'Études Scéniques et Audiovisuelles (USJ, Beirut)
INSAS	Institut National des Arts du Spectacle et Techniques de Diffusion (Brussels)
IT	information technology
JCC	Journées Cinématographiques de Carthage (Tunis)
JSFF	Jordanian Short Film Festival (Amman)
LAU	Lebanese American University (Beirut)
MEIFF	Middle East International Film Festival (Abu Dhabi)
NFS	National Film School (now National Film and Television School) (Beaconsfield, UK)
OGC	Organisation Générale du Cinéma (General Organisation for Cinema) (Syria)
OGCT	Organisme Général du Cinéma et du Théâtre (General Organisation for Cinema and Theatre) (Iraq)
OPEC	Organisation of Petroleum Exporting Countries
PFLP	Popular Front for the Liberation of Palestine

NB: The École de Vaugirard is now the École Nationale Supérieure Louis-Lumière.

PLO	Palestine Liberation Organisation	UCLA	University of California, Los Angeles
RTBF	Radio Télévision Belge Francophone (Belgium)	UNESCO	United Nations Educational, Scientific and Cultural Organization
RTF	Radio-Télévision Française (Paris)	USJ	Université Saint-Joseph (Beirut)
UAE	United Arab Emirates	VGIK	Vsesoyuznyi Gosudarstvennyi Institut Kinematografii (All-Union State Cinema Institute) (Moscow)
UAR	United Arab Republic (linking Egypt and Syria, 1958–1961)		

Arab Filmmakers
of the
Middle East

INTRODUCTION:
Filmmaking in
Divided Lands

"Middle East" is self-evidently a Western term,
and dates from the beginning of this century. It is
a striking testimony to the former power and continuing influence of the West that this parochial
term, meaningful only in a Western perspective,
has come to be used all over the world. It is even
used by the peoples of the region it denotes to
describe their own homelands. This is the more
remarkable in an age of national, communal, and
regional self-assertion, mostly in anti-Western
form.

BERNARD LEWIS, *THE MULTIPLE IDENTITIES OF
THE MIDDLE EAST* (1998: 3)

This dictionary is concerned with the films
directed by Arab filmmakers in and from
the Middle East. It excludes filmmakers from
the Maghreb and from Egypt (except for the
handful of Egyptian filmmakers who have
made the occasional film for Middle Eastern
producers), as these have already been dealt
with in an earlier volume, *Dictionary of African Filmmakers.*[1] Though—like Israel—most
of the countries with which we are concerned
here achieved independence after the end of
World War II in the 1940s, their story has
nothing to match the tale of Zionist triumph,
which Ahmad H. Sa'di characterizes as "the
standard narrative of glorious rebirth, a story
of exile and return after millennia, with a people of memory and suffering redeemed by belonging to their own modern nation-state with
all its accoutrements: sovereignty, dignity, a
flag, an anthem, a mythical past, and future
prospects. A noble but embattled state."[2] For
the dispossessed Palestinians, so neatly erased
from this grand narrative, the story of the past
60 years has been almost the exact reverse.

Even for those Arabs who do belong to a
recognized national state, the story has been
almost as bleak, with a unified Arab identity
denied by the divisive actions of the European

powers, which, after World War I, arbitrarily
set their borders and systems of government
and, without consultation, introduced Israel
into their midst. It is a story of internal feud-
ing and repeated defeat and humiliation at the
hands of Israel and its all-powerful patrons.
The fragmented history of Arab Middle Eastern cinema—with its powerful documentary
component—reflects all too clearly the fragmented history of the Arab peoples and is indeed comprehensible only when this history is
taken into account. While neighboring countries, such as Turkey, Israel, and Iran, have coherent national film histories which have been
comprehensively documented, the Arab Middle East has been given comparatively little attention. Jacques Mandelbaum has gone so far
as to deny the very existence of cinema there,
arguing that if we were to keep to "a classic
definition of cinema, essentially measurable
in terms of industrial weight, national production and aesthetic affirmation," we would
have to conclude that "cinema no longer exists in the Middle East, in so far as it has ever
existed, outside Egypt."[3] This all-too-common
dismissive attitude is one which this study is
designed to counteract.[4]

FIRST CONTACT WITH THE CINEMA

The invention of the cinematograph by the Lumière Brothers in 1895 came at a time when the world was organized very differently from the way it is today. This was the height of imperial power for the European nations, which together colonized or controlled three-quarters of the world's population. It was three years before the United States of America would emerge in 1898 as a major imperialist power, with overseas ambitions and "interests," in the Spanish-American War, which led to the annexation of the Philippines and the effective colonization of Cuba. Indeed, for the first 10–15 years of the cinema's existence, there was no Hollywood in the sense that we understand it today: "French films dominated the American market and so determined, in part, what would become an 'American' cinema."[5]

In 1895, most of what we now think of as the Middle East formed part of the Turkish Ottoman Empire, which had its capital in Istanbul, the ancient city of Constantinople. Since the height of its powers at the end of the eighteenth century, the Ottoman Empire had been in steady decline throughout the nineteenth century, first driven from its territories in Christian Europe, then having its North African provinces and, above all, Egypt—submitted to European colonization or "protection." But in the period up to the outbreak of the First World War, the Turks still controlled the area now occupied by the modern states of Saudi Arabia, Iraq, Syria, Lebanon, Jordan, and Israel-Palestine, an area in which, as Stewart Ross notes, "the governments of the Great Powers of Europe showed no special interest" and "that of the United States even less."[6]

It was therefore to the palace in Istanbul that the Lumière Brothers turned, when the operator Alexandre Promio was dispatched on his visit to Egypt and Turkey in March–April 1897, with instructions to follow the normal company practice of organizing film shows and also shooting material for inclusion in the Lumière catalogue back in Paris (the Lumière *cinématographe* doubled as camera and projector). Screenings were set up in the palace and at the residences of prominent citizens,

and a first public screening was arranged at the Spontek Restaurant in a cosmopolitan district of Istanbul. Other Lumière operators also visited Istanbul in the late 1890s, including Félix Mesguich, Francis Doublier, Charles Moisson, and Marius Perrigot. They all stopped there during trips to Moscow, still ruled by the tsar. The resulting shots taken in the Ottoman Empire appeared in the Lumière catalogue from 1897.

The Pathé representative in the Ottoman Empire, a Polish Jew with Rumanian nationality, Sigmund Weinburg, was also apparently active as early as 1897 and indeed had a more lasting impact on the introduction of cinema to Turkey, by setting up the first permanent public cinema in 1908. He also initially headed the army film unit, which pioneered filmmaking in Turkey at the beginning of the First World War, before being expelled as an alien. Though the sultan, Abdul Hamid II, was a passionate supporter of photography, he disliked the cinema and offered no support to the foreigners who were seeking to introduce it into his realm. Promio is quoted as saying:

> I have little to say about my trip to Turkey, except that I had great difficulty in introducing my camera. At the time, in Abdul Hamid's Turkey, any hand-cranked instrument was regarded with suspicion; we had to get the French Embassy to intervene and then also slip a few coins into an official's palm, just to get free access.[7]

We do not know exactly where Promio went during his trip through the Ottoman Empire, but Jean-Claude Seguin suggests Damascus, Jerusalem, and Bethlehem, as well as the cities of Smyrna, Beirut, and Jaffa mentioned by Promio himself.[8] Thus several of the future states of the Middle East can trace their contact with the cinema—if only momentarily—back to the 1890s. Seguin also notes that Promio set the pattern for later European filmmakers visiting the East, in that his "animated views are inscribed in the Orientalist tradition strongly rooted in painting and literature."[9]

THE END OF EMPIRE AND THE ERA OF EUROPEAN MANDATES

The weaknesses of the Ottoman Empire—like those of its European parallel, the Austro-Hungarian Empire—became apparent when the two entered World War I on the side of Germany. Defeat left Turkey at the mercy of its wartime enemies, and the victorious European states, France and Britain, occupied the whole Middle East and proceeded to impose their will upon the remains of the Empire. One of the many crucial European decisions and agreements regarding the Middle East had already been made in 1917, with the unilateral declaration of support for the establishment of a Jewish homeland in Palestine by the British foreign secretary, Arthur Balfour. This declaration led directly to the establishment of Israel in 1948 and changed the course of history in the Middle East forever. Chillingly, Balfour is quoted as saying that,

> In Palestine we do not propose even to go through the form of consulting the wishes of the present inhabitants of the country . . . Zionism, be it right or wrong, good or bad, is rooted in age-old traditions, in present needs, in future hopes, of far profounder import than the desires and prejudices of the 700,000 Arabs who now inhabit that ancient land.[10]

Within the Ottoman Empire, a specific Arab nationalism had been slow to develop. Observing that "the initial Arab antagonism towards the Turks was more cultural than social or political," Peter Mansfield argues that what was most resented was "the 'Turkification' of the educational system and the replacement of Arabic by Turkish for all except religious studies." In practice, "a large share of political power passed into the hands of the local elite of shaikhs, *ulama* and landowners."[11] Anti-Turkish sentiment was muted too, because the Arabs had traditionally seen their governing co-religionists as a bulwark against an increasingly expansionist Christian Europe.

In the early 1920s, when Turkey transformed itself in defeat from an empire and caliphate into a modern secular nation-state built on the European model, various proposals were put forward by Arab leaders for the reshaping of their own lands. But emboldened by the increasing retreat of the United States into isolationism after the wartime interventionist idealism of Woodrow Wilson, the French and British governments felt able to ignore Arab wishes (just as Balfour had done in 1917). The changes they made while their troops occupied the Middle East met with far greater opposition than Turkish rule had ever faced. There were revolts against the French in Syria in 1920, 1925, and 1926, a major uprising against the British in Iraq in 1920, and continual fighting in Palestine, which stemmed from Arab opposition to increasing Jewish settlement. But French and English power prevailed.

The American academic Justin McCarthy, for whom "the division of the Arab world by the European conquerors was a disaster that continues to our day,"[12] raises the intriguing question of what might have been, if "the obvious alternative" to the Ottoman Empire in the Middle East had been created, namely a single Arab state. He argues incontrovertibly that "a state that included the Ottoman Arab provinces would have been less linguistically and ethnically varied than the Ottoman Empire." Could it have developed into a nation-state? Yes, he argues: "common language, history, customs, and often a dominant religion are the building blocks of nationalism. The Arabs had all these."[13] Certainly the new nation-state of Indonesia, as Benedict Anderson points out, was created in the 1940s out of far less promising material: "enormous size, huge population (even in colonial times), geographical fragmentation (about three thousand islands), religious variegation (Muslims, Buddhists, Catholics, assorted Protestants, Hindu-Balinese, and "animists"), and ethnolinguistic diversity (well over a hundred distinct groups). Furthermore, as its hybrid pseudo-Hellenic name suggests, its stretch does not remotely correspond to any precolonial domain."[14] Insofar as nationalism needs the stimulus of foreign aggression in order to grow, the British and French provided this in abundance in the Middle East, both during their military occupation and immediately after.

What a potential Arab nation lacked, because their rulers were Turks, not Europeans, was a European-style colonial map, of the kind which, in Indonesia, "worked on the basis of a totalizing classification" (173) so as to "prefigure the official nationalisms of Southeast Asia" (174). As Anderson points out, the apparently innocent practice common to European imperial states of coloring their colonies on maps (pink-red for British colonies, purple-blue for French, yellow-brown for Dutch) had an unanticipated outcome: "Dyed this way, each colony appeared like a detachable piece of a jigsaw puzzle" (175). The image shifted from being the map of an existing reality to becoming the sign of an imaginary unity: "Instantly recognisable, everywhere visible, the logo-map penetrated deeply into the popular imagination, forming a powerful emblem for the anticolonial nationalisms being born" (175).

Apart from this lack of a map to define its precise boundaries and differentiate it from its neighbors, for many Arabs, "the Arab nation" was a notion totally compatible with Benedict Anderson's definition of what constitutes a unified nation: "an imagined political community—and imagined as both inherently limited and sovereign."[15] The notion of a unified Arab nation even had some political currency. The followers of Hussein, the sharif of Mecca, had proclaimed him "King of the Arab Countries" in 1916, though this was highly controversial. Britain had never formally recognized the title, but "it had encouraged him to believe that it would."[16] William Polk points to the useful Arabic distinction between this notion of the Arab nation or pan-Arabism (*qawmiyah*), which the Europeans opposed, and the "particularist nationalism"[17] of the emergent states (*wataniyah*), which—on the principle of divide-and-rule—they fostered. McCarthy is unequivocal that "uniting all of what had been the Ottoman Arab world would have been possible. What stood in the way of

an Arab state was not internal barriers. External forces kept the Arabs apart." From the European point of view, the problem with a unified Arab state, was that such a state would "have been large enough . . . to have some power in the world."[18] Certainly the establishment of the state of Israel would have been far more hazardous, if it had had to be imposed upon a united Arab nation.

When the European colonialists took over from the Turks, they proceeded as they had done decades earlier with regard to Africa; they "created theoretical states on maps, regardless of economic and social realities, then enforced their creation."[19] But this time they chose to hide their colonial ambitions by using the institutions of the newly established League of Nations to create mandates validating their actions. On this basis, the French and the British took upon themselves not just the definition and boundaries of the new states but also the choice of their systems of government and the identity of the rulers who were installed. What had been Greater Syria was divided up to create three new states, Syria and Lebanon under French mandates and Palestine under the British, who promptly subdivided their area to create a fourth state, Trans-Jordan. Also under British mandate was the newly created state of Iraq, put together from three ethnically and religiously diverse Ottoman provinces, centered on Mosul, Baghdad, and Basra, respectively. The mandates were finalized by the mid-1920s, but though the ostensible aim was for these new states to be led toward independence, this occurred only in the very changed circumstances of the late 1940s. No account was taken of Kurdish demands for their own independent state in the north, while the new Middle Eastern arrangements totally ignored Saudi Arabia, out of which Ibn Saud was to create a fully independent state by 1932, and the already independent North Yemen, presumably because both were judged too difficult to colonize.

Given the upheavals of this pre-independence period, it is remarkable that any film activity at all occurred. There seems indeed to have been no film activity in Iraq until after independence in 1945, but Syria and Lebanon both have pioneers to rank with Albert Samama Chikly in Tunisia and the Egyptians Mohamed Bayoumi and Mohamed Karim. In Syria, Ayoub Badri's first fictional film, *The Innocent Victim* (1928) achieved some success, but his first feature, *The Call of Duty* (1937), like Ismaïl Anzur's *Under the Skies of Damascus* (1931), was a commercial failure. Both were silent features that found themselves in competition with the first Egyptian sound films. In Lebanon, Jordano Pidutti achieved some success with two little comedies, *The Adventures of Elias Mabrouk* (1929) and *The Adventures of Abou Abeid* (1931), as did Julio De Luca and Karam Boustany with a first Lebanese sound film, *In the Ruins of Baalbeck* (1933). A further Lebanese pioneer, Ali al-Ariss, was less fortunate. He had to leave his first feature, *The Flower Seller* (1943) unfinished, and he is reported to have protested outside the cinema screening his second feature, *The Planet of the Desert Princess* (1946), because it had been re-edited by the producer.[20] Palestine too has its pioneer filmmaker, Ibrahim Hassan Sirhan, who was virtually unknown until he was rediscovered by the Iraqi filmmaker Qassim Hawal in the Shatila refugee camp in the late 1970s. Sirhan had apparently begun by documenting King Saud's visit to to Palestine in 1935 and went on to make a number of documentaries and a couple of little-known features in Jordan, to which he was driven into exile.[21]

POST-INDEPENDENCE

As Ghada Karmi makes clear, the very nature of the Zionist project made war (or abject submission) inevitable for the Arabs. What the Zionists envisaged was "a project that was bizarre and, on the face of it, unworkable, namely to set up an ethnically defined, Jews-only collective existing on a land belonging to another people and to their exclusion." Since this new state was supposed, "irrespective of native opposition, to prosper in perpetuity," and the

original inhabitants were deemed "ethnically unacceptable," it could clearly "only be realised by a mixture of force and coercion."[22] The new Arab nation-states of the Middle East emerged only in the mid-1940s: Iraq achieved its independence in 1945, Syria and Lebanon obtained theirs in 1946, the same year that the Hashemite Kingdom of Trans-Jordan was created (to be renamed Jordan in 1948). Even before they could accustom themselves to their new, artificial, boundaries and their imposed systems of government, they were plunged into war, when the state of Israel was formally established in 1948.

It can be argued that this was a war of the Arabs' choosing and that they should therefore accept the consequences. But it is hard to imagine how they could have reacted otherwise to a partition of Palestine, in which they had not been consulted, and the expulsion—largely into their own territories—of some 750,000 Palestinians, in a process codenamed by the Israelis at the time as "Plan D," but which we now know as "ethnic cleansing." Whatever the rights or wrongs of the founding of Israel, for the Palestinians the year 1948 means only one thing: *nakba*, catastrophe. The ill prepared, disunited, and badly led Arab troops were no match for an Israeli army strengthened by the inclusion of the Hagana and Irgun paramilitary forces. The eventual truce in 1949 left Israel firmly established and with its boundaries extended to take in another 20 percent of what the United Nations had intended to be Palestinian territory.

The 1948–1949 Arab-Israeli war was just the first of a seemingly endless series of international wars, invasions, conflicts, and expulsions to have plagued the Middle East over the past 60 years. There were three further general Arab-Israeli conflicts: the Suez invasion in 1956, the Six-Day War in 1967, and the renewed Arab invasion (the Jom Kippur War), which brought the Arabs some limited success, in 1973. Before this, in 1970, the events of "Black September" had brought conflict between Jordanians and Palestinians, and the expulsion of the latter to Lebanon, where their presence became one of the triggers for the 15-year civil war which began in 1975. In 1981,

Israel seized the Golan Heights from Syria and bombed an alleged nuclear weapons plant in Iraq. Israel's first invasion of Lebanon (Operation Litani in 1978) was followed by a second (Operation Peace for Galilee in 1981). This led to a partial occupation of Lebanon which lasted 9 years, and was followed by a third full-scale invasion, in 2007 (the 33 Day War). 2008 saw a massive Israeli invasion of Gaza.

From 1980 to 1988, Iraq was at war with Iran, in a conflict that caused tremendous losses to both sides. Palestinian militants responded to Israeli state aggression with a first intifada in 1987, followed by a second, beginning in 2000 and still continuing 8 years later, up to the Israeli assault on Gaza. Iraq's invasion of Kuwait in 1990 triggered the United States–led Desert Storm response of 1991, which was followed by the Second Gulf War, designed finally to overthrow Saddam Hussein, in 2003. These are merely the major international conflicts which created death and destruction throughout the area. As we now turn to the individual countries of the Arab Middle East, we shall find that they were all also plagued by internal conflicts—coups, regional strife, and even, in the case of Lebanon, full-scale civil war—which inevitably shaped and distorted both civil and cultural life, including the film production which concerns us here.

LEBANON

Whereas the English imposed bedouin kings on their mandated territories of Iraq and Trans-Jordan, the French tried to establish democratic republics in the areas they controlled. Nowhere was the constitution bequeathed on independence more finely tuned and elaborately balanced than in Lebanon, a wholly artificial state carved out of the old Syrian province, in which, at the time, just over half the population was Christian (Maronites

and Catholics with traditional links to France, as well as Protestants with ties to the United States). The remainder of the population was diverse: both Sunni and Shia Muslims, Druze, Jews, and a number of tiny groups. The French sought an intricate system of checks and balances: "The post of president traditionally went to a Maronite, that of prime minister to a Sunni Muslim, with the speaker of the chamber of deputies being a Shia."[23] Such a complex system might have worked in a stable world, but the Middle East, as we have seen, was a world in constant turmoil. Discussing what she terms "the Hollow State," Sandra Mackey argues—with some justification—that "the Lebanon the French had created was little more than a precariously balanced collective of economically and politically linked autonomous societies living in a weak, schizophrenic state."[24]

Though the French-imposed system actually fostered the sectarianism (the division between Maronite, Shia, and Sunni) that would eventually tear the country apart, it seemed at first to offer positive advantages. Christian-dominated Lebanon adopted a pro-Western stance and tried to stand aside from the basic quarrels between Arabs and Jews in the Middle East (it took no part in the wars of 1967 and 1973). The recipe seemed to work and Lebanon prospered, so that, by the mid-1960s, "Beirut had morphed into a glitzy, Mediterranean metropolis, a Mecca for the international set, a haven for exiles of the region's political wars, and a brothel of business, where cash transcended law and ethics."[25] Moreover, "if Beirut had pulsated in the 1960s, it vibrated in the early 1970s," as the 1973 oil boom in the Gulf took effect.[26]

It is against this background that the early development of post-independence cinema in Lebanon—so different from that elsewhere in the Middle East—must be assessed. The beginnings in the 1950s were hesitant: Michel Haroun, a recruit from the theatre, made just one feature, Georges Kahi directed his first film in literary Arabic before turning to Lebanese dialect for his subsequent works, while Georges Nasser, having presented his feature debut at Cannes, shot his second film in French, in the vain hope of attracting an up-market audience at home. Hady Zaccak observes that these early filmmakers "drew their subjects from Lebanese reality, putting the emphasis on the beauty of the landscape, village life, Lebanese dress and popular musical traditions as well".[27] But the pioneer director who found the path to popular success and established commercial filmmaking in Lebanon was Mohamed Selmane, who had trained in Egypt and subsequently adapted Egyptian popular film styles in a highly successful career that embraced thirty feature films shot over a period of 25 years.

The development of commercial filmmaking in Lebanon during the 1960s and early 1970s was aided by the disruption caused by the nationalization of film production in Egypt, with the setting up of the General Organisation for Cinema (1963–1971)—though the Egyptian studios still managed to produce 720 features in the period 1960–1975. For their part, Lebanese producers made 105 features in the same period, new cinemas sprang up in Beirut and elsewhere, and audience numbers soared. The major commercial directors, whose careers all extended into the 1980s—Mohamed Selmane and Rida Myassar, followed in the early 1970s by Samir al-Ghoussayni—all produced a spate of films. Co-productions with Egypt and Syria were undertaken and this was, in one sense, the golden age of Lebanese cinema.

But, as Zaccak notes, the growth in production was merely in quantity, not in quality. Many of the films were based on Egyptian or Western commercial formulas, with no specific Lebanese identity (even the dialogue of many films was in Egyptian dialect), and the key development required—the creation of the infrastructure needed for a film industry to rival Egypt—could not be achieved. There were a number of cultural initiatives—the Beirut Ciné Club was founded in 1957, the first International Film Festival to be held in the Arab world took place in 1971, the Arab Film and Television Centre was established thanks to Unesco initiatives in 1962, followed by the

The Broken Wings (1962, Lebanon)

Youssef Maalouf had worked in the Egyptian feature-film industry for 10 years when, in 1962, he arrived in Lebanon to direct the first of the ten films he was to make there, and in Syria, in the course of the next decade. *The Broken Wings* is virtually the only readily available film from the era when Beirut set out to rival Cairo as the center of Arab film. The English subtitled version of *The Broken Wings* does not contain full credits and attributes the script to Khalil Gibran, the celebrated author of *The Prophet*. But since the writer died in 1931, it seems inevitable that the script, though based on his autobiography, was in fact adapted by a professional screenwriter. Whatever the case, the film captures the full flavor of Gibran's floridly lyrical style through its static declamatory dialogue, full of aphorisms and lofty sentiments, and through the overlaying of Rachmaninoff's Second Piano Concerto at emotional high points throughout. Maalouf directs the studio set movie with fluid assurance and has made a thoroughly professional job of reshaping the material into the conventional form of an Egyptian film melodrama, even finding space for a lengthy belly-dancing scene (one of the rare moments of oriental music in the film). The story, with occasional first person voice-over comments by the author, tells of Gibran's first great love, for the beautiful Selma, in the context of turn-of-the century Christian Lebanon. The lovers, who fall in love at first sight, are separated when her wealthy father is persuaded by the bishop to marry her off to the bishop's nephew, who is a gambler, drunkard, and womanizer. The broken wings of the title are those of women in an unenlightened patriarchal society, against which Gibran rails in vain. Selma is idealized as a passive victim of oriental despotism whose predicable fate, death in childbirth, forms the film's emotional climax.

West Beyrouth (1998, Lebanon)

Ziad Doueiri, who was 12 when the Lebanese Civil War broke out in Beirut and lived there for a further 8 years, returned after 15 years in the United States to recreate his childhood years in *West Beyrouth*. During his years of absence, he had studied film at UCLA and worked in Hollywood, most notably as camera assistant to Quentin Tarantino. These experiences find their direct reflection in the film, which follows closely the experiences of the exuberant and rebellious middle-class schoolboy Tarek, his close friend Omar, and a Christian refugee, May, as they live through their adolescent experiences and obsessions at the very moment the war breaks out. The film captures brilliantly the initial uncertainties of the time, for adults and children, as events unfold around them without logic or meaning. Tarek's own personal rebellion at his French-language school, with which the film opens, is soon drowned by the chaos in the streets of what is now marked off by the fighting as "West Beirut." Perhaps because he has chosen to tell his film through the eyes of adolescents totally lacking political or religious insights and has included presumably autobiographical elements (such as the boys' obsession with Super 8 filming), Doueiri adopts an upbeat and positive attitude toward the horrors perpetrated in the city. Significantly, no one close to Tarek is either killed or wounded, and his parents, though left destitute and confused, are unbroken by events. Doueiri films with an often handheld camera and uses a jagged editing style to create closeness to the characters. He captures the exuberant flow of events and skilfully uses music to blend his enacted story with real documentary and newsreel archive footage. No side is blamed and no political points are made. Instead, Doueiri seeks out absurd and comic touches, such as the adoption by fighters on all sides of a woman's brassiere as the emblem or flag to indicate to each other that they are visiting the neutral space of the brothel, not engaged in hostile acts and therefore not to be shot by snipers. *West Beyrouth* was clearly conceived as entertainment which would also offer insights into the unique reality of the Lebanese Civil War years. In this, Doueiri is totally successful.

Centre National du Cinéma (CNC), attached to the Ministry of Information, in 1964.[28] But key newcomers of the 1960s tended to come not from these developments but from television.

The incident which plunged Lebanon into sudden and unexpected civil war in 1975 was no more than a trivial fishing dispute, but it brought to the fore a number of key underlying issues. The major problem was the threat to Maronite supremacy caused by demographic changes (which saw the nine hundred thousand Maronites outnumbered in a population of some three and a half million) and the arrival of a new wave of Palestinian immigrants (after the events of "Black September" had caused the Palestine Liberation Organisation's [PLO's] expulsion from Jordan) who organized themselves as a "state within a state" in Lebanon, as they had done in Jordan. Once violence began, the government had neither the authority nor the military resources to restore order, so that soon the various armed militias were at war, each defending its own territorial areas and what it saw as its own specific interests: "The Druze and some Lebanese leftists fought for power in the Lebanese system. Other Lebanese Muslims fought for radical reform and a Lebanon stripped of its Western identity. The Palestinians fought for their own nationalism. Some Christians fought for political reform and Arab identity. The Maronites fought for their vision of Christian Lebanon".[29] The Israelis, the Americans, and the Syrians all intervened militarily in the civil war, while both Iran and Iraq provided financial assistance to combatants. There is much truth in the traditional Arab joke quot-

Under the Bombs (2007, Lebanon)

Philippe Aractingi has 20 years of experience in documentary filmmaking from a production base in France and has recently developed an interest in improvisation. These two concerns were brought together in 2006, in the last days of the Israeli 33 Day invasion of Lebanon and during the ensuing uneasy truce. With two professional actors, Aractingi set out to make a road movie, tracing two people's journey from Beirut to the South, through the shattered landscape of Lebanon immediately after the Israeli assault. The two protagonists are contrasting figures. Zeina is a rich Lebanese Shiite expatriate, returning from Dubai to search for her son, Karim, lost with her sister in the bombing of their native village of Kherbet Selm. Tony is a working-class Christian taxi driver, also from the South, initially concerned primarily with being well paid for risking his life on a trip refused by all his colleagues. The film sensitively traces the growing relationship between the two, powered by Tony's obvious sexual attraction for his passenger. Under the tension of the journey, they move from initial hostility to emotional closeness, gradually revealing their personal lives to each other. Eventually, it is Tony who drives the search forward, only for the child eventually found to turn out to be not Karim but his traumatized friend, whose family was slaughtered in the same assault which killed Zeina's sister. More important than this central dramatic core is the series of glimpses the film offers of the impact of the Israeli onslaught on ordinary Lebanese civilians. The couple's journey takes them through a landscape of horror, where whole communities have been devastated. Apart from the central couple and the hotel receptionist with whom Tony has a brief sexual fling, all the characters are people directly living the disaster. The images of human suffering are particularly harrowing, because these are real victims, filmed at the very moment when they are having to come to terms with the loss of their families. This human immediacy has a devastating impact on the viewer: as Philippe Aractingi has said, the experience of *Under the Bombs* was less that of making a film than that of living the film.

ed by Ross: "God laughed when He created the Sudan and wasn't thinking when He created Arabia; so what were You doing, asked the bemused Lebanese, when You created our beautiful land of cedar trees, blue seas and cool breezes? Ah, God smiled, just wait until you see who I've given you as neighbours."[30]

Funded through extortion, the plundering of the state's resources, and foreign assistance, the militias were initially rich. As a result, ever more powerful and destructive weapon systems were introduced into the civil conflict, and the savagery of the combatants rose steadily. The Lebanese civil war lasted fifteen years in all, and finally came to an end only when the state had been bankrupted, the economy ruined, and vast swathes of the country, and especially Beirut, had been totally devastated. Little beyond destruction had been achieved. Perhaps one hundred fifty thousand people had been killed and 15 percent of the population driven into exile. A war which was "anchored in no coherent set of ideas" ended, 15 years later, "with no resolution of the issues that had ignited it." The Lebanese civil war had, in short, "been destructive and futile, ugly and unfinished. It ended only because the Lebanese became numb to each other".[31]

The civil war inevitably brought the collapse of existing Lebanese commercial filmmaking structures, as studios and cinemas were destroyed and filmmakers scattered. But under the pressure of events, a new generation of filmmakers emerged, whom Zaccak terms "the filmmakers of the Lebanese intelligentsia," their arrival heralded by Maroun Bagdadi's premonitory feature, *Beirut Oh Beirut*

(1975). Like Bagdadi, who studied filmmaking in Paris, all the new group had studied in Europe: Jean Chamoun, Jocelyne Saab, and Randa Chahal-Sabbag in Paris, and Borhan Alawiya in Brussels. Only Saab, who had studied economics at the Sorbonne, was not a professionally trained filmmaker. Many of their films were made with foreign finance— often from European television sources. But even when living in exile, their commitment to their country and its predicament, matched with a deep concern for the Palestinian cause, is very clear from the documentaries they made during the civil war period. This group is the one which dominates much of what we think of as Lebanese filmmaking.

The terms of the ceasefire which brought fighting to an end in 1990 did nothing to cure the inherent structural weaknesses of the Lebanese state. Huge efforts at reconstruction were made, particularly under the impetus of the Sunni billionaire businessman and sometime prime minister Rafik Hariri. But by the time Hariri was assassinated in 2005, many of the problems which had plagued Lebanon in the late 1970s had returned. The Iranian-backed Hezbollah grew to a position where it could taunt the Israelis and provide the trigger for a renewed Israeli invasion of southern Iraq in 2007, which killed thousands of innocent Lebanese in an all-out land and air bombardment which lasted 33 days. But Hezbollah emerged undefeated (if not victorious) from the conflict—the first time an Arab force had stood up to the full might of the Israeli war machine—and, like the PLO before it, set out to create a "state within a state" (perhaps more aptly named "a state within a no-state") in Lebanon. But this time the threat was even more daunting: the destruction of the Lebanese secular Western-style democracy and its replacement with a theocracy based on the Iranian model.

During the time of transition and unease after the end of the civil war, many of the documentarists of the 1970s turned to feature filmmaking. Their efforts have been supported by a diverse range of, mostly younger, feature filmmakers. Layla Assaf, who trained in Sweden, made numerous documentaries for Swedish television before completing her first feature in Lebanon. But many of the newcomers have no background at all in documentary filmmaking: Samir Habchi, who studied in Russia, Jean-Claude Codsi, a graduate of the Institut National des Arts du Spectacle et Techniques de Diffusion (INSAS) in Belgium, Josef Farès, who has lived since a child in Sweden, and Ziad Doueiri, who was brought up and educated in the United States. Equally striking is the work of those new filmmakers based in France—Danielle Arbid, Michel Kammoun, and Philippe Aractingi—along with that of the actress Nadine Labaki, who is based in Lebanon but wrote her first feature, *Caramel* (2007), in Cannes. Much of the work of these filmmakers is couched as entertainment and unashamedly seeks an international audience, even if, as Lina Khatib concludes, "the Civil War has become *the* defining feature of Lebanese cinema."[32]

SYRIA

Though the constitution bequeathed to Lebanon by the French caused (and continues to cause) huge problems, there was no internal dispute about the boundaries of the new state. The dominant Maronites were happy to accept the notion of a Greater Lebanon ("le Grand Liban"), since it added the coastal towns of Tripoli, Sidon, and Tyre to their traditional autonomous heartland of Mount Lebanon. In contrast, the Syrians did not accept the restricted territory bequeathed to them in the French partition of the ill-defined "Arab state." In part, this may be attributed to the fact that, in the immediate aftermath of the fall of the Ottoman Empire and before the formalization of the mandate, there was briefly an independent "Greater Syria," which held elections for a National Syrian Congress in May 1919, formed a national government in Damascus in December that year, and, in March 1920, chose, as its king, the amir Feisal, third son

The Extras (1993, Syria)

Nabil al-Maleh is a pioneer of Syrian cinema who contributed one episode to the first collective film produced by the state film corporation and directed its first full-length feature, *The Leopard* (1972). But like virtually all Syrian directors, he has had trouble with the film authorities and the censor, and he returned from years in exile to direct his fifth, and to date final, feature, *The Extras,* in 1993. After a fairly frenetic credit sequence, which edits together key images from throughout the film, *The Extras* is a virtually real-time study of 2 hours spent together in a friend's flat by two young people, shot through only by brief images of the man's imaginings of his own force and prowess. Though they have known each other for 8 months, this is the couple's first time alone together (there is a marvellous moment when she removes her headscarf and he sees her luxuriant black hair for the first time). The film as a whole is a masterly depiction of their awkwardness and insecurity, the result of living in a society which allows them no personal freedom. Their very different temp-eraments are gradually revealed, both to each other and to us. Nada, a widow who lives with her domineering brother, is the more mature, and, in their longest embrace, Salem falls asleep like a child in her arms. Salem, a would-be actor at the National Theatre who earns his living by working in a petrol station, is more dynamic, acting out an elaborate marriage proposal and staging play excerpts for her. But to her consternation, he can play only bit parts, doomed and ignoble figures. From early on in the narrative, the interior of the flat has been under threat from sinister and powerful state policemen lurking outside to catch and persecute the blind oud player who lives next door. Their intrusion leads to Salem's humiliation, which Nada observes. Though she pretends all is well, there seems little hope for their relationship, as they go their own ways at the end of the film. Combining precise observation, sensitive acting, and a perceptive use of sound, *The Extras* is a powerful study of the impact on ordinary people of a harsh and repressive regime.

of Sharif Hussein of Mecca and leader of the bedouin revolt against the Ottomans.[33] But, within months, the European provisions of the Treaty of San Remo were imposed (against fierce and continuing Arab opposition), and the Arab world was divided into the mandated territories which now form the independent states of the Arab Middle East. Feisal was promptly expelled by the French, but, in compensation, was made king of the newly created mandated territory of Iraq by the British.

When Syria became independent in 1946, it continued to have problems with its national identity. Though lacking in the manpower and national resources to achieve its ambitions, it became a major proponent of war against Israel and of pan-Arab unity. In 1958, it even merged with Nasser's Egypt (with which it has no land borders) to form the United Arab Republic, but this union dissolved in acrimony 3 and a half years later. Syria has continued to seek to influence developments in neighboring countries, stationing troops in Lebanon for 29 years and acting as a major sponsor of the insurgents in occupied Iraq, prompting Fouad Ajami's remark that "Syria's main asset, in contrast to Egypt's preeminence and Saudi wealth, is its capacity for mischief."[34] Internally Syria was in complete disarray for the first 25 years of its existence, since, as Barry Rubin notes, it had "twenty different cabinets and four different constitutions" in the first decade of existence (1946–1956) and it suffered "ten successful coups and a lot of failed ones" in the period up to 1970.[35]

Unsurprisingly, there is little film production in Syria before 1970: one feature in the 1940s, two in the 1950s, and just five in the 1960s. Syrian cinema of the time was best known for the comedies starring Dureid Lah-

The Night (1992, Syria)

Mohamed Malas's second feature film, *The Night*, is the first part of a projected trilogy, of which his first feature, *City Dreams* (1984), forms the second stage. The third part, *Cinema al-Dunya*, has not been realized. *The Night* covers the events of a decade or more of Syrian history (1936–1948) and reflects the tortured politics of these years. It also relates the lives and dreams of its two central characters, a mother, Wissal, and her only son, who both figure as voice-over narrators for some of the film's episodes. Beyond this, the dominant figure in the whole is the often absent father, Alalla, whose life is closely enmeshed with the events of the times, particularly those involving Palestine. The film is also markedly autobiographical, set in Koneitra, the director's own birthplace and a town occupied by the Israelis since they seized the Golan Heights in the 1967 war. The literary nature of the narration reflects Malas's own ambitions as a writer: he has revealed that he turned to cinema because the only scholarships for study abroad in 1968 were for the Soviet film school, the VGIK, in Moscow. *The Night* opens with Wissal and her son looking up at the night sky, and the narrative begins with her memories and dreams of her dead husband. They met when he passed through Kuneitra in 1936, on his way to fight the British and the Jews in Palestine, and he married her, at her father's request, on his return as a broken man from the fighting. Alalla's life is a turbulent one. Though he lives in Kuneitra, he is always a transient figure, and he is twice imprisoned by the authorities. His son, also called Alalla, struggles to come to terms with his father's life, and the latter part of the film becomes his story and his memories, real or imaginary. Visually, the film is very formally composed, and the narrative, full of echoes and repetitions, operates on a number of levels simultaneously. As a whole, *The Night* is a complex interweaving of intense personal experiences within the family and startling political transitions in the street outside.

ham and Nouhad Kalahi, who had begun their joint career on Syrian television, but whose feature films were largely co-productions directed either by the Lebanon-based Egyptian Youssef Maalouf or by Lebanese directors. In 1963, power was seized by the Baath Party (the name means "renaissance" or "awakening"), which has been characterized by William Polk as "authoritarian, somewhat mystical, vaguely socialistic but determinedly pan-Arabist."[36] The change did not bring stability to Syria, but it did lead to a major development in Syrian cinema, namely the founding that year of the General Establishment for Cinema (referred to by French critics as the Organisation Nationale du Cinéma), set up on the Egyptian model, to oversee film production, distribution, import, and export. The organization's first feature production was *The Lorry Driver* (1966), directed by the Yugoslav filmmaker appointed to oversee its activities, variously referred to by Yves Thoraval as Boshko Votchinitch, by Mahmud Abdel Wahed as Bosko Vucinitch, and by Rasha Salti as Poçko Poçkovic. In 1969, the General Establishment was granted a monopoly of film production and the following year released *Men Under the Sun*, a three-part feature directed by three Syrian newcomers, Nabil al-Maleh, Mohamed Shahin, and Mohamed Muwaddin.

When Hafiz al-Assad took control of Syria in a coup by the radical wing of the Baath Party in 1970, he imposed absolute authority on Syrian internal affairs, while continuing Syria's now traditionally aggressive foreign policy and maintaining close ties with the Soviet Union (the source of government weaponry). Constant features of his 30-year reign were the advocacy of pan-Arabism of one form or another and the ongoing domination of Lebanon, by means of threats, secret service operations, the funding of terrorist activities and

The Nights of the Jackal (1989, Syria)

Abdellatif Abdelhamid is by far the most prolific of Syria's internationally known directors, with eight features in 20 years. His films are immediately accessible, and he is one of the most popular directors with Syrian audiences. The pattern was set with his first feature, *The Nights of the Jackal,* which is a basically realistic tragi-comedy, set in 1967 in the arid countryside near the port of Lattakia, where the director was born. But the film also has a touch of pure fantasy. At night, the farm is surrounded by jackals, whose howling cannot be silenced except by high-pitched whistling, which only the hero's wife, Um Kamel, can manage. Kamel himself cannot whistle, though his wife makes it clear that she regards this as a man's responsibility. By day, Kamel's apparent authority is restored, as he leads his family out to the fields, pompously riding a donkey. But the daytime world too is full of unseen dangers, and gradually the basis of Kamel's authority is destroyed, as he loses the members of his family, one by one. His older daughter gets married, but the sec-ond one gets pregnant, elopes, and is later slaughtered in an "honor killing." His westernized elder son abandons his university studies, while the reliable second son is conscripted and killed, resulting in the death of Um Kamel too. When Kamel grows tomatoes, they fall in price in the state-controlled market; when he volunteers for military service, he is promptly dismissed. His one recognized skill is repairing radios. He carries his own with him at all times, enjoying the stirring music and believing the patriotic propaganda. But toward the end of the film, the radio also lets him down, bringing only news of the Arabs' humiliating defeat at the hands of the Israelis. When his final child, his youngest son, Bassam, leaves him, Kamel is totally alone. He had tried buying a whistle on a trip to Lattakia, but the jackals were not deceived. Now, still unable to whistle, he succumbs to the night and the jackals. Beneath the surface farce, *The Nights of the Jackal* has a serious message about the place of the traditional Arab male, and of Syria, in the modern world.

actual military occupation. Al-Assad came from the minority Alawite sect in Syria. As outsiders to the dominant Sunni Muslim community, the Alawites had been recruited into the armed forces by the French during their years of rule. Al-Assad rose steadily through the ranks from squadron leader to head of the air force and he had, by the time of the coup, become minister of defence.

Al-Assad's dictatorial rule gave Syria a hitherto unknown national stability, but this has only been achieved at the cost of brutal repression (with particular ferocity directed against the Muslim Brotherhood), massive state control and heavy censorship; his approach has been characterized as "one part realism, one part ideology, and one part family-based mafia."[37] A basic component of his rule has been the Baath Party, in power when he took control. The party took as its organiza-tional model the Soviet Communist Party, in which "the key is to control all the commanding heights of the society: army, economy, media, education, religion, and so on, both to use them for promoting the regime and to keep them out of anyone else's hands."[38] In this, al-Assad succeeded totally, and the result is a society marked by authoritarian control and massive state propaganda, arbitrary imprisonment, and torture, which is, at the same time, "a society in which the people generally accept the regime's stories."[39] It was hoped that when his son Bashar succeeded Hafez al-Assad as president after his death in 2000, there would be some softening of the regime's stance and some recognition of past errors (as has occurred in Morocco since Mohammed VI succeeded his father, the autocratic King Hassan II, who ruled from 1962 to 1999). But this was not to be, with Bashar telling a journalist in

2001: "The development of civil society institutions must come at a later stage. And they
are not therefore among our priorities."[40]

The cinema which emerged under al-
Assad's rule is, as Rasha Salti notes, highly
paradoxical: while not an industry, it performs
the role of "a national repository of aspirations
and sentiments"; though a state-sponsored
cinema, it is also "the premier realm of artistic
expression in contemporary cinema," offering
"a lucid, intelligent and subversive critique of
the state."[41] The filmmaker Hala al-Abdallah
Yakoub offers a striking characterization of
the two contradictory realms of Syrian cinema: "an open realm, charged with courage
and freedom, creativity and imagination, defiance and provocation" and "a closed realm,
encumbered with fear and ambivalence, echo
and emptiness, confinement and absence."[42]
The pioneering Nabil al-Maleh, who trained at
Filmov Akademie Múzickych Umení (FAMU)
in Czechoslovakia, was one of the first to experience the state's displeasure, when his second
feature led to him being banned from working
for the state organization for 5 years. For the
past two decades he has lived in exile, though
returning to Syria to direct the masterly study
of the impact on personal relations of a totally
repressive society, The Extras (1993).

Throughout the years of Hafez al-Assad's
rule, the General Establishment for Cinema
maintained an approach committed to the regime's causes (such as Palestine and pan-Arab
unity) and favored the adaptation of major
works of contemporary Syrian literature (such
as the novels and stories of Ghassan Kanafani and Hanna Mina). It imported directors
from other Arab countries in the early years:
the Egyptians Tewfiq Saleh and Seif-Eddine
Chawkat, the Iraqis Qays al-Zubaydi and Qassim Hawal, and the Lebanese Borhan Alawiya
all worked there between 1969 and 1974. But
it also trained two generations of Syrian filmmakers by offering bursaries for study in the
Soviet Union (at film schools in Kiev or Moscow). This shared training has given rise to a
distinctive Syrian approach, while still enabling the leading filmmakers to have highly

individual personal styles. Though itself a
tightly controlled state institution, the General Establishment has offered its filmmakers
considerable freedom in the films they made,
even if these works have been subsequently
banned or denied screenings in Syria by the
state censors.

Attention in the West was initially captured by two filmmakers who made their
feature film debuts in the early 1980s, Samir
Zikra with The Half-Metre Incident (1983) and
Mohamed Malas with City Dreams (1984), followed 8 years later by The Night (1992). They
were joined later in the decade by Oussama
Mohammad, whose debut film, Stars in Broad
Daylight, appeared in 1988. But though they
form a closely knit trio, collaborating on each
other's works, they have made only three or
four features features apiece in 30 years, often
with gaps of 10 years or more between productions. Omar Amiralay, the sole documentarist
in the group, who trained in France, has chosen to live in exile there since the early 1980s,
after his first feature-length work, Everyday
Life in a Syrian Village (1974), was banned.
Among Syrian directors of the 1980s, only
Abdellatif Abdelhamid has managed to direct
a succession of eight features, from The Nights
of the Jackal (1989) to Days of Boredom (2008).
There have since been further striking debuts
by directors trained in Moscow in the 1990s
and 2000s, but neither Riyad Shayya (Al-Lajat,
1995) nor Nidal al-Dibs (Under the Ceiling,
2005) has been able to complete a second feature. In the last decade, thanks to the growth
of Syrian television and the advent of digital
technology, new possiblities of production
outside the General Establishment for Cinema
have arisen. A number of Syrian newcomers, most still in their twenties and thirties
and many based abroad, are active, making
short fictional and documentary works, with
the path to feature-length output pioneered
by the Paris-based Hala al-Abdallah Yakoub
with her experimental video autobiography, I
Am the One Who Brings Flowers to Her Grave
(2006).

IRAQ

The cinemas of Syria and Iraq, like the political development of the two countries and the careers of their respective long-serving dictators, offer fascinating parallels and stark contrasts. While Syria's initial problem was that of coming to terms with its constrained boundaries, Iraq had to fuse three Ottoman provinces (*vilayets*), centered respectively on Mosul, Baghdad, and Basra, that had not previously formed a single unit and to attempt to unite three very diverse communities (Sunni, Shia, and Kurd). The years of the mandate were years of continual Arab revolt, and, like Syria, Iraq took years to find a national identity. In the 1920s and 1930s, the British treated Iraq much as they treated Egypt, offering its pro-Western monarch notional independence, while ensuring that "what they most wanted would be kept safe—lines of transportation, British oil companies, and military control."[43] The British, like the French, "did not plan to advise and assist, but to rule."[44] As Gertrude Bell, who was intimately involved in the creation of Iraq, wrote in 1920, "The underlying truth of all criticism—and it's what makes the critics so difficult to answer—[was] that we had promised self-governing institutions, and not only made no step towards them, but were busily setting up something quite different."[45] The British authority extended into the early 1940s, when, after a nationalist coup, they reinstated the royal family of Feisal II (who had become king in 1939) and restored the authority of the pro-Western prime minister Nuri al-Said. Iraq became fully independent in 1945 as a monarchy, and this situation lasted, despite nationalist unrest, until 1958, when a military coup by the so-called Free Officers abolished the monarchy and executed both the royal family and the prime minister.

There seems to have been no filmmaking in Iraq before independence in 1945, and the late 1940s features which did emerge were shot either as co-productions by experienced Egyptian directors or by a Frenchman (identified by Yves Thoraval as André Chotin),[46] who was invited to shoot the first feature at the newly opened Baghdad studios. The first feature to claim Iraqi identity is Abdl Khaliq al-Samari's *Regrets* (1955). There was no support for filmmaking from the royal government, and only fourteen features were made in 1945–1959, with Hyder al-Omer being the sole director to complete two features. The two films which critics pick out from the period are Abdl Jabar Wali's *Who Is Responsible?* (1956) and Kameran Hassani's *Saïd Effendi* (1957).

The 1958 coup did not produce a stable Iraq. There were regular assassination attempts on whoever assumed power, and further coups in 1963, which brought the Baath Party to power for the first time, and in 1968, which reestablished its rule. Brigadier Qasim was succeeded by Colonel Abdus-Salam Arif, who was killed in an air crash and followed as president by his brother, Abdur-Rahman Arif, who was overthrown in a Baath Party coup, led by General Hassan al-Bakr. Successive governments, all dominated by Sunni officers, were thrown off course by external events—the 1967 Arab-Israeli war, the relationship with Egypt, pan-Arabism or the oil crisis—but it was internal problems, first with the Kurds and then with the Shia majority, which brought Saddam Hussein, for 11 years al-Bakr's seemingly loyal deputy, to power in 1979. His response to personal authority was the immediate execution of all possible rivals and a purge of opposition supporters throughout the country.

As in Syria, it was a change of government through military action which precipitated the establishment of a state media organization in 1959. But the title of this, the General Organisation for Cinema and Theatre, points to the lack of autonomy of filmmaking in Iraq at this time. As in Algeria, the state organization's focus kept shifting: in 1972 it was fused with the Radio and Television Organisation and then, in 1975, split off again. In its early years it was principally a documentary producer (three hundred documentaries had been made by 1970),[47] and its first three feature films were not released until 1969–1970. State production after 1972 began with the first important production of Mohamed Choukri Jamil, who, like his colleague Fayçal al-Yassiri, worked mainly

Clash of Loyalties (1983, Iraq)

Mohamed Choukri Jamil began his career as a documentary filmmaker for British oil companies and received his training as a filmmaker in England. His early feature films of the 1970s include two adaptations of Iraqi novels, *The Thirsty Ones* (1972), dealing with the plight of the peasantry in a time of drought, and *The Walls* (1979), which explores the urban struggle against the monarchy in the early 1950s. His most ambitious film, *Clash of Loyalties,* is a big-budget international co-production, made from an original script and in two versions (Arabic and English), with a huge budget provided by the Iraqi government. The handling of the spectacular battle scenes is impressive. *Clash of Loyalties* deals with the Iraqi revolt in 1920 against the imposition of the British mandate in Iraq. But rather than exploring the complex national and political tensions that exist in relation to this crucial historical moment, Jamil opted for an epic treatment in the manner of David Lean, drawing heavily on the camerawork of

English director of photography Jack Hilyard and on Ron Goodwin's very Western musical score. One Iraqi critic has maintained that the leader of the revolt is depicted like the hero of a Hollywood Western and complained of the falsification of the role of King Faisal—seen here as a leader of the nationalist revolt, rather than as the compliant would-be ruler to be imposed by the British. While the mass of the Arab people is reduced to mere extras dying spectacularly in desert battles, most of the film's focus is on the highly personalized internal clash among the British, with Oliver Reed dominating the strong English acting participation in the film. Despite this concentration on the British occupiers, many of the key historical figures who shaped the fate of Iraq, such as Sir Arnold Wilson, are omitted, and the crucial role of Gertrude Bell is downplayed. For all its impressive spectacle, *Clash of Loyalties* offers only limited insight into the historical realities of 1920.

for the public sector in the following years. From 1959, the private sector continued to operate alongside the state organization, producing almost three times more features than the ten produced by the General Organisation before 1977, when a virtual state monopoly was introduced. Nineteen eighty and eighty-one were key years for the state organization, with films produced by two major Egyptian filmmakers, *The Long Days* by Tewfiq Saleh and *The Battle of Al-Qâdissiya* by Salah Abou Seif, as well as the founding of the state film production company, Babylon/Babil.

For the new Iraqi president, Saddam Hussein, 1980 was the year he began the Iran-Iraq war, invading a country over three times the size of Iraq in an assault which Saddam expected to last a month and lead to the overthrow of the Khomeini regime, but which instead dragged on for 95 months.[48] The war, "one of the most costly, cruel and protracted

of modern wars,"[49] resulted in huge suffering for both nations, who fought with the utmost determination and ruthlessness. As a result, there were atrocities on both sides, especially Saddam Hussein's use of poison gas attacks, a tactic which he later applied to dissident populations within Iraq. Half-a-million people died, but in the end, "the war was a draw. Neither country lost much territory, nor was there any change of regime in either nation. The conflict enabled Khomeini to consolidate the Islamic revolution. And Iraq emerged as the most powerful military force in the region, outstripping Turkey and Egypt."[50]

With the state now bankrupt and with his army as his sole (if expensive) asset, Hussein decided on a new war. He had been supported by the West throughout the Iran-Iraq conflict and received very ambiguous responses to his new plans. So, on August 2, 1990, he launched his attack on neighboring Kuwait. This attack

Dreams (2005, Iraq)

Mohamed al-Daradji's experiences while making *Dreams,* recounted in his documentary *War, Love, God and Madness,* show the difficulties in filming in Iraq after 2003. As well as facing logistical and casting problems, al-Daradji was arrested by the Iraqi police, shot at by the insurgents, kidnapped and beaten by militants, and then subjected to 5 days of maltreatment by the American military. What enabled him to survive was his Dutch passport. These experiences find their reflection in the film, but its focus is on the sufferings of the Iraqi people, rather than on political issues. *Dreams* has a complex time structure, beginning with the Americans' "shock and awe" bombing of Baghdad in 2003, and ending with the appearance of U.S. troops on the streets of Baghdad. The central figures are a doctor and two patients at a Baghdad psychiatric hospital destroyed by the U.S. bombing, and the early parts of the film comprise flashbacks to 1998, which trace the previous lives of the three and their sufferings under the Saddam Hussein regime. Dr. Mehdi had his hopes of progression blocked because his father was a communist, executed by the Baathist regime. Ali is a patient because of his experiences as a conscript: being bombed by the Americans, losing his best friend in battle, and being tortured as a deserter. Most touching is the tale of the young Shia woman, Ahlaam (the name means "dreams" in Arabic), who was driven to her collapse when her husband was arrested and shot on their wedding day. The tale of her love for Ahmed and the preparations for their wedding are told lyrically and shot in warm colors, but the visual quality of the film becomes far bleaker, as the impact of the Saddam Hussein regime and then the U.S. invasion is shown. Ali makes a partial recovery and is able to help rescue some of the patients who have fled from the bombed and looted hospital. But Ahlaam, clearly the symbol of a tortured Iraq, is left to wander in her wedding dress through the empty streets of a nightmarish Baghdad, where she is raped and abandoned. There is little hope for her at the end of the film, as she looks out over the 2003 Baghdad skyline from a deserted rooftop.

on a fellow Arab state and the brutal occupation that followed provoked an immediate response from a startled world community. The United States, keen to protect its ally (and oil supplier) Saudi Arabia, organized United Nations Security Council resolutions and a coalition of world governments for its biggest military operation since the Vietnam War. With total air supremacy and the failure of Iraq to use any of its alleged weapons of mass destruction, the coalition forces destroyed the bulk of the Iraqi forces within a hundred hours. But the Security Council resolutions did not allow for regime change, so the defeated Hussein was able to survive and subsequently to wreak a savage revenge on those—the Shia in the south and the Kurds in the north—who, wrongly expecting coalition support, had risen in opposition. President George Bush's decision not to overthrow Saddam Hussein left half completed a mission which his son, George W. Bush, was more than happy to attempt to finish 12 years later.

In the circumstances, it is not surprising that Iraqi filmmaking has declined since 1980 (little more than a feature a year, including documentaries shot in exile, for the past 28 years). Yves Thoraval picks out the work of four "auteurs"—Mohamed Choukri Jamil, Fayçal al-Yassiri, Qays al-Zubaydi, and Qassim Hawal—but these do not have the shared background and collective identity characteristic of their contemporaries in Syria. Jamil trained in the United Kingdom, while al-Yassiri and al-Zubaydi (who has worked largely in Syria) both studied in East Germany and Hawal (much of whose work concerns Palestine) is a product of the Baghdad Academy of Fine

Kilometer Zero (2005, Iraq)

Hiner Saleem, a Kurdish refugee who eventually settled in Paris, set his first feature in the Kurdish community in Paris and depicts the journey of a refugee couple in his second. The bulk of *Kilometer Zero,* his fourth feature, takes place in Kurdistan, where it was shot. The time of the action is 1988, during the Iran-Iraq War and a few weeks after Saddam Hussein launched his poison-gas attack on the Kurdish village of Halabja. Yet the film is shot in a sequence of formally controlled shots and edited with a slow rhythm, which matches perfectly the temperament of its thoughtful, somewhat passive hero, Ako. His dreams of escape are hindered by his wife's bedridden old father, so Ako finds himself conscripted into the Iraqi army, to fight for a cause that is not his. War is depicted as a tragic farce, boredom interspersed with sudden bombardments, endured by men who dream of a Europe symbolized for them by Anita Ekberg emerging from the Trevi Fountains in *La dolce vita.* Ako is given the task of returning a dead Kurdish "martyr" to his home village and the core of the film is his uneasy relationship with the Iraqi taxi driver, as they drive through an empty desert landscape. They meet dozens of similar taxis on a journey that emphasizes their similarities as ordinary people and their irreconcilable enmity as Arab and Kurd. Eventually they split up, abandon the coffin, and Ako is reunited with his family, only to be bombed again before being miraculously transported to Paris at the joyous moment of the fall of Baghdad. The film is marked by bickering incomprehension (between Ako and his father-in-law and later between him and the Arab driver) and shot through with moments of desperate farce (Ako attempting to get his leg shot off so he will be discharged from the army, the constant reappearance of lorries bearing a statue of Saddam Hussein, Ako's dancing battle with the Iraqi flag). *Kilometer Zero* is a film that celebrates the spirit of the Kurdish people under Saddam Hussein's rule but also shows their inseparable difference from the Iraqi Arabs who rule them.

Art. Their concerns are disparate, and Hawal describes Jamil and al-Yassiri's 1970s works as "faithful to the party line" and as "ideological films." He has even complained that Jamil reshot one scene of his 1977 feature, *The Houses in That Alley,* when Hawal himself refused to meet the censor's demands.[51]

What has emerged since the 1980s, however is a "cinema of the diaspora, making the most of experimental, documentary and short films, often working in difficult conditions with low budgets of around 10,000 dollars, and then being faced with great difficulty in obtaining screenings."[52] Among those cited by Hawal who have made feature-length works are Maysoon Pachachi (in the United Kingdom), Samir (Switzerland), Saad Salman (France), and Jano Rosebiani (Germany). Four further foreign-based filmmakers—the team of Hussein Hasan Ali and Masoud Arif Salih (France), Kassim Abid (United Kingdom), and Mohamed al-Daradji (the Netherlands and the United Kingdom)—have been active since 2004. Though he does not deal with these filmmakers explicitly, this is the kind of diasporic filmmaking so ably analyzed by Hamid Naficy,[53] as is indicated by the titles of two 2000s features—Saad Salman's *Baghdad On/Off* and Samir's *Forget Baghdad* (both 2002)—and the subject matter of two short films—Abbas Fahdel's *Back to Babylon* (2002) and Tarek Hashim's *16 Hours in Baghdad* (2004)—each chronicling the filmmaker's return home after 20 or so years.

PALESTINE AND JORDAN

One of the advocates of a single Arab state, of which he assumed he would become ruler, was Hussein, the sharif of Mecca and notional head of the bedouin tribes, who had allied himself with the British in World War I. Ironically, two of his sons were among those most involved in the division of Arab lands into the separate states which they remain today. One of the first acts of the British on taking up their mandate was to split Palestine, by dividing off the territories across the River Jordan to become a separate entity. At the time, this portion of Palestine east of the Jordan River was "a largely worthless, mainly desert kingdom."[54] Its rule was entrusted to Hussein's second son, Abdullah, who had threatened trouble by taking his bedouin followers to aid his brother Feisal, who had just been ousted by the French in Syria (Feisal was later made king of Iraq). The main concern of the British in Jordan was security (particularly against the bedouin), hence their support for the creation of Abdullah's army, the Arab Legion, organized by a British officer, John Baggot Glubb (better known as Glubb Pasha). Abdullah subsequently conspired with the Israelis in the lead-up to the 1948 war and, when assassinated in Jerusalem, left the kingdom to his mentally unbalanced son, Talal, who was forced to abdicate a year later. But against all odds, the pro-Western Hashemite Kingdom of Jordan, independent since 1946, survived and prospered under Abdullah's grandson, Hussein, whose army was strong and loyal enough to oust the Palestinians threatening to take over the state in the 1970 "Black September" fighting.

Filmmaking in Jordan has been very limited. In the 1950s and 1960s, there are two, little documented, features produced by the Palestinian pioneer Ibrahim Hassan Sirhan, who had been driven into exile into what was then Trans-Jordan, a patriotic piece by the Palestinian-born Mohamed Kaouach, and two 1969 works on the Palestine liberation struggle by Abdel Wahab al-Hindi. More recently, but 16 years apart, there have been two features whose status as "Jordanian" has been contested, the French-financed *An Oriental Story* (1991), directed by Najdat Ismaïl Anzur, who has dual Jordanian-Syrian nationality, and *Captain Abu Raed* (2007), made by Amin Matalqa, who was brought up and trained in the United States, where he is now resident and where he found funding for his film. In 2007, the locally based Mahmoud Massad made a first feature-length Jordanian documentary, *Recycle*, shot on video but transferred to 35mm film. In addition, in the 2000s, there has been a mass of short documentary work shot on video, particularly by those associated with the Amman Filmmakers Cooperative, set up by Hazim Bitar in 2003.

Edward Said has emphasized that, after the 1880s, Palestinian history "takes a course peculiar to it, and quite different from Arab history," since "the defining characteristic of Palestinian history—its traumatic national encounter with Zionism—is unique to the region."[55] Under the terms of the mandate, the British were obliged to set up a Jewish state in the now diminished Palestinian territory. Their progress toward this led to complaints of bias from both Jews and Arabs, and the years of the mandate were marked by continual disorders, in particular those of 1936–1939, which are referred to by the Arabs as the Great Arab Revolt, and which the Jews call the Riots.[56] Ghada Karmi captures perfectly the impact of the 1948 creation of Israel, the Palestinian *nakba* or catastrophe, in which the Arab world found itself confronted with an "alien" creation: "Its governing ethos was European and the bulk of its population was also European . . . The Arabs could neither understand it nor deal with it."[57] The Arab armies were comprehensively defeated by the well-organized and intensely motivated Jewish forces, and, within the boundaries of the new Israel, ethnic cleansing on a massive scale was undertaken, resulting in the expulsion of an estimated 750,000 Palestinians from their lands. Much of this took place between the expiry of the mandate and the United Nations proclamation of the state of Israel on May 14, 1948. During this 5-month period, "the irreg-

Fertile Memory (1980, Palestine)

Michel Khleifi's first feature-length documentary, *Fertile Memory*, is one of the founding films of Palestinian cinema. Khleifi, who was born in Nazareth, was one of a number of Arab filmmakers who studied filmmaking at INSAS in Brussels and went on to work initially for Belgian television. In *Fertile Memory*, he juxtaposes the personal stories of two Palestinian women who are completely unknown to each other. One is Roumia, a widowed grandmother in Jaffa who works in an Israeli clothing factory. She has lived in poverty since the family's land was expropriated by the Israelis (who have founded a kibbutz on it). After 30 years, she still clings to the land but also to the old ways of living, disapproving of young people's lives in general, and her own daughter's remarriage in particular. The other, younger, woman, Sahar, lives a very different life as a divorced single mother in Ramallah, teaching at Bir Zeit University and working as a novelist. Both are victims of the assumptions of Arab patriarchal society (one accepting, at her own cost, the other rebelling, and thereby causing herself new problems), as well as of the the Israeli occupation, which denies Roumia her land rights and involves Sahar, even if she is not herself a militant, in the student struggle. *Fertile Memory* not only comprises two very different stories, it also involves two documentary procedures, with Sahar questioned by an unseen interrogator, while Roumia gives her own account, largely in voice-over, and participates in what seem to be staged scenes of domestic life. One focus of the film is on the everyday gestures of the two women, but Khleifi has said that he intended the film to be not just about women but also for women. In *Fertile Memory*, Khleifi's fluent camerawork and evocative use of music also offer a lament for Palestine's lost lands and autonomy. Throughout this beautifully edited film, there is a concern with the dignity of simple interior spaces and the beauty of the empty landscape. The inclusion toward the end of black-and-white newsreel footage of the Israeli response to the first intifada adds a fresh poignancy to Khleifi's restrained, contemplative stance.

ular Palestinian forces were crushed, Palestinian society was pulverised, and the first wave of refugees was set in motion."[58]

In the aftermath of the shattering defeat in the 1948 war, the age of exile, refugee camps, and statelessness began for the Palestinians. For the Arabs as a whole, the years between 1948 and 1967, which Ilan Pappe calls "the Age of Partition," were immensely difficult, since Palestine "now became a new geo-political entity, or rather three entities": the West Bank "fully annexed to Jordan, but without the population's consent or enthusiasm," the Gaza Strip "in limbo under military rule, its inhabitants prevented from entering Egypt proper," and Israel itself, "bent on Judaizing every part of Palestine, and building a new living organism, the Jewish community of Israel."[59] In this period, as in the years before 1948, there was virtually nothing that can be deemed Palestinian cinema, with Gertz and Khleifi refering only to the work in Jordan of Ibrahim Hassan Sirhan and Mohamed Kaouach.[60]

The third Arab-Israeli war (the Six-Day War in 1967), unlike the second (the Suez crisis), had a profound effect on Palestinian life and on resistance to Israel. It led to the Israeli occupation of Palestinian lands which persists today and to the Palestinians realizing "for certain that there was little or no chance of fellow Arabs coming to their rescue."[61] Palestinian organizations retreated to Jordan and reshaped themselves there. But their efforts were fragmented. The overall umbrella organization, the PLO, was dominated by Yasser Arafat's Fatah group, but there were dozens of other guerrilla groups operating indepen-

Paradise Now (2005, Palestine)

In interviews dealing with *Paradise Now,* Hany Abu Assad has said that his intention was to do for suicide bombers what Coppola's *Godfather* films had done for gangsters. In fact, by drawing on his skills at depicting the detail of everyday life and at the mixing of documentary and fiction, Abu Assad has made a much more compelling and involving work, particularly for Western audiences used to the media demonization of Islamic terrorists. Though he begins with the obligatory scene of an Israeli border crossing point, the director's emphasis throughout is less on the physical oppression by the military occupiers (who caused huge disruptions to the actual shooting) than on the psychological effects of occupation and imprisonment on those who endure it. In a film concerned with murderous violence, the key moments are not those of physical action. They are the long-held, silent close-ups of faces: those of the people closest to the protagonist, Saïd, immediately before the film's climax, and the extreme close-ups of Saïd's own eyes throughout the film, par-

ticularly early on, when he has his photograph taken, and at the end, when he is about to detonate the bombs which will kill him and a busload of Israeli soldiers. From the start, the emphasis is on the futile emptiness of the lives of Saïd and his friend Khaled, which offers them no real future. The director's own viewpoint, that there is an alternative to violence, can come only from Suha, the pretty girl who is an outsider to Nablus and to whom Saïd is immediately drawn (as she is to him). There is no attempt in the film to glorify suicide bombing—the camera does not work when Saïd and Khaled record their suicide videos, and both would-be bombers draw back from their first attempts. Saïd was born in a refugee camp and experienced his father's execution as a collaborator when he was just 10. When he finally articulates the hopelessness of his situation, his decision to respond to the humiliation and violence he has experienced by a suicide bombing becomes only too understandable.

dently, the best known of which was George Habash's Popular Front for the Liberation of Palestine (PFLP). The Palestinians' constant harassment of Israel and its activities within Jordan (where it became virtually "a state within a state") brought it into conflict with King Hussein. The hijacking of four Western airliners led first to a bloody confrontation in September 1970 ("Black September") and then to the expulsion of Palestinian organizations to Lebanon.

It was during the late 1960s, in Amman, that Palestinian cinema was born, with the efforts of the photographic archivist Sulfa Jadallah Mirsal and two exiled Palestinians working for Jordanian television (from which they acquired their equipment), Mustafa Abu Ali and Hani Johariya. At this point the definition of Palestinian cinema was unambiguous. It was for Fatah in Amman that they made *No*

to the Defeatist Solution (1969), and when Fatah was relocated to Beirut, they moved there too to make *With Blood and Spirit* (1971). But later, particularly after the dispersion of Palestinians after their expulsion from Lebanon in 1975, "revolutionary Palestinian cinema" takes on a much broader geographical identity, both in terms of filmmakers and of funding and commissioning sources. Gertz and Khleifi reckon that over sixty documentary films were made before 1982.[62] Some of these were the work of Palestinians such as Abu Ali, Ghalib Sha'ath, and Ismaïl Chammout, but others were directed by filmmakers from other Arab states, such as the Lebanese Rafic Hajjar, Fu'ad Zantut, and Jean Chamoun, the Jordanian Adnan Madanat, and the Iraqis Samir Nimr, Qays al-Zubaydi, and Qassim Hawal (who also later made the feature film *Return to Haifa* [1981], from the novel by Ghassan Kana-

Divine Intervention (2002, Palestine)

Elia Suleiman's second feature-length film, *Divine Intervention,* confirms his place as the most idiosyncratic of Palestinian filmmakers. It is both highly personal (dedicated to the memory of his father) and totally stylized, with the actions of Israeli soldiers constantly choreographed into balletic movements. The film has no linear narrative but is structured as a succession of often absurd or extravagant incidents. It opens with the frustrations of the father, mouthing obscenities as he drives past his smiling neighbors, and ends with the filmmaker sitting side by side with his mother in the kitchen, watching a boiling pressure cooker. The action in between is watched over, as always in Suleiman's films, by the director in person as the silent and totally impassive ES, here accompanied by his unnamed girlfriend (played by Manal Khader). The film begins in Nazareth showing a life reduced to violent repetitive rituals, turning neighbor against neighbor in a series of senseless acts, all filmed without comment or explanation with a static, long-held camera. The life of ES in Jerusalem is equally frustrating: since Manal lives in Ramallah, they can meet only in the car park of an Israeli checkpoint, expressing their passion only through their clasped and caressing hands as they sit, otherwise motionless, side by side. The potential violence contained in all the scenes of everyday life finds glorious expression in a series of wonderful gags and fantasies. A date pip tossed casually from his car by the impassive ES on his very first appearance blows up an Israeli tank in a huge explosion. The elegant Manal, walking fearlessly through the checkpoint, reduces the Israeli guards to juddering wrecks and brings the observation tower crashing down. A red balloon adorned with a cartoon of Yasser Arafat's face is released by ES and flies triumphantly over Jerusalem, finally stroking the El Aksa mosque. In the long penultimate parody sequence, Manal appears as an avenging Palestinian ninja figure, moving with surreal grace and magically destroying a team of trainee Israeli snipers with the emblems of Palestinian national identity.

fani). In addition, there were a number Lebanese feature films which used Palestine as the background for melodramatic action films, and two outstanding works by "outsiders": the Iraqi feature *The Duped* (directed by the Egyptian Tewfiq Saleh, 1972), and the Syrian feature *Kafr Kassem* (made by the Lebanese documentarist Borhan Alawiya, 1974). Both dealt powerfully with Palestinian subjects.

The fourth Arab-Israeli conflict (the Jom Kippur War) in 1973 and the Organisation of Petroleum Exporting Countries (OPEC) oil embargo redressed somewhat the balance between the Arabs and Israel and its Western supporters, but the uneasy peace was shattered by the outbreak of civil war in Lebanon in 1975. The PLO was deeply involved in this, and it was a Fatah attack on Israel which provided the trigger for a first Israeli invasion of Lebanon in 1978. The second (full-scale) Israeli assault in 1981 succeeded in expelling the PLO from Lebanon, leaving the Palestinian refugees in the Sabra and Shatilla camps totally at the mercy of Maronite forces, which, with the complicity of the Israelis, slaughtered thousands of men, women, and children. It seemed difficult to imagine a bleaker period for the Palestinians than the 1970s.

Yet, from the 1980s, the Israelis increased their pressure on the Palestinians in the West Bank and Gaza Strip, which they had occupied and administered since the 1967 war. They could not simply annex the territories, since this would have threatened the Jewish majority in an enlarged Israeli state, so they attempted a dual strategy, "to destroy all opposition to Israeli rule, and persuade Palestinians that life would be better for them outside Israeligoverned territory."[63] But the very brutality of their efforts had the opposite effect: it fostered the Palestinians' sense of national identity and led to the emergence of two groups violently opposed to Israel's very existence, Hamas and Islamic Jihad. In 1987, the oppression sparked off spontaneous protests, particularly by the young and by children, which became known as the intifada, which resulted in 626 Palestinian deaths, with 37,500 wounded and 40,000 arrested. The various attempts at a political solution, culminating in the Oslo Accords in the 1990s and more recently the so-called Road Map, have changed little for the Palestinians, as the Israelis continue their policy of building new settlements on the West Bank and of intensifying their occupation. At the time of writing, after the Israeli assault on Gaza toward the end of 2008, there exists no sign of the emergence of any kind of viable state for the Palestinians.

Against this discouraging background, the emergence of a new generation of Palestinian filmmakers was heralded by Michel Khleifi's feature-length documentary *Fertile Memory* (1980) and two further internationally shown fictions, *Wedding in Galilee* (1987) and *The Tale of the Three Jewels* (1996). Some of the newcomers who followed him shared Khleifi's film school background (he had trained at INSAS in Belgium). Maï Masri (much of whose exclusively documentary work has been done with her husband, the Lebanese filmmaker Jean Chamoun) studied at the University of San Francisco and Ali Nassar at Vsesoyuznyi Gosudarstvennyi Institut Kinematografii (VGIK) in Moscow. But many of the other new Palestinian directors lacked this background. What they all had in common was a concern with creating images documenting Palestinian life. As Said has pointed out, "the whole history of the Palestinian struggle has to do with the desire to be visible." Sixty years after the founding of Israel, the struggle continues to counteract the old Zionist slogan that Palestine was "a land without people" seemingly designed for "a people without a land."[64] Among those who have consistently worked in documentary are Nizar Hassan and the actor-

turned-filmmaker Mohamed Bakri. Most of the other key figures in Palestinian cinema have followed the same trajectory as Khleifi in moving from documentary in the 1980s to fiction in the 1990s: among them, Ali Nassar and Elia Suleiman, along with Rashid Masharawi and Hany Abu Assad (who both received some technical training in the Netherlands). Many of these filmmakers have lived, or are now resident, abroad, and much of their funding has come from European television sources. Indeed, Palestinian filmmakers, working under very difficult circumstances and often at great physical risk in a context which ex-President Jimmy Carter has likened to South African apartheid, have to take their funding where they can find it. Those who are Israeli citizens and have taken funding from Israeli government sources have on occasion been subjected to unjustified criticism by journalists from other parts of the Arab world, whose individual compromises with their own domestic autocratic regimes are often no more defensible. But the commitment of Palestinian filmmakers to the cause of their people—along with their talent—is unquestionable. As Gertz and Khleifi observe, since the 1980s, Palestinian cinema "has been striving to maintain a heterogeneous and open nature." The films have been produced "in an era of distress, when the fate of occupation and repression is shared by an entire nation struggling to crystallize its oneness in face of the outside Other." Simultaneously, Palestinian cinema "attempts repeatedly, in every possible way, to break down this image, to take it apart and to reassemble it, drawing from a mosaic of classes, generations, genders, regions, and nations."[65]

THE GULF

Developments in the Gulf over the past 90 years have been quite separate and totally different from those elsewhere in the Arab Mid-

The Cruel Sea (1972, Kuwait)

Khalid al-Siddick's independently produced first feature, made after a number of short films, looks at Kuwait's past, before the exploitation of the oil which was to make it rich, and specifically at the struggles of the pearl fishermen against the sea, which is depicted as savage and all-powerful. The film begins and ends with long-held images of the waves, and, throughout, the hardship of the men battling against natural forces is emphasized. Moussaid's father was crippled both by the sea, which has ruined his eyesight, and a shark, which bit into his shoulder. But the film is also a merciless depiction of a traditional society structured according to wealth rather than merit, in which there is no place for women's individual wishes or desires. Al-Siddick's approach is basically realistic (visually more in the manner of Visconti than Rossellini), and some of the strongest sequences have a documentary-style authenticity: the cramped life of the men during their 4-month voyage on board the tiny fishing boat is parallelled by the ceremonies on shore organized collectively by the women—the noisy ritual of a wedding ceremony (where the bride's desires are of no concern) and a chilling sequence on the beach where a kitten is drowned to ensure the men's safe return. The narrative set against this background is a simple and conventional one: two young people, Moussaid and Noura, are in love, but they are separated by the social forces which keep her cloistered at home and by the poverty which drives him out to seek his fortune at sea. His efforts lead seemingly inevitably to his death but would in any case have been in vain, since Noura is married against her will in his absence. Her wedding night with a rich, much older merchant is depicted unambigiously as a socially sanctioned rape: her own mother signals to the musicians to play louder, so as to drown out the daughter's screams. The generation gap is also revealed in Moussaid's struggle against his father for permission to become a diver (parallelled, al-Siddick tells us, by his own struggle to become a filmmaker against his own father's wishes).

dle East (though Kuwait did share the common Middle Eastern experience of invasion by overwhelming forces, when Saddan Hussein launched his assault in 1990). When the Ottoman Empire disintegrated in 1918, there was no move to impose a European solution on Saudi Arabia or North Yemen—they were simply ignored—and they achieved their independence in 1932 and 1919, respectively. The five smaller states bordering the Persian Gulf, which with Saudi Arabia make up the Gulf Cooperation Council—Oman, the Trucial States (subsequently the United Arab Emirates—UAE), Qatar, Bahrain, and Kuwait—were all British protectorates and enjoyed treaties which prevented them from being absorbed by their much larger neighbors (Iraq had what it saw as historic claims to the territory of Kuwait, for example). At the time they were backward states, often the personal property of their ruling families, insignificant on the world stage and religiously conservative in ways that made their development on Western democratic lines inconceivable (the links between the Saudi ruling family and fundamentalist Wahabi Islamic sect are well known).

All this changed with the discovery of oil in the 1930s and its exploitation after World War II. By the time the Gulf states achieved independence in the 1960s and 1970s, some of them were among the richest states in the world in terms of per capita income, and Saudia Arabia, Kuwait, and the UAE were on the way to becoming major forces in the world capitalist financial system, their power as oil-producing states revealed through the actions of the oil cartel OPEC. Much of the Gulf states's immense wealth may have been

A New Day in Old Sana'a (2005, Yemen)

The London-born Bader Ben Hirsi chronicled his personal discovery of Yemen, in
the company of the English traveller Tim
Mackintosh-Smith, in his documentary
*The English Sheikh and the Yemeni Gentle-
man.* In *A New Day in Old Sana'a,* he tells
a fictional tale of Yemeni life obliquely, using an Italian photographer, Federico, as
his (English-speaking) narrator. Set in the
picturesque old capital city of Sana'a, the
film tells a tale of passion and misunder-
standing, setting the power of love against
the force of tradition. Federico's assistant
Tariq falls passionately in love with his
upper-class fiancée Bilquis (whom he has
never met) when he sees her—unbeliev-
ably—wearing the dress he has bought
her and dancing bareheaded in the street
after dark. He is quite unable to cope with
the totally unexpected impact of love, but,
to make things worse, he is mistaken: the
woman who has captured his love is in
fact Ines, a humble girl without a family,
who works as a *managasher,* applying the
local variant of henna (jet-black *naqsh*)
to other women, especially to brides.
Tariq's carefully chosen dress, which Ines
is briefly accused of stealing, has in fact
been thrown out into the street by Bilquis,
as "only fit for a bedouin." The film captures well both the women's world of gossip and emotion, jealousy and intrigue,
and the emotional immaturity of a young
man like Tariq. Ben Hirsi constructs a deftly
shaped lighthearted narrative, broken up
by snatches of questioning voice-over by
a narrator intrigued by his discoveries of
an unknown culture, and enlivened by musical interludes. Inevitably, tradition wins
out in the end, and Tariq listens to reason
and returns to his fiancée, while the dis-
appointed Ines, we are told, returns every
night to wait at the bridge which was to
have been their rendezvous and the start
of their new life together.

wasted, but much has also been invested in
hospitals, schools, universities, and television
organizations, leading to profound and un-
predictable social changes, including those involving the media. As Nada Mourtada-Sabbah
and her colleagues observe, "a market economy armed with sophisticated media cease-
lessly bombards the citizens and expatriate
workers alike with messages of consumer (and
secular) behaviour. Very few people can ignore
the visual images seductively enacting dramas
before them."[66]

Television networks were initially set up
largely to transmit imported material, but
local production has increased, with the Al
Jazeera news network based in Qatar leading
the way by becoming a force in world news
broadcasting and, more recently, in documentary production. The newly educated young,
in particular, are keen to enter the modern
media world, and the new education system,
in the UAE, for example, has provided young
men and women with production skills in
video and with the desire to make full use of
them. Though barely two dozen feature films
have been made in the Gulf since Khalid al-
Siddick's pioneering *The Cruel Sea* in 1972,
there is every reason to expect a surge in production in the coming years.

Yemen's development has been quite different from that of its neighbors. Divided in
the nineteenth century, the largely unacces-
sible and reclusive North became independent when the Ottoman Empire disintegrated,
while the South remained a British colony,
better known as Aden. The North (the Yemen
Arab Republic) promptly plunged into civil
war, while Aden successfully fought against
the British for its independence, to emerge
as the People's Democratic Republic of Yemen. But this independence came to be de-
pendent on Soviet aid, and when that ceased
after the end of the cold war, it was conquered
and swallowed up by its much larger northern
neighbor in 1990. Unsurprisingly, the only Yemeni cinema is a cinema of individual exiles.

MIDDLE EASTERN FILMMAKING

As it has done since the beginning of the sound era, Egypt continues to dominate Arab cinema. The three thousand plus Egyptian feature films produced since the 1920s amount to three times the number produced in all the rest of the Arab world put together and, in terms of box office receipts, the gap is far wider still. But there has been a continuous tradition of filmmaking in both the Arab east (the Mashreq) and the Arab west (the Maghreb) since independence, tentative at first, but well established by the 1960s and 1970s and often flourishing in the last decade. In terms of output, at around five hundred feature films in total, the cinemas of the Mashreq (Lebanon, Syria, Iraq, Palestine, and Jordan) are broadly comparable to those of the Maghreb (Algeria, Morocco, and Tunisia), and their shared characteristics, as well as the differences between them, are instructive.

There are many features common to both Maghreb and Mashreq, the first of which has already been noted: the work of the tiny handful of pioneers from the 1920s silent era and the early years of of sound which was spread thinly across the Arab world. Only in Egypt and, to a certain extent in Lebanon, does this pioneering activity lead directly to some kind of national cinema. Outside these two countries, this pioneering work was followed by years of silence, and when filmmaking did resume, it was from a quite different base.

Across the many divisions of the Arab world, a shared sense of commitment is apparent whenever cinema has been called upon to play its part in the struggle for independence and against violence. Cinema in Algeria has its roots in liberation struggle of the late 1950s and in the filmmaking undertaken as part of the Front de Liberation Nationale (FLN) struggle by a number of young Algerians, inspired by the French activist René Vautier. So too, at the origins of Palestinian cinema in the 1970s, we find militant filmmakers directly linked to the groups involved in the liberation struggle (the PLO, the PFLP, etc.) and working partially under the umbrella of the Palestinian Film Unit, which was established in 1972.

Though without such precise political affiliations, Lebanese and other Arab documentarists raised their voices against the civil war which erupted in 1975. In Algeria, the initial militant impulse finds its immediate echo in Ahmed Rachedi's pioneering compilation film *Dawn of the Damned,* the first major film of the newly independent Algeria. But subsequently, in Algeria, this militant phase—like the work of the Middle Eastern pioneers—has little direct influence on what is to follow. But in Palestine and Lebanon, the committed activity of the 1970s forms the basis for the powerful surge of documentary filmmaking across the Arab Middle East, which in turn helps shape the more tentative emergence (or re-emergence) of fictional feature filmmaking from the early 1980s.

Another shared characteristic of filmmaking across the Arab world is the pioneering role played by Europeans at the beginnings of feature filmmaking. The origins of Egyptian cinema lie essentially in Cairo's cosmopolitan expatriate community. In Algeria, it was a Frenchman, Jacques Charby, who shot the first Algerian-produced feature film after independence. It was another Frenchman, André Chotin, who shot the first feature at the newly established Baghdad Studio in Iraq in 1948, just as the German Fritz Kramp was chosen to inaugurate the Misr Studios in Cairo with *Weddad* in 1936. Subsequently European directors working in the Arab world have largely found their production funding at home and aimed their work at a wider audience. But various European film-funding bodies, particularly in France, have played a continuing vital role in the development of Arab cinema outside Egypt. For example, the French Fonds Sud, set up in 1984 and just one of the numerous French film production aid agencies, has contributed to films by fifty-one Maghrebian and thirty-two Middle Eastern Arab filmmakers, many of them resident in Europe. Certain Egyptian "outsiders"—Youssef Chahine, Youri Nasrallah, Asma El-Bakri, Atef Hetata, and Khaled El-Hagar—have received similar assistance. The challenges these filmmakers face in maintaining authentic links to their homelands, while simultaneously engaging with foreign audiences, are very real, but are, in many cases, very successfully overcome.

The situation of all these filmmakers is similar, in that they have to operate as individual auteurs seeking foreign funding for their work, but their personal reactions, and hence their filmic approaches and styles, are very different. These vary sharply from country to country, in response to particular opportunities—especially with regard to film training—and due to the impact of conflict and oppression (as chronicled above) in the specific context within which they have had to operate. While it is possible to generalize meaningfully about Maghrebian cinema as a whole, the work of contemporary Arab filmmakers of the Middle East is much more tied to local developments within their countries of origin. Hence the need to deal with each country or area independently and to bear constantly in mind the specific political and economic context.

Authoritarian regimes are the norm in the Arab world, and attempts to establish state monopolies for filmmaking have been widespread. But whereas the authorities in Algeria, Tunisia, and Morocco looked for inspiration to the Paris Centre National de Cinématographie (CNC), the newly established Baath regimes in both Syria and Iraq looked to the Egyptian model, the General Organisation of Egyptian Cinema set up in Cairo in 1961. Similarly, while no major Egyptian filmmaker has worked in the Maghreb since independence (Youssef Chahine's *Gamila the Algerian Woman* was shot in Egypt in 1958, when the war was still raging), about twenty Egyptians—including some of the leading figures in Arab cinema—have directed mainstream feature films for local producers in Lebanon, Syria, and Iraq.

These differences indicate the further key underlying distinction between the two areas. Whereas the Maghreb has largely turned its back on Egypt (from whose popular film audiences its particular forms of spoken Arabic largely cut it off) and adopted almost exclusively the model of auteur film production which has its origins in France, some of the filmmaking developed in the countries

of the Mashreq relates much more directly to that of Egypt. In the 1960s, with the disruption caused to commericial filmmaking by the establishment of the state monopoly in Egypt, there was a serious attempt in Lebanon to build filmmaking on an industrial model, so as to rival the Cairo studios. Filmmakers whose careers resemble those of the prolific mainstays of Egyptian production emerged, headed by a trio of Lebanese—Mohamed Selmane, Samir al-Ghoussayni, and Rida Myassar—each of whom spent 20 years or so making up to two dozen commercial features for distribution throughout the Arab world. The Lebanese pattern was also followed sporadically—and with markedly less international success—in Syria and Iraq.

As part of the highly professional organization of its film industry, Egypt has developed an accepted path to filmmaking: years of study at the Higher Film Institute in Cairo, followed by a period of work as an assistant director and the making of two or three short films. None of the governments in the rest of the Arab world has made use of this pattern of training, and only a tiny handful of filmmakers from the Maghreb or the Arab Middle East, none of them major figures, have studied in Cairo (two Moroccans, Imane Mesbahi and Hassan Moufti, the Palestinian Ghalib Sha'ath, and Khalid al-Zadjali, who made the first Omani feature in 2006).

In the Maghreb, the preferred pattern has been very different and study in either France or Belgium has become something of the norm. In the mid-1970s, the Syrian Omar Amiralay and a group of Lebanese filmmakers followed this pattern of training and indeed remained resident in Europe, among them the documentarists Borhan Alawiya, Jean Chamoun, and Jocelyne Saab, as well as the feature filmmakers Maroun Bagdadi and Randa Chahal-Sabbag. But otherwise there has been no uniformity in the training of filmmakers in the Middle East and, from the beginning, directors there have had very diverse introductions to filmmaking.

The aspirations toward establishing commercial patterns of film production, especially in Lebanon, meant that a number of filmmakers there learned their craft as assistant directors, sometimes in the Egyptian studios. Among the pioneers of Middle Eastern Arab filmmaking, those who went abroad to study travelled in very different directions. The Iraqi Mohamed Choukri Jamil received most of his training in London (as a result of working initially as a documentary filmmaker for the oil companies), the Kuwaiti Khalid al-Siddick studied at Poona in India, while Nabil al-Maleh from Syria followed courses at FAMU in Czechoslovakia and the Lebanese feature filmmaker Ziad Doueiri studied in Los Angeles. Whereas the Palestinian documentarist Ali Nassar studied in Moscow, his compatriot Maï Masri graduated from the University of San Franscisco. The filmmaker who pioneered the breakthrough for the Palestinian feature film, Michel Khleifi, studied at the Belgian film school, INSAS, but most of the Palestinians who followed him a decade or more later lacked this film school background. Rashid Masharawi and Hany Abu Assad both had only limited technical training as cameramen in the Netherlands, while the other 1990s debutants—Palestine's most original feature filmmaker, Elia Suleiman, and the leading documentarists, Nizar Hassan and the actor Mohamed Bakri—were self-taught film directors. By contrast, virtually all the key Syrian directors—beginning with Samir Zikra, Mohamed Malas, Oussama Mohammad, and Abdellatif Abdelhamid—trained in the Soviet Union.

In the Maghreb, the pattern which predominates is that of the European-trained filmmaker who turns almost immediately to feature filmmaking, often with partial funding from Europe and sometimes from a production base there. By contrast, a dozen or more Middle Eastern Arab filmmakers have devoted decades of their lives to documentary work, making a large number of highly individual non-fictional films, some of feature length and all reflecting the complexities of life in this troubled region, before turning to fictional feature filmmaking. Among these, in addition to Alawiya, Saab, Chamoun, and Amiralay, are the Palestinians Maï Masri and

Samir Nimr and the Iraqis Qassim Hawal and Qays al-Zubaydi.

Edward Said argued in 2000 that "the greatest single fact of the past three decades" was "the vast human migration attendant upon war, colonisation and decolonisation, economic and political revolution, and such devastating occurrences as famine, ethnic cleansing and great power machinations."[67] Arab filmmakers from the Maghreb and the Middle East have been caught up in this international development, and, in the 2000s, their filmmaking has become, to a considerable extent, a cinema of diaspora, with residence abroad and the receipt of funding from foreign sources becoming almost the norm. Looking from a 2000s perspective, Andrea Khalil sees contemporary North African filmmakers as "part of the Maghrebi diaspora." They "travel back and forth between Europe or North Amerca and their North African origins," looking "to each shore of the globe's waters with the other side already imprinted on their field of vision."[68] The same is true in the Middle East, especially with regard to the younger filmmakers from Syria and Iraq.

The diaspora extends throughout the Middle East and into the present. The only Yemeni features, for example, have been made by Bader Ben Hirsi, resident in London where he was born, and Khadija al-Salami, who works at the Yemeni embassy in Paris. The latest Iraqi feature filmmaker, Mohamed al-Daradji, found funding first in the Netherlands and then in the United Kingdom, where he now lives. The Jordanian graduate of the American Film Institute, Amin Matalqa, worked from a base in Los Angeles to make his first feature. Similarly, the Lebanese Wajdi Mouawad and Syrian Ruba Nadda live in Canada, while the Syrian Hala al-Abdallah Yakoub works as a producer in Paris.

Filmmakers of this kind, living in enforced exile or, at best, working abroad for financial reasons, are a common feature of the contemporary international film scene. At the same time, there is in the Arab Middle East and even more in the Gulf at the present time, a constant stream of graduates from local media training establishments within the Middle East itself: the Academy of Fine Arts in Baghdad (often known by its French acronym, ALBA [Académie Libanaise des Beaux Arts]), the media department, Institut d'Études Scéniques et Audiovisuelles (IESAV), of St. Joseph's University in Beirut, and the Higher Technical Colleges (separate for men and women) in Dubai and Abu Dhabi. There are also invaluable individual training efforts, such as the Amman Filmmakers Collective, animated by Hazim Bitar, and the Independent Film and Television Academy, run by Maysoon Pachachi and Kassim Abid, in Baghdad.

But if their backgrounds, opportunities, and locations are very diverse, there are common cultural factors which shape and influence many of the filmmakers of both Maghreb and Mashreq. The Tunisian filmmaker Nouri Bouzid set this out eloquently in his piece on "New Realism in Arab Cinema: The Defeat-Conscious Cinema" in the 1980s.[69] For someone of Bouzid's generation (he was born in 1945) the key defeat is 1967, but the issue is, as he sees, "not a circumstantial crisis, centralized in one country, but rather a historical, structural crisis rooted in the cultural degeneration which the Arab-Islamic countries have been experiencing for many centuries now."[70] After independence, cinema became for young filmmakers "a social necessity," and it was in their hands that it "began to assume a vital role."[71] Bouzid includes a number of (unsourced) quotations from his Middle Eastern contemporaries about the importance of cinema for them. Michel Khleifi: "One of the many questions that have preoccupied me is how to portray the Palestinian reality—so as to change it." Mohamed Malas: "Our generation has only lived a series of defeats. Questioning and discussion through cinema have become a must if we are to stand on our own feet." Borhan Alawiya: "We must work toward the prevention of real defeat, which is division and then annihilation."[72]

Looking at the work of his own generation in the Arab world outside Egypt, Bouzid feels that the new cinema "developed the ego of the director, allowed his creative energy to pour forth and enabled him to express his opinions freely—refusing guardianship and not heeding the censors who continued to watch him and take him to task over everything he said—and intended to say." It was this quality which gave the new films "a distinctly and intimately personal flavour . . . making the *auteur* director the pivotal element in the film."[73] Bouzid's assessment of the situation in the late 1980s (the piece was first published in Arabic in *Al-Tariq* in 1988) still holds good 20 years later. What characterizes much of the new Arab cinema is its "attempt to say something new":

> Fixed models and clichés are discarded and, instead, topics and approaches are as varied as the directors themselves, each making films that carry their own mark and are expressive of their particular feelings and thoughts, sorrows and joys, and sense of self-respect.[74]

NOTES

1. Roy Armes, *Dictionary of African Filmmakers* (Bloomington: Indiana University Press, 2008).
2. Ahmad H. Sa'di, "Reflections on Representations, History, and Moral Accountability," in Ahmad H. Sa'di and Lila Abu-Lughod, eds., *Nakba: Palestine, 1948, and the Claims of Memory* (New York: Columbia University Press, 2007), 287–288.
3. Jacques Mandelbaum, "Au Moyen-Orient, tous les cinéastes sont des Palestiniens," in Jean-Michel Frodon, ed., *Au sud du cinéma* (Paris: Cahiers du Cinéma / Arte Éditions, 2004), 63.
4. In a similar vein, the Arab Middle East is accorded just three pages in André Z. Labarrère's 603-page *Atlas du cinéma* (Paris: Librairie Française, 2002), 351–353.

5. Richard Abel, *The Red Rooster Scare: Making Cinema American, 1900–1910* (Berkeley: University of California Press, 1999), xi.

6. Stewart Ross, *The Middle East Since 1945* (London: Hodder Education, 2006), 17.

7. Cited in Jean-Claude Seguin, *Alexandre Promio ou les énigmes de la lumière* (Paris: Éditions L'Harmattan, 1999), 85.

8. Ibid., 88.

9. Ibid.

10. Cited in Sa'di, "Reflections," 289.

11. Peter Mansfield, *The Arabs* (Harmondsworth, England: Penguin Books, 1980), 185.

12. Justin McCarthy, *The Ottoman Peoples and the End of Empire* (London: Arnold, 2001), 163.

13. Ibid., 163–164. For an opposing view, see William R. Polk, *Understanding Iraq* (London: I. B. Tauris, 2006), 104–107.

14. Benedict Anderson, *Imagined Communities: Reflections of the Origin and Spread of Nationalism*, 2nd ed. (London: Verso, 1991), 120.

15. Ibid., 6.

16. Peter Mansfield, *A History of the Middle East*, 2nd ed. (Harmondsworth, England: Penguin Books, 2003), 156.

17. Polk, *Understanding Iraq*, 106.

18. McCarthy, *The Ottoman Peoples*, 163–164.

19. Ibid.

20. Hady Zaccak, *Le Cinéma libanais, itinéraire d'un voyage vers l'inconnu (1929–1996)* (Beirut: Dar el-Machreq, 1997), 16.

21. Nurith Gertz and George Khleifi, *Palestinian Cinema: Landscape, Trauma and Memory* (Edinburgh: Edinburgh University Press, 2008), 13–14.

22. Ghada Karmi, *Married to Another Man: Israel's Dilemma in Palestine* (London: Pluto Press, 2007), 1.

23. Ross, *The Middle East*, 29–30.

24. Sandra Mackey, *Mirror of the Arab World: Lebanon in Conflict* (New York: W. W. Norton, 2008), 48.

25. Ibid., 65.

26. Ibid., 66.

27. Zaccak, *Le cinéma libanais*, 23.

28. The Arab Film and Television Centre, Beirut, published the proceedings of three roundtable conferences it sponsored on *Arab Cinema and Culture* in 1962, 1963, and 1964, and, as the Interarab Centre of Cinema and Television, it also published Georges Sadoul's *The Cinema in the Arab Countries* (1966).

29. Mackey, *Mirror*, 105.

30. Ross, *The Middle East*, 29. Though totally apposite, this is, of course, an international—not specifically Arab—joke. On the evening I typed this I heard it again on television (with different vegetation and climate), this time told about Wales.

31. Mackey, *Mirror*, 143.

32. Lina Khatib, *Lebanese Cinema: Imagining the Civil War and Beyond* (London: I. B. Tauris, 2008), 188.

33. McCarthy, *The Ottoman Peoples*, 166.

34. Cited in Barry Rubin, *The Truth about Syria* (New York: Palgrave Macmillan, 2007), 2.

35. Ibid., 36.

36. Polk, *Understanding Iraq*, 109.

37. Rubin, *The Truth*, 126.

38. Ibid., 44.

39. Ibid.

40. Rasha Salti, *Insights into Syrian Cinema* (New York: Arte East / Rattapallax Press, 2006), 61.

41. Ibid., 21–22.

42. Ibid., 167.

43. McCarthy, *The Ottoman Peoples*, 175.

44. Ibid., 176.

45. Cited in Georgina Howell, *Daughter of the Desert: The Remarkable Life of Gertrude Bell* (London: Macmillan, 2006), 325.

46. Yves Thoraval, *Les écrans du croissant fertile* (Paris: Éditions Séguier, 2002), 18.

47. Shakir Nouri, *À la recherche du cinéma irakien (1945–1985)* (Paris: Éditions L'Harmattan, 1986), 65.

48. Dilip Hiro, *Iraq: A Report from the Inside* (London: Granta Publications, 2003), 28–29.

49. Ross, *The Middle East*, 124.

50. Hiro, *Iraq*, 32.

51. Kassem Hawal, "Regard sur le cinéma irakien," in *Septième Biennale des cinémas*

arabes (Paris: Institut du Monde Arabe, 2004), 101.

52. Ibid.

53. Hamid Naficy, *An Accented Cinema: Exilic and Diasporic Filmmaking* (Princeton, N.J.: Princeton University Press, 2001).

54. McCarthy, *The Ottoman Peoples,* 173.

55. Edward Said, *The Question of Palestine* (London: Routledge and Kegan Paul, 1980), ix.

56. Gertz and Khleifi, *Palestinian Cinema,* 54.

57. Karmi, *Married to Another Man,* 11.

58. Avi Shlaim, "No Sentiments in War," *Guardian* (London), May 31, 2008, 8.

59. Ilan Pappe, *A History of Modern Palestine: One Land Two Peoples* (Cambridge: Cambridge University Press, 2006), 140.

60. Gertz and Khleifi, *Palestinian Cinema,* 19–20.

61. Ross, *The Middle East,* 90.

62. Gertz and Khleifi, *Palestinian Cinema,* 22.

63. Ross, *The Middle East,* 146.

64. Edward Said, preface to *Dreams of a Nation: On Palestinian Cinema,* by Hamid Dabashi (London: Verso, 2006), 2.

65. Gertz and Khleifi, *Palestinian Cinema,* 8.

66. Nada Mourtada-Sabbah, Mohamed al-Mutawa, John W. Fox, and Tim Walters, "Media as Social Matrix in the United Arab Emirates," in Alanoud Alsharekh and Robert Springborg, eds., *Popular Culture and Political Identity in the Arab Gulf States* (London: Saqi and London Middle East Institute SOAS), 2008, 121.

67. Edward Said, *Reflections on Exile* (London: Granta Books, 2001), xiv.

68. Andrea Khalil, introduction to *North African Cinema in a Global Perspective: Through the Lens of Diaspora* (London: Routledge, 2008), ix.

69. Nouri Bouzid, "New Realism in Arab Cinema: The Defeat-Conscious Cinema," *Alif* 15 (1995): 242–250.

70. Ibid., 242.

71. Ibid., 243.

72. Ibid., 243.

73. Ibid., 247.

74. Ibid., 250.

Part One

Dictionary of Filmmakers

Abbas, Hiam. Palestinian filmmaker and actress. Born in 1960 in Nazareth, she has lived in France since 1989. She studied photography before turning to acting in 1983. Since playing the lead in Michel Khleifi's Palestinian *Wedding in Galilee* (1987), she has starred in a dozen or more major Arab films, including two Lebanese productions—Rashid Masharawi's *Haifa* and Danielle Arbid's *Raddem;* two Tunisian features—Raja Amari's *Satin Rouge,* and Moufida Tlatli's *Nadia and Sara;* two dealing with the immigrant community in France—Christophe Ruggia's *Le Gône de chaaba* and Bourlem Guerdjou's *Living in Paradise;* as well as Ahmed Boulane's Moroccan feature *Ali, Rabia and the Others,* and the Egyptian Yousry Nasrallah's *Gate of the Sun.* Short films: *Bread / Le pain / al-Khubz* (2000, 18', 35mm), *The Eternal Dance / La danse éternelle / al-Raqisa al-abadiya* (2003, 26', 35mm).

Abbas, Hussain Ghulom (Abu Jalal). Bahraini filmmaker. Born in 1947, he studied filmmaking in Tehran and worked there for some years. He also worked in television. Short films: *Black Bag* (1968), *Compunction* (2005, 52', DVD).

Abbas, Mustafa. Emirati filmmaker. He studied filmmaking at the Hollywood Film Institute and has written and directed a number of amateur films. Short film (with English dialogue): *100 Miles* (2007, 26', Mini DV).

Abboud, Anne-Marie. Lebanese filmmaker. She studied filmmaking at Fine Arts Institute in Beirut. Short fictional film: *Portrait of Memories* (2000, 17').

Abboud, Marwa. Emirati filmmaker. Born in 1983, she studied at the American University of Sharjah. Short documentary film: *Egoism* (2004, 11', Mini DV).

ABBOUD, TAYSIR. Lebanese filmmaker. Feature films: *The Madness of Adolescent Girls / La folie des adolescentes / Jounoun al-mourahikat* (1969), *The Bells of Return / Les cloches du retour / Ajrass al-awda* (1969), *Forgive Me, My Love / Pardonne-moi mon amour / Samehni habibi* (1981).

Abdalla, Hussain Nabil. Emirati filmmaker. Born and raised in the UAE, of Palestinian descent, he studied at the American University of Sharjah. Short films: *'48 and After* (2007, 2', DVD), *Too Much Work* (2007, 1', Mini DV).

Abdallah, Ghassan. Syrian filmmaker. Short fictional film: *Daydreams / Ahlam mountasaf al-daheera* (2005, 7', 35mm).

Abdallah, Mona. Emirati filmmaker. She was born in 1988 in Benghazi, Libya, and lived in Lebanon before moving to the UAE. She studied at the American University of Sharjah. Short films: *Bait* (2007, 3', Mini DV), *Break In* (2007, 3', Mini DV), *Aftermath* (2007, 2', Mini DV).

ABDALLAH, SAMIR. Palestinian filmmaker. Born in 1959 in Denmark, he has lived in France since the age of 6 and has French nationality. He has made numerous short documentary films. Feature-length documentaries: *We Shall Return One Day / Nous retournerons un jour* (with Walid Charara, 1998, 90', video),

Writers on the Borders, a Journey to Palestine / Écrivains des frontières (with Jose Reynes, 2004, 80', DV Cam), *After the War . . . / Après la guerre, c'est toujours la guerre* (in Lebanon, 2008, 82', DigiBeta).

ABDELAZIZ, FALEH. Iraqi filmmaker. Feature film: *Return to the Countryside / Retour à la campagne / Al-awda lil rif* (1963, 35mm).

Abdelhadi, Walid. Palestinian filmmaker. Short film: *Nour's Dream* (2006).

ABDELHAMID, ABDELLATIF. Syrian filmmaker. Born in 1954 in Lattakiah, he first studied Arabic literature at university in his hometown, then filmmaking at the Moscow film school, VGIK, where he graduated in 1981. He has appeared as an actor in films by Mohamed Malas and Oussama Mohammad. His short and documentary films include three made during his studies: *Good Night / Bonne nuit / Tushibuna . . . ala-Khayr, An Old Lesson / Une ancienne leçon / Darsun qadima, Upside Down / Sens dessus dessous / Ra'as ala aqib* (1981). After graduating, he made further documentaries: *Desires* a.k.a. *Wishes / Désirs / Umnyat* (1983), *Our Hands / Nos mains / Aydeena* (1984, 21'). In 1985, he wrote and directed a television serial, *Two Weeks and Five Months / Usbu'an wa khamsat shuhur.* Feature films: *The Nights of the Jackal / Les nuits du chacal / Layali ibn awa* (1989, 95', 35mm), *Verbal Messages / Lettres orales / Rasa'il al shafahyya* (1991, 105', 35mm), *The Rising Rain / La montée de la pluie / Su'ud al-matar* (1996, 90', 35mm), *Breeze of the Soul / Le souffle de l'âme / Nassim ar-ruh* (1998, 90', 35mm), *Two Moons and an Olive Tree* a.k.a. *Qamaran and Zeltouna / Deux lunes et un olivier / Qamarn wa zayrunah* (2001, 90', 35mm), *At Our Listeners' Request / Au plaisir des auditeurs / Ma yatlubuhu al-mustami'un* (2003, 89', 35mm), *Out of Coverage / Hors réseau / Kahref al-taghtiya* (2007, 100', 35mm), *Days of Boredom / Jours d'ennui / Ayyam al-dajar* (2008).

Abdelrahman, Firas. Palestinian filmmaker. Short film: *Rachel's War* (2003).

Abdelwahed, Naima. Emirati filmmaker. Short film: *Anti-Gendercide* (with Farha Moon, 2007, 1', Mini DV).

Abdou, Sara Tarek. Emirati filmmaker. Studied at the American University of Sharjah. Short fictional film: *Eruption* (2006, 3', Mini DV).

Abdul Azeem, Hani. Emirati filmmaker. Short documentary films: *Medicine School: A Story of Success* (2001, 13', Beta SP), *The Emirates Date Factory in Al-Sad* (2001, 20', Beta SP).

ABDULAMIR, LAYTH. Iraqi filmmaker. Born in 1957 in Iraq, he studied film at the Sorbonne in Paris (1977–1980) and at the Fine Art Institute in Kiev (1980–1986). He made three short films, *Night Chat, President,* and *Death,* in 1982–1985. He subsequently worked in Kiev and then for French and Dubai television. Short fictional films: *The Cradle / Le berceau* (1985, 21', Beta SP), *Sunflower* (2005, 20', 16mm). Feature-length documentary: *Iraq: The Song of the Missing Men / Irak, le chant des absents* (in France, 2005, 93', DV Cam).

Abdulaziz, Samantha. Emirati filmmaker. She studied at the American University of Sharjah. Short fictional film: *Where the Lost Things Go* (2007, 4', Mini DV).

Abdulkhalek, Heba. Emirati filmmaker. Short film: *Don't Drink and Drive* (with Bandar al-Mandeel, 2000, 1', Mini DV).

Abdulla, Abdulla Abdulaziz. Qatari filmmaker. He studied at the Higher Institute of Arts in Kuwait. He works for Qatar TV and is also a stage director. Short film: *From the Darkness to the Bright* (2005, 7', Mini DV).

Abdulla, Hafez Ali. Qatari filmmaker. Born in 1975 in Doha, in Qatar, he studied drama at the California Arts Institute and then directing at the Chapman University in California. He has made a number of short fictional films, including *Faces of Qatar / Visages du Qatar* (2001), *For You Alone / Pour toi seul* (2002), *I'm* *at Home / Je suis chez moi* (2003), *Taxi Driver / Chauffeur de taxi* (2005, 19', Beta SP).

Abdulla, Suhail Matar. Emirati filmmaker. Studied at Dubai Men's College. Short films: *Mis-Used Freedom* (2007, 2', DV Cam), *Innocent Souls* (2007, 2', DV Cam).

Abdulla, Wedima Bilal. Emirati filmmaker. She studied at Abu Dhabi Women's College. Short fictional film: *Kid's Revenge* (2003, 2', DV Cam).

Abdullah, Bilal. Emirati filmmaker. An actor in ten short films. Short fictional film: *Sunset* (2002, 51', DV Cam).

Abdullah, Khalid. Emirati filmmaker. Studied at the American University of Sharjah. Short film: *Alcoholism* (with Fatma Almushrrakh, 1', Mini DV).

Abdullah, Yahya. Jordanian filmmaker. Born in 1978 in Lebanon, he studied literature at the University of Amman in Jordan, where he now teaches. He also studied filmmaking in Paris and works as a literary critic. He has made a number of short films: *The Arab Citizen / Le citoyen arabe*, *Gentle Grandmother / La gentille grand-mère* (2004), *Family-Sized Middle East / À l'échelle familale* (2004), *Six Minutes / Six minutes* (2005, 15', DV Cam), *Colouring / Coloriage* (2005), *Hello, Hello / Allô, allô* (2005), *A Man in a Cup / Un homme dans la tasse* (2005, 5', Beta SP), *Six Minutes* (2005, 15', video), *Pummelo* (with Aseel Mansour, 2008, 29', DigiBeta), *SMS* (2008, 17', video).

Abdulrahman, Dawood Mohammed Hassan. Emirati filmmaker. He studied at Dubai Men's College. Short films: *Al Bidyah Mosque* (2002, 6', Beta SP), *Sooner or Later* (2003, 1', DV Cam), *Faith and Friendship* (2003, 18', DV Cam), *Innocent Dreams* (2004, 6', DV Cam).

Abed, Adel. Emirati filmmaker. Short film: *The Soul* (2001, 12', Beta SP).

Abi Aad, Serena. Lebanese filmmaker. Short film: *The Lullaby* (2007, 19').

Abi Khalil, Jad. Lebanese filmmaker. Born in 1973 in Beirut, he studied filmmaking at IESAV in Beirut. Short films: *Mediterranean Hereditary Blood Medicines / Les médecines sanguines héréditaires méditerranéennes* (1997), *Just as My Confessor Told Me / Tel que mon confesseur me l'a rapporté* (1999, 21', 35mm), *Sorry / Dommage / Rahet ya haram* (2002, 17', video). *Your Majesty Mr. President* (2003, 50'), *Thirty* (2003, 14').

Abi Samra, Maher. Lebanese filmmaker. Born in 1965 in Beirut, he studied at the Academy of Fine Arts in Beirut. Short films, mostly documentaries: *Syndromes of Return / Syndromes de retour* (1993), *Building on the Waves / Bâtir sur les vagues* (with Jérome Allamargot and Aldo Pancari, 1995, 26', 16mm), *Hezbollah: Party of Gods / Hezbollah: parti de dieu* (1996), *Shatila Roundabout / Rond-point Chatila* (2004, 51', video), *Merely a Smell* (2007, 11').

Abi Wardeh, Hady. Lebanese filmmaker. Studied filmmaking at IESAV in Beirut. Short fictional film: *Broken Dream / Rêve brisé* (2000, 14').

ABID, KASSIM. Iraqi filmmaker. Studied at the Institute of Arts in Baghdad and at VGIK in Moscow. He has lived in the United Kingdom since 1982. In 2003, with Maysoon Pachachi he set up an Independent Film & TV College in Baghdad. He has also taught at the Birzeit University in Palestine. Short films: *Amid the Alien Corn / Dans les champs étranges de maïs* (1991, 38', 36mm), *Naji al-Ali, an Artist with Vision / Naji al-Ali, un artiste visionnaire* (1998, 60', Beta SP), *Surda Checkpoint* (2005, 30', video). Feature-length documentary: *Life After the Fall / La vie après la chute / Hatay ma baad al-suqoot* (2008, 155', DigiBeta).

ABOU SAMAH, NICOLAS. Lebanese filmmaker. He worked in television. Feature film: *Charbel / Charbel* (1966, 35mm).

ABOU SEIF, SALAH.* Egyptian filmmaker who directed one Iraqi feature film: *The Battle* *of Al-Qâdissiya / La bataille d'Al-Qâdissiya / al-Qâdissia* (1981).

Abou Zeid, Ahmad. Palestinian filmmaker. Short film: *Palestine, 52 Years of Occupation / Palestine, 52 ans d'occupation* (2000, 10', Beta SP).

Aboubayda, Abdulrahman. Emirati filmmaker. Short film: *Careless Driving* (2007, 1', Mini DV).

Aboujarad, Mohamed. Jordanian filmmaker and member of the Amman Filmmakers Cooperative. He studied at Yarmouk University and works as a computer network administrator. Short film: *What a Job / Quel boulot* (with Hazim Bitar and Omar Saleh, 2006, 7', DV Cam).

Aboulhosn, Zeina. Lebanese filmmaker. Documentaries: *Zeid's Little Bomb* (2006, 5'), *Staying Alive* (2006, 8'), *I Remember Lebanon* (2006, 6').

Abousaif, Sajeda. Jordanian filmmaker and member of the Amman Filmmakers Cooperative. She studied Islamic jurisprudence and works as a teacher. Short films: *Free to Fly* (with Alabbas Sa'ed, 2006, 6'), *Emergency* (2007).

Abu al-Ala, Amjad. Emirati filmmaker. He studied mass communication at UAE University and subsequently worked in television. Student films: *In the End of the Fall* (2001, 8', Beta SP), *The Slump on Cannes Roads* (2003, 14', Beta SP), *On the Pavement of the Soul* (2004, 31', DV Cam). Short fictional films: *Coffee and Orange* (2005, 19', Mini DV), *Feather of the Birds* (2006, 32', Mini DV).

Abu Ali, Khadija. Palestinian filmmaker. Wife of Mustafa Abu Ali. Documentaries: *Children, but . . . / Des enfants, mais . . . / Atfal, wa lakin* (1981, 23', 16mm), *Women for Palestine / Nisaa'on min Filastin* (1982).

Abu Ali, Mustafa. Jordanian filmmaker. Husband of Khadija Abu Ali. Founder of the Palestine Film Organisation. Many of his early films were made collectively under his leadership. Short films: *The Palestinians' Right / Le droit palestinien / al-Hak al-falastini* (1969, 8'), *Reportage / Ribottâj* (1969), *No to the Defeatist Solution / Non à la solution défaitiste / Lâ li-l hall es-simy* (collective, 1969, 20', 16mm), *With Our Souls, with Our Blood* a.k.a. *With Blood and Spirit / De toute mon âme et avec mon sang / Bi al-ruh, bi al-dam* (collective, 1971), *Fatah Land / Le Fathahland / al-Arqoub* (1972, 25', 16mm), *Zionist Aggression / Agression sioniste / 'Adwan sahyuni* (1972, 22', 16mm), *The Achilles Heel / al-Arqub* (1972), *Scenes from the Occupation of Gaza / Scènes d'occupation à Gaza / Mashahid min al-ihtilal fi Ghazeh* (1973), *Palestinian Newsreels 1 & 2 / Actualités Palestiniennes 1 & 2 / Jarida filistin eth-thawra-l-muçawara* (1974), *They Do Not Exist / Ils n'existent pas / Laysa lahum wujud* (1974, 26', 16mm), *On the Road to Victory / Le chemin de la victoire / Tariq al-nasr* (1975, 15', 16mm), *Tel al-Za'tar* (with Jean Chamoun and Pino Adriano, 1977), *Palestine in the Eye / Filastin fi al-'ayn* (1977).

Abu Alwan, Amani. Lebanese filmmaker. Born in 1977 in Beirut, she studied at IESAV, then worked in the theatre and for television as a sound engineer, assistant director, and editor. Documentary: *Zanzoun* (2000, 21', Beta SP).

ABU ASSAD, HANY. Palestinian filmmaker. Born in 1961 in Nazareth, he worked initially as an aeronautical engineer in the Netherlands, where he subsequently trained as a cameraman. On his return to Palestine, he worked as a television producer, turning to cinema to collaborate with Rashid Masharawi. He worked as assistant on the latter's documentary, *House, Houses* (1991), then produced *Long Days in Gaza* (1991) and Masharawi's first feature, *Curfew* (1993). Abu Assad began his own directing career in 1991, with the short documentary *To Whom It May Concern* (1991, 15'), followed by two fictional shorts, including *A Paper House / Une maison en papier / Bayt min waraq* (1992, 28', 16mm). His documentaries include *Sanctuary / Sanctuaire / Taht al-mahjar* (2000), *Nazareth 2000 / Nasseriyya 2000* (2001, 55'). His first feature was a Dutch-language comedy romance. Feature films: *The Fourteenth Chick / Le quatorzième poussin / Het veertiende kippetje* (1998, 88'), *Ford Transit* (2002, 81', documentary), *Rana's Wedding / Le mariage de Rana / Urs Rana* (2002, 90', 35mm), *Paradise Now / al-Jinna alaam* (2005, 90', 35mm).

Abu Dayyeh, Mohamed. Palestinian filmmaker. Short film: *My Dad Is Late / Mon père est en retard / Ta'akhar abi* (2003).

Abu Diqqa, Wael. Palestinian filmmaker. Short films: *Exile / L'exile / al-Ghyrba* (1998), *Checkpoints / Points de contrôle / al-Hawajiz* (2000).

Abu Ghoush, Dima. Palestinian filmmaker. Shorts: *At the Checkpoint / Au point de contrôle* (2004), *Good Morning, Qalqiliya / Bonjour, Qaqiliya / Sabah al-khayr Qalqiliya* (2004, 26', video), *My Palestine* (2007, 10').

Abu Goumazah, Khalid Mahmoud. Emirati filmmaker. He studied at the American University of Sharjah. Short film: *Choose Your Path* (with Joud Odeh, 2007, 1', Mini DV).

Abu Haidar, Lamia. Lebanese filmmaker. Debut documentary: *Lost Childhood / Enfance perdue* (with Maria Ousseimi, 1992, 40', 16mm).

Abu Hanna, Umayya. Palestinian filmmaker. Born in 1961 in Haifa, Israel, where she was educated, she moved in 1981 to Helsinki, where she studied radio and television journalism. She has worked as a radio and television reporter in Finland. Documentary: *My Homeland* (1993).

Abu Hmud, Saed. Palestinian filmmaker. Short film: *Second Halftime* (2005).

Abu Nawas, Shamma. Emirati filmmaker. She studied communication technology at Dubai Women's College. Short film: *I'm a Man / Ana rajol* (with Sahar al-Khatib, 2006, 19', Mini DV).

Abu Rish, Darwish. Palestinian filmmaker. Short film: *The Man from Haifa / L'homme de Haïfa / Haifawi* (1999).

Abu Sa'da, Ahmad. Palestinian filmmaker. Short films: *A Guerrilla's Diary / Youmiyyat fida'i* (1969), *On the Vanguard / Ma'a al-tala'i* (1970).

Abu Salem, François. Palestinian filmmaker. Documentaries: *Bread and Salt / 'Aysh wa milh* (1976), *Jerusalem . . . Gates of the City / Jérusalem . . . Les portes de la ville / al-Quds abwab al-madina* (1995).

ABU WAEL, TAWFIK. Palestinian filmmaker. Born in 1976 in Um El-Fahem, he graduated in film studies from Tel Aviv University and worked in the university archive, 1996–1998. Then, in 1997–1999, he taught drama at the Hassan Arafa School in Jaffa. Short films: *Waiting for Saladin / En attendant Saladin / Fintithar Salah-Eddin* (2001, 53', Beta SP), *Diary of a Male Whore / Journal d'un prostitué mâle / Yaw'miyat a'hir* (2001, 14', Beta SP), *The Fourteen / Le quatorze / Rabe 'ashar* (2002, 13', video). He also contributed one episode to the collectively made video documentary *One More Time (Five Stories about Human Rights in Palestine / Une fois encore (cinq histoires sur les droits de l'homme en Palestine)* (with Nada al-Yassir, Ismaïl Habash, Abdel Salam Shehada, Najwa Najjar, 2002, 57', Beta SP). Feature film: *Thirst / La soif / 'Atash* (2004, 110', 35mm).

Aburahme, Dahna. Palestinian filmmaker. Of Palestinian origin, she grew up in Amman, Dubai, and Beiruit, and studied video and media in New York. Short films: *Palestine Is Waiting / La Palestine attend* (with Annemarie Jacir and Suzy Salmy, 2003), *Until When . . .* (2004).

Adam, Hermeen Kamel. Emirati filmmaker. Short film: *Katkoot* (with Salma Khaifa Al-Darmaki, 2007, 26', DVD).

Adel, Jaidaa. Emirati filmmaker. Short film: *Sense of Detection* (with Ramzy Shuhaiber, 2007, 8', Mini DV).

Adelkrim, Tarek. Iraqi filmmaker. Documentary: *Art in the Conflict / L'art dans le combat / Fan wa maraka* (1969).

Adhami, Reema. Emirati filmmaker. Short film: *Enigmatic* (2007, 6', Mini DV).

Adwan, Abdel Menem. Palestinian filmaker. Now living in Europe and working mainly in television. Documentary: *About the Other / Au sujet de l'autre / 'An al-'akhar* (2004, 13', Mini DV).

Agha, Akram. Saudi filmmaker. Short film: *Intabih* (2005, 3', video).

AGRAMA, FAROUK.* Egyptian filmmaker who made one Lebanese feature film: *The Conquerors / Les conquérants / al-Kahiroun* (1966, 35mm).

Ahmad, Asma. Emirati filmmaker. Short film: *Mission of Hope / Mashroo' amal* (with Aisha Mohamed Obaid al-Muhairi, 2008, 21', Mini DV).

Ahmad, Nazima. Emirati filmmaker. She studied at the American University of Sharjah but has spent most of her life in Pakistan. Short animated film: *Compact Void* (2006, 2', DV Cam).

Ahmaro, Amir. Palestinian filmmaker. Short documentary film: *Prayers for the Patient* (2007, 24').

Ahmed, Abdul Rahman Abubaker. Emirati filmmaker. Born in 1969, he studied mass communication at UAE University. Short films: *Impossible Interview* (2001, 26', Beta SP), *Khararif* (2002, 12', Beta SP).

Ahmed, Abdullah Hassan. Emirati filmmaker. Born in 1978 in the UEA, he works as director for the Sama television channel in Dubai. Also worked as cameraman on a number of short films. Short films: *The Nail / L'ongle* (2002, 6', Beta SP), *The Swing / L'oscillation* (2003, 21', DV Cam), *The Rise of the Doing* (2004, 25', Mini DV), *Fan Clip* (2004, 4', Mini DV), *01'03* (with eleven other directors, 2004, 12', Mini DV), *Yahoo* (2004, 35', DV Cam), *Amen / Ameen* (2005, 15', Mini DV), *Al-Fustan* (2005, 28', Mini DV), *Small Sky / Petit ciel / Sama sagheera* (with Omar Ibrahim, 2006, 14', Mini DV), *Summer Birds* (2007, 19', Mini DV).

Ahmed, Ahmed Abdulla. Emirati filmmaker. He studied at Dubai Men's College. Short film: *Innocent Eyes* (2005, 3', Mini DV).

Ahmed, Asma. Emirati filmmaker. She studied at Dubai Women's College. Short film: *Speeding* (2006, 1', Mini DV).

Ahmed, Bader. Emirati filmmaker. He studied at Dubai Men's College. Short film: *Speed Maniacs* (2006, 11', Mini DV).

Ahmed, Imad. Palestinian filmmaker. He worked as a cameraman for news and documentaries in Ramallah. Documentaries: *Local / Mahalli* (with Ismaïl Habash and Raed al-Helou, 2002), *Poppa / Papa / Buba* (2004).

Ahmed, Roqia Murad Mohammed. Emirati filmmaker. She studied at UAE University. Short animated films: *Drop of Water* (2004, 2', DVD), *Suffering of a Blind Boy* (2004, 5', DVD).

Ahmed, Yousef Hussain. Emirati filmmaker. He studied at Dubai Men's College. Short films: *Before You Drive* (2002, 1', DV Cam), *Statistics* (2002, 1', DV Cam).

Ajajah, Mahmoud Salem Ba. Saudi filmmaker. He has worked extensively in theatre and television. Short films: *Affiliation* (with Mahdi Ali Ali and Dalia Bakhet, 2007, 9', Mini DV), *Full Moon Night / Laylat al-badr* (2007, 31', Mini DV), *A Child's Task* (2008, 18', Mini DV).

Ajffar, Ali Mohammad. Kuwaiti filmmaker. Born in 1960, he became an amateur filmmaker while still at college. Short film: *Matrix Reloaded* (2006, 26', DV Cam).

Ajram, Ajram. Lebanese filmmaker. Born in 1969 in South Lebanon, he studied at the Institute of Dramatic Art and worked on cultural programs for children. Short films: *The Nightmare / Le cauchemar* (1996), *Abdo* (with Tania El Khoury, 25', Beta SP).

Akad, Bachar. Syrian filmmaker. Short documentary film: *Pages from the Golan / Pages du Golan / Çafahätun mina-l Julan* (1974).

Akaf, Kamel. Iraqi filmmaker. Documentary: *A People's Tragedy / La tragédie d'un peuple / Massat chaab* (1968).

Akaron, Myrna. Lebanese filmmaker. Short fictional film: *Adult Story / Conte d'adulte* (2000, 14').

AKIKI, PHILIPPE. Lebanese filmmaker and actor. He worked as an actor and also as director of photography for several pioneer filmmakers, including Michel Haroun (*Red Flowers*, 1957). He directed just one feature and died in 1995. Feature film: *The Realm of the Poor / Le royaume des pauvres / Mamlakat al-foukara* (1967).

AKKACHI, MAROUAN. Syrian filmmaker. Feature film: *The Hero's Stormcloud / La nuée du héros* (1974, 35mm).

AKKAD, MUSTAPHA. Syrian filmmaker. Born in 1933 in Aleppo, he studied filmmaking at UCLA. He worked as assistant to Sam Peckinpah on *Ride the High Country* before setting up his own production company to make documentary and fictional films. He later produced John Carpenter's *Halloween* in the United States. His own two feature films as director are international co-productions made with Hollywood stars. He was killed in a terrorist attack in Jordan in 2008. Feature films: *The Message / Le message / al-Risala* (1975, 35mm), *Lion of the Desert / Le lion du désert / Omar al-Mukhtar* (1980, 117', 35mm).

AL-ABDALLAH YAKOUB, HALA. Syrian filmmaker. Born in 1956 in Hama, she studied first agricultural engineering at the University of Damascus and then anthropology at the EHESS in Paris and filmmaking at the Université de Paris VIII. She worked as assistant to Oussama Mohammad for *Stars in Broad Daylight* and Mohamed Malas for *The Night*. She joined Ramad Films in Paris and worked as producer for its founder, Omar Amiralay, on several films. Documentary feature films: *I Am the One Who Brings Flowers to Her Grave / Je suis celle qui porte les fleurs vers sa tombe* (with Ammar al-Beik, 2006, 110', video), *Hey! Don't Forget the Cumin / Hé! N'oublie pas le cumin* (2008, 66', DigiBeta).

Al-Abdool, Ali. Emirati filmmaker. He has worked extensively in television and commercials. Fictional film: *Wayfarer* (1989, 75', Beta SP).

Al-Abdooli, Khalil Ibrahim. Emirati filmmaker. He studied at Dubai Men's College. Short films, one documentary: *The Raging Bulls of Fujairah* (2002, 5', Beta SP), and two fiction: *Who Let the Dog Out* (2003, 19', DV Cam), *Devil's Wood* (2004, 16', DV Cam).

Al-Abidi, Hisham Mansour. Saudi filmmaker. Short fictional film: *Gregeaan Mbarak* (2005, 14', DV Cam).

Al-Adwani, Humaid. Omani filmmaker. He studied film and media production in Australia and works at Sultan Qaboos University. His short film was made in collaboration with an independent woman filmmaker from Australia. Short film: *For Night Another Sun* (with Tani Bodini, 2006, 7', DV Cam).

Al-Aidarous, Khadher. Emirati filmmaker. He studied at Columbia University, Hollywood, and at the American Film Institute in Los Angeles and subsequently worked in television in Abu Dhabi. Short documentary film: *Innocent Voices* (2003, 37', DigiBeta).

Al-Akawi, Alaa Mohammed. Emirati film-maker. Of Syrian origin, but raised in the UAE, he studied at the American University of Sharjah. Short films: *Reincarnation* (2004, 21', Mini DV), *Spiritual Hunt* (2004, 14', Mini DV).

Al-Ali, Ali. Bahraini filmmaker. Short films: *Alyaqada* (2006, 27', DV Cam), *The Radical Solution* (2007, 34', DV Cam), *Bloodlust* (2007, 15', DV Cam), *Abbass Homeland* (2007, 12', DV Cam).

Al-Ali, Masoud Amralla. Emirati filmmaker. Short fictional film: *Al-Rumram* (1994, 24', Hi-8).

Alameer, Ali Hasan Mohamed. Saudi film-maker. Born in 1981, he began his career in 1995. Short fictional and experimental films: *The Lost Dream* (2003, 30', DV Cam), *Child of Heaven* (2006, 21', Mini DV).

Al-Ameri, Saeeda. Emirati filmmaker. She studied at Abu Dhabi Women's College. Short documentary film: *Al Shallah* (2000, 5', DV Cam).

Al-Amoodi, Reem. Emirati filmmaker. She studied at Dubai Women's College. Short films: *Paranoia* (2006, 1', Mini DV), *Hard to Fix* (2006, 1', Mini DV).

Alamuddin, Rana. Lebanese filmmaker. She studied audio-visual media and worked as a journalist for the *Beirut Times*. Short films: *Boys First . . . Ladies After* (1998), *Murur al-kiram* (1999).

AL-ANSARI, MOHAMED. Iraqi filmmaker. Feature film: *Life's Lesson / La leçon de vie / Ababathu al-hayat* (1958, 35mm).

Al-Aqeeli, Sara. Emirati filmmaker. She was born in 1978 in Dubai. Short fictional film: *Swing* (2002, 8', Mini DV).

AL-ARISS, ALI. Pioneer Lebanese filmmak-er. Born in 1909, he worked in the theatre in Egypt before returning to Lebanon to make two feature films. After a further documen-tary film, Al-Ariss abandoned the cinema. He died in 1965. Feature films: *The Flower Seller / La vendeuse de fleurs / Bayyaat al-ward* (1943, 35mm), *Kawkab, Princess of the Desert / Kaw-kab, princesse du désert* a.k.a. *L'étoile du Sa-hara / Kawkab amirat as-sahra* (1946, 35mm).

Al-Arouj, Meshari. Kuwaiti filmmaker. Has worked for some years as cameraman and graphic designer in Kuwaiti TV. Short animat-ed film: *No Random Fishing* (2006, 2', DVD).

Al-Ashoor, Zinab. Emirati filmmaker. Born in 1980, she studied at Abu Dhabi Women's College. Short films: *Romantic Poetry* (2001, 7', DV Cam), *Cornflakes* (2001, 1', DV Cam), *Cru-el Reality* (2002, 7', DV Cam), *All That Glitters Is Not Gold* (2002, 5', DV Cam).

Al-Ashqar, Akram. Palestinian filmmaker. Documentary: *First Picture* (2006, 27'). Con-tributed *Red, Dead and Mediterranean* (1' 25") to the collective film *Summer 2006, Palestine* (2006, 35', Beta SP).

Al-Askari, Lama. Emirati filmmaker. Born in 1985 in Abu Dhabi, of Palestinian/Lebanese origin, she studied at the American University of Sharjah. Short fictional film: *Her* (2004, 5', Mini DV).

Alatar, Mohamed. Palestinian filmmaker. Documentary: *Jerusalem . . . the East Side Sto-ry* (2008, 56').

Al-Awadi, Nadia Ahmed. Emirati filmmaker. She studied at Dubai Women's College. Short documentary film: *Between Dream and Real-ity of an Airhostess* (2001, 4', Beta SP).

Al-Awadi, Walid. Kuwaiti filmmaker. Born in 1965 in Kuwait, he studied filmmaking in New York. Documentaries: *A Moment in Time* (1995), *Dreams without Sleep* (2002), *Storm from the South* (2006, 55', Beta SP). Also a nar-rative feature: *Sedra* (2000).

Alawar, Hamad Mansoor. Emirati filmmaker. He studied computer animation at Miami International University of Art and Design. Short animated films: *Once upon a Seed* (2005, 5', DVD), *Hammer and Nails / Matraqa wa Masamir* (2008, 6', Mini DV).

Al-Awar, Maryam. Emirati filmmaker. She studied at Dubai Women's College. Short films: *Osteoporosis* (2004, 1', Mini DV), *The Journey* (2005, 13', Mini DV).

ALAWIYA, BORHAN. [Known in France as Borhan Alaouié.] Lebanese filmmaker. Born in 1941 in Southern Lebanon, he studied filmmaking from 1968 to 1973 at INSAS in Belgium, where he made two short films, *Poster versus Poster / Afiche contre afiche* (1971, 25', 16mm) and a documentary on a Belgian village, *Fourrière* (1971, 60', 16mm). His first feature, and best-known film, *Kafr Kassem,* which won the top prize, the Tanit d'or, at the Journées Cinématographiques de Carthage in Tunis in 1974, was produced by the Syrian General Cinema Organisation. Throughout his career—even after his feature debut—he has continued to make shorter documentaries, including *Letter in a Time of War / Lettre d'un temps de guerre / Risala min zaman al harb* (1984, 55', 35mm), *Letter in a Time of Exile / Lettre du temps de l'exil / Risala min zaman al-manfa* (1985), *For the Attention of Madame the Prime Minister / À l'attention de Madame le premier ministre* (1982), *The Aswan High Dam / Assouan, le haut barrage sur le Nil / al-Sad al-âli* (1991), *To You, Wherever You Are / A toi où que tu sois / ilayk aynama takoun* (2001, 52', video). He also contributed one episode, *The Eclipse of a Dark Night / L'éclipse d'une nuit noire / Fi al-layati al-damâ,* to the Tunisian-produced collective film *After the Gulf? / La guerre du Golfe . . . et après / Harbu al-khalîj wa ba'du?* (1992). In 2008, he made a short fictional film: *Mazen and the Ant / Mazen et la fourmi* (2008, 21') in Qatar. Feature films: *Kafr Kassem* (in Syria, 1974, 100', 35mm), *It Is Not Enough for God to Be with the Poor / Il ne suffit pas que Dieu soit avec les pauvres / La yakfi an yakoun allah maal foukara* (1976, 70', 16mm) (documentary), *Beirut: The Encounter*

/ Beyrouth, la rencontre / Beirut, al-liqa (1981, 90', 35mm), *Khalass* (2007, 101', 35mm).

Alayan, Muayad Mousa. Palestinian filmmaker. Short films: *Qater al-nader* (2007, 25'), *Lesh sabreen* (2008, 20').

Alaywan, Fouad. Lebanese filmmaker. Born in 1964 in Beirut, he studied at a university in Montana and has U.S. citizenship. In Beirut he has made several reports for Future Television. Fictional shorts: *Nostalgia for a Sick Country / Nostalgie pour un pays malade* (1991, 18', Beta SP), *Blue Night, The Wind from Beirut / Le vent de Beyrouth / Hawa Beirut* (2002, 15'), *See You Later / Ila al-leqa'a* (2006, 25', 35mm).

AL-AZZAWI, KAMEL. Iraqi filmmaker. Born in 1926, he studied filmmaking and then worked as assistant director on five films in Egypt. Director of the film department at the Baghdad Institute of Fine Arts, he also worked as an actor and stage director. Short film: *Sulayman the Wise / Souleymane le sage / Souleymân al-hakim* (1956). His sole feature film, an intended superproduction, was a financial disaster. Feature film: *Nebuchadnezzar / Nabuchodonsor / Nabuoched nosser* (1962, 35mm).

Al-Badran, Mansour. Saudi filmmaker. Short film: *Anglizi* (2008, 8', DV Cam).

Al-Banna, Shoug. Emirati filmmaker. Born in 1985. Short film: *Will the Dream Ever Come True?* (2006, 1', Mini DV).

Al-Basha, Mohamed. Saudi filmmaker. A writer who has also worked in television. Short fictional films: *Around Us* (2006, 18', Mini DV), *Angels without Wings* (2007, 4', DVD).

Albatashe, Jasim. Omani filmmaker. He studied drama and works as television actor and director. Short film: *The Disaster* (2007, 20', DV Cam).

Albatashi, Abdullah. Omani filmmaker. Born in 1977 in Oman, he is a poet, playwright, and television director. Short film: *Bint Garba* (2007, 16', DV Cam).

Al-Baw, Darin Ali. Palestinian filmmaker. Born in 1979, she studied at the American University in Sharjah. Short documentary film: *Identity* (2004, 34', DV Cam).

AL-BAYATI, DIA. Iraqi filmmaker: Feature film: *The Al-Ahrar Bridge / Le pont d'al-Ahrar / Jisr al-Ahrar* (1971, 35mm).

Al-Bazi, Baz Shamoun. Iraqi filmmaker. Resident in Canada since 1996. Short films: *Desire and Clay* (1997, 30', Super 16), *Where Is Iraq? Where Is Iraq?* (2004, 20', Beta SP).

AL-BEIK, AMMAR. Syrian filmmaker. Also photographer and video artist. Born in 1972 in Damascus, he began as a photographer before turning to film in 1997. Short films and documentaries: *Harvest of Light / Moisson de lumière* (1997), *They Were There / Ils étaient là* (2000, 8', Beta SP), *16mm* (2001), *The Golden River / Le fleuve d'or* (2002), *Boulevard Assad* (2002), *My Ear Can See / Mon oreille peut voir* (2002, 8', Beta SP), *When I Colour My Fish / Quand je colorie mon poisson* (2002, 1', DV Cam), *Clapper / Le Clap / Klakeit* (2003, 58', Beta SP), *Jerusalem HD* (2008, 22'). Feature-length documentaries: *I Am the One Who Brings Flowers to Her Grave / Je suis celle qui porte les fleurs vers sa tombe* (with Hala al-Abdallah Yakoub, 2006, 110', video), *Samia* (2008, 40', DigiBeta).

Al-Bloshi, Yusef Mohamed. Omani filmmaker. He studied media in Cairo, worked as a playwright and in television, and also works for the Ministry of Education. Short films: *Leaves Tears* (2005, 40', Mini DV), *Warrior Breathes* (2007, 12', DV Cam).

Al-Bloushi, Abdalla Mohamed. Emirati filmmaker. He studied at Abu Dhabi Men's College. Short film: *A Gurm* (2005, 3', Mini DV).

Al-Braikhi, Shaikha Rashed. Emirati filmmaker. She studied at Abu Dhabi Women's College. Short films: *Bazaar* (with Fatema Salem al-Shabibi and Amani Ahmed al-Lawghani, 2003, 3', DV Cam), *L'or torrent* (with Amani Ahmed al-Lawghani, 2004, 1', Mini DV).

Al-Buloshi, Khadija Hussain. Emirati filmmaker. Born in 1985, she studied at Dubai Women's College. Short films: *Florist* (with Alia al-Shamsi, 2005, 10', Mini DV), *Through Child's Eyes* (with Alia al-Shamsi, 2005, 6', Mini DV), *Fly Fly Fly = Die* (with Alia al-Shamsi, 2006, 2', Mini DV), *No Vacancy* (with Alia al-Shamsi, 2006, 13', Mini DV).

Al-Buna, Ma'moun. Palestinian filmmaker. Documentary: *Martyrs on the Road to Palestine / Les martyrs sur le chemin à la Palestine / Shuhada 'ala tariq filastin* (1975, 7').

Al-Bunni, Maamoun. Syrian filmmaker. He studied filmmaking at the École Nationale Supérieure Louis-Lumière in Paris. He has since made several short documentary films, including *Dead for Palestine / Morts pour la Palestine* (1973), *A Day in a Child's Life / Une journée de la vie d'un enfant,* and *The Peasant Woman / La paysanne / Al-mar'a al-rifiya* (1979). He has also worked for Syrian and Gulf television.

Albzzaz, Abdulla Mohammad Jawad. Bahraini filmmaker. Born in 1983, he studied at the University of Bahrain. Short films: *Till When?* (2004, 16', Mini DV), *Tree* (2006, 2', Mini DV), *2008* (2007, 2', Mini DV).

Al-Dabbagh, Noor. Saudi filmmaker. Documentary: *Seeing through the Sand* (2008, 50').

Aldaheri, Saeed. Emirati filmmaker. Born at Al-Ain, he studied at Bristol University in the United Kingdom. Short films: *The Final Conflict* (2002, 9', video), *The Kidnapped* (2003, 40', DV Cam), *01'03* (2004, with eleven other directors, 12', Mini DV), *Subarashii* (2004, 4', video), *The Parrot,* (2004, 6', DV Cam), *Snow* (2005, 6', Mini DV), *Stain* (2005, 6', Mini DV), *The Rescue / al-Faza'a* (2008, 18', Mini DV).

Al-Dakheel, Khalid. Saudi filmmaker. Short animated films: *Cats Benefits* (2006, 7', DVD), *Sida* (2006, 5', DVD).

AL-DARADJI, MOHAMED. Iraqi filmmaker. Born in 1978 in Baghdad, he studied stage production at the Baghdad Institute of Fine Arts and received a technical training in filmmaking at the Media Academy in Hilversum in the Netherlands. He also studied at Leeds Metropolitan University in the United Kingdom. He worked as cameraman and then as director of photography on a dozen shorts, documentaries, and commercials. He also made two short films, *The War / La guerre* (2003) and *The Faith / La foi* (2005). His first feature film was produced with funding from Dutch and UK sources. Feature films: *Dreams / Rêves / Ahlaam* (2005, 110', 35mm), *War, Love, God and Madness / Guerre, amour, dieu, et folie* (2009, 72') (documentary), *Son of Babylon / Fils de Babylone / Ibn Babil* (2009, 90').

Al-Darmaki, Salma Khaifa. Emirati filmmaker. Short films: *Katkoot* (with Hermeen Kamel Adam, 2007, 26', DVD), *My Palestine* (2008, 35', Mini DV).

Al-Dawud, Hikmat. Palestinian filmmaker. Documentary: *Forever in Memory / Abadan fith-thakira* (1983).

Al-Deek, Yousef. Palestinian filmmaker. Documentary: *Case* (2005).

Aldeen, Baqer Sadiq Zain. Bahraini filmmaker. He studied mass communications at the University of Bahrain and works as a journalist. Short film: *Bahrain Municipal Experience* (2006, 21', DV Cam).

Al-Demashqi, Nedhal K. Saudi filmmaker. He studied in the Czech Republic and in the United Kingdom and worked on several films in Europe. Short films: *Street Dreamer* (2005, 9', DV Cam), *Hjab and the Inherited Treasures* (2006, 66', DV Cam).

Al-Dhabaan, Abedel Muhsen. Saudi filmmaker. Short film: *Three Men and a Woman* (2009, 13', Mini DV).

Al-Dhahery, Hessa Abdulla Rashed. Emirati filmmaker. She studied at Abu Dhabi Women's College. Short documentary film: *Guy's Day Out* (2005, 6', DV Cam).

Al-Dhahiri, Ahmed Saeed Ali. Emirati filmmaker. Short film: *Be Merciful* (2007, 13', DVD).

Al-Dhahri, Hiba Ahmad. Emirati filmmaker. She studied at Dubai Women's College. Short film: *Melting Candle* (2003, 4', Beta SP).

Al-Dhanhani, Heba. Emirati filmmaker. She studied at Dubai Women's College. Short film: *Adolescent Colors* (with Wafa Faisal, Maitha Ebrahim, Nada Salem, Hana Abdullah Mohammed al-Mulla al-Muhairi, 2005, 28', DV Cam).

AL-DIBS, NIDAL. Syrian filmmaker. Born in 1960 in Syria, he studied architecture in Damascus and filmmaking at the VGIK film school in Moscow. He worked as assistant to Oussama Mohammad and Abdellatif Abdelhamid. He made several short films: *Winter Sonata / Sonate d'hiver* (1992), *Collage* (1994), *Oh Night / O nuit, ô regard / Ya leil ya ain* (1999, 12', 35mm), *Black Stone / Pierre noire / Hajar aswad* (2005, 60'). Feature film: *Under the Ceiling / Sous le toit / Tahta al-saqf* (2005, 95', 35mm).

AL-DIJAILI, ZUHAIR. Iraqi filmmaker. Feature film: *Mutawa and Bahia / Mutawa et Bahia / Mutawa wa Bahia* (with Sahib Haddad, 1982, 35mm).

AL-DIN JASSEM, BORHAN. Iraqi filmmaker. Feature films: *The Will of the People / La volonté du peuple / Iradat al-chab* (1959, 35mm), *The Path of Love / La voie de l'amour / Darb al-Hub* (1966, 35mm), *Baghdad Nights / Les nuits de Bagdad / Layali Bagdad* (1975, 35mm).

Al-Doseri, Ebrahim Rashid. Bahraini filmmaker. Also a composer, author, and radio and television writer, he works for the Ministry of Education. Short films: *The Cage* (2005,

17', DVD), *A Cord from Al Muharra* (2006, 18', DV Cam), *Other Time* (2006, 47', DV Cam), *A Flower* (2007, 13', DVD), *Light Fingers* (2007, 12', DVD), *Ash of the Years* (2008, 12', Mini DV).

Al-Doseri, Munira. Emirati filmmaker. She studied at the American University of Sharjah. Short fictional films: *A Tail Apart* (with Miriam al-Sabah, 2004, 4', Mini DV), *Faithless* (with Miriam al-Sabbah, 2004, 4', Mini DV).

Al-Duwaisan, Faisal S. Kuwaiti filmmaker. Short musical video: *Singing Nemo* (2006, 3', Mini DV).

Aleddin, Ghasoub. Palestinian filmmaker. Documentary: *Escape / Evasion / Hurub* (2004).

Al-Emadi, Ahmed Abdullah. Emirati filmmaker. He studied at Abu Dhabi Men's College. Short films: *The Present Completes the Past* (2006, 5', DigiBeta), *Coastal Zone in Dubai* (2006, 6', DigiBeta), *Dubai Green City* (2006, 13', DigiBeta), *Za'abeel Park* (2006, 6', DigiBeta).

Al-Enzi, Meshal Mogamed. Saudi filmmaker. He studied at the Imam Mohamed Bin Saud Islamic University and worked as a newspaper journalist and television reporter. Short fictional films: *Taxi* (2004, 20', DigiBeta), *Democracy Dimocratiya* (2006, 5', HDV).

Al-Eyaf, Abdullah. Saudi filmmaker. Born in 1976 in Al-Hassa in Saudi Arabia, he studied mechanical engineering. He worked as an engineer before turning to journalism and the cinema and becoming a film critic for *Al-Watan*. Documentaries: *Cinema 500 km / Cinéma 500 km* (2006, 45', Beta SP), *A Frame / Etaar* (2007, 19', Mini DV), *Rain / Matar* (2008, 23', Beta SP).

Al-Falahi, Rashid Harib. Emirati filmmaker. Short film: *Prices Crisis* (2007, 9', DVD).

Al-Faqih, Dara. Emirati filmmaker. Short film: *Nour* (2007, 6', Mini DV).

Al-Faqih, Rowan. Palestinian filmmaker. Born in 1974 in Jerusalem, she is one of the founders of the Palestinian Filmmakers' Collective. Her first documentary was a Palestinian-Swiss co-production. Documentary: *Summer of '85* (2005). Contributed *Security Leak* (2' 48") to the collective film *Summer 2006, Palestine* (2006, 35', Beta SP).

Al-Fardan, Khalid. Emirati filmmaker. He studied at the Abu Dhabi Men's College. Short film: *Between Yesterday and Today* (with Mohamed Najm al-Qubaisi and Mohamed Abdullah al-Qubaisi, 1998, 2', DV Cam).

Al-Farjani, Amen. Emirati filmmaker. Studied at UAE University. Short film: *Migrants in Their Own Country* (2001, 14', Beta SP).

Al-Flasy, Latifa Saeed. Emirati filmmaker. She studied at Dubai Women's College. Short animated film: *A Day in Time* (2004, 2', Mini DV).

Alfounz, Tanjour. Syrian filmmaker. Short film: *Little Sun* (2008).

Al-Gargawi, Yasser. Emirati filmmaker. Short films: *Arabia's Wildlife Centre* (2001, 4', DV Cam), *Superstition between Reality and Fantasy* (with Khalid Alrayhi, 2002, 15', Beta SP).

Al-Ghaferi, Samira. Emirati filmmaker. Born in 1975 in Abu Dhabi, she studied at the University of Al-Ain, UAE. Short films: *Zionism Campaign* (with Bassam Mesalatie, 2006, 22', HD), *For the Sake of Democracy* (with Bassam Mesalatie, 2007, 5', HD), *For Release* (with Bassam Mesalatie, 2007, 5', HD), *Small Terrorists* (with Bassam Mesalatie, 2007, 7', HD).

Alghamdi, Bandar. Emirati filmmaker. He studied at the University of Sharjah. Short film: *Smoking Rose* (2006, 2', Mini DV).

AL-GHANEM, NUJOOM. Emirati filmmaker. Born in Dubai, she is also a poet, with six published collections of poems. She worked as a journalist and studied media production at Ohio University and at Griffith University in

Australia. She has undertaken various media activities in the Emirates. Two short fictional films: *Ice-Cream / La glace* (1997, 7', Beta SP) and *The Park / Le parc* (1997, 12', Beta SP), and a documentary: *Between Two Banks / Entre deux rives* (1999, 20', Beta SP). Feature-length documentary: *Al-Mureed* (2008, 87', DigiBeta).

Al-Gheilan, Gamal. Bahraini filmmaker. Short film: *Yassin* (2009, 25', HD Cam).

AL-GHOUSSAYNI, SAMIR. Lebanese filmmaker. Born in 1948 in Baakline, he began his career as script boy and as assistant director to Taysir Abboud. Following the success of his first feature, he made some twenty-four commercial feature films between 1972 and 1994, some co-produced with Syria. Feature films: *The She-Cats of Hamra Street / Les chattes de la rue Hamra / Kotat charé al-Hamra* (1972, 35mm), *The Captive / La captive / al-Asira* (1973, 35mm), *Cherwale and Mini-skirt / Cherwale et mini-jupe / Cherwale wa mini-jupe* (1973, 35mm), *The Postman / Le facteur / Said al-barid* (1973, 35mm), *Grand Prix / Grand prix / al-Jaiza al koubra* (1974, 35mm), *Winter Women / Femmes d'hiver / Nisa'a lil chitaa* (1974, 35mm), *Life Is a Melody / La vie est une mélodie / al-Dounya nagham* (1975, 35mm), *Does / Biches / Ghezlane* (1976), *Days in London / Des jours à Londres / Ayyam fi London* (1977, 35mm), *Fish Filet / Filet de poisson / Samak bila hassak* (1977, 35mm), *A Beauty and Some Giants / Une belle et des géants / Hassnaa wa amalika* (1980, 35mm), *The Adventurers / Les aventuriers / al-Moughamiron* (1981, 35mm), *Women in Danger / Des femmes en danger / Nisaa fi khatar* (1981, 35mm), *The Island Devil / Le diable de l'île / Chaitane al-jazira* (1981, 35mm), *The Affair / L'affaire / al-Safaka* (1982, 35mm), *Women's Intrigue / La manigance des femmes / Loubat al-nisaa* (1982, 35mm), *The Hero's Return / Le retour du héros / Awdat al-batal* (1983, 35mm), *The Siren / La sirène / Arouss al-bahr* (1984, 35mm), *The Gipsy and the Heroes / La gitane et les héros / al-Ghajaria wal abtal* (1985, 35mm), *The Seductress and the Adventurer / La séductrice et l'aventurier / al-Fatina wal moughamer* (1985, 35mm), *Fadous and the Hitchhiker / Fadous et l'autostoppeuse* (1989, 35mm), *Uncle Vania & Co.'s Circus / Le*

cirque de l'oncle Vania et cie / Cirque al-ame Vania wa chourakah (1991, 35mm), *Mr. Gold / Monsieur Gold / Mr. Gold* (1993, 35mm), *Operation: Golden Phoenix / Opération: Golden Phenix / Amaliat al-taer al-zahabi* (1994, 35mm).

Alhabbash, Isma'il. Palestinian filmmaker. Documentary: *The New Apartment / ash-Shakkato-l-jadeeda* (2002).

Alhaddad, Fathia. Kuwaiti filmmaker. She studied in France and works as writer and journalist. Short film: *40 Years After the Storm* (2006, 21', Mini DV).

Al-Haddad, Mohamed Fouad. Emirati filmmaker. Short fictional film: *The Rain* (2002, 16', video).

Al-Haj, Ahmad Ali. Emirati filmmaker. Short documentary films: *Falconry and the CITES Treaty* (2002, 6', Beta SP), *The Ostrich* (2003, 7', DV Cam).

Al-Hajri, Saeed. Emirati filmmaker. Studied at the Dubai Men's College. Short documentary film: *3adi.com* (2000, 22', DV Cam).

Al-Halami, Sultan. Emirati filmmaker. He studied at the American University of Sharjah. Short fictional film: *Victims* (with Saoud Alkaabi, 2007, 1', Mini DV).

AL-HALIBI, HASSAN. Bahraini filmmaker. Feature film: *Four Girls / Quatre filles* (2008, 144').

Al-Hamad, Salama. Emirati filmmaker. Short fictional film: *Hair Today, Gone Tomorrow* (2001, 4', DV Cam).

Al-Hamadi, Ali. Emirati filmmaker. He studied at Abu Dhabi Men's College. Short films: *Proud of My Heritage* (1999, 4', DV Cam), *Electronic Chat* (2000, 13', DV Cam), *Learning without Borders* (2001, 1', DV Cam).

Al-Hamli, Reem. Emirati filmmaker. She studied at Abu Dhabi Women's College. Short animated film: *Error Message: Access Denied* (2005, 4', Mini DV).

Al-Hamly, Aisha. Emirati filmmaker. She studied at Abu Dhabi Women's College. Short films: *A Cat's Life* (2000, 3', DV Cam), *Omani Fashion* (2000, 2', DV Cam), *Dr. Martin* (2001, 6', DV Cam).

Al-Hammadi, Abdulla Ahmed. Emirati filmmaker. He studied at Dubai Men's College. Short film: *Animal Rights* (2006, 1', Mini DV).

Al-Hammadi, Hamad. Emirati filmmaker. Short fictional film: *Ashes / Ramad* (2007, 10', Mini DV).

Al-Hammadi, Khadeeja Mohammed. Emirati filmmaker. Born in 1982 in Abu Dhabi, she studied at the Abu Dhabi Women's College. Short films: *Sunshine Tours* (2001, 1', Beta SP), *The Doomed* (2003, 8', DV Cam).

Al-Hammadi, Khalid Ahmed. Emirati filmmaker. He studied at UAE University. Short films: *What Is After the Explosion?* (with Maryam Bin Fahad, 2004, 39', DV Cam), *High Peak and Pure Intent* (2005, 3', DV Cam), *Him* (2005, 25', DV Cam).

Al-Hammadi, Mariam Dawood. Emirati filmmaker. Born in 1982 in Abu Dhabi, she studied at Zayed University. Short films: *A Moment* (2004, 1', Mini DV), *To Where!* (2005, 4', Mini DV), *Sir Bani Yas* (2005, 5', Mini DV), *E* (2005, 1', Mini DV).

Al-Hammadi, Rana Mohamed. Emirati filmmaker. She studied at the Abu Dhabi Women's College. Short film: *A Point of No Return* (with Eiman Ahmed Ghanem and Dana Ali al-Hosani, 2003, 2', DV Cam).

Al-Hammady, Mohamed Abdullah. Emirati filmmaker. Born in 1988, he is also an actor and dramatist. Short films: *Houjas* (2007, 20', HDV), *Mariam's Paradise* (2008, 18', Digi-Beta).

Al-Hani, Hassanain. Iraqi filmmaker. He studied at the Independent Film & TV College in Baghdad. Short documentary film: *A Stranger in His Own Country* (2007, 10').

Al-Hashemi, Abeer. Emirati filmmaker. She studied at Dubai Women's College, Short films: *A Shock of Life* (2005, 8', Mini DV), *One Drop* (2005, 1', Mini DV), *Less Is More* (2006, 1', DV Cam).

Al-Hashemi, Buthaina. Emirati filmmaker. She studied at Dubai Women's College. Short films: *A Spinster Miss* (2002, 8', Beta SP), *Poverty in the UAE* (with Amena Saif al-Suboosi and Mariam Jassim al-Sarkal, 2002, 6', Beta SP).

Al-Hashimi, Tariq. Emirati filmmaker. Born in 1987, he studied at Dubai Men's College. Short films: *Brotherhood Takes a Friend or Two* (with Waleed Masood Badri, 2006, 3', Mini DV), *Speeding Kills* (2008, 3', Mini DV).

Al-Hassan, Areej. Emirati filmmaker. Short film: *Child Labor* (with Farah Kassem, 2007, 1', Mini DV).

Al-Hassan, Azza. Palestinian filmmaker. Born in 1971 in Amman, Jordan, to Palestinian parents who moved to Beirut when she was born and back to Amman when the Israelis invaded Lebanon in 1982. Her father was one of the leaders of Fatah. She studied film and sociology in Glasgow and television documentary at Goldsmiths' College, London. She has worked for Arab satellite televison stations, travelling between London, Jordan, Dubai, and Ramallah. Documentaries: *Arab Women Speak Out / Des femmes arabes parlent / al-'Arabiyyat yatakallimna* (1996, 40', Beta SP), *Title Deeds from Moses / Un acte de Moïse / Kushan Musa / Kushan musa* (1999, 29', Beta SP), *Sindbad Is a She* (1999, 30', Beta SP), *The Place / La place / al-Makan* (2000, 7', Beta SP), *Newstime / L'heure des nouvelles / Zaman al-akhbar* (2001, 52', Beta SP), *3cm Less / 3cm de moins / Talata sintimetar* (2003, 60', Beta SP), *Kings and Extras: Digging for a Palestinian*

Image / Des rois et des figurants / Muluk wa kumbars (2004, 62', Beta SP), *Forgotten Images / Sowar manisiyah* (2004).

Alhebsi, Abeer. Emirati filmmaker, Studied at the UAE University. Short animated films: *The Hypothetical Learning* (2004, 2', DVD), *Brief About Japan* (2004, 2', DVD).

Al-Helou, Raed. Palestinian filmmaker. Worked as a cameraman in Rammallah. Documentaries: *Gaza Tea Boy / Ba'i' al-shay fi Ghazza* (1997), *Local / Mahalli* (with Imad Ahmed and Ismaïl Habash, 2002), *Hopefully for the Best / Pour le meilleur, espérons / Laalo khayr* (2004, 42', video).

AL-HINDI, ABDEL WAHAB. Jordanian filmmaker, born in Palestine. Feature films: *The Road to Jerusalem / La route de Jérusalem / al-Tarikila al-Qods* (1969), *Struggle till Liberation / Lutte jusqu'à la libération / Kifah hatta al-Tahrir* (1969).

Al-Homoud, Bader Abdul Majeed. Saudi filmmaker. Short film: *Pigeon of War* (2006, 24', Mini DV).

Al-Hosani, Dana Ali. Emirati filmmaker. She studied at the Abu Dhabi Women's College. Short film: *A Point of No Return* (with Eiman Ahmed Ghanem and Rana Mohamed al-Hammadi, 2003, 2', DV Cam).

Al-Hulaybi, Hussain Abbas. Bahraini filmmaker. Born in 1977 in Bahrain, he studied mass media and public relations. He is also a stage director. Short film: *Black Day* (2004, 12', DV Cam).

Alhuraiz, Mohammad. Emirati filmmaker, He studied at Dubai Men's College. Short animated films: *Karth-O-Mania—One* (2004, 3', Mini DV), *It's Truffle Season My Boy!* (2005, 5', DV Cam).

Alhusaini, Zeyed (Z.). Kuwaiti filmmaker. He has lived in Kuwait, Spain, and the United States and studied at Arizona State University and Columbia University Film School. He has directed music videos and teaches at Kuwait University. Short fictional film: *Just Like You Imagined* (2004, 10', 35mm).

Ali, Emad. Iraqi filmmaker. He studied at the Independent Film and Television Academy in Baghdad. Documentary: *A Candle for the Shabandar Cafe* (2007, 23').

Ali, Hafiz Ali. Qatari filmmaker. He studied at the California Arts Institute and Chapman University. He has directed TV shows in the United States and Qatar. Short film: *Cab Driver* (2005, 19', 16mm).

ALI, HUSSEIN HASAN. Iraqi filmmaker. Born in 1974 in Duhok in Kurdish Iraq, he has made three short fictional films. He also acted in a dozen téléfilms for Iraqi television. His co-directed first feature was produced by a French-based company. Feature film: *Narcissus Blossom / Le temps des narcisses / U nergiz biskvin* (with Massoud Arif Salih, 2005, 80', 35mm).

ALI, JAF'AR. Iraqi filmmaker. Born in 1933, he studied filmmaking in Iowa, taught at the Baghdad Fine Art Academy, and founded a theatre group. Feature films: *The Bus Driver / Le contrôleur d'autobus / al-Jabi* (1969, 55', 35mm), *The Turning / Le tournant* a.k.a. *Le virage / al-Monataf* (1974, 100', 35mm), *The Bride from Kurdistan / La mariée du Kurdistan / Arusat Kurdistan* (1992).

Ali, Khalid. Emirati filmmaker. Short films: *The Last Call* (1998, 16', S-VHS), *Sharks and Divers* (2001, 26', Beta SP).

Ali, Mahdi Ali. Qatari filmmaker. He studied engineering in Qatar. Short film: *Affiliation* (with Mahmoud Salem Ba Ajajah and Dalia Bakhet, 2007, 9', Mini DV).

Ali, Majeed Radhi. Bahraini filmmaker. Short fictional film: *Resident Evil* (2006, 7', Mini DV).

Ali, Reem. Syrian filmmaker. He studied at the Institute of Drama and Theatre in Damascus. Short fictional film: *Zabad* (2008, 42', video).

Ali, Safa Mohamed. Iraqi filmmaker. Feature films: *The Last Decision / La dernière décision / Hobat al-madlum* (1961, 35mm), *Sultana* (1962, 35mm), *Gazala* (1967, 35mm).

Ali, Sheefa Abdulla. Emirati filmmaker. She studied at Abu Dhabi Women's College. Short films: *Crazy (Women) Drivers* (2002, 3', DV Cam), *The Lie* (2003, 6', DV Cam), *Letter to God* (2003, 7', DV Cam), *Dad, Stay with Me* (2004, 4', DV Cam).

Alibrahim, Faisal. Kuwaiti filmmaker. Born in 1978 in Kuwait. He studied film at California State University. Short film: *Karma* (2007, 10', HD).

Al-Imam, Borhan Jassem. Iraqi filmmaker. Feature film: *Chazhra the Bedouin / Chazhra la bédouine / Chazhra al-badawia* (1962, 35mm).

Alireza, Hani. Emirati filmmaker. Short film: *September 12th* (with Theyab al-Tamimi, 2005, 11', Mini DV).

Al-Jabri, Adel. Emirati filmmaker. Short films: *Smoking Kills Too* (2007, 2', Mini DV), *Reuse, Recycle* (2007, 2', Mini DV), *Speeding Kills* (2008, 3', Mini DV).

Al-Jabri, Hamad. Emirati filmmaker. Short experimental films: *Path* (2004, 2', DV Cam), *Nothing* (2004, 45', DV Cam), *Loneliness* (2005, 6', Mini DV), *Voice of the Rocks* (2005, 3', Mini DV).

AL-JADER, SAMI. Iraqi filmmaker. Feature film: *The Path of Evil / La voie du mal / Trik al-char* (1967, 35mm).

AL-JAFARI, KAMAL. Palestinian film-maker. Born in 1972 in Ramala, Palestine, he graduated from the Academy of Media Arts in Cologne. Short films: *The Jahalin / al-Jahalin* (2000), *Visit Iraq* (2003, 25', 35mm). Feature-

length documentary: *The Roof / Le toit / al-Sateh* (2008, 63', video).

AL-JANABI, FAWZI. Iraqi filmmaker. Feature film: *For the Homeland / Pour la patrie / Min ajl al-watan* (1962, 35mm), *The Seekers / Les chercheurs / al-Bahithun* (1978).

Al-Janabi, Kutaïba. Iraqi filmmaker. Born in Baghdad, he now lives in London, where he works for MBC television. After studying filmmaking in Budapest in the 1980s, he made firstly fictional shorts: *Still Life / Nature morte* (1997, 12', 16mm), *No Man's Land* (1998, 5', color), *The Train / Le train* (1999, 9', Beta SP), *Transient* (2003, 5', DV Cam), Documentaries: *My Friend Nassir* (2003, 7', DV Cam), *Against the Light* (2007, 15').

AL-JANABI, MOHAMED YOUSSEF. Iraqi filmmaker. Feature film: *The Searchers / Les chercheurs / Al-bahitun* (1978, 35mm).

Al-Janahi, Nawaf. Emirati filmmaker. Born in 1977 in Abu Dhabi, he studied film in the United States, where he made three Super 8 films: *The Source, My Love, The Confrontation* (all 1998). He has worked for Abu Dhabi television and as cameraman on a number of shorts. Short fictional films: *Obsession* (2002, 18', Mini DV), *On a Road* (2003, 4', Mini DV), *Souls* (2006, 15', Beta SP), *Mirrors of Silence / Miroirs du silence / Maraya al-samt* (2006, 16', Beta SP).

Al-Jassim, Mohammad. Emirati filmmaker. Short film: *Life of Stock Market* (2007, 12', Mini DV).

Al-Jermi, Hiba Saleh. Emirati filmmaker. She studied mass communcation at UAE University. Short documentary film: *Al-Gars* (with Fatima al-Ziyoudi, 2007, 5', DVD).

Al-Jisr, Rachad. Lebanese filmmaker. Born in 1965 in London. Studied architecture in Florence and became a photographer. Short films: *Sweet Little Sister, Distant Shadows / Ombres lointaines* (with Akram Zaatari, 1993, 11', Beta SP).

Al-Joundi, Dima. Lebanese filmmaker. Born in 1966 in Arnoun, Lebanon, she studied philosophy in Beirut until 1984, when she began her studies of filmmaking at INSAS in Brussels. She worked in a variety of production roles, worked for Young Asia TV, and made reports and documentaries for television. After a year in Colombo, Sri Lanka, where she produced documentaries, she returned to Beirut. There she organized film festivals and became the first woman to produce and distribute films through her company, Crystal Films, producing, among others, Nigol Bezjian's feature, *Ayroum* (2005). Documentaries: *Between Us Two . . . Beirut / Entre nous deux . . . Beyrouth / Bayni wa baynak . . . Bayrut* (1993, 52', 16mm), *The Silk Route in Anatolia / La route de la soie en Anatolie* (1995, 52', 35mm), *The Mask of the Night / Le masque de la nuit* (1996, 20', Beta), *Maid for Sale / Bonne à vendre* (2005, 53', video).

Al-Junaibi, Abdullah Moumen. Emirati filmmaker. Short fictional films: *When?* (2002, 8', Beta SP), *Sunset* (2002, 51', DCV Cam).

Al-Junaibi, Afrah. Emirati filmmaker. Short documentary film: *Conflict of Suffering* (2008, 5', video).

Al-Juneidi, Laith. Palestinian filmmaker. He studied visual culture at Coventry University in the United Kingdom. His student films include a short fictional film: *Trainspoofing,* and two documentaries: *Church@21stCentury* and *War vs. Peace* (2001, 12', Mini DV).

Al-Kaabi, Abdulla Matar. Emirati filmmaker. Born in Fujairah, he studied at the American University of Sharjah. Short film: *A Student Film That Never Happened* (2006, 9', Mini DV).

Alkaabi, Saoud. Emirati filmmaker. Short fictional film: *Victims* (with Sultan al-Halami, 2007, 1', Mini DV).

Alkalbani, Khalid Salem. Omani filmmaker. Short fictional films: *The Bus* (2006, 7', DV Cam), *Whiteness* (2009, 9', HD Cam).

Al-Karimi, Nada Mohamed. Emirati filmmaker. She studied communication science in Dubai. Her first short won a prize at the Beirut Documentary Film Festival. Documentary: *Death by Pleasure / La mort par plaisir / al-Maout lel mota'a* (2004, 10', Beta SP).

Alkarimi, Nadia Mohamed. Emirati filmmaker. She studied at Dubai Women's College. Short documentary films: *Emirati Hijab in Emirati Eyes* (2004, 10', Mini DV), *Dying for Fun* (2005, 10', Mini DV).

Al-Katheeri, Ali Hassan. Emirati filmmaker. Short fictional film: *The Honour of Land* (2005, 7', DV Cam).

Al-Katheery, Howaida Ali. Emirati filmmaker. Studied at Abu Dhabi Women's College. Short films: *Farewell* (1999, 4', DV Cam), *Cultural Foundation* (2000, 1', DV Cam), *The Yemeni Diaspora* (2001, 5', DV Cam).

ALKAWEY, MAROUN. Syrian filmmaker. Feature film: *The Heroic Airforce Formations / Les héroiques formations aériennes / Kharq el-akhtâr* (1974, 35mm).

Al-Keisri, Sabah. Emirati filmmaker. Studied at UAE University. Short film: *Oud Fragrance* (2000, 11', Beta SP).

Alketbi, Fatima Saif. Emirati filmmaker. Short documentary film: *Lost Identity,* (2007, 23', DVD).

Al-Khaja, Khahida. Emirati filmmaker. She studied at Dubai Women's College. Short films: *The Old Days* (2003, 8', Beta SP), *Jinni: Fact or Fiction?* (2004, 10', Mini DV).

AL-KHAJA, MAHER. Emirati filmmaker. Feature film: *The Fifth Chamber Ouija / La cinquième chambre d'Ouija* (2009, 128', HD Cam).

Al-Khaja, Nayla. Emirati filmmaker. She studied mass communication at Dubai Women's College and at Ryerson University, Toronto, and set up her own production company in Dubai. Student films: *Red* (2002), *Free Me Cockroach* (2003). Short films: *Unveiling Dubai* (2004, 46', DigiBeta), *Arabana* (2006, 6', 35mm).

Al-Khaja, Reef. Emirati filmmaker. She studied at Abu Dhabi Women's College. Short films, one documentary: *Royal Oman Symphony Orchestra* (with Ameena Abdulla al-Mazrouie, 2003, 11', DV Cam), and two fictional: *Rebirth* (2004, 7', DV Cam), *People* (2004, 7', DV Cam).

Al-Khajah, Farid. Emirati filmmaker. He studied at the American University of Sharjah. Short films: *Happy People* (2005, 7', Mini DV), *Digital Predestination* (2007, 11', DVD), *The Last Bahraini* (2007, 6', HDV), *The Hadith in Contemporary Times* (2008, 32', HD).

Al-Khaldi, Susan. Emirati filmmaker. She studied at Abu Dhabi Women's College. Short documentary film: *The Golden Mask: The Burgah* (1999, 5', DV Cam).

Al-Khalifi, Abdulrahman. Kuwaiti filmmaker. Short fictional films: *The Lost Years* (2008, 17', Mini DV), *Whispers of Sin* (2009, 31', HD Cam).

Al-Khatib, Basil. Palestinian filmmaker. Documentaries: *Amina . . . A Palestinian Story / Amina . . . une histoire palestinienne / Amina . . . Hikaya filstiniyyah* (1982), *Curse / La'na* (1984).

Al-Khatib, Dhafir. Iraqi filmmaker. Documentary: *Who Are They Flying the Flags For? / Pour qui hisse-t'on les drapeaux* (1994, 20', 16mm).

Al-Khatib, Nabil Issa. Palestinian filmmaker. Documentary: *Return of the Deer / Le retour des gazelles / 'Awdat al-ghazala* (2003).

Al-Khatib, Sahar. Emirati filmmaker. Studied communication technology at Dubai Women's College. Short film: *I'm a Man / Ana rajol* (with Shamma Abu Nawas, 2006, 19', Mini DV).

AL-KHAYALI, ABDERRAHMAN. Syrian filmmaker. Feature film: *Three Operations in Palestine / Trois Opérations en Palestine / Thalath amaliyyatdâkhil Filistin* (with Mohamed Salah, 1969, 90', 35mm).

Al-Khayat, Yasser. Emirati filmmaker. He studied at Dubai Men's College. Short film: *Friendship* (2008, 1', DVD).

Al-Khoori, Khawla Zainal. Emirati filmmaker. She studied at Abu Dhabi Women's College. Short films: *Fatherhood* (2002, 3', DV Cam), *A Hard Lesson* (2002, 3', DV Cam), *Dinner Invitation* (2003, 5', DV Cam), *Al-Msafer* (2003, 6', DV Cam).

Al-Khoori, Thuraya. Emirati filmmaker. Born in 1980, she studied at Abu Dhabi Women's College. Short films: *Persian Carpet* (2001, 8', DV Cam), *Boss* (2001, 1', DV Cam), *Sooner or Later?* (2002, 6', DV Cam).

Al-Khouri, Alia. Emirati filmmaker. She studied at the Abu Dhabi Women's College. Short documentary film: *Always in Mind* (2000, 4', DV Cam).

Al-Kiyumi, Dawood. Omani filmmaker. Short film: *Realism Beats / al-Eqaya afthal* (with Yasir al-Kiyumi, 2007, 1', DigiBeta).

Al-Kiyumi, Yasir. Omani filmmaker. Short film: *Realism Beats / al-Eqaya afthal* (with Dawood al-Kiyumi, 2007, 1', DigiBeta).

Al-Kout, Meqdad. Kuwaiti filmmaker. Also actor and assistant on commercials. Short films: *Shards of Peace* (2006), *The Beauty of Khaled's Mind* (2007, 12', HD), *Paradoxes / Mufaraqat* (2008, 24', DigiBeta).

Alkubaisi, Meshaal Ali. Qatari filmmaker. He has worked for Qatar TV and Al Jazeera. Short documentary film: *Jusasiyah* (2006, 7', Mini DV).

Alkury, Dalia. Jordanian filmmaker and member of the Amman Filmmakers Cooperative. Born in 1980, of Jordanian/Palestinian origins and Canadian nationality. She studied at Wilfrid Laurier University, Canada, and at Goldsmiths' College in London. Short documentary films: *It's MY Grapevine* (2003), *Made in China* (2004, 3', DV Cam), *Arab Terrorist Management Camp* (2004), *Like Many of Us, Nayef Has a Mobile* (2004), *Smile You're in South Lebanon / Souriez vous êtes au Sud Liban* (2008, 53', video).

Al-Lawghani, Amani Ahmed. Emirati filmmaker. She studied at Abu Dhabi Women's College. Short films: *Bazaar* (with Fatema Salem al-Shabibi and Shaikha Rashed al-Braikhi, 2003, 3', DV Cam), *L'or torrent* (with Shaikha Rashed al-Braikhi, 2004, 1', Mini DV).

Al-Leem, Juma Hmaid. Emirati filmmaker. Short documentary films: *The Dream Has Come True* (2002, 9', Beta SP), *Economic Crime in a Time of Globalism* (2002, 9', Beta SP).

Allooh, Mohamed. Emirati filmmaker. Short documentary film: *Confessions of Muhaura's Idiot* (2002, 33', Beta SP).

AL-MAHLED, KHALDOUN. Syrian filmmaker. Feature film: *Good Night / Bonne nuit* (1975, 35mm).

Al-Mahmoud, Khalid. Emirati filmmaker. Born in 1976 in Abu Dhabi, he studied mass communications at Denver University in the United States and filmmaking at the New York Film Academy. He now lives and works in the Emirates. Cameraman on a number of shorts. Short films: *Business and Personal* (1999), *Boulevard of Broken Dreams* (2001, 4', 16mm), *Dream in a Box* (2003, 6', DV Cam), *Breakfast* (2004, 1', Mini DV), *01'03* (with eleven other directors, 2004, 12', Mini DV), *The Barber* (2005, 16', Mini DV), *Celebration of Life* (2005, 5', Mini DV), *A Fictional Story: Woman and Boy* (2007, 5', Mini DV), *Bint al-Nokhitha* (2008, 17', DigiBeta).

Almahmoud, Khalid. Qatari filmmaker. Born in Qatar, he works as a broadcast journalist for the Al Jazeera network. He studied filmmaking at the London Film Academy and

has also written plays and published poetry. Short film: *Terrorism-Tourism / Irhab-seyaha* (2008, 3', DigiBeta).

Al-Mahrouqi, Khaled Saleem. Emirati filmmaker. He studied at Dubai Men's College. Short films: *Whispers* (2005, 5', Mini DV), *Fatal Flaw* (2005, 6', Mini DV).

Al-Majid, Basheer. Iraqi filmmaker. Born in 1977 in Iraq, he is director, actor, writer, poet, and journalist and teaches at the Faculty of Fine Arts in Baghdad. He starred in Mohamed al-Daradji's feature film *Dreams*. Short fictional film: *Personal Calendar / Taqweem shakhsi* (2007, 9', DV Cam).

AL-MALEH, NABIL. Syrian filmmaker. Born in 1939 in Damascus, he began his career as a caricaturist and painter. He travelled widely in Europe and studied filmmaking at FAMU in Prague. His diploma film, *Aleppo / Halab*, won a prize at the Karlovy-Vary Festival. He made numerous short documentaries and fictional films: *Colour and Life / Couleur et vie / Lawn wa hayât* (1966), *Damascan Rhythm / Rythme damascène / Iqa'a Dimashq* (1970), *Napalm* (1970, 90"), *Days of History / Jours d'histoire / Aiyyam li al-tarikh* (1971), *The Eternal Game / Le jeu éternel / al-Lu'aba abadia* (1972), *The Rock / Le roc / al-Sakher* (1978, 17'), *The Circle / Le cercle* (1978), *The Window / La fenêtre / al-Nâfidha* (1978), *Images That Remain / Des images qui restent* (1978, 35mm), as well as the fictional short *The Crown of Thorns / La couronne d'épines / Ikil al-shuk* (1968, 18'). He contributed one of three episodes, *Childbirth / L'accouchement / al-Makhad*, to the first feature produced by the General Organisation for Cinema: *Men Under the Sun / Des hommes sous le soleil / al-Sayyid al-taqaddumi* (with Mohamed Shahin and Mohamed Muwaddin, 1970, 108', 35mm). His private-sector James Bond parody was made with the popular comedian, actor, and director Doureid Lahham. He left Syria in the 1980s, teaching in Texas and at UCLA, before moving to Europe, There he lived in Geneva and in Athens, where he made his feature-length documentary. He returned to Damascus to make his fifth feature,

The Extras, and a further, unreleased, feature, *The Hunt Feast*, in 2004. Feature films: *The Leopard / Le léopard / al-Fahd* (1972, 110', 35mm), *The Progressive / Le Progressiste / al-Sayyid al-taqaddumi* (1974, 35mm), *Jealous James Bond / James Bond le jaloux / Ghawar James Bond* (1974, 35mm), *Fragments of Images / Fragments d'images / Baqaya suwar* (1980, 128', 35mm), *Story of a Dream / Histoire d'un rêve / Ta'rick hulm* (1983), *The Extras / Les figurants / al-Kombars* (1993, 105', 35mm).

Al-Mandeel, Bandar. Emirati filmmaker. Short film: *Don't Drink and Drive* (with Heba Abdulkhalek, 2000, 1', Mini DV).

Al-Mansoor, Asma. Emirati filmmaker. Short film: *My Future Career* (with Noura al-Mehairi, 2005, 3', Beta SP).

Al-Mansoori, Mariam Abdulla. Emirati filmmaker. Born in 1980, she studied at Abu Dhabi Women's College. Short films: *Local Women Horseriders* (2001, 9', DV Cam), *Smoggles* (2001, 1', DV Cam), *What Happened to Our Men?* (2002, 5', DV Cam).

Al-Mansour, Haifaa. Saudi filmmaker. Born in Saudi Arabia, she studied first English literature at the American University in Cairo and then management and human resources at the University of Minnesota. Short films: *Who? / Qui?* (2003, 7', Mini DV), *The Bitter Departure / Le départ amer* (2003), *Crossed Reflections / Réflexions croisées* (2004, 15', Beta SP), *The Only Way Out* (2004, 15', 16mm), *Women without Shadows / Femmes sans ombre* (2005, 45', Beta SP).

AL-MANSOUR, KHAIRIYA. Iraqi filmmaker. Born in 1958 in Baghdad, she studied first at the Academy of Arts in Baghdad and then at the Cairo Higher Film Institute. She worked as assistant to leading Egyptian directors, including Salah Abou Seif, Tewfiq Saleh, and Youssef Chahine, before returning to Iraq to direct documentaries: *This Is My Village / C'est mon village* (1981, 15', 35mm), *Basma* (1981, 10', 16mm), *Determination* (1983, 12', 35mm),

three 15-minute documentaries about the Nairobi World Conference on Women (1983), *The Daughter of Mesopotamia* (1984), *The Student and the Battle* (1986, 30', 35mm), *The Churches of Iraq* (1988, 30', 35mm), *The Wells of Iraq* (1988, 30', 35mm), *Magical Fingers* (1989, 15', 35mm), *The Lady of Ages* (1990, 30', 35mm), *Look!* (1991, 30', 35mm), *White Dreams* (1991, 30', 35mm), *The Call of Iraq* (1991, 30', 35mm), *The Builders* (1996, 30', 35mm), *Cinema Lover* (1997, 10', 35mm), *The Dream, The Memory* (1998, 15', 35mm), *One Day in Baghdad* (1998, 15', 35mm), *The Memory of An Eye* (1999, 15', 35mm), *Adoration and Creativity* (2000, 30', 35mm), *Angels Do Not Die* (2000, 22', 35mm), *The Last Painting* (2000, 7', 35mm). Feature films: *20/20 Vision / Sitta 'ala sitta* (1988, 90', 35mm), *100 Percent / Miya 'ala miya* (1992, 105', 35mm).

Al-Mansouri, Nayef. Emirati filmmaker. He studied at Abu Dhabi Men's College. Short documentary film: *Facing the Inevitable* (with Abdallah Bastaki, 2005, 25', Mini DV).

Al-Marri, Rashid. Emirati filmmaker. He studied at Dubai Men's College. Short films: *Speed Kills* (2006, 1', Mini DV), *Dubai Men's College Then and Now* (2007, 19', HD), *The Mandoobs* (2008, 17', HD).

Al-Marri, Roudha. Emirati filmmaker. She studied at Dubai Women's College. Short films: *Violence against Women* (2005, 1', Mini DV), *The Mannequin* (2005, 7', Mini DV).

Al-Marzouqi, Amena Abdul Aziz. Emirati filmmaker. She studied at Abu Dhabi Women's College. Short documentary films: *Wasta: Above the Law* (2002, 3', DV Cam), *The War through Children's Eyes* (2003, 5', DV Cam), *The Wing of Mercy* (2003, 5', DV Cam).

Almarzouqi, Hind Mohammed. Emirati filmmaker. She studied at Abu Dhabi Women's College and subsequently worked in television. Student films: *A Day in a Reporter's Life* (2000, 5', DV Cam), *National Day* (2000, 3', DV Cam), *Experience in Life* (2000, 3', DV Cam),

Behind Closed Doors (2000, 12', Beta SP), *Al-Liwa* (2001, 9', DV Cam), *The Showjumper* (2001, 5', DV Cam).

Al-Marzouqi, Salah Mohamed. Emirati filmmaker. He studied at the Abu Dhabi Men's College and later worked as editor and graphics consultant. Student films: *Orange* (2002, 3', Beta SP), *Sultan al-Nbata Adventures* (2003, 9', video), *My Brothers* (2003, 22', Beta SP). Short films: *The Arrest Night of al-Nbata* (2005, 13', Mini DV, animation), *Tekra* (2005, 4', DV Cam), *Soul Colours* (2006, 4', DV Cam).

Al-Marzouqi, Samir Hussain. Emirati filmmaker. He studied at Dubai Men's College. Short films: *A Money Trip* (2005, 13', Mini DV), *Higher Colleges of Technology Student Council* (2005, 6', Mini DV).

Al-Mashni, Mahmoud Yousouf. Emirati filmmaker. He is a member of the Arabic Animation Society in Cairo. Short animated films: *Mercy within Us* (2001, 3', Beta SP), *I Grow* (2001, 4', Beta SP), *Words We Love* (2001, 3', Beta SP), *My Grandfather* (with Omar Sabah, 2001, 4', Beta SP), *Uncle Salem's Farm* (2001, 12', Beta SP), *My Mother* (2002, 3', Beta SP), *A Home Near Jerusalem* (2002, 3', Beta SP), *Our Beautiful Woods* (2002, 11', Beta SP), *My Rights* (with Omar Kawan, 2003, 4', DV Cam).

Al-Masri, Izzidin. Palestinian filmmaker. Short film: *Rainbow Dress / Thawb al-qaws quzah* (2004).

Al-Massoudi, Saad. Iraqi filmmaker. He has worked as a journalist and film critic and made several films for Iraqi television. Documentary: *al-Mandayoun* (1998, 51', video).

Al-Mayahi, Asad Salem. Emirati filmmaker. He studied at Abu Dhabi Men's College. Short documentary film: *Al-Ain City* (2003, 5', Beta SP).

Al-Mazrooie, Ahmed Rashed. Emirati filmmaker. Born in 1984, he studied at Dubai Men's College. Short film: *Ashes to Ashes* (with Hassan Ibrahim Hassan Ismail, 2007, 4', Mini DV), *Enough* (2007, 2', Mini DV), *Discrimination* (2007, 14', Mini DV).

Al-Mazrouei, Afra. Emirati filmmaker. She studied at Abu Dhabi Women's College. Short film: *Traditional Dances in the UAE: Al-Harbia* (with Salama al-Romaithi, 2004, 10', Mini DV).

Al-Mazrouie, Ameena Abdulla. Emirati filmmaker. Born in 1982, she studied at Abu Dhabi Women's College. Short films: *Kid's Smoking* (2002, 6', DV Cam), *Does Technology Control the World?* (2003, 2', DV Cam), *The Well* (2003, 8', DV Cam), *Royal Oman Symphony Orchestra* (with Reef al-Khaja, 2003, 11', DV Cam), *Ayaam* (2004, 6', DV Cam).

Al-Medfa, Sahar. Emirati filmmaker. Short film: *The Pebble* (2007, 5', DVD).

Al-Mehairi, Noura. Emirati filmmaker. Short film: *My Future Career* (with Asma al-Mansoor, 2005, 3', Beta SP).

Almehdi, Zainab. Emirati filmmaker. Born in 1986 in the United States, she studied at the American University of Sharjah. Short fictional film: *Get Real* (2006, 6', Mini DV).

Al-Mehrizi, Badria Mohammed. Emirati filmmaker. She studied at Dubai Women's College. Short films: *Stop Drugs* (2001, 8', Beta SP), *Seatbelts Will Save Your Life* (with Mariam Jassim al-Sarkal and Shaikha al-Manouri, 2002, 9', Beta SP), *Child Abuse* (2003, 5', Beta SP), *Falcon Hunting* (2003, 10', Beta SP).

AL-MERAIKLY, KHALIFA. Qatari filmmaker. Feature film: *Threads Beneath Sands / Des fils sous le sable / Khyoot taht al rimal* (2006).

Al-Mohaishi, Bashir Hassan. Saudi filmmaker. Born in 1980, he studied fine art at King Saud University, Riyadh. Short fictional films: *My Lord, Send Me Back* (2005, 38', Mini DV), *Soil Complaint* (2007, 35', DVD).

AL-MOHEISSEN, ABDULLAH. Saudi film-maker. Born in 1947 in Saudi Arabia, he studied philosophy and film in London. On his return to Saudi Arabia, he set up an advertising company, equipped with the first film studios in the kingdom. He made a number of short films: *Islam: A Bridge to the Future / Islam, un pont pour l'avenir, The Killing of a City / L'assassinat d'une ville, The Shock / Le choc.* Feature film: *Shadow of Silence / Les ombres du silence / Dhalal al-samt* (2006, 110', 35mm).

Al-Moherat, Firas Abd al-Jalil. Jordanian filmmaker. Worked in television and made his short film in the UAE. Short documentary film: *The Death Is Coming from Horses* (2006, 26', DigiBeta).

Al-Moodi, Reem. Emirati filmmaker. She studied at Dubai Women's College. Short films: *Paranoia* (2006, 1', Mini DV), *Hard to Fix* (2006, 1', Mini DV).

Al-Motiri, Rja Sair. Saudi filmmaker. Also journalist. Short film: *Margin* (2007, 4', Mini DV).

Al-Muathen, Amira. Emirati filmmaker. She studied at Dubai Women's College. Short film: *Thalessemia* (2007, 1', DV Cam).

Al-Muhairi, Aisha Mohamed Obaid. Emirati filmmaker. A media student who graduated in 2008. Short film: *Mission of Hope / Mashroo' amal* (with Asma Ahmad, 2008, 21', Mini DV).

Al-Muhairi, Amna Ateeq. Emirati filmmaker. She studied at Abu Dhabi Women's College. Short documentary films: *Harley Davidson* (2001, 4', DV Cam), *Zayed: Always in Our Hearts* (2006, 13', DV Cam).

Al-Muhairi, Ayesha Mohammed. Emirati filmmaker. Born in 1986, she studied at Dubai Women's College. Short film: *Would You Give Up Your Home?* (2006, 2', Mini DV).

Al-Muhairi, Fadel Saeed. Emirati filmmaker. Born in 1979 in Abu Dhabi, he studied filmmaking at the American University of Shar-jah. Student films: *Tolerance* (2002, 3', DV Cam), *Al-Ra'aboob* (2003, 34', DV Cam), *Xs* (2003, 15', DV Cam), *Once upon a Night* (2003, 25', DV Cam). Short films: *Al-Ghaith* (2004, 38', Beta SP), *Under Construction / Kaid al-insaha'a* (2006, 18', DVD), *Ras Harba* (2008, 57', HDV).

Al-Muhairi, Hamda Mohamed. Emirati filmmaker. She studied at Abu Dhabi Women's College. Short fictional films: *The Little Boy* (2002, 3', DV Cam), *A Father's Loss* (2002, 4', DV Cam), *Our Right to Ride* (2009, 51', HD Cam).

Al-Mulla al-Muhairi, Hana Abdullah Mohammed. Emirati filmmaker. Born in 1984 in Dubai, she studied at Dubai Women's College. Short films: *Adolescent Colors* (with Maitha Ebrahim, Nada Salem, Wafa Faisal, Heba al-Dhanhani, 2005, 28', DV Cam), *Give Them Way* (2006, 7', Mini DV).

Al-Mulla, Alya Mohamed Ali. Emirati filmmaker. She studied at the American University of Sharjah. Short film: *Workers at Nine Ball Café* (with Vivian Mamdouh Ibrahim, 2003, 15', DV Cam).

Al-Mulla, Fatma. Emirati filmmaker. She studied at the American University of Sharjah. Short films: *Marriage and Appearances among the UAE Youths* (2006, 4', Mini DV), *Al-Amal* (2006, 13', Mini DV), *The Pearl* (2006, 16', Mini DV).

Al-Mulla, Saoud Mohamed Ali. Emirati filmmaker. He studied at Abu Dhabi Men's College. Short film: *See You There* (2002, 10', DV Cam).

Al-Murry, Saeed Salmeen. Emirati filmmaker. Born in 1968 in the UAE. Short films: *Sand Remains* (2004, 38', DV Cam), *Walls* (2005, 40', DVC Pro), *A Traveler* (2005, 9', Mini DV), *Hoboob* (2005, 22', DVC Pro), *Erj-al-Tein* (2006, 10', DVC Pro), *The Blood Wedding* (2007, 21', DV Cam), *Al-Ghobna* (2007, 13', DigiBeta), *Mariam's Daughter / La fille de Mariam / Bint Mariam* (2008, 27', DigiBeta).

Almushrrakh, Fatma. Emirati filmmaker. She studied at the American University of Sharjah. Short film: *Alcoholism* (with Khalid Abdullah, 1', Mini DV).

Al-Mutawa, Ahmed. Emirati filmmaker. He studied at the Academy of Art University in San Francisco and took courses at UCLA, while working on various U.S. productions. Short films: *Moments!* (2006, 4', 16mm), *Palaces of Sand* (2006, 4', 16mm).

Al-Mutawa, Hafsa. Emirati filmmaker. She studied at Dubai Women's College. Short film: *Thalassemia* (2006, 1', DC Cam).

Al-Naboulsi, Khalil Sameer. Emirati filmmaker. He studied at UAE University. Short fictional film: *Between Rita and My Eyes* (2004, 24', DV Cam).

Al-Nazwani, Ahmed Hassan. Emirati filmmaker. He studied at UAE University. Short fictional films: *From Birth* (2003, 8', Beta SP), *In the Fire's Womb* (2004, 16', DV Cam), *In Brackets* (2005, 6', Mini DV).

Al-Nejaim, Abdulaziz Nasser. Saudi filmmaker. Born in 1986 in Riyadh, he worked in theatre and film while still a student at Imam Islamic University. Short fictional films: *Disobedience* (2007, 20', Mini DV), *The Note* (2008, 5', Mini DV).

Al-Neyadi, Yaser Saeed. Emirati filmmaker. Also child actor. Short fictional films: *Person of Cup* (2006, 4', Mini DV), *The Dreams Seller* (2006, 18', Mini DV), *And He Returned* (2007, 25', Mini DV), *Letters to the Sky* (2008, 18', Mini DV), *Temporary Drought* (2009, 15', HD Cam).

Al-Nizer, Ali Khalifa. Emirati filmmaker. He studied at the Dubai Men's College. Short film: *A Race Home* (2002, 6', Beta SP).

Al-Obaid, Mohammed Mahde. Saudi filmmaker. Short animated film: *Namool Adventures* (2008, 19', Mini DV).

AL-OBALI, JAWAD. Iraqi filmmaker. Feature film: *Painful Nights / Les nuits de douleur / Layali al-adab* (1963, 35mm).

AL-OBEIDI, ABDI JABAR. Iraqi filmmaker. Feature film: *At Dawn / À l'aube / Maa al-fahr* (1964, 35mm).

AL-OBEIDI, KAMEL. Iraqi filmmaker. Feature film: *The Hand of Fate / La main du destin / Yad al-qadar* (1964, 35mm).

Alomain, Abdullah Ibrahim. Saudi filmmaker. Short film: *A Message to a Writer* (2008, 3', Mini DV).

Alomary, Mohammed. Qatari filmmaker. Born in Jordan. Short documentary film: *Souk Waqif* (with Dawoud Hassan, 2007, 10', DV Cam).

AL-OMER, HYDER. Iraqi filmmaker. Feature films: *Fitna and Hassan / Fitna et Hassan / Fitna wa Hassan* (1950, 35mm), *Take Pity on Me / Ayez pitié de moi / Irhamoini* (1958, 35mm).

Al-Otaiba, Mohammed. Emirati filmmaker. He studied at the New York Film Academy and made *Empty Clip* (2003) in the United States. Short films: *Afghan Days* (2004, 31', Mini DV), *Petra 2025 AD* (2006, 5', Mini DV).

Alotaibi, Faisal Shahid. Saudi filmmaker. Documentary producer for Saudi and Emirati television. Short documentary film: *Bride of Mountains and Archeology* (2006, 43', DV Cam).

Alowais, Nasir. Emirati filmmaker. Underwater wildlife videographer. Short film: *The Unexplored Socotra* (2005, 13', DV Cam).

Al-Qadami, Jaafar. Bahraini filmmaker. Short documentary film: *Hearts Imprint* (2006, 10', DV Cam).

Al-Qallaf, Hussain. Emirati filmmaker. Short film: *HIV+* (2008, 1', Mini DV).

Alqasab, Mohammad Noaman. Bahraini filmmaker. Also an actor. Short fictional films: *The Unknown Step* (2001), *I Will Keep on Loving You* (2003, 15', DV Cam), *Knife* (2004, 8', Mini DV), *The Last Match* (2005, 22', Mini DV), *Follow* (2006, 6', Mini DV), *Leave a Legacy* (2007, 5', Mini DV), *The Debarred Area* (2007, 28', Mini DV).

Al-Qasimi, Aisha. Emirati filmmaker. Born in 1982 in Sharjah, she studied at the American University of Sharjah. Short films: *Nike* (2004, 1', Mini DV), *Next* (with Dareen al-Sarraj, 2004, 11', Mini DV), *Another Day* (with Dareen al-Sarraj, 2004, 4', Mini DV), *When a Girl* (with Dareen al-Sarraj, 2004, 7', Mini DV).

Al-Qassimi, Maryam. Emirati filmmaker. Short film: *Global Warning* (with Mamoun Alzoughbi, 2007, 1', Mini DV).

Al-Qassimi, Maysoon. Emirati filmaker. She is a poet, novelist, and conceptual artist who has lived mostly in Egypt. Her film was made in the UAE and Egypt. Short film: *Thread After Thread* (2005, 12', Beta SP).

Al-Qassimi, Salem Faisal. Emirati filmmaker. Born in 1984, he studied at the American University of Sharjah. Short films: *My Way* (2003, 8', DV Cam), *Static Identity* (2004, 3', Mini DV).

Al-Qattan, Omar. Palestinian filmmaker. Born in in 1964 in Lebanon of Palestinian parents, he studied filmmaking at INSAS in Belgium, where his graduation film was *Tale of a Blind Man and a Paralytic / Conte de l'aveugle et du paralytique* (1988, 16'). He has lived in England since 1975. He worked with Michel Khleifi as executive producer of *The Tale of the Three Jewels* (1996) and *Mixed Marriages in the Holy Land* (1995). Documentaries: *Jerusalem / Jérusalem* (1998, 25'), *Dreams and Silence/ Rêves et silence / Ahlma fi fairagh* (1991, 52', 16mm), *Going Home / Le retour / al-'Awda* (1995, 50', Beta SP), *Diary of an Art Competition (Under Curfew) / Yaomiyyat musabiqa faniyya taht al-hisar* (2002, 17', Beta SP).

Al-Qood, Bader Johar. Emirati filmmaker. Short fictional film: *Jerusalem, Who Will Defend You Now?* (2002, 3', video).

Al-Qubaisi, Mohamed Abdullah. Emirati filmmaker. He studied at the Abu Dhabi Men's College. Short film: *Between Yesterday and Today* (with Khalid al-Fardan and Mohamed Najm al-Qubaisi, 1998, 2', DV Cam.

Al-Qubaisi, Mohamed Najm. Emirati filmmaker. He studied at the Abu Dhabi Men's College. Short films: *Between Yesterday and Today* (with Khalid al-Fardan and Mohamed Abdullah al-Qubaisi, 1998, 2', DV Cam), *Adnoc Ad* (1999, 1', DV Cam).

Al-Qubaisi, Nadir. Emirati filmmaker. She studied at Abu Dhabi Women's College. Short film: *Al Alali* (2002, 1', DV Cam).

Al-Rabeea, Saif Fadhel. Emirati filmmaker. He studied at Sharjah University. Short film: *My Emirates* (2006, 4', Mini DV).

AL-RAHEB, WAHA. Syrian filmmaker, writer, and actress. She was born in 1960 in Cairo, daughter of Syrian parents. Her father was a diplomat, so she went to school in various cities, including Moscow and Khartoum. She studied at the Fine Art Academy in Damascus and at the Université de Paris VIII. She lives in Damascus and works there as an actress and director in Syrian television. She has also appeared in various films, including Mohamed Malas's *City Dreams* and written screenplays and a book on women in Syrian cinema. She has made a number of téléfilms (*Blue Glass Pearls / Perles de verre bleu*, 1997, and *A Suitcase for the New Year / Une valise pour la nouvelle année*, 1999), a seven-part television series, *Family House / Maison de famille* (2001), and a TV children's series, *This Is the One / Tilka al-lati* (2004). One short fictional film: *An Optional Exile* (1987), and a documentary film: *Our Grandmothers / Nos grand-mères* (1987, 30', 35mm). Feature film: *Dreamy Visions / Visions chimériques* a.k.a. *Vision de rêve / Ra'a halima* (2003, 125', 35mm).

Al-Rahman, Nasser Jaber. Emirati filmmaker. Short film: *Educational Contrasts* (2007, 20', Mini DV).

Al-Rahman, Saleh. Emirati filmmaker. Born in 1980. Short fictional film: *Star of Stars* (2006, 17', Mini DV).

Al-Rahmy, Adnan. Jordanian filmmaker. Documentary: *Cherif Hussein / Le Cherif Hussein / al-Cherif Hussein* (1969).

Al-Rais, Maria Mohammad. Emirati filmmaker. She studied at Dubai Women's College. Short films: *Gossip* (2006, 1', Mini DV), *Killing Lives* (2006, 1', Mini DV).

Al-Rasheed, Amjad. Jordanian filmmaker. Short fictional films: *Disturbance* (2007, 7'), *Dali* (2008, 25').

Al-Rawas, Amer. Omani filmmaker. Born in 1980 in Oman. Short films: *Between Lines and Mirrors* (2005), *Belooh* (2008, 5', DVD).

AL-RAWI, ABDELHADI. Iraqi filmmaker. Born in 1938, he trained in the USSR. Documentary: *What Have You Done for Palestine / Qu'avez-vous fait pour la Palestine / Madha qadamta li Filistin* (1973). Feature films: *Love in Baghdad / L'amour à Bagdad / al-Hubb fi Baghdad* (1986), *The House / La maison / al-Bayt (1988), Iftarid nafsaka Sa'idan* (1990).

Alrayhi, Khalid. Emirati filmmaker. Born in 1979 in Ajam in the UAE, he studied applied media at the Dubai Men's College and worked as an animator and graphic designer. Also editor on a number of shorts. One short animated film: *The Day* (2001, 7', video), and two fictional shorts: *Superstition between Reality and Fantasy* (with Yasser al-Gargawi, 2002, 15', Beta SP), *An Hour* (2003, 7', Beta SP).

Al-Redha, Mohamed Jasim. Emirati filmmaker. He studied at the Dubai Men's College. Short film: *Free to Be Free* (2007, 3', DV Cam).

Al-Reyami, Hamad Saif. Emirati filmmaker. Born in 1974, he studied media at the Abu Dhabi Men's College and subsequently worked in television. Student films: *Abu Dhabi Cinemas* (2002, 3', DV Cam), *Taxi Driver* (2002, 5', DV Cam), *F2 Grand Prix* (2002, 6', DV Cam), *Memories / Yaadien* (2002, 5', DV Cam), *The Nightmare* (2003, 34', DV Cam), *Debtor* (2004, 19', DV Cam). Short films: *Emirate Drums in France's Neighbourhood* (with Juma al-Sahli, 2005, 15', DV Cam), *Tones* (2005, 9', DV Cam), *Umm al-Dowais . . . In Their Eyes* (2006, 10', DV Cam), *Khalaas* (2006, 2', DV Cam), *Tuna* (2006, 20', Mini DV), *Sewage* (2007, 7', DV Cam).

Al-Reyami, Omar. Emirati filmmaker. Born in Al-Ain, he studied at the American University of Sharjah. Short fictional film: *Registration Day* (2004, 7', Mini DV).

Al-Reyami, Salem Ghaleb. Emirati filmmaker. He studied at the Abu Dhabi Men's College. Short films: *Shop Clerk* (2002, 3', Beta SP), *Trouble Maker* (2005, 10', DV Cam).

Al-Rifai, Yahya Basheir. Emirati filmmaker. He studied at UAE University and has worked as cameraman on numerous short films. Short fictional films: *Association* (2003, 5', Beta SP), *Behind the Walls* (2004, 11', Beta SP), *Strong* (2005, 1', Beta SP).

Al-Riffaei, Hussain. Bahraini filmmaker. Short fictional film: *Dinner* (20', DigiBeta).

Al-Robea, Omar Abdalaziz. Saudi filmmaker. He trained in the theatre. Short film: *Msear* (2007, 7', Mini DV).

Al-Romaithi, Fatima Khalifa. Emirati filmmaker. She studied at the Abu Dhabi Women's College. Short films, one documentary: *Arabian Eyes* (1999, 5', DV Cam), and one animation: *Driving the Boat / Khlid Bu Tilah* (2007, 7', DVD).

Al-Romaithi, Rashed Mohamed. Emirati filmmaker. He studied at Ajman University. Short film: *Heritage Village* (2002, 9', Beta SP).

Al-Romaithi, Salama. Emirati filmmaker. She studied at Abu Dhabi Women's College. Short film: *Traditional Dances in the UAE: Al-Harbia* (with Afra al-Mazrouei, 2004, 10', Mini DV).

Al-Roumi, Adnan. Jordanian filmmaker. Documentaries on Palestine: *Twenty Years / Vingt ans / Ichrouna am* (1968, 16mm), *Meeting at Ajloun / Rencontre à Ajloun / Liqâ fi Ajloun* (1968, 28').

Al-Roumi, Meyar. Syrian filmmaker. Born in 1973 in Damascus, he studied filmmaking at the Université de Paris VIII and FEMIS in Paris. Short documentaries: *The Object of Desire / L'objet du désir* (1997), *A Silent Cinema / Un cinéma muet / Sinima samta* (2001, 29', Beta SP), *Waiting for the Day / L'attente du jour* (2003, 53', Beta SP), *Rabia's Journey / Le voyage de Rabia* (2006, 23', Beta SP), *Six Ordinary Stories / Sitat qosas adiyyah* (2007, 59', Video HD).

Al-Roumi, Mohamed. Syrian filmmaker. Born in 1945 in Syrian Mesopotamia, he lives between Paris and Damascus and has worked professionally as a photographer since the beginning of the 1970s, selling his work internationally. Short documentary film: *Blue-Grey / Bleu-gris* (2004, 23', Beta SP), and a short fictional film: *A Journey to the End of the World*.

Al-Rumaithi, Shamma Mohamed. Emirati filmmaker. She studied at Abu Dhabi Women's College. Short documentary films: *Ghareem Alshooq: Abdullah Al-Rumaithi* (2000, 1', DV Cam), *Desert Rose* (2001, 6', Beta SP), *The Trackers* (2001, 5', DV Cam).

Al-Saadi, Rasha Ali. Emirati filmmaker. She studied at Abu Dhabi Women's College. Short films: *A Woman's Journey* (2003, 4', DV Cam), *Mixing in the UAE* (2004, 13', DV Cam).

Al-Sabah, Miriam. Emirati filmmaker. She studied at the American University of Sharjah. Short fictional films: *A Tail Apart* (with Munira al-Doseri, 2004, 4', Mini DV), *Faithless* (with Munira al-Doseri, 2004, 4', Mini DV).

Alsabahi, Arwa. Emirati filmmaker. Studied at the American University of Sharjah. Short film: *Anti-Smoking* (with Ahmad Essam, 2007, 1', DVD).

AL-SABOUNI, BILAL. Syrian filmmaker. He graduated from the Cairo Higher Film Institute in 1970, where his graduation film was *Suspension Points / Points de supension / Alâmatu istifhâm* (1970). He worked for several years as assistant director and made a number of shorts and documentaries: *The New Dawn / Le nouvel aube / Fajrun jadîd* (1972), *Petrol / L'essense / al-Bitrûl* (1975), *Nuclear Medicine / La médecine nucléaire / al-Tibbu al-nawawi* (1978). He also shot one episode, *The Sprig of Mint / Le brin de la menthe / U'd al-n'ana'a*, of the collective film *Shame / La honte / al-'Ar* (1974), with Wadeih Yousef and Bashir Safia. Feature film: *The Fifth Arm of the Prison / La cinquième citadelle / al-Qal'a al-khâmisa* (1979, 90', 35mm).

Al-Sahen, Ibrahim. Iraqi filmmaker. Short fictional about the Palestinian struggle: *It Happened in June / C'est arrivé en juin / Waqa'a fi huzeirân* (1973).

Al-Sahli, Juma. Emirati filmmaker. He studied at the Abu Dhabi Men's College. He also appeared as an actor in numerous shorts. Short films: *Education* (2003, 3', Beta SP), *Emirate Drums in France's Neighbourhood* (with Hamad Saif al-Reyami, 2005, 15', DV Cam), *Sara's Secrets* (2005, 23', DV Cam), *An Empty Bottle* (2005, 19', DigiBeta), *The Return of Umm al-Dowais* (2007, 40', DigiBeta), *Paradise Evening* (2009, 19', HD Cam).

AL-SAIDI, WIAM. Lebanese filmmaker. Feature films: *Red on the Snow / Rouge sur neige / Dimaa al-talj* (1963, 35mm), *Darbat al-wade'* (1963, 35mm), *Al-Marmoura* (1985, 35mm), *At the Time of Pearls / Au temps des perles / Ayyam al-loulou* (1986, 35mm), *Me, the Radar / Moi, le radar / Ana al-radar* (1986, 35mm), *Shame, Restoum / La honte, Restoum / Ayb ya Restoum* (1987, 35mm), *For Whoever Sings of Love / Pour qui chante l'amour / Liman youghanni al-hub* (1991, 35mm).

AL-SAÏFI, HASSAN.* Egyptian director of two Syrian feature films: *The Two Friends / Les deux amis* (1970, 35mm), *Men's Nights / Nuits des hommes* (1975, 35mm).

AL-SALAMI, KHADIJA. Yemeni filmmaker. Born in 1966 in the village of Mabar in North Yemen, she began hosting a weekly children's television show for Yemeni Television in Sanaa at the age of 11. She moved at the age of 16 to the United States, where she studied at the University of Washington and UCLA. She now lives in Paris, where she works in the communication and cultural service of the Yemeni embassy. She has made a number of short documentaries: *Women of Yemen / Femmes du Yémen / Mar'a fi Yemen* (1990, 24', Beta SP), *Hadramout, Crossroads of Cultures / Hadramout, carrefour des civilisatisations / Hadramawt, multaqa al-hadarat* (1991, 45', Beta SP), *Land of Saba / Terre de Saba / Ard al-saba* (1997, 55', Beta SP), *Yemen of a Thousand Faces* (2000), *Women and Democracy in Yemen / Les femmes et la démocratie au Yémen / al-Mar'a wa-l dimuqratiya fi-l Yemen* (2004, 54', Beta SP), and *A Stranger in Her Own City / Une étrangère dans sa ville / al-Ghariba fi madinatiha* (2005, 28', Mini DV). In 2005, she co-wrote a book with Charles Hoots: *Pleure, ô reine de Saba*. Feature-length documentary: *Amina* (2006, 75', DV Cam).

Al-Saleh, Nouri. Kuwaiti filmmaker. Directed a documentary on Palestine for Kuwaiti television: *Fatima el Bernaoui* (1968, 25').

Al-Salty, Jassim Mohamed. Emirati filmmaker. Studied applied media studies at the Dubai Men's College. Short films: *Fish Market* (2004, 5', Mini DV), *Al-hellah* (2005, 18', Mini DV).

AL-SAMARI, ABDL KHALIQ. Iraqi filmmaker. Feature film: *Regrets / Nadam* (1955).

AL-SAMARI, HUSSEN. Iraqi filmmaker. Feature film: *Tiswahen* (1957), *The Reward / La récompense / Al-jaza* (1970, unreleased).

Al-Sanousi, Mohamed. Kuwaiti filmmaker. Born in 1940, he studied filmmaking in the United States before making the first Kuwaiti short film, *The Storm / La tempête / al-Asifa* (1964).

AL-SARAJ, ABDEL KARIM. Iraqi filmmaker. Feature film: *The Path of Darkness / La voie des ténèbres / Tariq al-dalam* (1970, 35mm).

Al-Sarkal, Mariam Jassim. Emirati filmmaker. She studied at Dubai Women's College. Short film: *Poverty in the UAE* (with Buthaina al-Hashemi and Amena Saif al-Suboosi, 2002, 6', Beta SP).

Al-Sarraj, Dareen. Emirati filmmaker. Born in 1981 in Sharjah, she studied at the American University of Sharjah. Short films: *Landrover* (2004, 1', Mini DV), *Next* (with Aisha al-Qasimi, 2004, 11', Mini DV), *Another Day* (2004, 4', Mini DV), *When a Girl* (with Aisha al-Qasimi, 2004, 7', Mini DV), *Level 7 Underground* (2004, 7', Mini DV).

Al-Sawalmeh, Mohamed. Palestinian filmmaker. He studied filmmaking in Moscow and has made a dozen documentaries on Palestinian society for the PLO and the Palestinian Ministry of Culture and Information, among the latter *Intifada* (1988), *The Coming Fire / Le feu qui progresse / al-Nahr al-qadima* (1998, 52', video), *The Doorman for the Numeral / Le portier du chiffre / Bawaba li al-raqam* (1998), *Night of the Soldiers / La nuit des soldats / Layla al-junud* (2002, 15', Beta SP).

Al-Sayed, Moza Ali. Emirati filmmaker. She studied at Dubai Women's College. Short films: *Desert Boys* (with Kadija al-Yousuf, 2004, 10', DV Cam), *His Abstract Life* (2005, 3', Mini DV).

Al-Shabibi, Fatema Salem. Emirati filmmaker. She studied at Abu Dhabi Women's College. Short film: *Bazaar* (with Shaikha Rashed al-Braikhi and Amani Ahmed al-Lawghani, 2003, 3', DV Cam).

AL-SHAIBANI, HANI. Emirati filmmaker. Born in 1974 in Dubai, he studied communication at Cairo University and then worked as film director for the police communications unit in Dubai. His short, *Jawhara*, won best short film prize at the Emirates Film Competition in Abu Dhabi and the MEIFF in Abu Dhabi. He has directed numerous short films and collaborated as writer, editor, or actor on several others. Short films: *Whirling* (1994, 4', video), *Message from Hell / Lettre d'enfer* (2000, 13', Beta SP), *Birthday, the Ring, and Other / Anniversaire, la bague et tant d'autres choses* (2001, 23', Beta SP), *A Warm Winter Night / Une nuit d'hiver chaude* (2001, 27', DV Cam), *Jawhara* (2003, 29', Beta SP), *01'03* (collective film with eleven other directors, 2004, 12', Mini DV), *Innocence* (2007, 3', Mini DV), *Young Sadness* (2009, 15', DigiBeta). Feature films: *A Dream* (2005, 71', 35mm), *Jumaa and the Sea / Jumaa et la mer / Jumaa wa al-bahr* (2007, 68'), *The Hotel* (2009, 57', DigiBeta).

Al-Shaibani, Mohammed. Emirati filmmaker. Short films: *Waiting for AUS* (2007, 11', Mini DV), *Game Plan* (2007, 2', Mini DV), *The In Out* (2007, 2', Mini DV).

Alshaibi, Sama. Palestinian filmmaker. Short experimental film: *All I Want for Christmas* (2007, 6').

Al-Shaikh, Hassan Abdulrahman. Emirati filmmaker. He studied at Dubai Men's College. Short fictional film: *Once a Child* (2006, 3', DV Cam).

Alshakaili, Hamad bin Salem. Omani filmmaker. Also playwright and theatre director. Short fictional film: *Before Sunset* (2006, 10', DV Cam).

Al-Shami, Abdallah. Emirati filmmaker. He studied at the American University of Sharjah. Short films: *Emes* (2004, 3', Mini DV), *The Stupor of Death* (2004, 3', Mini DV).

Al-Shamsi, Abdallah Rashid. Emirati filmmaker. Born in 1988, he studied at Sharjah University. Short film: *The Watch* (2006, 29', Mini DV).

Al-Shamsi, Alia. Emirati filmmaker. Born in 1985, she studied at Dubai Women's College. Short films: *Florist* (with Khadija Hussain al-Buloshi, 2005, 10', Mini DV), *Through Child's Eyes* (with Khadija Hussain al-Buloshi, 2005, 6', Mini DV), *Fly Fly Fly = Die* (2006, 2', Mini DV), *No Vacancy* (with Khadija Hussain al-Buloshi, 2006, 13', Mini DV).

Al-Sharif, Shamsa. Emirati filmmaker: She studied at Dubai Women's College. Short films: *Unpretty* (2005, 4', Mini DV), *Non-Verbal Language* (2005, 2', DV Cam), *The Bride Has It All* (2007, 10', DV Cam).

Al-Shateri, Hana. Emirati filmmaker. She studied at UAE University. Short fictional films: *The Beginning of an End* (2007, 8', DV Cam), *Something* (2008, 8', Mini DV).

AL-SHAWWA, ZUHAYR. Syrian filmmaker. Feature films: *The Green Valley / La vallée verte / al-Wadi al-akhdar* (1950, 35mm), *Beyond the Borders / Au-delà des frontières / Wara al-hudud* (1963, 35mm), *Satan's Game / Le jeu de Satan / La'bat al-shaytan* (1966, 35mm).

Al-Shayeb, Ibtisam Ahmed. Emirati filmmaker. Studied at UAE University and worked in television from the mid-1990s. Short documentary films: *Memory of a Wall* (2001, 17', DigiBeta), *The Return* (2002, 11', Beta SP).

Alshehhi, Rashid Abdullah Abdul Aziz Al-fahad. Emirati filmmaker. He studied computer science at university. Short film: *Boat Story* (2005, 10', Mini DV).

Al-Shehhi, Walid. Emirati filmmaker. He works at the Higher Colleges of Technology, Ras al-Khaima. He has also worked as editor on a number of short films. Short films: *Epitaphs* (2001, 6', Mini DV), *The Martyr* (2001, 15', Mini DV), *Faces and Windows* (2003, 54', DV Cam), *Aushba's Well* (2004, 17', video), *Signs of the Dead* (2005, 26', Mini DV), *Ahmed Suliman* (2006, 19', Mini DV), *The Wa-*

ter Guard (2007, 11', Mini DV), *Door / Baab* (2008, 20', DigiBeta).

Al-Sheihk, Mustafa. Emirati filmmaker. Short films: *Ali and the Magic Lamp* (2003, 27', Beta SP), *The Alive Dead* (2003, 10', DV Cam).

Al-Shemsi, Jassim Ali. Emirati filmmaker. He studied at Dubai Men's College. Short films: *Concentrate More* (2002, 1', DV Cam), *Obey the Traffic Laws* (2002, 1', DV Cam), *Beauty by Design: The Mosques of Sharjah* (2003, 15', DV Cam).

Al-Shirawi, Ahmed Mohammed. Emirati filmmaker. He studied at UAE University. Short film: *Hassan Sharif* (2004, 9', DV Cam).

Al-Shirqawi, Bakr. Palestinian filmmaker. Documentary film: *War in Lebanon / La guerre au Liban / al-Harb fi Lubnan* (co-dir., 1977).

AL-SIDDICK, KHALID. Kuwaiti filmmaker. Born in 1945 in Kuwait City, he abandoned the business studies in Bombay (Mumbai) proposed by his father to study photography and then filmmaking at the Poona Institute in India. He worked in television in the Emirates and also took film courses in England, the United States, and Italy. He made a number of short films: *The Falcon / Le faucon / al-Saqr* (1965, 35mm), *The Last Voyage / Le dernier voyage / al-Rihla al-akhîra* (1966, 35mm), *Faces of the Night / Visages de la nuit / Wufûhu al-layl* (1968, 35mm), *The Canal / Le canal / al-hufra* (1969), *The Stage of Hope / La scène de l'espérance / Masrah al-amal.* His first feature is a realistic study of fishermen's lives, his second, a Sudanese co-production, is adapted from the novel by the Sudanese writer Tayeb Saleh (who also wrote *Season of Migration to the North*), while his third was shot in India and is based on a story by Boccaccio. Feature films: *The Cruel Sea / La mer cruelle / Basya bahr* (1972, 90', 35mm), *The Wedding of Zein / Les noces de Zein / Urs al-Zayn* (1976, 105', 35mm), *Chahin / Shâhîn* (1985).

Al-Suboosi, Amena Saif. Emirati filmmaker. She studied at Dubai Women's College. Short documentary film: *Poverty in the UAE* (with Mariam Jassim al-Sarkal and Buthaina al-Hashemi, 2002, 6', Beta SP).

Alsuwaidi, Oshba Ahmad. Emirati filmmaker. She studied at Dubai Women's College. Short film: *Crystal Meth* (2006, 1', DV Cam).

Al-Suwaidi, Rehab Ibrahim. Emirati filmmaker. She studied at Dubai Women's College. Short film: *They Made the Cat Eat My Tongue* (2006, 1', Mini DV).

Al-Suwaidi, Saeed Mohamed. Emirati filmmaker. He studied at Dubai Men's College. Short film: *My Immortal* (2004, 5', DV Cam).

Al-Suwaidi, Salwa Hassan. Emirati filmmaker. She studied at Abu Dhabi Women's College. Short documentary film: *Still We Struggle* (2000, 12', DV Cam).

Al-Suwaidi, Sumaya. Emirati filmmaker. She studied at Abu Dhabi Women's College. Short fictional film: *Sabny* (2001, 3', DV Cam).

Al-Tahri, Jihan. Lebanese filmmaker. Documentary film: *Africa—Shuffling the Cards / L'Afrique en morceaux, la tragédie des grands lacs* (with Peter Chappell, 1982, 57').

Al-Tamimi, Theyab. Emirati filmmaker. He studied at the American University of Sharjah. Short films: *Newsnews* (2004, 10', Mini DV), *September 12th* (with Hani Alireza, 2005, 11', Mini DV).

AL-THAWADI, BASSAM. Bahraini filmmaker. Born in 1960 in Bahrain, he studied at the Cairo Higher Institute of Cinema and then worked as a documentary filmmaker for the Ministry of Information and Bahraini television. Three shorts: *The Masked Man / Le masqué / Al-qinqâ'u* (1982, 16mm), *Angels on Earth / Les anges sur la terre / Malâikatu al-ard* (1983, 16mm), and *The Confession* (1984, 34', DVD). Director of the first Bahraini feature.

Feature films: *The Obstacle* a.k.a. *The Barrier /
L'obstacle / Al-hajiz* (1990, 88', 35mm), *Visitor
/ Visiteur* (2002, 86', 35mm), *A Bahraini Tale
/ Un conte de Bahrain / Hekaya Bahrainiya*
(2008, 96', 35mm).

AL-TOUKHI, AHMED.* Egyptian filmmaker who made two Lebanese feature films:
Burning Heart / Cœur brûlant / Fi kalbiha nar
(1960, 35mm), Birth of the Prophet / Naissance du prophète / Mawled al-rassoul (1960,
35mm).

AL-TRAIFI, MOHAMED. Emirati filmmaker. Born in 1976 in Sudan, he worked in
theatre as a playwright and in technical roles.
Short films: *Candle for My Sweetheart* (2003,
50', DV Cam), *Cigarettes* (2004, 13', HD), *Pay
for Their Eyes* (2004, 19', DV Cam). Feature
film: *Haneen* (2006, 92', video).

AL-TUHAMI, FOUAD.* Egyptian filmmaker
who made one Iraqi film. Feature film: *The Attempt / L'essai* a.k.a. *L'expérience / al-Tajruba*
(1977).

Altunayan, Mousa Jafer. Saudi filmmaker.
Short film: *Leftover Food* (2007, 9', DVD).

ALWAN, AMER. Iraqi filmmaker. Born in
1957 in Babylon, he studied at the National
School of Dramatic Art and the Audio-Visual
School in Baghdad, then worked as writer-di-
rector in Iraqi television. He left Iraq in 1940 to
study the philosophy of art in Paris. In France
he made a number of short films and documentaries, as well as working on a feature film
with André Téchiné. Documentary: *The Children of the Embargo / Les enfants de l'embargo*
(2000, 26', Beta SP). His sole feature is a French
co-production. Feature film: *Zaman, The Reed
Man / Zaman, l'homme aux roseaux* (2003,
77', 35mm).

Alwan, Hussein. Iraqi filmmaker. Short fictional film on the Palestine struggle: *The Cur-
rent / Le courant / al-Sakya* (1973).

Al-Yakoubi, Nasser. Emirati filmmaker. Born
in the Emirates, he studied at the Radio and
Television Academy in Egypt. Short films: *The*

*Bleeding, The Martyr, The Decision, Roots and
Seeds, Mountain Sheik / Sheik al-jabal* (2008,
11', Mini DV).

Al-Yaqobi, Naser. Emirati filmmaker. He
studied documentary filmmaking in Egypt.
Also an actor. Short film: *Sneaker* (2007, 13',
Mini DV).

AL-YASEN, MOHAMED AL-DIN. Iraqi
filmmaker. Feature film: *I Am Iraq / Je suis
l'Irak / Ana al-Irak* (1960, 35mm).

AL-YASEN, MOHAMED MONIR. Iraqi
filmmaker. Feature film: *Doctor Hassan /
Docteur Hassan / Doctor Hassan* (1958, 35mm).

Al-Yassir, Nada. Palestinian filmmaker. Short
films: *Mirage / Sarab* (2000), *Four Songs for
Palestine / Quatre chants pour la Palestine /
Arba'a aghani li Filastin* (2001, 13', Beta SP),
Paradise / Naim paradise (2001), *All That Re-
mained* (2005). Also contributed one episode
to the collectively made video documentary
*One More Time (Five Stories about Human
Rights in Palestine / Une fois encore (cinq his-
toires sur les droits de l'homme en Palestine)*
(with Ismaïl Habash, Tawfik Abu Wael, Abdel
Salam Shehada, Najwa Najjar, 2002, 57', Beta
SP).

AL-YASSIRI, FAYÇAL. Iraqi filmmaker.
Born in 1923, he trained in the German Democratic Republic and in Austrian television,
in Vienna, worked in Iraqi television and in
what was then East Berlin. Then he directed
téléfilms in Damascus (his first television feature was never released). He is also a pioneer
of the animated film in Iraq, and has made
various television series for the Gulf. Shorts:
Abdallah's Story / L'histoire d'Abdallah (in the
RDA), *The Awe-inspiring Meeting / La rencontre grandiose* (for television), *All Is Well / Tout
va bien / Nahnou bi kheir* (1969, 11'), *The Stra-
tegic Aims / Les buts stratégiques / al-Ahdaf al-
istratijyiyya* (1974), *Our Children's New Toys /
Les nouveaux jouets de nos enfants* (1974, 9').
Feature films: *The Man / L'homme / al-Rajul*
(1968), *Love and Karaté / L'amour et karaté /
Hubb wa karati* (1973), *Hamidou's Return / Le*

retour d'Hamidou / Awdat Hamidu (1974), *A Very Particular Love* / *Un amour tout particulier* / *Gharâmiât khasa jidan* (1974), *The Head* / *La tête* / *al-Ras* (1976, 35mm), *Lovers on the Road* / *Les amants en route* / *Ushâqalâ al-tariq* (1977, 35mm), *The River* / *Le fleuve* / *al-Nahr* (1977, 90', 35mm), *The Sniper* / *Le canardeur* a.k.a. *Un jour à Beyrouth* / *al-Qannes* (1980, 35mm), *The Princess and the River* / *La princesse et le fleuve* / *al-Amira wal-Nahr* (animated feature, 1982, 35mm).

Al-Yousuf, Khadija. Emirati filmmaker. She studied at Dubai Women's College. Short films: *Desert Boys* (with Moza Ali al-Sayed, 2004, 10', DV Cam), *The Other Side* (2005, 5', DV Cam).

Al-Zaabi, Fatima. Emirati filmmaker. She studied at Abu Dhabi Women's College. Short documentary film: *Millennium Marriage* (2000, 3', DV Cam).

AL-ZADJALI, KHALID. Omani filmmaker. Born at Muscat in Oman, he studied at the Cairo Higher Film Institute, graduating in 1989. He became a scriptwriter and producer in the television service of the Sulinate of Oman and was also involved in student and drama organizations. Feature film: *The Dawn* / *L'aube* / *Al-Boom* (2006, 110', 35mm).

Al-Zain, Osama. Palestinian filmmaker. He studied at the American University in Washington, D.C., where he now lives. Documentaries: *Reflection* (2002, 1', Beta SP), *Transparency* (2002, 30', DV). Feature-length documentary: *Palestine Post-9/11* / *La Palestine après le 11 septembre* (2005, 73').

Al-Zamel, Tareq. Kuwaiti filmmaker. He studied filmmaking in the United States and now works in television and at the American University of Kuwait. Short film: *Under the Sky of Kuwait* (2006, 50', Bigi Beta).

Alzarooni, Essa. Emirati filmmaker. He studied at Sharjah University. Short fictional film: *Lost in Communication College* (2006, 5', Mini DV).

Al-Zarouni, Azza. Emirati filmmaker. Studied at the Abu Dhabi Women's College. Short experimental films: *Blue* (2000, 3', DV Cam), *Finally* (2001, 3', DV Cam).

Al-Zeidi, Faleh. Iraqi filmmaker. Feature film: *Afra and Bader* / *Afra et Bader* / *Afra wa Bader* (1963, 35mm).

Al-Zeidi, Tawfik. Saudi filmmaker. Work in television. Short fictional film: *The Fabricated Crime* / *Al-Garima al-murakaba* (2006, 22', DV Cam).

Al-Ziyoudi, Fatima. Emirati filmmaker. She studied mass communcation at UAE University. Short documentary film: *Al-Gars* (with Hiba Saleh al-Jermi, 2007, 5', DVD).

Al-Zobaïdi, Sobhi. Palestinian filmmaker and actor. Born in 1961 in Jerusalem, he studied economics at the University of Bir Zeit and filmmaking at the University of New York. He worked as an actor from 1982 till 1994. He has made several documentaries on Palestine, including *My Very Private Map* / *Ma carte géographique à moi* / *Kharitati-l-khassa jiddan* (1998, 21', video), *Women in the Sun* / *Femmes au soleil* / *Nisa fi alshams* (1999, 57'), *Ali and His Friends* / *Ali et ses amis* / *Ali wa-ashabhu* (2000, 12', Beta SP), *Light at the End of the Tunnel* / *La lumière au bout du tunnel* / *Du'fi akhar al-nafaq* (2000, 47', Beta SP), *Looking Awry* / *Décale* / *Shawwal* (2001, 34', video), *Crossing Kalandia Roadblock* / *Ubur Kalandia* (2002, 52', video), *A Caged Bird's Song* / *La chanson un oiseau en cage* / *Uqiyyata'ir sijjin* (2003), *A Long Arab Film* / *Un long film arabe* / *Film arabi tawil* (2006).

Alzoughbi, Mamoun. Emirati filmmaker. Short film: *Global Warning* (with Maryam al-Qassimi, 2007, 1', Mini DV).

Al-Zouki, Hicham. Syrian filmmaker. Born in 1968 in Damascus, where he studied English literature. In 1999, he completed his film at the Film and TV Academy in Oslo, where he is now based. Short films and documentaries:

Nostalgia / La nostalgie (1998), *The Door / La porte / Doren* (1999, 7', 35mm), *Ghetto* (2000, 3'), *Eternally Aliens* (2002, 25', DigiBeta), *Just a City / Juste une ville / Moujarad madina* (2003, 13', DV Cam), *The Wash / Le Lavage / Vaskeriet* (2006, 35', 35mm).

Al-Zubaidi, Saad Hassan. Yemeni filmmaker. He studied filmmaking in Moscow and has completed one 60' film.

AL-ZUBAYDI, QAYS. Iraqi filmmaker who worked largely in Syria and directed one Syrian feature film: *Al-Yazirli* (1974). Born in 1939 in Baghdad, he trained as a cameraman and editor from 1959 to 1968 at Babelsberg in what was then East Germany (RDA). Worked in Syrian television, making a number of documentaries, including his first, *Far from the Homeland / Loin de la patrie / Ba'id . . . an al-watan* (1969. He also worked extensively as editor, director, and scriptwriter for Syrian television and the National Cinema Organisation. Much of his work is focused on Palestinian issues. He has continued working as a film editor for other directors, for example, on Nabil al-Maleh's *Crown of Thorns,* Omar Amiralay's *Daily Life in a Syrian Village,* Maroun Bagdadi's Lebanese *Beirut Oh Beirut,* and Mohamed Malas's *The Night.* Short films include: *Far From the Homeland / Loin de la patrie / Ba'idan an-il ardh* (1969, 11'), *The Visit / La visite / al-Ziyara* (1972, 15'), *Palestinian Children's Testimonies in a Time of War / Les témoinages des enfants palestiniens à l'heure de la guerre / Shahâdat al-atfâl fi zaman al-harb* (1972, 25'), *A Voice from Jerusalem / Une voix de Jérusalem / Sawt min al'quds* (1977), *An Opposite Seige / Hisar moddad* (1978), *The Nation of Barbed Wire* a.k.a. *Barbed Wire Homeland / La nation aux barbelés / Watan al-aslak al-sha'ika* (1980, 60'), *Opposition / L'opposition / Muwajihha* (1984), *Dossier of a Massacre* a.k.a. *Slaughter File / Dossier d'un massacre / Milf al-mujazirra* (1984), *Colours / Couleurs / Al-wân* (1988). His sole fictional feature film was made in Syria. Feature films: *Al-Yasseri* (1974, 35mm), *Palestine: A People's Record* a.k.a. *Palestine: The Chronicle of a People / La Palestine,* *chronique d'un peuple / Filstin, sjil sha'* (1984, 110', 35mm) (documentary).

AL-ZUHAIR, AMER. Kuwaiti filmmaker. Feature-length documentary: *When the People Spoke / Lorsque le peuple a parlé / Indama rtakalam al-sha'ab* (2007, 83').

Al-Zuhairi, Bahram. Iraqi filmmaker. Studied at the Independent Film & TV College in Baghdad. Short documentary film: *Leaving* (2007, 23').

Amin, Jamal. Iraqi filmmaker. Documentary: *Spare Parts / Pièces détachées* (2006, 28', video).

AMIRALAY, OMAR. Syrian filmmaker. Born in 1944 in Damascus, he studied first at the Fine Art Academy in Damascus, then drama at the Sorbonne and filmmaking, in 1967, at IDHEC in Paris. On his return he made three documentaries in Syria: *Film Essay about the Euphrates Dam / Essai sur un barrage de l'Euphrate / Muhawwalu sudd al-furat* (1970, 13'), a first feature-length documentary and *The Hens / Les poules / al-Fara'ij* (1977, 45', video). He then directed a documentary on the socialist revolution in Yemen, *About a Revolution / Au sujet d'une révolution / An al-thawra* (1978, 35', Beta SP), and a study of the civil war in Lebanon, *Some People's Misfortunes / Le malheur des uns / Maçaibu qawmin* (1982, 50', 16mm). In the 1980s he worked largely for French television and later set up his own production company, Ramad Films, in Paris. His documentaries include *A Scent of Paradise / Un parfum de paradis / Ra'ihat al-janna* (1982, 40', Beta SP), *The Sarcophagus of Love / Le sarcophage de l'amour / al-Hub al-mawud* (1984, 52', 16mm), *Video on the Sand / Vidéo sur sable / Vidio ala'l rimali* (1984, 45', Beta SP), *The Intimate Enemy / L'ennemi intime / al-'Arduu al-hamim* (1986, 55', 16mm), *Islamic Renewals / Renouveaux islamiques* (1986, 52', video), *The Lady from Shibam / La dame de Shibam* (1988, 13', 16mm), *For the Attention of Madam Prime Minister Benazir Bhutho / À l'attention de Madame le Premier Ministre Benazir Butho* (1989, 52', Beta SP), *On a Day of Ordinary Vio-*

lence, *My Friend Michel Seurat* / *Par un jour de violence ordinaire, mon ami Michel Seurat* / *Fi awm min ayyam al-unf al-adi* (1996, 50', Beta SP), *There Are Still So Many Things to Say* / *Il y a encore tant de choses à raconter* / *Hunalia ashiya' kathira kana yumken an yatahadath 'anha al-mare'* (1997, 50', Beta SP), *The Dish of Sardines* / *Le plat de sardines* / *Tabaq al-sardin* (1998, 18', video), *The Man with the Golden Soles* / *L'homme aux semelles d'or* / *Rajol al-hitha' al-thahabi* (2000, 55', Beta SP), and *Flooding in the Land of the Baa'th Party* / *Déluge au pays du Baas* / *Tufan fi balad el-ba'th* (2003, 46', Beta SP). He also co-directed two documentary portraits, with Mohamed Malas and Oussama Mohammad, *Shadows and Light* / *Nouron wa thilal* (1991, 52', Beta SP), on the pioneer filmmaker Nazir Shahbandar, and *Fateh al-Moudarress* (1995, 52', Beta SP). Feature-length documentary: *Everday Life in a Syrian Village* / *La vie quotidienne dans un village syrien* / *Al-hayat al-yawmiya fi qaria Suriya* (1974, 80', Beta SP).

Amiri, Noura. Emirati filmmaker. She studied at Dubai Women's College. Short documentary film: *This Working Life* (2004, 16', Mini DV).

Amman Filmmakers Cooperative. A remarkable and highly active experiment in filmmaking by ordinary people, set up in 2003 and run by Hazim Bitar. The members include: Yahya Abdullah (teacher), Mohamed Aboujarad (computer network administrator), Sajeda Abousaif (teacher), Dalia Alkury (public sector), Muna Asmar (graphic designer), Rifqi Assaf (director and writer), Reem Bader (retail sector), Ala' Diab, (graphic designer), Yazan Doughan (student), Hussam Hamarneh (hardware store manager), Mais Hamarneh (n/a), Ahmad Humeid (co-founder SYTAX), Saleh Kasem (student), Razan Khatib (IT manager), Suhad Khatib (graphic designer, filmmaker), Aseel Mansour (IT consultant), Aseel Qader (student), Ahmed Humeid (n/a), Ammar Quttaineh (stockbroker), Nesreen Rafeeq (self-employed), Alabbas Sa'ed (teacher), Ja'far Safwan (student), Omar Saleh (telecom engineer), Ghassan Salti (n/a), Bashar Sharaf (freelance filmmaker), Hamza Soufan (student), Najah Taffal (artist, teacher at deaf women clubs), Amr Toukhy (commercials production), Rawan Zeine (public relations consultant), Rabee' Zureikat (advertising executive), Sima Zureikat (writer and editor). Collective films: *Death by Chocolate* (2004, 4', Mini DV) (AFC Class of May '04), *My Name Is Mohamed* (2008, 10') (Rania Okla, Yacoub Haddad, Baan S. Shibab, Sinan Najm Abdullah, Yahya T. Hassan), *Ya Halawood* (2008, 10') (Nadia Odeh, Fathi Hueimel, Rabee Zureikat, Suhayb Ja'araat, Qusai Oshibat, Osama Oshibat).

Amrallah, Massoud. Emirati filmmaker. Born in 1967, he obtained a diploma in communication at the University of the Emirati and then studied filmmaking in the United States in 1988. He wrote a number of dramas and documentaries for television. He is also a poet and writer and one of the organizers of the Gulf States Film Festival and the Dubai International Film Festival.

Amro, Hind. Emirati filmmaker. Short documentary film: *Dream of Masafi* (2004, 22', Beta SP).

AMROUCHE, NASSIM. Jordanian filmmaker. Feature film: *Goodbye Gary* / *Adieu Gary* (2009, 75', 35mm).

Andoni, Raed. Palestinian filmmaker. As an independent producer he set up his own company, Dar Films, in 1999. Documentary: *Improvisation, Samir and His Brothers* / *Improvisation, Samir et ses frères* / *Irtijal* (2005, 57', Beta SP).

Andoni, Saed. Palestinian filmmaker. Born in 1972 in Bethlehem, he studied filmmaking at Goldsmith's College in London, and worked as a documentary film editor. Short films: *Jamal, a Tale of Courage* / *Jamal, une histoire de courage* / *Jamal, qissa shuja'a* (2000), *Number Zero* / *Numéro zéro* / *'Ala sifr* (2002, 27', Beta SP), *The Last Frontier* / *La dernière frontière* / *al-Hudud al-akhira* (2002, 32', Beta SP), *Ertijal* (2005, 60', Beta SP).

Annadawi, Nizar. Iraqi filmmaker. Short documentary film: *Out of the Frame* (2008, 22').

ANZUR, ISMAÏL. Syrian pioneer filmmaker. His sole film, the first silent feature to be made in Syria, was a financial disaster, since it coincided with the first Egyptian sound films. He subsequently worked very successfully in television. His son, Najdat Ismaïl Anzur, has directed one of Jordan's few feature films. Feature film: *Under the Skies of Damascus / Sous le ciel de Damas / Tahta sama' Dimask* (1931, 60', 35mm).

ANZUR, NAJDAT ISMAÏL. Jordanian filmmaker. Born in 1954 in Damascus, son of the first Syrian director Ismaïl Anzur, he has lived in Jordan since 1971. He has obtained Jordanian citizenship and worked there in television production. Feature film: *An Oriental Story / Une histoire orientale / Hikâya sharqiyya* (1991, 75', 35mm).

Aoun, Chadi. Lebanese filmmaker. Short animated film: *Ahawa* (2002, 5').

ARACTINGI, PHILIPPE. Lebanese filmmaker. Born in 1964 in Beirut, he studied at the CLCF in Paris, graduating in 1984. He began working for Lebanese television in 1985, shooting reports and documentaries on the war in Lebanon, some of which were shown internationally. He later moved to Paris, where he has worked in television for many years. His documentaries include *A Year Already / Un an déjà* (1986), *Cannes 88* (1988), *You Carry on Living / On vit toujours* (1988), *Refugees in South Beirut / Refugiés à Beyrouth-Est* (1988), *The House of the Future / La maison du futur* (1989), *Free Flight / Libre vol* (1991, 18', Beta SP), *The Kadicha Valley / La vallée de Kadicha* (1991), *Living / Vivre* (1991), *Car Connection* (1991), *The Bus / L'autobus* (1991), *Through the Mothers' Looks / Par le regard des mères* (1992, 52', Beta SP), *The Redeployed / Les Reconvertis* (1992), *Beirut Today / Beyrouth aujourd'hui* (1993, 13', video), *Beirut of Stones and Memories / Beyrouth de pierres et de mémoires* (1993, 18', Beta SP), *The Child Acrobat's Dream / Le*

rêve de l'enfant acrobat (1997, 50', video). He also made two fictional pieces for Canadian television: *Ramadan, Pyramid Guide / Ramadane, guide des pyramides* (1993) and *Jamal, Petrol Seller / Jamal, le vendeur de gas-oil* (1993). Feature films: *The Bus / L'autobus / Bosta* (2005, 112', 35mm), *Under the Bombs / Sous les bombes / Taht al-qasef* (2007, 98', 35mm).

Arasoughli, Alia. Palestinian filmaker. Born in Acre, she grew up in Lebanon before moving to the United States. She has worked as teacher of film and the sociology of culture, organizer of events concerning film, and editor of the book *Screens of Life: Critical Film Writing from the Arab World*. Short films: *Torn Life / Vie déchirée / Hayat mumazzaqa* (1993, 23', video), *This Is Not Living / C'est pas une vie / Hay mish eishi* (2001, 42', Beta SP), *Between Heaven and Earth / Entre ciel et terre / Ma bayn al-sama' wa al-ard* (2003, 30', video), *A Testimony of Birth / Shahadat milad* (2003, 17', video), *Are We Supposed to Fly? / Bidna ntir tayr?!* (2005, 14', video), *Stories from Behind the Wall* (2006, 24'), *After the Last Sky / Ba'ad al-samaa'al-akhira* (2007, 55', video), *The Clothesline* (2006, 14', video).

ARBID, DANIELLE. Lebanese filmmaker. Born in 1970 in Beirut, she studied literature and journalism and worked as a French journalist for 5 years. She has lived in Paris since the mid-1980s. She has made short fictional films: *Demolition / Démolition / Raddem* (1998, 17', 35mm), *The Trafficker / Le passeur / al-Ma'addi* (1999, 13', 35mm), *The Foreign Woman / L'étrangère / al-Ghariba* (2002, 46', 35mm), *Mutuality / La mutuelle / al-Naql* (13'); and documentaries: *Alone with the War / Seule avec la guerre / Halat harb* (2000, 58', Beta SP), *At the Borders / Aux frontières* (2002, 60', Beta SP), *Living Room Conversation / Conversation de salon* (2002, 9', Beta SP). She has also been involved with interactive art and video installations. She contributed two collaboratively made videos, *Airport 1* (40") and *Starry Night* (45"), to the collective project *Videos Under Siege* (DIFF 2008, 39', video). Feature films: *In the Battlefields / Dans les champs de bataille /*

Maarik hob (2004, 90', 35mm), *A Man Lost /
Un homme perdu* (2007, 97', 35mm).

Arif, Farah Ibrahim. Saudi filmmaker. She
works as presenter on children's television.
Short animated film: *The Past Returns* (2006,
15', DVD).

Arif, Sameer Ibrahim. Saudi filmmaker. He
work as an editor and animator in television.
Short films: *Jeddah's Football Champions
Competition* (2006, 16', DV Cam), *Hard Way /
Tareeqa sa'aba* (2006, 18', DVC Pro).

Arraf, Suha. Palestinian filmmaker. Lives in
Jerusalem, working as a journalist and filmmaker. Documentaries: *Take My Sister and
Give Me Yours* (1997), *The Gypsy Quarters*
(1998), *End of the Line* (1999), *Fatima* (2000),
Her Story / Qissatuha (2000), *Holy Fire* (2001),
The Cinder Keepers (2001), *I Am Palestine*
(2003, 16', Beta SP), *Ramallah Short Cuts,
Summer 2001* (2003, 6') *Good Morning Jerusalem / Bonjour, Jérusalem / Sabah al-kkatr ya
al-Quds* (2004, 52'), *Hard Ball* (2006, 52').

Arsan, Ayham. Syrian filmmaker. Short fictional film: *Behind the Faces / Derrière les visages* (2005, 12', 35mm).

Arshi, Ahmed. Emirati filmmaker. Short
film: *Al-Hamra Island in the Eyes of Emirati
Filmmakers* (with Ahmed Zain, 2009, 25', HD
Cam).

Arya, Pranav. Emirati filmmaker. He studied
at the American University of Sharjah. Short
fictional film: *Jane Doe* (2004, 3', Mini DV).

Asaf, Ravin. Iraqi filmmaker. Feature film:
The Smell of Apples / Le parfum des pommes
(2008, 85').

Asfour, Georina. Palestinian filmmaker.
Short film: *Neighbours* (2008, 13').

Ashoor, Mohamed. Emirati filmmaker. Short
film: *Zayed: Dignity and Originality* (with Sameer Saeed, 2001, 36', Beta SP).

Ashour, Montiana Bahgat. Emirati filmmaker, Studied at the American University
of Sharjah. Short films *Tarha* (2006, 7', Mini
DV), *Still "Sukoon"* (2007, 2', Mini DV).

Asmar, Muna. Jordanian filmmaker and
member of the Amman Filmmakers Cooperative. She studied at Yarmouk University, and
works as graphic designer. Short films: *A Rock
and a Hard Place* (2003), *A Couple and a Silver
Roof* (with Sima Zureikat, 2003).

ASSAF, LAYLA. Lebanese filmmaker. Born
into a Christian family in 1947 in Beirut, she
trained in a range of media (publicity, photography, journalism and film) in Sweden. She
made about a hundred documentaries from
1979, including *Before the Catastrophe* (with
Ragnau Hedlund, 1986, 52'), and shot the first
of several fictional films, *Martyrs / Choucha-
da,* for Swedish television in 1988. Feature
film: *The Freedom Gang / Le gang de la liberté
/ al-Sheikha* (1994, 87', 35mm).

Assaf, Rifqi. Jordanian filmmaker and member of the Amman Filmmakers Cooperative.
He studied at the Applied Science University, Jordan, and works as director and writer.
Short films: *The Last Patch* (with Omar Saleh,
2006), *Amman in Red* (2006), *The View* (with
Hazim Bitar, 2008, 17').

ASSAF, ROGER. Lebanese filmmaker. A
major figure in Iraqi theatre, founder of the
Studio of Dramatic Art in Beirut and teacher
at the Fine Art Academy, he was active in the
theatre both before and after his sole feature
film, made with players from the Théatre al
Hakawati. Documentary: *Sirhan and the Pipe
/ Sirhan wal-masoura* (collective, 1973). Feature film: *Maaraka / Maaraké* (1984, 120',
16mm blown up to 35mm).

Ataya, Abdullah. Emirati filmmaker. He
studied at the University of Sharjah. Short
fictional films: *Forgotten Red Roses* (2005, 14',
Mini DV), *Show Off Shadow* (2007, 3', video).

Ataya, Amina. Emirati filmmaker. Born in Dubai, she studied at the University of Sharjah. Student film: *Among the Clouds* (2002, 15', S-VHS). Short fictional films: *Sadness Thief* (2004, 20', DV Cam), *Silk Strings* (2005, 35', Mini DV), *Always Happens in 16.9* (with Salwa Mohammed, 2007, 11', Mini DV, in Egypt).

Ateek, Rehab Omar. Emirati filmmaker. She studied at Abu Dhabi Women's College. Short films: *The Car or the Wife?* (2000, 13', DV Cam), *Distant Lives* (2001, 6', DV Cam), *Between Two Suns / Bain shamsain* (2006, 18', DV Cam).

Attalah, Muawia. Jordanian filmmaker. Short fictional film: *Espresso* (2008, 7').

Attallah, Hanna Selim. Palestinian filmmaker. Short fictional film: *The Shadow of Time / L'ombre du temps / Khayalat azmina* (2000, 13').

Attieh, Rania. Lebanese filmmaker. Short fictional film: *Tripoli, Quiet / Trablos al-hada* (with Daniel Garda, 2009, 15').

Attieyeh, Ruba. Lebanese filmmaker. Ducumentary: *Remembrance* (2000, 37', Beta).

Awad, Abdullah. Saudi filmmaker. Short film: *Quran Light* (2005, 1', Super 16).

Awadallah, Hala. Emirati filmmaker. Born in Egypt, but brought up in the UAE. Short fictional film: *Deep Sight* (2004, 7', Mini DV).

Awjeh, Abdel Raheem. Lebanese filmmaker. Short fictional film: *Globalisation* (2002, 3').

Awwad, Gibril. Palestinian filmmaker. Documentaries: *Berlin Trap / Piège à Berlin / Berlin al-masida* (1982), *Good Morning, Beirut / Bonjour, Beyrouth / Sabah al-khayr ya Bayrut* (1983).

Awwad, Nahad. Palestinian filmmaker. She studied filmmaking in Canada and in Denmark and has worked in film and television since 1997. Documentaries: *Lions / Asud* (2001, 10', video), *Going for a Ride? / Mashiyyin?* (2003, 15', video), *25 Kilometres / Chamsa wa'ashrun kilometer* (2005, 15', video), *The Fourth Room / La quatrième chambre* (2005, 25', video), *Five Minutes from Home / A cinq minutes de chez moi* (2008, 52', video). Contributed *Not Just At Sea* (2' 56") to the collective film *Summer 2006, Palestine* (2006, 35', Beta SP).

Ayache, Mohamed. Palestinian filmmaker. Short documentary film: *Oum Jaber / Um Jaber* (2000, 21', Beta SP).

Ayish, Samya. Emirati filmmaker. She was born in 1983 in the United States, of Palestinian origin, and studied at the American University of Sharjah. Short fictional films: *A Letter to a UN Official* (2004, 12', Mini DV), *Dear Women . . .* (2004, 8', Mini DV), *Prison of Freedom* (2005, 7', Minin DV).

Azar, George. Palestinian filmmaker. Documentary: *Gaza Fixer* (2007, 22', video).

Bachiri, Naima. Yemeni filmmaker. She lives currently in Geneva. Documentary: *Jewish, Arab, Yemenite / Yahudi, 'arabi, yamani* (1989, 52').

Bader, Kaltham. Emirati filmmaker. Studied at Zayed University. Short film: *Healthy Pregnancy* (2003, 10', DV Cam).

Bader, Nidhal. Bahraini filmmaker. Born in 1976, he works as an electrical engineer. Short film: *The Open Door* (2007, 7', DVD), *Coffee Shops, Refused or Accepted* (2007, 18', Hi-8).

Bader, Reem. Jordanian filmmaker and member of the Amman Filmmakers Cooperative. She studied at the University of Dubai. Short films: *And Life Goes On / Et la vie continue* (2004), *Civilisation 101* (2006).

Badr, Layali. Palestinian filmmaker. Sister of Liana Badr. Born in 1957 in Jerico, she wrote books for children and ran a children's theatre. After training in East Berlin, she worked for children's television in Syria and, since 1997, in Egypt. Short films, mostly for children: *The Path to Palestine / Le chemin vers la Palestine / al-Rariq ila Filastin* (1985, 8', 16mm animation), *The Little Bride / al-'Arusa al-bahira* (1993, 30', video), *The Riddle / al-Lughuz* (19894), *A Planet All Our Own* (1995), *The Fairy Tale Keys* (1997).

Badr, Liana. Palestinian filmmaker. Sister of Layali Badr. Born in 1952 in Jerusalem, she studied philosophy and psychology at Beirut University. She worked as a journalist until the 1982 Israeli invasion, when she moved to Tunis. Later, she returned to Palestine to work for the Palestinian Authority. She has also written several novels, three of which have been translated into English: *A Compass for the Sunflower* (1989), *A Balcony over the Fakihani* (1993), and *The Eye of the Mirror* (1994). Documentaries: *Fadwa, a Palestinian Poet / Fadwa, une poétesse de la Palestine / Fadwa, hikayat sha'ira min Filastin* (1999, 52', Beta SP), *The Olive Trees / Les oliviers / Zaytunat* (2000, 37', Beta SP), *The Green Bird / L'oiseau vert / al-Tir al-akhdahar* (2002, 50', Beta SP), *Zaytounat / Zaytounat* (2002, 37'), *Siege: A Writer's Diary / Siège / Hisar Mudhakarat katiba* (2003, 33', Beta SP), *The Gates Are Open, Sometimes! / Les passages sont ouverts, parfois* (2006, 42' Beta SP). Contributed *Football on a Thursday Afternoon* (2' 08") to the collective film *Summer 2006, Palestine* (2006, 35', Beta SP).

Badr Khan, Salah al-Din. Palestinian filmmaker. Short film: *Night Dream / Rêve de nuit / Hilm layla* (1946).

BADRAKHAN, AHMED.* Egyptian filmmaker responsible for one of the first Iraqi feature films: *Cairo-Baghdad / Le Caire-Bagdad / Al-Kahira-Bagdad* (1945).

BADRAKHAN, SALAH.* Egyptian filmmaker responsible for one Lebanese feature: *Summer in Lebanon / L'été au Liban* (1946, 35mm).

BADRI, AYUB. Syrian filmmaker. With a group of friends—Ahmed Tello, Mohamed Elmradi and Rashid Jalal—set up a production company to make the first Syrian film, *The Innocent Victim / L'accusé innocent / al-Muttaham al-bary* (1928). Later, in the 1930s, he directed Syria's second (silent) feature. Feature film: *The Call of Duty / L'appel du devoir / Nada 'al-wajeb* (1937).

Badri, Waleed Masood. Emirati filmmaker. He studied at Dubai Men's College. Short film: *Brotherhood Takes a Friend or Two* (with Tariq al-Hashimi, 2006, 3', Mini DV).

BAGDADI, MAROUN. Lebanese filmmaker (1951–1993). Born in 1951 in Beirut within a Christian family, he first studied law and political science in Beirut, then filmmaking at IDHEC in Paris. Back in Lebanon he made a series of 16mm television reports for television. After a pioneering first feature, he continued to make television documentaries. Documentaries: *Nine and a Half / Neuf et demi* (1974, television), *Seven and a Half / Sept et demi* (1974, television), *The South Is Doing Well, and You? / Le Sud va bien, et vous?* (1976), *The Silent Majority / La majorité silencieuse* (1976), *Kafr Kala* (1976), *Ninety / Quatre-vingt-dix* (1988), *The Most Beautiful of Mothers / La plus belle des mères* (1978, 25', 16mm), *We Are All for the Homeland / Nous sommes tous pour la patrie* (1979), *Story of a Village and of a War / Histoire d'un village et d'une guerre* (1979), *Homage to Kamal Joumblat / Hommage à Kamal Joumblat* (1979), *Murmurs / Murmures* (1980), *Nostagia for a Land at War / Nostalgie d'une terre en guerre* (1980, 25', 16mm), *Follow the Road / Poursuivre la route* (1982), *New Year Speech / Discours du nouvel an* (1982), *The Reconstruction of the Commercial Centre / La reconstruction du centre commercial* (1983), *War on War / Guerre sur guerre* (1984). In 1984 he settled in Paris, where he made feature-length téléfilms: *Lebanon, The Land of Honey and Incense / Liban, Pays de miel et de l'encens / Loubnan balad al-assal wal bakhour* (1987, 95', Super 16), *Marat* (1989, 90', 35mm), and *Slowly Slowly in the Wind* (1990).

He died in a mysterious accident on his return to Beirut to shoot a new film in 1993. Feature films: *Beirut Oh Beirut / Beyrouth ô Beyrouth / Beirut ya Beirut* (1975, 110', 35mm), *Little Wars / Petites guerres / Houroub saghira* (1982, 108', 35mm), *The Veiled Man / L'homme voilé / al-Rajul al-muhajjah* (1987, 93', 35mm), *The Scarecrow / L'épouvantail* (1990, 35mm), *Outside Life / Hors la vie / Kharifi al-hayat* (1990, 97', 35mm), *The Girl from the Air / La fille de l'air* (1992, 103', 35mm).

BAHRI, ALFRED. Lebanese filmmaker. Feature film: *The Mute Man and Love / Le muet et l'amour / al-Akhrass wal hub* (1967, 35mm).

Bakhet, Dalia. Lebanese filmmaker. Short film: *Affiliation* (with Mahdi Ali Ali and Mahmoud Salem Be Ajajah, 2007, 9', Mini DV).

BAKRI, MOHAMED. Palestinian filmmaker. Born in 1953 in Bina Village, Galilee (Israel), he studied at the University of Tel-Aviv and worked as stage and screen actor. He appeared in numerous international feature films: Costa-Gavras's *Hannah K* (1983, France), Uri Barbash's *Beyond the Walls* (1984, Israel), Amos Gitai's *Esther* (1986, Israel), Erik Clausen's *Rami og Julie* (1988, Denmark), Isadore Musallam's *Foreign Nights* (1989, Canada), Eran Riklis's *Cup Final* (1991, Israel), Uri Barbash's *Beyond the Walls II* (1992, Israel), Michel Kleifi's *The Tale of Three Jewels* (1994, Palestine), Ali Nassar's *The Milky Way* (1994, Palestine), Rachida Krim's *Sous les pieds des femmes* (1995, France), Rashid Masharawi's *Haifa* (1996, Palestine), Benny Toraty's *Desperado Square* (1997, Italy), Hannah Elias's *The Olive Harvest* (2001, Palestine), Saverio Costanzo's *Private* (2004, Italy), Paolo and Vittorio Taviani's *The Lark Farm* (2007, Italy), and Rashid Mashawara's *Leila's Birthday* (2008, Palestine). Feature-length documentaries: *1948* (1998, 54', Beta SP), *Jenin, Jenin / Jénine, Jénine / Jenin, Jenin* (2002, 54', Beta SP), *Since You Left / Depuis que tu n'es plus là / Min youm ma ruhat* (2006, 58', DV Cam).

Balwai, Riyadh. Bahraini filmmaker. Short film: *The Devil's Lake* (2005, 16', DVD).

Bani, Abbas. Iraqi filmmaker. Short animated film: *Beirut Summer 82 / Beyrouth Été 82* (1985, 10', 35mm).

BARAKAT, HENRI. Egyptian director of several Lebanese feature films in the 1960s and 1970s: *Safar Barlek / Safar Barlek* (1967), *The Watchman's Daughter / La fille du gardien / Bint al-hares* (1968), *The Visitor / La visiteuse* (1972), *My Darling / Ma chérie* (1973), and *The Best Days of My Life / Les plus beaux jours de ma vie* (1973).

Barakat, Ray. Lebanese filmmaker. Studied at ALBA. Short fictional film: *Visions* (2000, 15').

Barakat, Sheila. Lebanese filmmaker. Born in 1968 in Beirut, she graduated from the Fine Art Academy in Beirut in 1992 and from FEMIS in Paris in 1994, where her graduation film was *Miro* (1994). Short fictional film: *Letter from Nabil / La lettre de Nabil / Risala min Nabil* (1995, 21', 35mm).

Barakat, Yahya. Palestinian filmmaker. Films: *The Path of Struggle / Le chemin de la lutte / Masira al-nidal* (1981), *Abu Salma* (1982), *Days of Cooperation / Jours de la coopération / al-Ayyam al-mushtaraka* (1989), *Rimal al-Sawafi* (1991), *In God's House / Dans la maison de dieu / Fi bayt Allah* (2003, 42'), *Rachel: An American Conscience* (2005).

Barrak, Rima. Palestinian filmmaker. Short film: *The Land of '48 / al-Ard al-'48* (2003).

Bassem, Hiba. Iraqi filmmaker. She studied at the Independent Film and Television Academy in Baghdad. Her second documentary was made for Al Jazeera International. Short documentary films: *Baghdad Days / Jours de Baghdad* (2005, 35', video), *Thinking About Leaving* (2007, 10').

Bassile, Raymond. Lebanese filmmaker. He studied at the London International Film School and made reports from Lebanon and some short documentaries for the German television company ZDF. He has also worked as assistant to Borhan Alawiya and Maroun Bagdadi. Documentary: *For Better and Worse*

/ *Pour le meilleur et pour le pire* (1997, 54', video).

Bastaki, Abdallah. Emirati filmmaker. He studied at Abu Dhabi Men's College. Short documentary films: *Kalba: Harmless Contradictions* (2004, 3', Mini DV), *Facing the Inevitable* (with Nayef al-Mansouri, 2005, 25', Mini DV), *Etisalat's Role in the Advancements of the UAE* (2005, 5', Mini DV), *To Whom Belongs the Kingdom This Day?* (2005, 10', Beta SP).

Bayous, Ghassan. Syrian filmmaker. Documentaries: *Liberation / La libération / al-Tah'rir* (1972), *Exhibition on the October War / Exposition sur la guerre d'octobre* (1974), *The New Nazism / Le nouveau nazisme* (1974).

Baz, Tina. Lebanese filmmaker. Contributed three collaboratively made videos, *Airport 1* (40"), *Starry Night* (45"), and *Beirut Ground Zero* (1'), to the collective project *Videos Under Siege* (DIFF 2008, 39', video).

Bazaid, Mohammad. Saudi filmmaker. Also journalist. Short fictional film: *Last Piece* (2005, 5', Mini DV).

Behbehani, Sadeq Hussain. Kuwaiti filmmaker. Studied at the Theater Arts Institute in Kuwait. Short film: *When?* (2007, 18', Mini DV).

Belaid, Sofiane. Lebanese filmmaker. Short film: *Sarkha* (1997, 18', video).

Belyouha, Salem. Emirati filmmaker. He studied at Dubai Men's College. Short documentary film: *The Future of Fitness* (2001, 6', Beta SP).

BEN HIRSI, BADER. Yemeni filmmaker. Born in 1968 in London of Yemeni descent, he studied at Goldsmiths's College, University of London. He continues to live and work in London. In 2000, he made a first 74 minute video documentary about his meeting with Tim Mackintosh-Smith, author of *Yemen: Journeys to the Land of the Dictionary,* and their joint exploration of Yemen. He has since made a further documentary, *A Girls' School at Taiz*

(2002), a Channel 4 television series, *Hadj: The Greatest Pilgrimage on Earth* and a fictional feature. Feature films: *The English Sheikh and the Yemeni Gentleman / Le cheikh anglais et le gentleman yéménite* (2000, 74', Beta SP) (documentary), *A New Day in Old Sana'a / Un jour nouveau dans le vieux Sana'a* (2005, 86', 35mm).

BEZJIAN, NIGOL. Lebanese filmmaker. He has made a docudrama: *The Apricot Path / Le Chemin des abricots* (2001, 35', Beta SP), and a documentary: *Verve / Avivn* (2002, 15'). Feature-length documentaries: *Muron* (2003, 90', Beta SP), *Ayroum* (2005).

Bin Amro, Manal Ali. Emirati filmmaker. She studied mass communications at UAE University. Short films: *Shoes* (2006, 6', Mini DV), *Stuck Face* (2007, 6', Mini DV).

Bin Fahad, Maryam. Emirati filmmaker. She studied at Dubai Women's College and subsequently at Leeds Metropolitan University—Northern Film School in the United Kingdom. Student films: *Lifeless* (2002, 5', DigiBeta), *Are They Forgotten?* (2002, 6', DV Cam). Short films in the United Kingdom: *Into the Unknown* (2004, 46', DV Cam), and in the UAE: *What Is after the Explosion* (with Khalid Ahmed al-Hammadi, 2004, 39', DV Cam), *Tough Moments* (2004, 7', DV Cam).

Bin Fahad, Nahla. Emirati filmmaker. Studied graphic design at the Abu Dhabi Women's College. Directed about 15 commercials. Short films: *The Nation's Beloved* (2003, 36', DV Cam), *Thousand Miles* (2004, 5', Beta Cam.

Bin Hafez, Moath. Emirati filmmaker. He studied at Dubai Men's College. Student films: *Suicidal Thoughts* (2005, 14', Mini DV), *Nothing* (2006, 4', DV Cam), *On the Line* (2007, 13', Mini DV), *Inequity* (2007, 10', DV Cam).

Bin Haider, Hussain. Emirati filmmaker. Short film: *The Roots* (2001, 8', DigiBeta).

Bin Owqad, Maitha Mohammed. Emirati filmmaker. She studied at Dubai Women's College. Short film: *Road Victim* (2006, 1', Mini DV).

Bin Sougat, Mohammed Abdulla. Emirati filmmaker. He studied at Dubai Men's College. Short films: *A Foot Behind* (2006, 6', DV Cam), *Do You Believe in Magic* (2006, 15', DVD).

Bishara, Amahl. Palestinian filmmaker. Short film: *Across Oceans, among Neighbours* (2002).

Bitar, Hazim. Jordanian filmmaker. Born in 1964 in Saudi Arabia of Palestinian/Jordanian descent, he has Jordanian and U.S. citizenship. Brought up in Saudi Arabia, he studied IT at Millersville University in Pennsylvania and management at George Washington University, Washington, D.C. On his move to Amman, Jordan, in 2003, he founded the Amman Filmmakers Cooperative and the Jordanian Short Film Festival. Short documentary films: *Uncivil Liberties: Secret Trials in America* (2000, 30', video—in the United States), *Jerusalem's High Cost of Living* (2002, 53', video), *Girls' Education Under Siege in Hebron* (2003, 5'), *Teaching Heyam: Girls' Education in Rural Syria* (2003, 12'), *JRF and Communities of Hope* (2004, 13'), *Growing Up in Amman's Suburbia* (2006, 9'), *Sharar* (with Ammar Quttaineh and Saleh Kasem, 2006, 17', Beta SP), *What a Job / Quel boulot* (with Omar Saleh and Mohamed Aboujarad, 2006, 12', DV Cam), *Three Eyes* (with Rawan Zeine, 2007, 5'), *Not My Turn* (with Rabee Zureikat, 2008, 6'), and a short fictional film: *The View* (with Rifqi Assaf, 2008, 17').

Bitrawi, Walid. Palestinian filmmaker. Short film: *And the Walled Enclosure / Wa mahuta bi an-aswar* (1998).

Bizri, Hicham. Lebanese filmmaker. Born in 1966 at Saïda, he studied filmmaking in Boston and New York, where he is now based. He has worked as assistant director, notably to Raoul Ruiz. Short films and documentaries: *The Ludicrous Man / L'homme ridicule* (1989), *One Day / Un jour* (1990), *Cypress Leaves / Les feuilles du cyprès* (1990), *Message from a Dead Man / Message d'un homme mort* (1992, documentary, 47', 16mm).

Bokhary, Lina. Palestinian filmmaker. Documentary: *Flood / Déluge / Fayd* (2002).

Bolooki, Ahmed Abdul Majeed. Emirati filmmaker. He studied at the American University of Sharjah. Short fictional film: *Close Your Eyes* (2004, 16', Mini DV).

Boulghourjian, Vatche. Lebanese filmmaker. Short film: *Ali the Iraqi* (2008, 22').

Bourjeily, Lucien. Lebanese filmmaker. Born in 1980 in Lebanon. Short film: *Under the Vine Tree / Sous la vigne / Tahta al-aricha* (2008, 9', Beta SP).

BOUSHAHRI, ABDULLAH. Kuwaiti filmmaker. Born in 1979 in Kuwait, he studied at Florida Atlantic University. Short films and documentaries: *Boiling Over* (2002), *Akthar* (2003), *Death of the Doll* (2003), *Tow Away Zone* (2003), *Kuwaiti Champion* (2004, 20', Beta SP), *Deserted* (2006, 6', HDV). Feature-length documentary: *Losing Ahmad / En perdant Ahmad* (2006, 68', Mini DV).

BOUSTANY, KARAM. Lebanese pioneer filmmaker. Co-directed the first Lebanese sound feature. Feature film: *In the Ruins of Baalbeck / Dans les ruines de Baalbeck / Bayn hayakel Baalbeck* (with Julio De Luca, 1933, 35mm).

BOUTROS, RAYMOND. Syrian filmmaker. Born in 1950 in Hama, he studied filmmaking at the University of Kiev, graduating in 1976. Made a number of short documentary films: *Ordinary Zionism / Le sionisme ordinaire / Subyûniya âdiya* (1974), *When the South Wind Blows / Lorsque souffle le vent du sud / Indama tabubbu rîh al-Janûb* (1976), *The Witness / Le témoin / al-Shahîd* (1986, 20'), *Whispers / Chuchotements* (1999, 30', 35mm). Feature films: *The Greedy Ones / Les gourmands* a.k.a. *Les algues d'eau douce / al-Tahalib* (1991, 90', 35mm), *The Displacement / Le déplacement / al-Tarhaj* (1997, 120', 35mm), *Hasiba* (2008, 135').

Brèche, Bass. Lebanese filmmaker. He was born in 1978 in Lebanon, where he studied drama, before moving to England to study film. He also worked as a film actor. Short film: *Both / Ala atabah* (2007, 11', 35mm).

Bu-Ali, Mohammed Rashed. Bahraini filmmaker. Born in 1984 in Bahrain. Short films: *Betwixt Them* (2006, 33', Mini DV), *From the West* (2006, 9', Mini DV), *Absence / Ghiyab* (2008, 10', Beta).

Buchakjian, Gregory. Lebanese filmmaker. Contributed *What, Shoes?* (2') to the collective project *Videos Under Siege* (DIFF 2008, 39', video).

Bukhamas, Yousef. Emirati filmmaker. Short fictional films: *Discerning Memory* (with Razan Takash, 2006, 10', Mini DV), *The Jumeira Job* (2007, 15', Mini DV).

BUNNI, AMIN. Syrian filmmaker. He studied filmmaking at IDHEC in Paris and then worked in Syrian television from 1968. Medium-length fiction: *To the Last Man / Au dernier homme / Hata al-rajoul al-akhir* (1972, 50'). He made a number of documentaries, including *Lessons in Civilisation / Leçons de civilisation / Durusum fi-l h'adhâra* (1973, 38'), *Palestine: The Roots / Palestine, les racines* (1973, 43'), *Quneitra, My Love / Quneitra, mon amour/ Quneitra h'abbibaty* (1974, 20'). Director of the second channel of Syrian television from 1992. Feature film: *Palestinian Memories / Mémoires palestiniennes* (1991, 70', 16mm).

Bustan, Sahar. Emirati filmmaker. Born in 1982 in Saudi Arabia and studied at American University of Sharjah. Short fictional film: *Trilogy* (2004, 6', Mini DV).

Cabral, Drina. Emirati filmmaker. She studied at the American University of Sharjah. Short fictional films: *Intentionally Untrue* (2004, 21', Mini DV), *Crimson of Regret* (2004, 8', Mini DV).

Cha'ar, Ala-Eddine. Syrian filmmaker. He studied filmmaking in Moscow and subsequently made a number of documentaries, including *The Exiled Willow Tree / Le saule exilé*

(1985, 23'), and a number of téléfilms. He has taught film analysis at the University of Damascus.

Chabaane, Mahmoud. Syrian filmmaker. He studied filmmaking in Moscow and subsequently worked as a documentary filmmaker for Syrian television. Documentary: *Message of Love for Syria / Message d'amour pour la Syrie* (with Haïdar Yaziji, 1992, 38').

Chabaane, Youssef. Palestinian filmmaker. He made one feature film, *The Road / La route / al-Tariq* (1973) in Libya.

Chahadat, Houssam. Syrian filmmaker. Born in 1966 in Syria, he studied film and television at the Munich Film Academy and acting at the Academy of Dramatic Arts in Damascus. Short films: *Sunkiss* (1994), *The Wedding* (1998), *Scheherezade's Daughters / Les filles de Schehérézade* (2000, 38', video), *If Life Becomes Cinema* (2000), *Just Get Married!* (2003, 20', Beta SP).

CHAHAL-SABBAG, RANDA. Lebanese filmmaker. Born in 1953 in Tripoli, with an Iraqi Christian mother and a Lebanese Muslim father, she studied in Paris, directing at the Université de Vincennes Paris VIII and filmmaking at the École de Vaugirard. She was based in Paris from 1982. Her feature film, *The Kite*, won the Silver Lion at the Venice Film Festival. She died in 2008. She made a number of film and video documentaries: *Little Steps / Pas à pas / Khutwatin* (1976, 110', 16mm), *The Lebanon of Old / Liban d'autrefois / Lubnan zaman* (1982, 10', 16mm), *Half Past Nine / 9 heures 30* (30 x 10 minutes television series) (1982), *Shaykh Imam / Shaykh Imam* (1984), *Our Imprudent Wars / Nos guerres imprudents / Hurubina al-taisha* (1995, 52', Beta SP), and *Souha, Surviving in Hell / Souha, survivre à l'enfer* (2000, 57', Beta SP). She directed a téléfilm: *The Infidels / Les infidèles* (1997, 86'). Feature films: *Screens of Sand / Écrans de sable / Shash min al-raml* (1991, 80', 35mm), *The Civilised / Civilisées / al-Moutahaddirat* (1998, 95', 35mm), *The Kite / Le cerf-volant / Tayyara min waraq* (2003, 80', 35mm).

Chahine, Carlos. Lebanese filmmaker. Lebanese-French film actor. Short film: *The North Road / La route du nord* (2008, 25', 35mm).

Chahine, Elias. Lebanese filmmaker. Short documentary films: The Man Walking on the Other Side of the Street / L'homme qui marche sur l'autre côté de la rue (2000, 27').

CHAHINE, YOUSSEF.* Egyptian filmmaker who directed two Lebanese produced features (the second shot on location in Spain) in the 1960s: *The Seller of Rings / Le vendeur de bagues / Biya al-khawatim* (1965) and *Golden Sands / Sables d'or / Rimal min thaheb* (1967).

CHAMCHOUM, GEORGES. Lebanese filmmaker. Born in 1946 in Niger, he studied at the CLCF in Paris. He produced Oumarou Ganda's *Saitane* in 1972 in Niger and published a review, *Film*, in Syria in 1974. He began with a short film, *Inside-Out* (1969), and made documentaries after his sole fictional feature, including *Lebanon, Why? / Liban, pourquoi? / Loubnan limaza* (1977, 35mm). Feature film: *Salam After Death / Salam après la mort / Salam baad al-mawt* (1971, 100', 35mm).

Chammas, André. Lebanese filmmaker. He studied at Fine Art Intitute in Beirut. Short film: *Wayn Yo?* (1998, 15', video).

Chammout, Ismaïl. Palestinian filmmaker. Also a painter. Documentaries about Palestine: *Youth Camps / Camps des jeunes / Mu'askinat al-shebab* (1972, 15', 16mm), *Memories and Fire / Souvenirs et feu / Zikriyyat wa nar* (1972, 20', 16mm), *The Urgent Call / L'appel urgent / an-Nida' al-milah* (1973, 7', 35mm), *On the Road to Palestine / Sur le chemin de la Palestine / Ala tarik filistin* (1974, 20', 35mm), *Tell al-Zaatar* (1976).

CHAMOUN, JEAN. Lebanese filmmaker. Husband of the Palestinian documentarist, Maï Masri. Born in 1944, he studied drama at the University of Lebanon and filmmaking at the Université Paris VIII. He participated in the collective film *Tel al-Za'tar* (with Mus-

tafa Abu Ali and Pino Adriano, 1977), about a beseiged Palestinian camp, and later made *Hymn for Freedom / La cantique des hommes libres / Anshuda al-ahrar* (1979). He subsequently collaborated on a series of documentaries with Maï Masri: *Under the Rubble / Sous les décombres / Tahatal ankad* (1983, 48', 16mm), *Wild Flowers: Women of South Lebanon / Fleurs d'ajonc: Femmes du Sud du Liban / Zahrat el koundoul* (1986, 71', 16mm), *War Generation—Beirut / Beyrouth, la génération de la guerre* (1988, 52', 16mm), *Children of Fire / Les enfants du feu / Atfâl jabal al nâr* (1990, 50', 16mm), *Suspended Dreams / Rêves suspendus / Ahlam mu'allaqa* (1992, 52', Beta SP), *Hanan Ashwari / Hanan Ashwari: femme de son temps* (1995), *Children of Shatila / Les enfants de chatila* (1998, 47', Beta SP), *Frontiers of Dreams and Fears / Frontières du rêve et de la peur / Ahlam al-manfa* (2001, 56', video), *The Magic Lantern / La lanterne magique* (2003), *Comedy in the Line of Fire / Sourire en flamme* (2006), *Reviving Memory / La mémoire renaissante* (2006). He returned to solo filmmaking with *Hostage of Time / L'otage de l'attente* a.k.a. *L'otage du temps / Rahinat el-intizar* (1994, 50', 16mm), *Facing the Destruction / En face de la destruction / Ma adhan fi wjh aal-dammar* (1999), *Land of Women / Terre de femmes / Ard ennissa'* (2004, 58', DV Cam). Feature film: *In the Shadows of the City / L'ombre de la ville / Taif al-madina* (2000, 100', 35mm).

CHAMS, HASSIB. Lebanese filmmaker. Feature film: *Abou Selim in the City / Abou Sélim en ville* (1963, 35mm).

Charaf, Wissam. Lebanese filmmaker. Short fictional film: *Hizz ya wizz* (2004, 26', 35mm).

CHARAFEDDINE, FOUAD. Lebanese filmmaker and actor. Brother of Youssef. Feature film: *The Cry / Le cri / al-Sarkha* (1991, 35mm).

CHARAFEDDINE, YOUSSEF. Lebanese filmmaker. Brother of Fouad. Feature films: *The Last Passage / Le dernier passage / al-Mamar al-akhir* (1981, 35mm), *The Decision / La décision / al-Karar* (1981, 35mm), *The*

Last Night / La dernière nuit / al-Layl al-akhir (1982, 35mm), *The Death Leap / Le saut de la mort / Kafzat al-mawt* (1982, 35mm), *Rendezvous with Love / Rendez-vous avec l'amour / Moad maa al-hub* (1982, 35mm), *Mr. Risk-Everything / Monsieur risque-tout* a.k.a. *Téméraire / al-Moujazef* (1983, 35mm), *My Eternal Love / Mon amour éternel* a.k.a. *Mon impérissable amour / Houbi lazi la yamout* (1984, 35mm), *The Vision / La vision / al-Rou'ya* (1985, 35mm), *The Woman Thief / La voleuse / al-Sarika* (1991, 35mm).

CHARARA, WALID. Lebanese filmmaker. Feature-length documentary: *We Shall Return One Day / Nous retournerons un jour* (with Samir Abdallah, 1998, 90', video).

CHAWKAT, SEIF-EDDINE. * Egyptian filmmaker who directed a number of Syrian features in the 1960s and 1970s. Feature films: *Love in Constantinople / Amour à Constantinople* (1967, 35mm), *Operations at 6 O'clock / Opérations à six heures / amalyat al-saa 6* (1969, 90', 35mm), *Mexico Trip / Des aventures comiques au Mexique* (1972, 105', 35mm), *Memories of a Night of Love / Souvenirs d'une nuit d'amour* (1973, 35mm), *The Beauty and the Four Looks / La belle et les quatre regards* (1975, 35mm), *Official Mission / Mission officielle* (1975, 35mm), *Arrivals from the Sea / Les arrivants par la mer* (1977, 35mm).

CHAWQI, KHAHIL. Iraqi filmmaker. Born in 1924 in Baghdad, he studied there at the Academy of Fine Arts and became one of the major actors in the national theatre. He made a number of film appearances, his best-known role being in Mohamed Choukri Jamil's *The Thirsty Ones / Les assoiffés / al-Damiun* (1972). He also worked in television and directed just one film for cinema release. Feature film: *The Night Watchman / Le veilleur de nuit / al-Haris* (1968, 90', 35mm).

Chlatt, Alias. Iraqi filmmaker. Short films on the struggle in Palestine, both fictional—The Beginning / Le commencement / al-Bidaya (1969), The Commandos / Les commandos / al-Khta'ib (1969)—and documentary—Fire Doesn't Destroy the Children's Dolls / Le feu ne détruit pas les poupées des enfants / al-Neiran la taakol luaeb el Atfäl (1973).

CHOTIN, ANDRÉ. * Born in 1898, he was the French director of a "bedouin drama" shot in Iraq before Iraqi production got under way. He died in 1954. Feature film: *Alia and Issa / Alia et Issa / Alya wa Issa* (1948, 32', 35mm).

Chouaib, Jihane. Lebanese filmmaker. Born in 1972 in Beirut, she left with her family for Mexico before arriving in France while still an adolescent. She studied philosophy before turning to filmmaking. Short fictional films: *The Chandeliers / Les lustrales* (with Lionel Delplanque, 1996), *Otto or The Jams / Otto ou les confitures* (2000), *Under My Bed / Sous mon lit* (2004, 44', 35mm).

Choucair, Cynthia. Lebanese filmmaker. Born in 1975 in Lebanon, she studied at ALBA and IESAV in Beirut. She has worked on many films and television programs. Short films: *Anonyms* (1998), *El Haouch* (1998), *Des choux et des chous?* (2000), *The Chair / La chaise / al-Kursi* (2002, 22', 16mm), *Travel / Safar* (with Dimitri Khadr, 2003, 28', DV Cam), *Elie Feyrouz* (2003).

CODSI, JEAN-CLAUDE. Lebanese filmmaker. Born in 1948 in Beirut, he studied at INSAS in Belgium and served as assistant to Borhan Alawiya on *Kafr Kassem* (1974). His diploma film at INSAS was the documentary: *The Tap / Le robinet / al-Hanafiyah* (1971). He contributed *Coffee and Cigarettes* (3') to the collective film *Summer 2006, Palestine* (2006, 35', Beta SP). Feature film: *The Story of a Return* a.k.a. *A Time Has Come / Histoire d'un retour* a.k.a. *Il est temps / Ana al-awan* (1994, 83', 35mm).

Copty, Fady. Palestinian filmmaker. Short film: *Alienation* (2007, 8').

DABAGUE, CHRISTINE. Lebanese filmmaker. Born in 1959 in Beirut, she studied philosophy at the Sorbonne in Paris and filmmaking at Hunter College in New York. She worked for 10 years in various production roles in the film industry and produced ten films. She also wrote short stories and made a number of films, both documentaries: *Bernt Naber* (1990), *Fields, the Anatomy of Morning* (1991, 15', 16mm), *Ceausescu* (1993), and a short fictional film: *The First Night / La première nuit* (1993). Feature film: *Zeinab and the River / Zeinab et le fleuve / Zaynab wa al-nahr* (1997, 80', 35mm).

DABIS, CHERIEN. Palestinian filmmaker. Born in Omaha, Nebraska, in 1976, she grew up in the United States and Jordan. She studied filmmaking at Columbia University, New York, and worked as a scriptwriter. Short film: *Make a Wish / Atmenah* (2006, 12', 35mm). Feature film: *Amerrika / Amreeka* (2009, 110', 35mm).

DAFFAR, HAYDER MOUSA. Iraqi filmmaker. Documentary feature film: *The Dreams of Sparrows / Rêves de moineaux* (2005, 72', Beta SP).

Dagher, Ely. Lebanese filmmaker. Short animated film: *Beirut* (2005, 5').

Damen, Rawan. Palestinian filmmaker. Studied mass communications at Leeds University in the UK. Short film: *Waiting for Light* (2000).

Damuni, Nicolas. Palestinian filmmaker. Based in France. Short film: *Returning Alone / Un seul retour / 'Awda wahida* (2002, 10' Beta SP).

Daou, Souad. Emirati filmmaker. Born in 1986 in the UAE, she studied at the American University of Sharjah. Short film: *Even-Out* (2006, 3', Mini DV).

Daoud, Hikmat. Palestinian filmmaker. Short film: The Beginning of Memory / Le début de la mémoire / Ibda' fi al-dhakira (1983).

Daoud, Iyad. Palestinian filmmaker. Short films: *The Agony . . . Dayr Yassin / Dayr Yassin, zamn al-waf'* (1998), *Jerusalem, the Promised of Heaven / al-Quds wa'ad al-sama* (1999).

Darwaza, Nazih. Palestinian filmmaker. Documentary: *Palestinian Diaries* (with Abdel Salam Shehada and Suheir Ismaïl, 1992, 52', Beta SP).

Darwaza, Sawsan. Palestinian filmmaker. Short films: *Artists Speak Out / Ma'i'a fannanun yaqulun* (2000), *The Square / al-Murabba'* (2003).

Darwish, Ziad. Palestinian filmmaker. Short films: *Still on the Land* (1989, 25'), *The People's Intifada / Intifada sha'ab* (1991), *Bayt Sahhur, City of Resistance / Bayt Sahhur madina al-samud* (1992), *Defiance / Murda* (1992, 19').

Daw, Salim. Palestinian filmmaker. Short and documentary films: *Keys / Mafateeh* (2003), *Mafateeh* (2006, 60').

Dayoub, Mohamed Youssef. Syrian filmmaker whose experimental videos have been made in the UAE. He studied at the Fine Art College of Damascus University. Short films: *Colour from the UAE* (2002, 13', DV Cam), *Dallah* (2005, 3', Mini DV), *Forming* (2005, 4', Mini DV), *Wind Drugget* (2005, 7', Mini DV), *To Moustapha Akkad: War and Peace* (2006, 6', Mini DV), *Coal and Water* (2006, 4', Mini DV), *Spectrums* (2008, 4', DVD).

DE LUCA, JULIO. Lebanese pioneer filmmaker. Co-directed the first Lebanese sound film in 1933. Feature film: *In the Ruins of Baalbeck / Dans les ruines de Baalbeck / Bayn hayakel Baalbeck* (with Karam Boustany, 1933, 35mm).

Debs, Jacques. Lebanese filmmaker. Born in 1957 in Beirut, he graduated from the Moscow film school VGIK in 1981. Documentaries: *Central Asia / L'Asie centrale* (1991), *The Trophy War / La guerre des trophées* (1992), *Goodbye Bakou / Adieu Bakou* (1994, 52', Beta SP), *European Muslims, Oriental Christians / Musulmans d'Europe, chrétiens d'Orient.* a.k.a. *Miroirs brisés* (2006, 135').

Deed, Wael. Lebanese filmmaker. Documentary: *Faces Hanging on the Wall / Visages collés au mur* (2006, 42', video).

DEHNI, SALAH. Syrian filmmaker. Also film critic and historian, as well as novelist. Born in 1925, he abandoned his medical training to study filmmaking at IDHEC in Paris. Back in Syria, he worked as a journalist for various newspapers and for Radio Damascus. He made six documentaries between 1961 and 1978, including *Water and Drought / Eau et sécheresse / al-Mâ'u wa al-jafaf* (1961), *Arab Antiquity / L'antiquité arabe / al-Athar al-arabiya* (1962), *Syrian Glass / Le verre syrien / al-Zujaj al-suri* (1966), *The Flower of Golan / La fleur du Golan / Zahratu al-julan* (1974, 20'), *Ibn al-Nafis* (1978, 22' + 11'). After completing his only feature film, he turned to film criticism and wrote a novel, *The Salt of the Earth*, and several books on the cinema. Feature film: *Heroes Are Born Twice / Les héros naissent deux fois / al-Abtal yuadun marrayayn* (1977, 110', 35mm).

Deis, Riyad. Palestinian filmmaker. Short film: *The Matchbox / al-Kibrita* (2004), *Easy Easy / Swesh Swesh* (2008, 22'). Contributed *Janan* (1' 50") to the collective film *Summer 2006, Palestine* (2006, 35', Beta SP).

Der-Ghougassian, Hagop. Lebanese filmmaker. Born in 1970 in Beirut, he studied at IESAV in Beirut and worked as reporter for Lebanese television. He also worked as an actor. Short fictional film: *Yva* (1993, 26', Super VHS).

Deyoub, Ali. Syrian filmmaker. Short fictional film: *Tarab* (2006, 4').

DHIADDINE, MOHAMED. Syrian filmmaker. Feature film: *Muse and Amber / Muse et ambres* (1973, 35mm).

Diab, Ala'. Jordanian filmmaker and member of the Amman Filmmakers Cooperative. Studied architecture at the University of Jordan, and works as a graphic designer. Short film: *True Italian . . . True Italian Car* (with Yazan Doughan, 2003).

Dib, Rolly. Lebanese filmmaker. Short film: *Casting* (2000, 13', video).

Dibs, Jasim Bou. Emirati filmmaker. Short fictional film: *The Neighbour* (1993, 17', Beta SP).

Dirbas, Sahera. Palestinian filmmaker. Short documentary film: *Stranger in My Home Jerusalem* (2007, 37').

Dora, Amin. Lebanese filmmaker. Short animated film: *Greyscale* (2003, 5').

DOUEIRI, ZIAD. Lebanese filmmaker. Born in 1963, he lived in Lebanon for 20 years and then went to study filmmaking in the United States, first at the University of San Diego, then at UCLA. Trained as a cameraman, he worked as assistant cameraman on all Quentin Tarantino's early films. He divides his life between France and the United States. Feature film: *West Beyrouth / Beyrouth al-gharbiya* (1998, 100', 35mm), *Lila Says That / Lila dit ça* (2004, 89').

Doughan, Yazan. Jordanian filmmaker and member of the Amman Filmmakers Cooperative. Studied architecture at the University of Jordan. Short film: *True Italian Man . . . True Italian Car* (with Ala' Diab, 2003).

Durra, Zeina. Palestinian filmmaker. Born in 1976 in London of Palestinian parents. She studied in Oxford and New York, with a master's in film from the Tisch School of Arts, where she made her thesis film. Short film: *The Seventh Dog / Sabe'e kaleb* (2005, 21', 35mm).

Dweik, Bara Fakhri. Emirati filmmaker. She studied at the American University of Sharjah. Short fictional film: *The Pain of Being Jane* (2004, 6', Mini DV).

Ebrahim, Maitha. Emirati filmmaker. She studied at Dubai Women's College. Short films: *Adolescent Colors* (with Wafa Faisal, Nada Salem, Hana Abdullah Mohammed al-Mulla al-Muhairi, Heba al-Dhanhani 2005, 28', DV Cam), *The Scar* (2005, 13', Mini DV), *A Roof Over Our Heads* (2005, 10', Mini DV), *Funky Hair Style* (2007, 7', DigiBeta).

Eid, De Gaulle. Lebanese filmmaker. Born in 1970 in Edbel in Lebanon, he has lived in France since 1990. He studied filmmaking at the University of Aix-en-Provence and then worked as assistant director to Jean-Daniel Pollet in 1994 and to Youssef Chahine for a number of films beginning with *Fate / Le destin* (1977). Short documentary film: *Accursed Exile / Maudit soit l'exil* (2002, 52', Beta SP).

Eid, Rana. Lebanese filmmaker. She studied audio-visual media in Beirut. Short films: *Kamal Joumblatt* (1998), *Letter to a Palestinian Friend / Lettre à un ami palestinien* (1999).

El Asmar, Rouba. Lebanese filmmaker. Studied at IESAV. Short fictional film: *Rehearsal / Répétition* (2000, 12').

El Bakri, Yassine. Iraqi filmmaker. Short fictional film adapted from a Ghassan Kanafani story: *The Plum Tree Flower / La fleur de prunier / Zahrat al-barquq* (1973).

EL BASSEL, KHATIB. Syrian filmmaker. Born in 1962 in Holland of Syrian parents, he studied filmmaking in Moscow, graduating in 1987. He has written a novel, *Dreams of the Sacred Plant*, and translated the autobiographies of Andrei Tarkowski and Ingmar Bergman. He has also made short films and television series. Feature film: *The Last Message / Le dernier message* (2000, 115', 35mm).

El Chamaa, Sabine. Lebanese filmmaker. She studied Communication Arts at Beirut University and film at the University of Southern California. She has worked as a freelance editor in Europe and the United States since 1997. Short fictional film: *How Beautiful the Sea / Qu'elle est belle la mer / Ma ahla al-bahr* (2003, 10', 35mm). Contributed *Black on White / Noir sur blanc* (3') to the collective project *Videos Under Siege* (DIFF 2008, 39', video).

EL GEMAYEL, SABINE. Lebanese filmmaker. After living in Iran and Lebanon as a child, she moved to Canada in 1987 and studied at Concordia University in Montreal. After graduating in 1993, she wrote and directed three short 16mm films before moving to Los Angeles the following year. She has edited a number of feature films, including the Palestinian Hanna Elias's *The Olive Harvest* (2002). Feature film: *Niloofar* (2008).

EL HABRE, SIMON. Lebanese filmmaker. Born in Beirut, he studied at the Fine Art Academy in Beirut, graduating in 2001. He has directed commercials and news reports for channels including MBC, Al Arabiya, and Al Jazeera and also worked as an editor on short films. Feature-length documentary: *The One-Man Village / Le village d'un seul homme / Samaan bildayaa* (2008, 86', HDCAM).

El Haddad, Laila. Palestinian filmmaker. Documentary: *Tunnel Trade* (with Saeed Taji Farouky, 2007, 22').

El Horr, Dima. Lebanese filmmaker. Short fictional film: *The Street / La rue / al-Havi* (1997), *Imm Ali Ready to Wear / Prêt à porter Imm Ali* (2003, 27', 35mm).

El Jeiroudi, Diana. Syrian filmmaker. Born in 1977 in Damascus, she studied English literature at the University of Damascus. She founded the only independent film production unit in Syria, Proaction Films. Short films: *The Pot / al-Qarura* (2004, 20', video), *Good Morning / Sabah al-khayr* (2004, 3', 16mm).

El Khoury, Nadyne. Lebanese filmmaker. She studied filmmaking at IESAV in Beirut. Made a first documentary in 1994, then the short fictional film *Wash No. 10,452 / Lessive 10.452 / Ghasil raqm 10452* (1995, 13', Beta).

El Khoury, Tania. Lebanese filmmaker. Born in 1976 in Beirut, she studied audio-visual media at IESAV and then worked as sound engineer and editor on several productions. One short fictional film: *Yasmina* (1999, 8'), and a documentary: *Abdo* (with Ajram Ajram, 2002, 25', Beta SP).

El Koury, Fouad. Lebanese filmmaker. Born in Paris of Lebanese parents, he studied civil architecture in London and then turned to photography. He has published a series of books of his photographs: *Beyrouth Centre Ville* (1991), *Palestine, l'envers du miroir* (1996), *Liban provisoire* (1998), *Suite égyptienne* (1996). Short films: *Quiet Days in Palestine / Jours tranquilles en Palestine* (1998, 13'), *Letters to Francine / Lettres à Francine* (2003, documentary, 43', Beta SP).

El Omari, Majdi. Palestinian filmmaker. He studied filmmaking at the Cairo Higher Institute of Cinema and at Concordia University in Montreal. Resident in Canada, he has filmed in Egypt, Tunisia, Canada and Palestine. Short films: *The Question of Assad / La question d'Assad / So'al Assad* (in Egypt, 1988, 15', 16mm), *The Quiver of the Branch by the Wind* (in Egypt, 1989, 25', 35mm), *The Evergreen Oak* (in Tunisia, 1993, 25', Beta SP), *About the Other / Au sujet de l'autre / 'An al-akbar* (in Canada, 1996, 60', Beta SP), *Traces in the Rock of Elsewhere / Traces dans le rocher du lointain / Athar 'ala sakhra al-Aqsa* (in Canada, 1998, 15', video), *At the Window* (Canada / Palestine, 2004, 30', Beta SP).

El Rahabani, Maounan. Lebanese filmmaker. Documentary: *The End of Summer / Fin de l'été* (1981, 35mm).

El Sanjak, Ibrahim. Emirati filmmaker. He studied at the American University of Sharjah. Short film: *Reoccurrence* (2003, 4', DV Cam).

El Yasin, Jamal. Palestinian filmmaker. Documentaries: *On the Borders of the Nation / Aux frontières de la nation / 'Alla hudud al-watan* (1993), *Announcement from the Mosques of Jerusalem / Bayan min maazin al-Quds* (1993).

El Yasir, Nada. Palestinian filmmaker. Short fictional film: *Four Songs for Palestine / Arba'aghani li Filastin* (2001, 13', Beta SP).

ELIAS, HANNA. Palestinian filmmaker. Born in 1957 in Jerusalem, he graduated from the UCLA film school in 1991. He made several documentaries, among them *Departure / Le départ / Rahîl* (1986), *The Roof / Le toit / al-Saqf* (1987), *The Morning / Le matin / al-Subh* (1991), *The Mountain / La montagne / al-Jabal* (1992, 34'), and *Road Blocks / Barrages routiers / Hawajiz al-tariqat* (2002, 30', Beta SP), as well as a Palestinian television series for children. He also worked on a United Nations program on women in Palestine. Feature film: *The Olive Harvest / La cueillette des olives / Mawsim al-zaytun* (2002, 83', 35mm).

Elly, Carmen. Emirati filmmaker. Her sole film, shot in the United States, is a short fictional film: *A Guy Walks into a Bar* (1997, 28', 16mm).

Eltaieb, Mina. Emirati filmmaker. She studied at the American University of Sharjah. Short experimental films: *Confiscated Footage* (with Reem Mohd, 2004, 10', Mini DV), *Perverse, Almost Religious* (2005, 4', DVD).

ERFAN, AHMED. Syrian filmmaker. Feature film: *The Passer-By / Le passant / Abir sabil* (1950, 90', 35mm).

Esber, Abeer. Syrian filmmaker. Short fictional film: *Tek . . . Tek* (2006, 13').

Essa, Rima. Palestinian filmmaker. Documentary: *Ashes* (2001, 37'), *Drying Up Palestine* (with Peter Snowdon, 2007, 28').

Essam, Ahmad. Emirati filmmaker. Studied at the American University of Sharjah. Short film: *Anti-Smoking* (with Arwa Alsabahi, 2007, 1', DVD).

Faddoul, Merva. Jordanian filmmaker. Documentary: *T for Middle Eastern* (2006, 12').

Fahdah, Youssef. Syrian filmmaker. A pioneer of Syrian cinema, he made a number of documentaries, including *The Beginnings of Cinema in Syria / Les débuts du cinéma en Syrie / Bidayat al-cinama fi Sourriya* (1964, 25').

He is in charge of the laboratories of the General Cinema Organisation.

FAHDEL, ABBAS. Iraqi filmmaker. Born in Iraq, he moved to France to study at the age of 18. He has worked as a journalist and critic. His first documentary deals with his own return to Iraq after a number of years. Documentaries: *Back to Babylon / Babylone* (2002, 52', Beta SP), *We, the Iraqis / Nous les Irakiens* (2004, 54', Beta SP). Feature film: *Dawn of the World / L'aube du monde* (2007, 97', 35mm).

FAHDI, JOSEPH. Lebanese filmmaker. He shot both his feature films in a wide screen format of his own devising: Libano Scope. Feature films: *For Whom the Sun Rises / Pour qui se lève le soleil / Liman tachrok al-chams* (1958, 35mm), *A Stranger in the House / Une étrangère à la maison / Fil dar ghariba* (1961, 35mm).

FAÏQ, TAHYA. Iraqi filmmaker. Feature film: *Warda* (1956, 97', 35mm).

Faisal, Wafa. Emirati filmmaker. She studied at Dubai Women's College. Short films: *Adolescent Colors* (with Maitha Ebrahim, Nada Salem, Hana Abdullah Mohammed al-Mulla al-Muhairi, Heba al-Dhanhani 2005, 28', DV Cam), *The Rock* (2005, 40', DV Cam), *Strong and Weak* (2006, 1', Mini DV).

Fakih, Nasser. Lebanese filmmaker. Born in 1970 in Beirut, he studied science and filmmaking at university in New York. He has worked as a reporter for Future Television in Beirut, for which he made the fictional short, *Luna Park* (1995, 6', Beta SP), and a documentary, *Superman* (1995, 5', Beta SP).

FANARI, MOHAMED MUNIR. Iraqi filmmaker. Born in 1949 in Syria, he studied filmmaking in Paris. He also worked for Iraqi television, where he made *A New Fascism / Un nouveau fascisme / Fashiya jadida* (1976). Feature film: *The Lover / L'amant / al-'Ashiq* (1986).

Faour, Ahmed. Emirati filmmaker. Of Palestinian origin, he studied at the American University of Sharjah. Short films: *You Can't Stop Time* (2003, 3', DV Cam), *Diary from Ramallah* (2004, 7', Mini DV), *Respite of the Human Mind* (2004, 5', Mini DV).

FARÈS, JOSEF. Lebanese filmmaker. Born in 1977 in Lebanon, he settled with his family in Sweden at the age of 10. At the age of 15, he began making amateur films and in 1998, at 21, he began formal film training. Between 1995 and 2002 he made numerous fictional shorts, including *Madmen / Fous*, *The Thief / Le voleur*, *The Filmmakers / Les Cinéastes*, *Come / Viens*. His first two features were well received in Sweden. Feature films: *Jalla! Jalla!* (2000, 88', 35mm), *The Cops / Les flics* (2003), *Zozo* (2005, 103', 35mm).

Farhat, Rana. Emirati filmmaker. Born and raised in the UAE though of Lebanese origin, she studied at the American University of Sharjah. Short fictional films: *Reality vs. Reality* (2004, 2', Mini DV), *Got a Lighter?* (2004, 7', Mini DV).

Farouky, Saeed Taji. Palestinian filmmaker. Short documentary film: *Tunnel Trade* (with Laila El Haddad, 2007, 22').

FATHALLAH, DALIA. Lebanese filmmaker. Documentary: *Chronicle of a Return to South Lebanon / Chronique d'un retour au Sud Liban / Mabrouk at tahrir* (2002, 59', Beta SP). Feature film: *Beirut between New York and Baghdad / Beyrouth entre New York et Bagdad* (2005) (documentary).

Fathallah, Zeina. Lebanese filmmaker. Born in 1967 in Beirut, she completed a master's degree in public health at the University of San Jose in California and a doctorate in economics and the management of health systems at the Université de Paris I. In 2000 she took a training course in directing organized by the French Cultural Centre in Lebanon, and became involved with the ecological movement, the Green Line, the subject of her first documentary. Short fictional film: *The Wedding Dress / La robe de mariée / Fustan al-'arus* (2000, 15', 16mm), documentary: *On the Green Line / Sur la ligne verte / 'Ala-l-khatt al-akdar* (2001).

Fawzi, Ali. Palestinian filmmaker. Documentary: *Palestinian Youth / Shahiba min Filastin* (1979).

Fayad, Bassem. Lebanese filmmaker. Also actor. Born in 1976 in Lebanon, he studied at IESAV in Beirut and a made a number of shorts there, including a fictional short, *Soha* (1997, 15', video). Documentary: *Beirut-Baghdad / Beyrouth-Bagdad* (2003, 50', DV Cam).

Fikree, Badr. Emirati filmmaker. He studied at Dubai Men's College and works for Dubai Petroleum Company. Short documentary film: *Behind Closed Doors* (2002, 6', Beta SP).

Fleifel, Mahdi. Palestinian filmmaker. Born in 1979 in Dubai of Palestinian origins, he moved in 1987 to Lebanon. He subsequently studied film in Copenhagen and at the International Film School of Wales. He now lives in Denmark. Four short fictional and experimental films during his studies: *A Perfect Day* (1998, 10'), *The Elevator* (2001, 2'), *It Is Me* (2002, 10'), and *Life in the Bathroom* (2002, 5'). Short films: *Shadi in the Beautiful Well* (2003, 11', Beta SP), *Hamoudi and Emil* (2004, 23', 16mm), *Arafat and I* (2008, 18').

FOUAD, AHMED. Egyptian director of one Syrian feature film: *The World in the Year 2000 / Le monde en l'an 2000* (1972, 35mm).

FOULADKAR, ASSAD. Lebanese filmmaker. Born in 1961 in Beirut, he studied drama in Lebanon, and filmmaking at the University of Boston,where he also worked for Arab-American Television. He teaches filmmaking at the American University in Beirut and at the University of Kaslik. He has made a number of short films and documentaries, most notably the short fictional film *Kyrie eleison* (1988, 24', Beta SP). He has also made series for television: *Ismail* (1997) and *Beautiful Madness* (2001). Feature film: *When Maryam Spoke Out / Quand Maryam s'est dévoilée / Lamma hikyit Maryam* (2001, 98', 35mm).

Freij, Issa. Palestinian filmmaker. Documentary: *Lost Freedom / al-Hurriyya al-da'i'a* (2000), *The Last Spring at Abu-Dis / Le dernier printemps à Abu-Dis* (2005, 28', video).

Fuda, Aymn Ibrahim. Emirati filmmaker. Short animated film: Tarik Ibn Ziad: The Knight of El-Aldalus / Faris al-andalus: Tarik Ibn Ziad (2006).

GARABÉDIAN, GARY. Lebanese filmmaker. He studied in the United States and worked for Lebanese television. He was killed in 1969, along with twenty others, in a fire during the shooting of a nightclub scene in his fifth feature. Feature films: *The Vigilant Eye / L'œil vigilant / al-Ayn al-sahira* (1963, 35mm), *O Night / O nuit / Ya leil* (1964), *Garo / Garo* (1965, 35mm), *Abou Selim in Africa / Abou Sélim en Afrique / Abou Sélim fi Afriquia* (1965, 35mm), *We Are All Freedom Fighters / Nous sommes tous des fédayins / Koullouna fidaiyyoun* (1969, 35mm).

Garda, Daniel. Lebanese filmmaker. Short fictional film: *Tripoli, Quiet / Trablos al-hada* (with Rania Attieh, 2009, 15').

Gargash, Lamya Hussein. Emirati filmmaker. Born in 1982, she studied audio-visual communication at the American University of Sharjah. Short fictional film: *Damp Soil* a.k.a. *Wet Tiles / Sol mouillé* (2003, 8', Beta SP), *Woman at Seven* (2005, 17', Mini DV)..

Gargash, Maha. Emirati filmmaker. Short films comprise an animation: *Great Civilisations* (1992, 9', video), and documentaries: *Wilfred Thesiger* (2000, 9', Beta SP), *Echo of Days: Traditional Dances and Chants in the Emirates* (2000, 30', Beta SP), *Heart of the Emirates' Mountains* (2000, 9', Beta SP).

Gargour, Maryse. Palestinian filmmaker. Born in Jaffa in Palestine, she studied at the French Press Institute and worked as a journalist and producer at the office of RTF in Beirut. She also worked for UNESCO. Documentaries: *A Palestinian Looks at Palestine / Une Palestinienne face à la Palestine* (1988, 28', Beta SP), *My Jaffa / Jaffa la mienne* (1998), *Far from Palestine / Loin de Palestine* (1999), *Blanche's Homeland / Le pays de Blanche / Watan Blansh* (2001, 28', Beta SP), *The Land Speaks Arabic / La terre parle arabe* (2007, 61', video).

Gebran, Jean. Lebanese filmmaker. Born in 1971 in Beyrouth, he studied physical sciences and sound. He worked within theatre and film in sound and as assistant director. Short fictional film: *Chabrouh* (1994, 17mm, Beta).

GEDEON, ANDRÉ. Lebanese filmmaker. Born in 1941 in Katuly in South Lebanon, he followed his initial studies of law with a diploma in filmmaking from FAMU, the Prague film school. He has also worked in the theatre, in television and in journalism. He made several short films in Prague (1968–1972): *A Dog's Life / Vie de chien, Death and Company / Mort et compagnie, Tenderness / Tendresse, The Old Lady Enjoys Herself / La vieille dame s'amuse, The Devil / Le diable / al-Shaytân*. Feature films: *Lebanon, In Spite of Everything / Le Liban, malgré tout / Loubnan roughma koula chai'* (1982, 120'), *Our Little Kings / Nos petits rois / Mulûkundâ al-sighar* (1983).

GERGIS, YOUSSUF. Iraqi filmmaker. Feature film: *Abou Hella / Abu hila* (with Mohamed Choukri Jamil, 1962).

Geries, Raneen. Palestinian filmmaker. Documentary: *Women's Testimonies of the Nakba* (2006, 10').

Ghaibeh, Lina. Lebanese filmmaker. Short animated film: *Seven Days a Week / Sept jours par semaine* (1987, 3').

Ghalayini, Razan. Jordanian filmmaker. Short fictional film: *Noor* (2008, 24').

Ghanayem, Samar. Emirati filmmaker. She studied at the American University of Sharjah. Short fictional film: *I Went Crazy Once* (2004, 2', Mini DV).

Ghandour, Amer. Lebanese filmmaker. Born in 1961 in Beirut, he studied at the École Supérieure de Réalisation in Beirut. He later worked as reporter for Lebanese and French television. Documentary: *Une femme* (1987, 20', 16mm).

Ghanem, Eiman Ahmed. Emirati filmmaker. She studied at the Abu Dhabi Women's College. Short film: *A Point of No Return* (with Rana Mohamed al-Hammadi and Dana Ali al-Hosani, 2003, 2', DV Cam).

Ghannam, Lubna. Emirati filmmaker. She studied at the American University of Sharjah. Short films: *The Grinder* (2007, 5', Mini DV), *Going Back* (2007, 2', Mini DV), *Squid Special* (2007, 3', Mini DV).

GHAYAD, GEORGES. Lebanese filmmaker. Worked initially in television. Feature films: *The Ghost from the Past / Le fantôme du passé / Chabah almadi* (1984, 35mm), *The Session Is Over / La séance est levée / Wa roufiat al-jalsa* (1986, 35mm).

GHAZI, CHRISTIAN. Lebanese filmmaker. Primarily a man of the theatre, he made one documentary on Palestine, *Why the Resistance? / Pourquoi la résistance? / Limâdha al-thawra* (1970), and two features, the second a Syrian co-production. Feature films: *The Freedom Fighters / Les fedayins / al-Fidaiyyoun* (1967), *A Hundred Faces for a Single Day / Cent visages pour un seul jour / Miat wajh li yom wahed* (1972, 72').

GHORAYEB, JOSEPH. Lebanese filmmaker. Feature film: *The Judgement of Fate / Jugement du destin / Hokm al-kadar* (1959, 35mm).

Ghorayeb, Samer. Lebanese filmmaker. Born in 1979 in Lebanon of Lebanese-Italian parents. Short film: *The Little Black Book / Le petit cahier noir* (2008, 27', 35mm).

Ghorra, Nadine. Lebanese filmmaker. Born in 1972, she graduated from Fine Art Academy in Beirut (ALBA) in 1999. One documentary, *Zahlé*, and a fictional short, *The Siren / La sirène / al-Huriya* (1999, fiction, 18', Beta SP).

Ghosh, Lekha. Emirati filmmaker. Short documentary film: *The Land of a Gazelle and Indian Bengali Expatriates* (2007, 37', Mini DV).

Ghsein, Ahmad. Lebanese filmmaker. Contributed . . . *False Connection* (4') to the collective project *Videos Under Siege* (DIFF 2008, 39', video).

Gloor-Fadel, Samira. Lebanese filmmaker. Born in 1956 in Beirut, she studied filmmaking at INSAS in Brussels and workled as a journalist. She currently lives in Switzerland. Her sole documentary is a conversation with the German director Wim Wenders: *Berlin cinema* (1997, 105', 35mm).

Gorani, Joude. Syrian filmmaker. Born in 1980 in Syria, she studied filmmaking at FEMIS in Paris, where she now lives. She worked as cinematographer on several documentaries: Nidal al-Dibs's *Black Stones,* Camilla Magid's *When I Evaporated* and Diana Eljeroudi's *Dols.* Her graduation film is the documentary: *Before Vanishing / Avant de disparaître / Qabla el-ikhtifa'* (2005, 18', video).

Habash, Ahmad. Palestinian filmmaker. Short films: *Moon Eclipse / Uful al-qamar* (2001, 50', DVD), *Coming Back / Iyab* (2003, DVD), *Animation Collection* (2003–2004, set of 1–5' animations), *Fatenah* (2009, 20'). Contributed *Flee* (3' 03") to the collective film *Summer 2006, Palestine* (2006, 35', Beta SP).

Habash, Ismaïl. Palestinian filmmaker. He worked as a cameraman in Ramallah. Short films: *There's Still Ka'ek on the Sidewalk / Ma zal ka'k alla al-rasif* (2000, 27'), *Apartment* (2001), *Local / Mahalli* (with Imad Ahmed and Raed al-Helou, 2002, 53'), *My Dream / Mon rêve / Amani* (2002, 17'), *Say Hi / Radfi al-salam* (2003). Also contributed one episode to the collectively made video documentary *One More Time (Five Stories about Human Rights in Palestine) / Une fois encore (cinq histoires sur les droits de l'homme en Palestine)* (with Nada al-Yassir, Tawfik Abu Wael, Abdel Salam Shehada, Najwa Najjar, 2002, 57', Beta SP).

Habash, Lubna Jasim. Emirati filmmaker. Short commercial: *The Beginning* (2002, 3', Beta SP).

HABCHI, SAMIR. Lebanese filmmaker. Born in 1961 in Lebanon, he studied filmmaking at the Kiev Higher Film Institute, then at VGIK in Moscow, where he made two short films, *Khayalat sahra* and *As sabi al-aarage.* In Lebanon he made two further short films, *The Obsession / L'obsession / Iz'aj* (1988) and *The Scarecrows / Les épouvantails* (1988, fiction, 25', 35mm), as well as television series and documentaries. His documentary *The Lady of the Palace* was produced by Misr International Films, Cairo. Feature films: *The Tornado / Le tourbillon / al-I'sar* (1992, 90', 35mm), *Meshwar* (2001), *The Lady of the Palace / Sayidat el-kasr* (2003, documentary, 58'), *Beirut Open City Beyrouth ville ouverte* (2008, 90', 35mm).

Habib, Mazin. Omani filmmaker. He studied computer science at the University of Arizona. Also a short story writer. Short fictional film: *The Return* (2006, 6', DV Cam).

HABIS, ZINARDI. Lebanese filmmaker. Feature films: *A Woman with a Monster / Une femme chez un monstre / Imra'a fi bayt imlak* (1983, 35mm), *At the Mercy of the Winds / Au gré des vents / Fi mahab al-rih* (1986, 35mm).

Habr, Mirella. Lebanese filmmaker. Short film: *Little Beirut* (2005, 13', video).

Haddad, Fadi G. Jordanian filmmaker. Short fictional films: *Once upon a Piano* (2008, 26'), *High Heels* (2009, 20').

Haddad, Maha. Lebanese filmmaker. She studied audio-visual media at IESAV in Beirut and works as a teacher. Short films: *TurieB / ThouryeB* (Beirut / Beyrouth spelled backward) (1998, 12'), *I'm Well, What About You / Je vais bien, et toi?* (2002, 24', 16mm).

HADDAD, MARWAN. Syrian filmmaker. He studied fimmaking in Germany and worked at first as a print journalist and then in radio. He is director general of the National Cinema Organisation in Damascus. Short films and documentaries (1969–1974): *Building and Defence / Construction et défense /Binâ wa difâ'a* (1969), *In a Working Class District / Dans un quartier polulaire / Fi hay sha'abi* (1972, 20'), *The Return / Le retour / al-Awda* (1974, 7'), *The Dream / Le rêve* (1974), *Damascus O Damascus / Damas ô Damas* (1978, 10'), *Youth / La jeunesse / al-Shabiba* (1975), *Faces and Colours / Visages et couleurs / Wajûh wa alwân* (1978), *Tumour / Tumeur* (1978). Feature films: *The Wrong Way / Direction opposée* a.k.a. *Sens interdit / al-Ittijâh al-mu'âkis* (1975), *Sweet Like a Berry, My Love / Doux comme un baie, mon amour* a.k.a. *L'amour framboise / Habibati ya hab al-tout* (1979, 97').

HADDAD, SAHIB. Iraqi filmmaker. Born in 1939, he studied fine arts and then filmmaking in Hungary. Assistant to the great Egyptian director Youssef Chahine on *The Ring Seller/ Le vendeur de bagues / Biya el-khawstim* (1965) in Lebanon. He also worked on the Lebanese Gary Garabedian's *We Are All Freedom Fighters* (1969). On his return to Iraq he worked as an editor and at the newsreel company. Feature films: *Another Day / Un autre jour / Yawm akhar* (1978, 35mm), *Mutawa and Bahia / Mutawa et Bahia / Mutawa wa Bahia* (with Zuhair al-Dijaili, 1982, 35mm), *Flat No. 13 / L'immeuble No. 13 / Imara rakm 13* (1986), *Borders in Flames / Frontières en flammes / Hudud al-mulahihah* (1986).

Haddad, Victor. Iraqi director. Documentaries: *Medacity / Mendacité / Tassawwul* (1969), *Games of Chess / Jeux d'échecs / La'b chitranj*

(1969), *American Football / Footbal américain / Kurat al-qadam al-Americia* (1973).

Hadeed, Aida Butti. Emirati filmmaker. He studied television and radio at the UAE University, graduating in 2001, and currently works as director for Sharjah TV. Short documentary film: *Mariam* (2003, 17', Beta SP).

HADJITHOMAS, JOANA. Lebanese filmmaker. Born in 1969 in Beirut, she has constantly worked in collaboration with Khalil Joreige. Both studied literature and film. Living between Paris and Beirut, they both now teach at IESAV in Beirut (scriptwriting and the aesthetics of the image, respectively). They have also made photographic and video installations. Short documentary films: *The Agony of the Feet, 333 Sycamore* (1994), *Mistaken Identities / Fautes d'identité* (1996), *Khiam / Khiyam* (2000, 52', video), *Ashes / Cendres / Ramad* (2002, 26', 35mm), *The Lost Film / Le film perdu / al-Film al-mafqud* (2003, 42', Beta SP). They contributed three collaboratively made videos, *Airport 1* (40"), *Starry Night* (45"), and *Beirut Ground Zero* (1'), to the collective project *Videos Under Siege* (DIFF 2008, 39', video). Feature films: *Around the Pink House / Autour de la maison rose / al-Beit al-zahr* (1999, 90', 35mm), *A Perfect Day / Un jour parfait / Yawm akhar* (2005, 88', 35mm), *I Want to See / Je veux voir* (2007, 75', 35mm).

Hafez, Lara Osama. Emirati filmmaker. Of Palestinian origin, she studied at the American University of Sharjah. Short fictional film: *Flesh and Dust* (2004, 6', Mini DV).

Hafez, Mohamed. Emirati filmmaker. He studied at the American University of Sharjah. Short fictional film: *Manic Monday* (2007, 7', DVD).

HAFEZ, NAGDI.* Egyptian filmmaker who made a number of Syrian feature films in the mid-1970s: *A Woman Alone / Une femme seule* (1971, 35mm), *Bridge of the Wicked / Le Pont des méchants* (1971, 35mm), *The Crisis of the Young / La crise des jeunes* (1972, 35mm),

Flat for Love / Appartement de l'amour (1973, 35mm), *The Prostitutes of the Al Aram Avenue / Les prostituées de l'avenue Al Aram* (1973, 35mm), *The Five Master Singers / Les cinq maîtres chanteurs* (1974, 35mm).

Hage, Merdad. Lebanese filmmaker. Resident in Canada. Short documentary film: *Meantime in Beirut / Entre-temps à Beyrouth* (2002, 29', Beta SP).

Haïdar, Sara. Lebanese filmmaker. Born in 1980 in Beirut, she has lived in Tunisia, Greece, Syria and Egypt. He studied cinema at IESAV in Beirut. Two short films: fiction—*Myell* (2003)—and documentary—*Tante Hala* (2004, 14', Beta SP).

Haji, Mohammed Abdul Rahim. Emirati filmmaker. Born in 1980, he studied at the Dubai Men's College. Short documentary films: *DMC Students from Hong Kong* (2001, 8', Mini DV), *Henna Designs* (2001, 4', Beta SP), *World Folkdance: The Philippines* (2002, 10', Beta SP).

Hajjaj, Nasri. Palestinian filmmaker. Documentary: *Shadow of Absence / L'ombre de l'absense / Dhil al-gheyab* (2007, 84', DigiBeta).

HAJJAR, RAFIC. Lebanese filmmaker. He lived for a while in Egypt. On his return, he made a series of documentaries exploring the situation in Palestine in the 1970s: *The Path / Le chemin / al-Tarîq* (1973), *Guns United / Les fusils unis / al-Banâdiq al-mutahida* (1973, 35mm), *May and the Palestinians / Mai et les palestiniens / Ayyar . . . al-filastiniyûn* (1974, 35mm), *The Intidada / L'intifada / al-Intfada* (1975, 35mm), *Born in Palestine / Né en Palestine / Mawlud fi Filastin* (1975), *Born in Palestine / Né en Palestine* (1975, 35mm) *News from Tel al-Za'tar / Khabar min Tel al-Za'tar* (1976), *The Game / Le jeu / al-La'eib* (1978, 20'). Feature films: *The Shelter / L'abri / al-Malja'* (1980, 35mm), *The Explosion / L'explosion / al-Infijar* (1982), *Fragile Houses / Maisons fragiles* a.k.a. *Maisons de papiers / Bouyout min warak* (1984, 35mm).

HAKKI, HAYTHAM. Syrian filmmaker. He studied filmmaking in Moscow and has directed both fictional and short documentary films: *Water and Fire / L'eau et le feu* (1974), *The Change / Le changement* (1974), *Special Mission / Mission spéciale* (1974), *The Barrier / Le barrage* (1975), *The Swing / La balançoire* (1979). *The Game / Le jeu* (1979). Since his feature film debut, he has since worked for Syrian television and for some Gulf television stations, making a number of works which have attracted national attention. He is the head of production at Orbit Television. Feature film: *The Report / Le rapport* (1979).

Hakki, Inas. Syrian filmmaker. Short film: *The Path* (27').

Halabi, Moutia. Lebanese filmmaker. Studied at IESAV in Beirut and worked as an assistant in Lebanese television. Short fictional film: *A Cry / Un cri* (1997, 18', video).

Haleed, Feruza. Emirati filmmaker. Studied at the American University of Sharjah. Short fictional film: *Mother in Palestine* (2004, 3', Mini DV).

Halil, Mahmud. Palestinian filmmaker. Documentary: *Tayseer / Tayseer* (2001).

Hallak, Orwa. Emirati filmmaker. He studied at the American University of Sharjah. Short films: *The Image* (2001, 13', video), *Under the Stairs* (2002, 25', Beta SP), *Paradox* (2003, 8', Mini DV).

Hamad, Sarra. Emirati filmmaker. Born in 1984 in Fujairah, UAE, she studied at the American University of Sharjah. Short film: *A Cheesy Dream* (2004, 4', Mini DV).

HAMADEH, KHALED. Syrian filmmaker. Born in 1930 in Damascus, he had professional training in film. He founded the film section of the School of Fine Art in Damascus and also headed the film section of Iraqi television. He made one fictional short—*Little Suns / Les petits soleils* (1969)—and some twenty documentary films, including *The Big Festival / Le grand festival* (1966), *A Green Road to the Sea / Une route verte vers la mer* (1968), *Petroleum in Syria / Le pétrole en Syrie* (1969), *Yes, We Are Arabs / Oui, nous sommes Arabes / Na'am nahnu arab* (1969, 10'), *Women in Syria / La femme en Syrie* (1969), *Theatre in Syria / Le théâtre en Syrie* (1970), *Children and the Festival / Les enfants et la fête* (1971), *The Ommayades Mosque / La mosquée des Ommayades* (1971), *Damascan Wedding / Noce damascène* (1971), *Damascan Houses / Maisons damascènes* (1972, 10'), *The Master / Le maître* (1973). Feature films: *The Knife / Le couteau / al-Sikkin* (1972, 90', 35mm), *Forbidden Love / L'amour interdit* a.k.a. *Amour défendu* (1977, 35mm).

Hamaideh, Yasmin. Emirati filmmaker. Born in 1985 in Doha, she moved to the UAE at the age of 5, and later studied at the American University of Sharjah. Short film: *Chances* (2006, 8', Mini DV).

Hamarneh, Hussam. Jordanian filmmaker and member of the Amman Filmmakers Cooperative. He studied at the University of Jordan and works as a hardware store manager. Short film: *Heartache* (with Mais Hamarneh, 2004).

Hamarneh, Mais. Jordanian filmmaker and member of the Amman Filmmakers Cooperative. She studied at the University of Jordan. Short film: *Heartache* (with Hussam Hamarneh, 2004).

Hamdan, Dima. Jordanian filmmaker. Short fictional film: *Gaza-London / Gaza-Londres* (2009, 15').

Hammad, Aya Kassem. Emirati filmmaker. Of Palestinian origin, she studied at the American University of Sharjeh. Short film: *The Remains of My Identity* (2006, 10', Mini DV), *Have You Ever* (2007, 11', Mini DV).

Hamza, Jaffar. Bahraini filmmaker. Short film: *Pen Martydom* (2005, 13', Mini DV).

Hamzeh, Nadia. Syrian filmmaker. She studied drama in Damascus and in Paris, and has worked as an actress in television and film. Short films: *Paloma* (2005, 21', Mini DV), *Strong and Weak* (2006, 1', Mini DV).

Hanoun, Khalil. Lebanese filmmaker. Born in 1969 in Beirut, he studied history at a Lebanese university and then drama the Fine Art Academy in Beirut. He has worked in advertising and for the television channel Future Television, and also published two books of poetry in Beirut: *A Lot of Desire* (1995) and *Remains* (1997). Short films: *It's Finished / C'est fini* (1995), *Tomorrow Perhaps / Peut-être demain* (1995, fiction, 9', Beta SP), *Utopia / Utopie* (1996), *Rain's Song* (1997), *To Whom it May Concern* (1998, 6', DV Cam), *Pringles* (2000), *Identity* (2004, 34', DV Cam).

Harb, Amal. Lebanese filmmaker. Born in 1967 in Beirut, she studied at the Fine Art Academy in Beirut. Short films: *The Time / Le temps* (1997, 3', video), *The Wall /Le mur* (1998, 12', video), *The Other Self* (1999, 17', Beta SP—silent).

HAROUN, MICHEL. Lebanese pioneer filmmaker who died in 1979. He was a highly successful stage actor and director who made just one film. Feature film: *Red Flowers / Fleurs rouges / Zouhour hamra* (1957, 35mm).

HARTYON, KARLO. Iraqi filmmaker. Born in 1933 into a family of Palestinian emigrants in Argentina, he studied filmmaking in Budapest. He later settled in Iraq, where he made two documentaries. Feature film: *A Little Strength / Un peu de force / Chaï min al-quwwah* (1988).

Hasen, Anwar. Palestinian filmmaker. Short fictional film: *Colours Under the Sun / Couleurs sous le soleil* (1995, 18').

Hashim, Tariq. Iraqi filmmaker. Based in Denmark. His first film is the story of his own return to Iraq after 23 years of exile. Short films: *16 Hours in Baghdad / 16 heures* *à Bagdad* (2004, 58', DV CAM), *WWW. Gil-gamesh.21* (2007, 52', Beta SP).

Hassairi, Faycal BK. Palestinian filmmaker. He worked a producer on Mohamed Bakri's *Jenin, Jenin.* Short documentary film: *Tresspassers Will Be Severely Tortured* (2003, 44', DigiBeta).

Hassan, Ahmed Juma. Emirati filmmaker. Born in 1988 in Dubai, he studied at the Dubai Men's College. Short film: *Brotherhood* (with Saif Ben Qumasha, 2007, 2', DV Cam).

Hassan, Amira Mohammad. Emirati filmmaker. Born in the UAE, of Palestinian origin, she studied at the American University of Sharjah. Short films: *I Am Palestinian* (2004, 14', Mini DV), *Multiple Masks* (2004, 9', Mini DV).

Hassan, Dawoud. Qatari filmmaker. Born in Egypt, also a journalist. Short documentary film: *Souk Waqif* (with Mohammed Alomary, 2007, 10', DV Cam).

HASSAN, NIZAR. Palestinian documentary filmmaker. Born in 1960 in the village of Mashad in the Nazareth area, he began his filmmaking career in the early 1990s, without formal training. His documentaries include: *Hands of Tomorrow / Mains de demain / Sawa'id al-ghad* (1991), *Women in a Man's World / Les femmes dans le monde des hommes / al-Nisa fi alam al-rîjal* (1991), *To His Mother . . . Fun and Games / A sa mère . . . Jeux et amusements / Ila ummhu . . . La'ab wa La'aab* (1991, 42'), *Bethlehem / Bethléem / Bayt Laham* (1992), *Independence / Indépendance / Istiqlal* (1994, 55', Beta SP), *Words / Paroles* (1995), *Challenge / Le défi / Tahaddi* (2001, 20', Beta SP), *Invasion / Envahissement / Ijtiyah* (2003, 60', Beta SP), *Abou Khahil's Grove / Karem Abou Khahil* (2005). Feature-length documentaries: *Jasmine / Yasmin* (1996, 80', video), *Myth* a.k.a. *Ostura / Mythologies / Ustura* (1998, 90', Beta SP), *Cut / Coupure* (2000, 70').

Hassan, Reem Ahmed. Emirati filmmaker. Born in 1987 in Alexandria, Egypt, she studied at the American University of Sharjah. Short fictional films: *Captured* (2007, 2', Mini DV), *Versus* (2007, 4', Mini DV), *Or?* (2007, 2', Mini DV).

Hassan, Samir. Jordanian filmmaker. Documentary: *After the Defeat / Après la défaite / Baad al-naksa* (1968, 40').

HASSANI, KAMERAN. Iraqi filmmaker. He studied in the United States and, on his return, co-founded the company which produced his three features. He abandoned filmmaking after the commercial failure of the final two of the three films. Feature films: *Saïd Effendi / Sa'id Afandi* (1957, 35mm), *Wedding Proposal / Projet de mariage / Mashro zawadj* (1962, 35mm), *Room No. 7 / Chambre No. 7 / Gorfa raqm sabaa* (1964, 35mm).

Hatoum, Mona. Palestinian filmmaker. Born in 1952 in Beirut, to Palestinian parents, she has lived in London since 1975. She studied at Beirut University and the Slade School of Art in London (till 1981). A sculptor and installation artist, she has taught at various European universities and travelled to Canada and the United States. Short films: *So Much I Want to Say* (1983, 5', video), *Changing Parts* (1984, 24', video), *Eyes Skinned / Les yeux voilés* (1988, 4', video), *Measures of Distance / Les mesures de la distance* (1988, 15', Beta SP), *Foreign Body / Corps étranger* (1994, video Installation).

HAWAL, QASSIM. Iraqi filmmaker who directed one Syrian feature film: *The Hand / La main / al-Yad* (1970). Born in 1940, he studied at the Academy of Fine Arts in Baghdad. He worked in the theatre and as a journalist for Iraqi television. He produced Khalil Chawqi's *The Night Watchman / Le veilleur de nuit (1968)* and in 1970 joined the Palestinian resistance, whose cause he defended in several films: *Daily Life in the Nahr El Bared Camp / La vie quotidienne au camp Nahr el Bared* a.k.a. *Le fleuve froid / al-Nahr al-bârd* (1971), *Ghassan Kanafani: The Word-Gun / Ghassan*

Kanafani, le mot-fusil / Ghassan Kanafani al-kalima boundouqiyaa (1973, 20', 16mm), *The Guns Will Not Remain Silent / Les fusils ne resteront pas en silence / Ian taskut al-banâdiq* (1973), *Why We Scatter Roses... Why We Carry Guns / Pourquoi nous éparpillons des roses ... pourquoi nous portons des fusils / Limadha nazra'u al-ward ... limadha nahmilu al-silâh* (1973, 25', 16 +35mm), *Our Little Houses / Nos petits maisons / Buyutuna al-saghîra* (1974), *The Marshes / Les marais / al-Ahwar* (1976, 42', Beta SP), *Lebanon, Tal al-Za'atar / Le Liban, Tal al-Za'ater / Lubnân Tal al-Za'atar* (1978), *New Life / Une nouvelle vie / Hayât jadida* (1978), *The Massacre of Sabra and Shatila / Le massacre de Sabra et Chatilla / Al-majzara, Sabra wa Shatîla* (1984), *The Palestinian Identity / L'identité palestinienne / al-Hawiyya al falastîniya* (1984). Feature films: *The Hand / La main / al-Yad* (in Syria, 1970), *The Houses in That Alley / Les maisons de cette ruelle / Bitut fi dhalika al-zuqaq* (1977, 90', 35mm), *Return to Haifa / Le retour à Haifa / A'id ila Hayfa* (1981), *Looking for Princess Leila / À la recherche de la princesse Layla / al-Baath... 'an Layla al-amiriyyah* (1992).

Hayat, Anwar Mohammad. Bahraini filmmaker. He worked as a cameraman. Short film: *Al-Fares* (2006, 14', DV Cam), *The Guide* (2007, 16', DVD).

Haydamous, Mounir. Lebanese filmmaker. Short fictional film: *Rain Maker / Le faiseur de pluie* (2002, 14', DV Cam).

Helal, Mohammed. Saudi filmmaker. Short film: *Mission in City Centre* (2008, 56', HD).

HINDASH, FADI. Jordanian filmmaker. Feature-length documentary: *Not Quite the Taliban / Pas encore le Taliban* (2009, 70').

Hlailaat, Khaled. Jordanian filmmaker. Short fictional film: *Justice of Vengeance* (2007, 45').

HOJEÏJ, BAHIJ. Lebanese filmmaker. Born in 1948 in Zahle, he studied philosophy, drama and filmmaking. He has worked largely

making documentaries for Lebanese television: *The Third Age / Le troisième age, The Theatre in Lebanon / Le théâtre au Liban, History of Lebanese Independence / Histoire de l'indépendance libanaise.* He has also worked for French television: *The Green Line / La ligne verte* and *Beirut Paris Beirut / Beyrouth Paris Beyrouth.* Other documentaries: *Twenty-four / Vingt-quatre / Arbaa wa ichreeh* (1971), *Beirut: The Dialogue of Ruins / Beyrouth, le dialogue des ruines* (1993, 52', 1993), *Kidnapped* (1999, 50', video). Feature film: *Belt of Fire / Ceinture de feu / Zinnar al-nar* (2003, 95', 35mm).

Hojeij, Mahmoud. Lebanese filmmaker. Born in 1975 in Lebanon, he studied art and communication at the Lebanese American University in Beirut, film at Sheffield Hallam University and completed his Doctorate in Switzerland. He now teaches at the American Lebanese University. Documentaries: *Wahdoun* (1997), *Spring* (1998), *Once / Il était une fois* (1997, 11', video), *Shameless Transmission of Desired Transformation per Day* (2000, 25', video), *We Will Win* (2006), *Memories of Ras Beirut: Wish You Were Here* (2006, 51'), *Ladies, Women, Citizens / Anisat, nisa'a, mouwatinat* (2007, 55', HDCam).

Homsy, Georges. Lebanese filmmaker. Short film: *Miracle* (2004, 25', 35mm).

Hosa, Mohamed Khalil. Emirati filmmaker. Studied media at Sharjah University. Short films: *The Treasure* (2005, 5', Mini DV), *The Sixth Finger* (2006, 2', Mini DV), *Derani Cola* (2006, 1', Mini DV), *Blood Spot* (2006, 14', Mini DV).

Hosni, Rami. Emirati filmmaker. Of Syrian background and resident in Saudi Arabia. Short fictional films: *Execution or Jail* (2006, 12', Mini DV), *Yalla Tourist Taxi* (2007, 1', Mini DV), *Twisted Roles* (2007, 2', Mini DV), *A Word to Regret* (2007, 7', Mini DV).

Hotait, Laila. Lebanese filmmaker. Her first documentary, made with her sister Nadia, explores postwar Lebanese cinema as an emigrant's cinema: *Beirut . . . Coming Back to You Is Not Painful* (with Nadia Hotait, 2005, 12').

Hotait, Nadia. Lebanese filmmaker. Her first documentary, made with her sister Laila, explores postwar Lebanese cinema as an emigrant's cinema: *Beirut . . . Coming Back to You Is Not Painful* (with Laila Hotait, 2005, 12').

Hreib, Walid. Syrian filmmaker. He studied editing in Germany and edited more than forty short films and features. Short films: *One Day at the Farm / Un jour à la ferme, Nostalgia / La nostagie, The Call / L'appel, al-Ajjaj, The Mahabba Festival / Le festival de Mahabba, A Brief Moment of Happiness / Un bref moment de bonheur* (2001, 7', 35mm), *One Square Metre / Un mètre carré* (2003, 10', 35mm).

Huda, Mohamed Abul. Emirati filmmaker. He was born in Jordan but raised in Sharjah, where he attended the American University. Short film: *Regret* (2005, 6', Mini DV).

Humaid, Ahmed Juma Bu. Emirati filmmaker. Short films: *(2) Suicide* (2007, 1', Mini DV), *Devil's Walk* (2007, 3', Mini DV).

Humeid, Ahmad. Jordanian filmmaker and member of the Amman Filmmakers Cooperative. He studied at the University of Jordan. Short films: *MetroPulse: A City in Motion* (1997), *Aqaba Now* (2003), *Books* (2003).

Hussein, Bassam. Syrian filmmaker. Short film: *al-Qinaa* (2004, 20', 35mm).

Hussein, Cherif Abdel. Iraqi filmmaker. Documentary: *The Path of Victory / Le chemin de la victoire / Tarik al-naçr* (1969, 8').

Hussein, Sherine Hesham. Emirati filmmaker. She studied at the American University of Sharjah. Short fictional film: *Illusion* (2004, 5', Mini DV).

Husseini, Oussama. Syrian filmmaker. He studied filmmaking in Paris. Documentaries: *Voyage to the Heart of History / Voyage au cœur de l'histoire* (1991, 45'), *The Silk Route / La route de la soie* (1992, 47').

Ibrahim, Hussain. Emirati filmmaker. Born in 1959, he has worked for Sharjah Radio and Abu Dhabi TV. Short films: *Emirates Dream: A Vision of Eternity* (2002, 18', Beta SP), *01'03* (with eleven other directors, 2004, 12' Mini DV).

Ibrahim, Lamya. Emirati filmmaker. She studied at the American University of Sharjah. Short fictional film: *Surreal Solitude* (2004, 10', Mini DV).

Ibrahim, Mohamed. Emirati filmmaker. Studied at the American University of Sharjah. Short film: *Stallion Tea* (2007, 1', Mini DV).

Ibrahim, Muneer M. Emirati filmmaker. Short film: *Inequity* (2006).

Ibrahim, Omar. Emirati filmmaker. Born in 1980, he is both actor and sound engineer. After working as assistant on several films, he made his own first short in 2005 and has contined working in various technical roles. Short films: *An Ordinary Day / Un jour ordinaire / Youm aadi* (2005, 10', video), *Small Sky / Petit ciel / Sama sagheera* (with Abdullah Hassan Ahmed, 2006, 14', Mini DV), *Winter / Shetaa* (2006, 22', Mini DV), *Supplication* (2008, 10', 35mm).

Ibrahim, Reham. Emirati filmmaker. Born in 1983, she studied at the American University of Sharjah. Short film: *Them* (2003, 12', DV Cam).

Ibrahim, Sultan Abdulsalam. Emirati filmmaker. Short documentary film: *RAD.10* (2007, 17', Mini DV).

Ibrahim, Vivian Mamdouh. Emirati filmmaker. She studied at the American University of Sharjah. Short film: *Workers at Nine Ball Café* (with Alya Mohamed Ali al-Mulla, 2003, 15', DV Cam).

Ibrahim, Yousef. Emirati filmmaker. Worked as scriptwriter on a number of short films from 2001 onward. Short fictional films: *The Last Bird* (1994, 24', video), *The Shadow* (1999, 10', video).

Ideis, Riyad. Palestinian filmmaker. Short fictional film: *Easy Easy* (2008, 22', video).

Irshaid, Nabila. Palestinian filmmaker. She was born in Osnabrück, Germany, and studied in Hamburg. Video art and installations. Short film: *Travel Agency / Agence de voyage / Wakalat safar* (2001, 14', Beta SP).

Isma'el, Suheir. Palestinian filmmaker. Worked as cinematographer. Documentaries: *Palestinian Diaries* (with Abdel Salam Shehada and Nazih Darwaza, 1992, 52', Beta SP), *Peace Chronicles: On the Edge of Peace* (1994, 105', video), *Administrative Detention / al-E'eteqal al-edari* (1998 26'), *Arab Diary / Yaomiyyat arabiyya* (2000).

Isma'il, Azz al-Din. Palestinian filmmaker. Short films: The Dream / Le rêve / al-Hilm (1994), Gaza 2006 (1996), Another World / Un autre monde / al-Alam al-Akhar (1999).

Ismail, Hassan Ibrahim Hassan. Emirati filmmaker. He studied at Dubai Men's College. Short films: *Mental Illness* (2007, 2', Mini DV), *Ashes to Ashes* (with Ahmed al-Mazrooie, 2007, 4', Mini DV).

ISSA, YOUSSEF.* Egyptian director of a Lebanese-Syrian co-production: *The Likeable Thief / Le voleur sympathique / al-Loss al-zarif* (1968, 35mm).

Jabbar, Ahmed. Iraqi filmmaker. He studied at the Independent Film and Television Academy in Baghdad. Short film: *Doctor Nabil* (2007, 15').

Jaber, Hiba Abdel. Emirati filmmaker. Born in Dubai, she studied at the American University of Sharjah. Short fictional film: *A Friend Indeed* (2004, 4', Mini DV).

Jaber, Jasim. Emirati filmmaker. Born in Bahrain in 1958, he studied at the Television and Film Academy in Cairo. After a first short film, he has worked in television: Bahrain TV (1977–87), Sharjah TV (1987–95), Dubai TV (from 1997). Fictional film: *The Last Mud* (1990, 60', Beta SP).

JACIR, ANNEMARIE. Palestinian filmmaker. Born in 1974 in Saudi Arabia, which she left at the age of 16 to study filmmaking at Columbia University in New York. She lived for a while between New York and Ramallah, but now, banned from Palestine, she is based in Amman. She has worked as an editor and taught film at the Universities of Columbia, Bethlehem, and Birzeit. Short films: *Interview* (1994, 4'), *Scratch* (1996, 5'), *A Post-Oslo History* (1998, 8', video), *Two Hundred Years of American Ideology* (2000), *The Satellite Shooters / Les chasseurs de paraboles / Sayyad al-satilayt* (2001, 16', 16mm blown up to 35mm), *Palestine Is Waiting / La Palestine attend / Filastin tantazir* (with Dahna Aburahme and Suzy Salmy, 2003, 9', Beta SP), *Like Twenty Impossibles / Comme vingt impossibles / Kanhun 'ashrun mustahil* (2003, 17', 35mm), *A Few Crumbs for the Birds / Quelques miettes pour les oiseaux* (with Nassim Amaouche, 2005, 29', 35mm), *An Explanation (and Then Burn the Ashes)* (2005, 6', 16mm). Contributed *Sound of the Street* (3' 06") to the collective film *Summer 2006, Palestine* (2006, 35', Beta SP). Her first feature was shown at the Cannes film festival. Feature film: *Salt of This Sea / Le sel de la mer / Milh hadha al-bahr* (2008, 109', 35mm).

Jadallah, Ahmad. Emirati filmmaker. He studied at the American University in Dubai. Short films: *Mission Impossible* (2005, 10', DVD), *AUD 101* (2006, 11', DVD).

Jadallah, Hadi. Palestinian filmmaker. Short fictional film: *Hijara* (2006, 18').

Jadallah, Ihab. Palestinian filmmaker. Fictional shorts: *The Shooter* (2007, 8'), *Hijara* (2007, 19').

Jadallah, Sulafa. Pioneer Palestinian film-maker. She participated actvely in the shooting and directing of many of Mustafa Abu Ali's collectively made documentaries of the early 1970s.

Jafarawi, Hussein. Jordanian filmmaker. Short fictional film: *They Say There Is No Work* (2008, 10').

Jahami, Mouneir. Syrian filmmaker. Documentary: *October's Harvest / La moisson d'octobre / H'açâd uktubar* (1974).

Jahry, Karsan. Syrian filmmaker. One documentary on Palestine for Syrian television. Documentary: *The Foreigners Don't Drink Coffee / Les étrangers ne boivent pas de café / al-Ghurabâ' la lachruhu na-l-qahwa* (1972, 46').

Jajeh, Jennifer. Palestinian filmmaker. She studied at UCLA and the Lee Strasberg Studio in New York, and is based in San Francisco. She works as an actress and arts administrator. Short films: *In My Own Skin* (co-dir., 2001, 16'), *Fruition* (2003).

JALAL, IBRAHIM. Iraqi filmmaker. Worked in television. Feature film: *Hamad and Hammud / Hamad et Hammud / Hamad wa Hammud* (1980).

Jamal, Ali. Emirati filmmaker. He is also an author, actor, and stage director who has worked in television and radio. Short films: *The Lot of Shammah / Nasseb Shamma* (2005, 18', HDV), *The Birthday Gift / Hadiyat eid al-milad* (2007, 40', Mini DV), *Brother / Akhoui* (2008, 16', HDV), *Crossing* (2009, 4', HD Cam).

JAMIL, MOHAMED CHOUKRI. Iraqi filmmaker. Born in 1936 in Baghdad, he trained as a documentary filmmaker with the oil companies, especially the Iraq Petroleum Company. Subsequently he studied filmmaking both in Cairo and at the National Film School in Beaconsfield, England. On his return to Iraq he worked as editor on Kamel al-Azzawi's disastrous superproduction *Nebuchadnezzar /*

Nabuchodonsor / Naboched Nosser (1962) and appeared as an actor in a comedy, *Abou Hella / Abu hila* (1962), for which some sources also name him as co-director. He also made a short fictional film: *He Who Hopes for Prosperity / Celui qui espère la prospérité* (1967, 35mm), and a number of documentaries: *Nostalgia for the Soil / Nostalgie de la terre / Hanîn al-ard* (1971, 30', 35mm), *Those who Excavate the Land / Ceux qui fouillent la terre / Rijâlun yarfuru amâkin fi al-ard* (1971, 19'), *Baghdad in a Mirror / Bagdad dans un miroir / Bagdad fil mir'at* (1972, 30', 35mm), *Man and Machine / L'homme et machine / Al-insan wal ala* (1972, 52', 35mm), *Problem / Problème / Warta* (1972, 35', 35mm), *Harsh Winter / Le rude hiver / ach-Chia'ec-Ca'b* (1974, 15'). Feature films: *The Good Omen / Le bon augure / Chaif Khir* (1969, 35mm), *The Thirsty Ones / Les assoiffés / al-Damiun* (1972, 35mm), *The Walls / Les murs* a.k.a. *Les remparts / al-Aswar* (1979, 94', 35mm), *Clash of Loyalties* a.k.a. *The Big Question / La grande question / al-Massala al-korba* (1983, 170', 35mm), *Mountain Knight / Le chevalier de la montagne / Faris al-jahal* (1987, 35mm), *King Ghazi / Le roi Ghazi / al-Malik Ghazi* (1990, 120', 35mm).

Janabi, Khaled Yousif. Bahraini filmmaker. Born in 1963 in Bahrain, he studied fine art at the University of Cairo. He worked as assistant director on Bassam al-Thawani's feature film, *Visitor* (2003). Short experimental film: *Poet* (2003, 6', Mini DV).

Janahi, Mohammed Yousif. Bahraini filmmaker. Works for Bahraini Television. Short films: *Roosters Blood* (1993), *Time Game* (1995), *The Paper* (1999), *Camera* (2001, 30', Beta SP), *01'03* (collective film made in UAE—12 directors, 2004, 13', Mini DV), *A Message* (2006, 12', HDV).

Jankot, Mutaz. Jordanian filmmaker. Born in 1978 in Amman, he began making amateur films. He later studied at the New York Film Academy and the Intermediate University College in Amman. He made over eleven documentaries before 2002. Short documentary film: *A Letter from Sarah* (2002, 11', Beta SO).

JARJOURA, KATIA. Lebanese filmmaker. Documentries: *Caught in Between / Entre deux fronts* (2001, 53', Beta SP), *Princes of War, Lords of Peace / Princes de la guerre, seigneurs de la paix* (2002), *The Call of Karbala / L'appel de Kerbala* (2004, 75', Beta), *Beirut ma Betmout* (2006, 7', Mini DV). Fictional feature: *Terminator* (2006, 75', Min DV).

Jaroon, Taj Elsir Idris. Emirati filmmaker. Short film: *Successes of Abdulrahman Madani* (2002, 17', Beta SP).

Jassim, Mohammed Ahmed Ali. Emirati filmmaker. He studied at Dubai Men's College. Short film: *Water Equals Life* (2006, 1', DV Cam).

Jawad, Nizar. Bahraini filmmaker. Born in 1979, he studied media at the University of Bahrain. Short films: *Confessions* (2005, 5', Mini DV), *The Flag* (2005, 7', DVD).

Jbawi, Mounir. Syrian filmmaker. Short animated film: *Digital* (2002, 6', 35mm).

Ji, Ghazi Buqjah. Emirati filmmaker. He worked with Syrian TV from 1982 and subsequently with Sharjah TV. Short films: *The Image* (2001, 11', Beta SP), *The Fort Talks* (2002, 10', Beta SP), *The Silence* (2003, 12', Beta SP).

Jingan, Abdullah. Emirati filmmaker. Short fictional film: *Al-Kyram* (2000, 16', video).

Johariya, Hani. Pioneer Palestinian filmmaker. Born in Jerusalem in 1939, he studied filmmaking in Cairo and London. He joined the Palestinian resistance in 1967, shot newsreel material and served as cameraman, assistant, or co-director on a number of the early 1970s films of Mustafa Abu Ali, Qays al-Zubaydi and Ghalib Sha'ath. He was killed in action in Lebanon in 1976

JOREIGE, KHALIL. Lebanese filmmaker. All his work has been made in collaboration with fellow Lebanese Joana Hadjithomas. Both studied literature and film. They have since worked together consistently and both now teach at IESAV in Beirut (scripwriting and the aesthetics of the image, respectively). Working between Paris and Beirut, they have also made photographic and video installations. Short documentary films: *The Agony of the Feet, 333 Sycamore* (1994), *Mistaken Identities / Fautes d'identité* (1996), *Khiam / Khiyam* (2000, 52', Beta SP), *Ashes / Cendres / Ramad* (2002, 26', 35mm), *The Lost Film / Le film perdu / al-Film al-mafqud* (2003). They contributed three collaboratively made videos, *Airport 1* (40"), *Starry Night* (45"), and *Beirut Ground Zero* (1'), to the collective project *Videos Under Siege* (DIFF 2008, 39', video). Feature films: *Around the Pink House / Autour de la maison rose / al-Beit al-zahr* (1999, 92', 35mm), *A Perfect Day / Un jour parfait / Yawm akhar* (2005, 88', 35mm), *I Want to See / Je veux voir* (2007, 75').

Jorgeige, Lamia. Lebanese filmmaker. Short documentary film: *Nights and Days* (2007, 17').

JOUJOU, FOUAD. Lebanese filmmaker. Worked in advertising. Feature films: *Kidnapped / Le kidnappé / al-Makhtouf* (1983, 35mm), *Karim Abou Chacra Does His Military Service / Karim Abou Chacra fait son service militaire / Karim Abdou Chacra fi khidmat al-alam* (1994, 35mm).

Kaadan, Soudade. Syrian filmmaker. Born in France in 1979, she has lived and studied in Syrian and Lebanon. She works in the audio-visual department of the Damascus Opera House and has made documentaries for television. Short documentary film: *Two Cities and a Prison / Madeedatain wa sijn* (2008, 39', DigiBeta).

Kaado, Sayed. Lebanese filmmaker. Born in 1974, he studied sociology in Beirut and then filmmaking at the Academy of Fine Arts. He has made a few fictional shorts: *Chance Visitors / Visiteurs par hasard* (1977), *Beirut / Beyrouth* (1978); and a dozen documentaries: *Night of Celebration / Nuit de fête* (1972), *A Madman's Dream / Le songe d'un fou* (1973),

Letter of Independence / Lettre d'indépendance (1990), *The Way of Return / La voie du retour* (1995), *Cana* (1997, 24', video), *Ta-Ka-Sim from Baghdad / Ta-Ka-Sim de Bagdad* (1999, 52', video), *Lift Up Your Head, Brother / Relève la tête mon frère* (2002, 48', Beta SP).

Kabeel, Mohammed. Emirati filmmaker. Short fictional film: *The Possessed* (2007, 9', Mini DV).

KADDO, MAHER. Syrian filmmaker. Born in 1949 at Deir-Ezzar. He studied film directing. Feature film: *Noises from All Sides / Le hénissement des directions* a.k.a. *Le périple / Sahil al-jibat* (1993, 97', 35mm), *Gate of Heaven / La porte au ciel / Bawabet al-janna* (2009).

Kadhmi, Majeed. Bahraini filmmaker. Short film: *The Unknown* (2008, 8', video).

Kadi, Sam. Syrian filmmaker, Short fictional film: *Schizophrenian* (2008, 27', video).

KAHI, GEORGES. Lebanese pioneer filmmaker. He came from the theatre and his debut feature was based on a play he had produced successfully in Beirut. He claimed it was the first film to be "entirely Lebanese in all its elements, both technical and artistic," but its release was marred by disputes among the twenty-two person theatrical collective that had produced it, and Kahi did not make another film for 5 years. Feature films: *Remorse / Remords / Azab al-damir* (1953, 35mm), *Memories / Souvenirs / Zikrayat* (1958, 35mm), *Days of My Life / Jours de ma vie / Ayyam min omri* (1959, 35mm), *Two Hearts, One Body / Deux cœurs, un corps* (1959, 35mm), *The White Poison / Le poison blanc / al-Sam al-abiad* (1961, 35mm), *The Devil's Cart / La charrette du diable / Arabat al-chaitane* (1962, 35mm), *Years / Des années / Sinine* (1962, 35mm), *You Are My Life / Toi, ma vie / Anta omri* (1964, 35mm).

Kaidy, Fadhil Abbas Mohammad. Emirati filmmaker. He studied at Dubai Men's College. Short film: *Hope* (2004, 2', Mini DV).

Kamal, Ahmed. Iraqi filmmaker. He studied at the Independent Film and Television Academy in Baghdad. Short documentary film: *Documentary Course March 2006* (2007, 15').

KAMMOUN, MICHEL. Lebanese filmmaker. Born in Sierra Leone in 1969, he studied mathematics in Beirut, followed by filmmaking at ESEC in Paris. Short fictional films: *Cathodic / Cathodique* (1994, 7', 35mm), *Shadows / Ombres* (1995, 6', 16mm blown up to 35mm), *The Shower / La douche* (1999, 10', 35mm), *Clowning Around: The Vanishing Rabbits* (2003). Contributed *A Minute of Silence for Lebanon* (1') to the collective project *Videos Under Siege* (DIFF 2008, 39', video). Feature film: *Falafel* (2006, 83', 35mm).

Kanaan, Leila. Lebanese filmmaker. Born in 1981 in Saïda, she studied economics in France, philosophy in Lebanon and then filmmaking at IESAV in Beirut. Short fictional film: *My Father's House / La maison de mon père / Beit bayyi* (2003, 21', Beta SP).

KANAAN, SOUHEIL. Syrian filmmaker. Feature film: *The Horsemen of Liberation / Les cavaliers de la libération* (1974, 35mm).

KANAM, KANAM. Syrian filmmaker. Feature film: *The Crossing / La traversée / al-Ekhtiraq* (1974, 90', 35mm).

Kandil, Tarek. Lebanese filmmaker. Short animated film: *Superhajja* (2006, 2').

Kansoul, Hala Abu. Emirati filmmaker. Born in 1985 in Dubai, she studied at the American University of Sharjah. Short films *The Message* (2007, 5', Mini DV), *Workaholic* (2007, 2', Mini DV), *Going Somewhere* (2007, 3', Mini DV).

KAOUACH, MOHAMED. Jordanian filmmaker. Feature film (on the struggle in Palestine): *My Beloved Homeland / Ma patrie bien aimée / Watani habibi* (1964).

Karam, Raïf. Lebanese filmmaker. Short animated films: *OK* (1993, 3.5', Beta SP), *Blackout* (1993, 3', Beta SP).

KARAMA AL-AMRI, SALEH. Emirati filmmaker. He studied media at the Emirates University and cinema at the New York Academy and worked as a journalist. One of the founders of the Abu Dhabi Theatre, for which he wrote and directed plays. He has also published a collection of short stories, *Sleepless Nights,* and scripted the film *Carriage of the Soul,* directed by the British director Conrad Clark. Short fictional and experimental films: *Al-Della: The Coffee Pot* (2002, 4', DV Cam), *Turnstile* (2003, 2', video), *The Heavy Snowball* (2003, 10', DV Cam), *Valentine* (2003, 4', 16mm), *Sticky Doll* (2003, 1', 16mm), *Count Bubble* (2003, 4', DV Cam), *Breathing Light* (2003, 17', DV Cam), *Where Is My Shirt?* (2003, 4', 16mm), *Mirror* (2003, 3', 16mm), *Time Left* (2004, 28',16mm). Feature film: *Henna* (2008, 75', HD).

Karim, Najm Abdel. Kuwaiti filmmaker. Directed a documentary on Palestine for Kuwaiti television: *Yes, No / Oui, non / Naam, lâ* (1972, 25').

Kasem, Saleh. Jordanian filmmaker and member of the Amman Filmmakers Cooperative. Born in France of Syrian descent, he studied at the Arab Academy for Financial Sciences, Jordan, and now lives between Aleppo in Syria and Amman in Jordan, where he studied information science, before turning to video. Short film: *Sharar* (with Ammar Quttaineh and Hazim Bitar, 2006, 15', Beta SP).

Kassem, Fadi. Lebanese filmmaker. Short fictional film: *All for the Homeland / Tous pour la patrie / Koullouna lil watan* (2002, 29').

Kassem, Farah. Emirati filmmaker. Short film: *Child Labor* (with Areej al-Hassan, 2007, 1', Mini DV).

Kat, Mouaffaq. Syrian filmmaker. Short films: *A Thousand and One Images / Les mille et une images* (1995, animation, 4', 35mm), Memoirs of a Primitive Man / Mémoires d'un homme primitif (1997, 19', 35mm).

Katbi, Dima Arabi. Emirati filmmaker. Born in Syria and growing up in Jeddah, Saudi Arabia, she studied at the American University of Sharjah. Short fictional films: *The Pathway* (2007, 4', Mini DV), *The Proposal* (2007, 4', Mini DV), *Over Excited* (2007, 2', Mini DV).

KAWAAN, SOKHEIE. Syrian filmmaker. Feature film: *Conqueror of Space / Conquérant de l'espace* (1975, 35mm).

KAWADRI, TAHSINE. Lebanese filmmaker. Feature film: *Love in Istanbul / L'amour à Istamboul / Gharam fi Istambul* (1966).

Kawan, Omar. Emirati filmmaker. He studied civil engineering at Baghdad University and has subsequently worked in the fields of graphics and animation. He scripted six short films for other directors before turning to direction. Short film: *My Rights* (with Mahmoud Yousouf al-Mashni, 2003, 4', DV Cam).

Kayali, Mohamed Salah. Palestinian filmmaker. Documentary: *Three Operations in Palestine / Trois opérations en Palestine* (1969).

Kayed, Hichem. Palestinian filmmaker. Born in Lebanon, where he now lives and works. Short films: *Our Dreams . . . When? / A quand nos rêves? / Ahlamna . . . Emta?* (2001, 16', video), *God Forbid!* (2001, 26', DV), *The Sugar of Yafa / Le sucre de Yafa / Sukkar Yafa* (2002, 32', DVD), *Childhood in the Midst of Mines / Tufula bayn al-algham* (2003, 18', DVD), *Lemonade* (2005, 12'), *Neither Here, Nor There* (2006, 45').

Kermani, Naser. Kuwaiti filmmaker. Short fictional film: *Clowns* (2003, 40', Beta SP).

Khadr, Dimitri. Lebanese filmmaker. Born in 1967, he studied film at Duncan of Jordaston College of Art, University of Dundee. Short documentaries: *Living Icons / Icônes vivantes* (1998, 51', video), *Travel / Safar* (with Cynthia

Choucair, 2003, 28', DV Cam), *Children of the Cedars / Les enfants du cèdre* (2004, 58', video).

Khalaile, Jamal. Palestinian filmmaker. Short fictional film: *Escape / Evasion* (2008, 17').

Khaled, Shadh. Emirati filmmaker. She studied at Dubai Women's College. Short documentary film: *What Makes a Successful Song?* (2006, 12' DV Cam).

Khalifé, Élie. Lebanese filmmaker. Born in 1964 in Beirut, he studied at the École Supérieure d'Art Visuel in Geneva. Short films: *May Day* (1988), *Thank You Natex / Merci Natex* (1998, 13', 35mm), *Beirut-Geneva / Beyrouth-Genève* (1989), *Nine Times St Anthony / Neuf fois Saint-Antoine* (co-dir., 1990), *Echoes / Échos* (1991), *Love's Messenger / Le messager de l'amour* a.k.a. *Le messager du vent / Mersal el hawa* (1993, 20', 16mm), *Taxi service* (with Alexandre Monnier, 1996, 12', 35mm), *Van Express* (2004, 21', 35mm).

KHALIL, FARES. Lebanese filmmaker. Feature film: *Childish Love / Amour d'enfants* (2008, 107').

Khalil, Mahmoud. Palestinian filmmaker. Short film: *Facilitation / Taysir* (1984).

Khalil, Mano. Syrian filmmaker. Documentary: *The Place Where God Sleeps / L'endroit où Dieu dort / Tam kde boh spi* (1995, 26', 16mm).

Khan, Jonathan Ali. Emirati filmmaker. Documentary: *Under a Desert Sun* (2005, 60', Beta SP).

Khanamirian, Elda. Lebanese filmmaker. Born in 1964 in Beirut, she studied filmmaking in the University of Boston and worked as a reporter in Lebanon and England. Short fictional film: *Reflections in Time / Réflexions dans le temps* (1989, 8', 16mm).

Khatib, Razan. Jordanian filmmaker and member of the Amman Filmmakers Cooperative. Born in 1974 in Amman, he studied at the Arab Institute for Banking and Financial Studies, Jordan, and works as an IT manager. Short films: *Nightmares of Reality* (with Aseel Mansour, 2003, 5', DV Cam), *Small Victories* (2004, 13', DV).

Khatib, Suhad. Jordanian filmmaker and member of the Amman Filmmakers Cooperative. She studied at the Applied Science University, Jordan, and works as a graphic designer. Short films: *Suwar* (2003), *Three Ghettos One Land* (2004).

Khill, Ibrahim. Palestinian filmmaker. Documentaries: *My City Nazareth / Ma ville Nazareth / Madinati al-Nassiriya* (1978), *Palestinians and Peace? / Les Palestiniens et la paix? / al-Filastiniyyun wa al-salam?* (1990), *Budding to Eternity / Bourgeonnement à l'éternité / Bur'am 'ila 'ahab* (1993), *Paul the Carpenter / Paul le charpentier / Bulus al-najjar* (1999, 52', 16mm).

Khlat, Yasmine. Lebanese filmmaker, actress, and novelist. Born in 1959 in Ismaïla (Egypt), she was raised in Lebanon, her parents' native country. She studied film at the Université de Censier in Paris. As an actress, she played the leading roles in a number of major Arab films: the Algerian Farouk Belloufa's *Nahla*, the Tunisian Abdellatif Ben Ammar's *Aziza* and the Syrian Mohamed Malas's *City Dreams* among them. Resident in Paris since the early 1990s, she published her first novel, *Le désespoir est son péché* in 2001. Documentary: *Our Night / Notre nuit / Leylouna* (1987, 52', video).

Khleifi, George. Palestinan filmmaker. Short films and documentaries: *The Hermit / al-Nasik* (1978), *Lands of Sea and Sand / Bilad al-bahr wa al-raml* (1982), *The Palestinian Evacuation from Beirut / Khuruj al-filastiniyyeen min Bayrut* (1982), *Children of Stones / Les enfants des pierres / Atfal al-hajjara* (with Ziad Fahoum, 1988, 28'), *Heart to Heart / Cœur à cœur / Min qalb 'ila qalb* (1990), *Jerusalem Under Seige / al-Quds that al-hisar* (1990, 15'), *The Source of a Precocious Childhood / Masadir al-tufula al-Mubakira* (1991), *Sunrise / L'aube / Shuruq* (1991), *The Player of the Small Flute / 'Azef al-nay al-saghir* (1995), *You, I and Je-*

rusalem / *Anta, ana al-Quds* (1997), *Mariam's Dog* / *Kalb Maryam* (with Tayseer Mashareqa, 2004). He is co-author, with Nurith Gertz, of *Palestinian Cinema: Landscape, Trauma and Memory*.

KHLEIFI, MICHEL. Palestinian filmmaker. Born in 1950 in Nazareth, he left Palestine in 1970 and later studied at INSAS in Belgium, graduating in 1977. He worked in Belgian television (RTBF), making several reports and documentaries, including *The West Bank: The Palestinians' Hope? / Cisjordanie, espoir palestinien? / al-Diffa al-qarbiyya . . . al-Amal al-filastiniyyah* (1978, 58'), *Israeli Settlements in the Sinai / Les colonies israéliennes dans le Sinaï / al-Mustawtinat al-Isa'iliyya fi Sina* (1978, 50'), *Ashrafiyya / Achrafieh / al-'Ashrafiyya* (1978), *Palestinians and Peace / Les Palestiniens et la paix / al-Finastiniyyun wa al-salam* (1978). Short films include *El Naim's Journey / La route d'El Naïm / Tariq al-na'im* (1981, 54'), *Maaloul Celebrates Its Destruction / Maloul fête sa destruction / Ma'aloul tah'tafel bidamariha* (1984, 30'), *Mixed Marriages in the Holy Land / Mariages mixtes en terre sainte / Az-zawajo -l-mamnou' fi-larabi-l-mokaddasa* (1995, 50', Beta SP). Through his production company in Belgium, Marisa Films, he has been involved in the production of his own first two features, as well as those of other INSAS graduates, such as the Tunisians Mahmoud Ben Mahmoud (*Traversées*, 1982) and Nejia Ben Mabrouk (*La trace*, 1983–1988). He won the top prize, the Tanit d'or, at the JCC in Tunis in 1988, with his second feature, *Wedding in Galilee*. Feature films: *Fertile Memory / La mémoire fertile / Al-dhâkira al-khisba* (1980, 99', 16mm), *Wedding in Galilee / Noce en Galilée / Urs fi al-Jalil* (1987, 112', 35mm), *Canticle of Stones / Cantique de pierre / Nashid al-hajjar* (1989, 106', 35mm), *Order of the Day / L'ordre du jour* (1993, 105', 35mm), *The Tale of the Three Jewels / Conte des trois diamants / Hikayat al-jawaher al-thalatha* (1996, 107', 35mm), *Road 181: Fragments of a Journey / Route 181, fragments d'un voyage en Palestine-Israël* (with Israeli director Eyal Sivan, 2004, 270', Beta SP).

Khory, Lina. Jordanian filmmaker. Short film: *West . . . East* (2006, 8').

Khouly, Kosaï. Syrian filmmaker. After graduating from the Conservatoire de Théâtre in 1999, he has acted in forty téléfilms, seven feature films and four plays. Short film: *Script / Scénario* (2005, 30', Beta SP).

Khouri, Asma Ahmed. Emirati filmmaker. She studied at Abu Dhabi Women's College. Short documentary films: *A Gift from God* (2002, 3', DV Cam), *Rite of Passage* (2002, 5', DV Cam), *Paths to Peace* (2003, 5', DV Cam).

Khoury, Amal. Jordanian filmmaker. Resident in the United States. Short documentary film: *Dear Karlo* (2000, 8', video).

Khoury, Buthina Canaan. Palestinan filmmaker. Short films: *Women in Struggle / Femmes en lutte / Nisa fi siraa* (2004, 56', video), *Maria's Grotto / Magharat Maria* (2007, 52', DigiBeta).

KHOURY, GEORGES. Syrian filmmaker. Feature film: *If I Die Twice I Would Love You / Je meurs deux fois je t'aimerais* (1975, 35mm).

Khoury, Rina. Palestinan filmmaker. Short films: *Balala Land* (2003), *West End* (2005).

KHOURY, SAMIR. Lebanese filmmaker. He studied filmmaking in Europe. Feature films: *The Lady with the Dark Glasses / La dame aux lunes noires / Saydat al-akmar as-sawda* (1971), *Wolves Do Not Eat Raw Meat / Les loups ne mangent pas la chair fraîche / Ziab la taakol al-lahm* (1972, 35mm), *Amanie Under the Rainbow / Amanie sous l'arc en ciel / Amanie taht kaws kouzah* (1984, 110').

Khoury, Talal. Lebanese filmmaker. Short film: *The Respectable Man / L'homme respectable* (2008, 13', video).

Kodeih, Rami. Lebanese filmmaker. Short fictional film: *A Sheherazade Tale* (2006, 22').

Konath, Ahmed Kabeer. Emirati Filmmaker. Short films: *Waves* (2002, 9', Beta SP), *A Soul in a City* (2005, 15', Mini DV).

KORKI, SHAWKAT AMIN. Iraqi filmmaker. His first feature was shown at the MEIFF in 2007. Feature film: *Crossing the Dust / À travers la poussière / Parinawa la ghobar* (2006, 76', 35mm).

KOSHAV. Syrian filmmaker. Feature film: *Women Naked without Sin / Femmes nues sans péché* (1967, 35mm).

Kotait, Ghassan. Lebanese filmmaker. Born in 1973 in Lebanon, he studied filmmaking at the Academy of Fine Arts (ALBA) in Beirut. Graduation film at the Academy: *After the Silence / Après le silence* (1996, 22', Beta SP). Short fictional film: *Lebanese Non-footage / Non métrage libanais* (with Wissam Smayra, 2003, 13', 16mm).

Kreidieh, Amir. Lebanese filmmaker. Studied at the Lebanese American University in Beirut. Documentary: *Abandoned Children / Enfants abanonnés* (1997, 5', video).

Lababidi, Aseel. Saudi filmmaker. Born in 1986 in Riyadh, she studied at the American University of Sharjah. Both her short films were made in the UAE. Short films: *Ashes of Remorse* (2006, 4', Mini DV), *A Vivid Deception* (2007, 7', Mini DV).

Labaki, Carmen. Lebanese filmmaker. Short film: *France in Lebanon / La France au Liban* (2001, 52', Beta SP).

LABAKI, NADINE. Lebanese filmmaker. Born in 1974 in Lebanon, she studied at IESAV in Beirut. Also an actress, she starred in Philippe Aractingi's *The Bus* (2005). She made two short films during her studies, one of which was *11 Pasteur Street / 11 rue Pasteur / 11, Shari' Bastoor* (1996, 12', video). She also made a number of commercials and short films featuring Middle Eastern singers. Feature film: *Caramel* (2007, 95', 35mm).

LABIB, HIKMET. Iraqi filmmaker. Lived for some time in Lebanon, the subject of some of his films. Feature films: *Autumn Leaves / Feuilles d'automne / Awrak al-kharif* (1963, 35mm), *The Seven O'clock Train / Le train de sept heures / Qitae al-saa sabaa* (1963, 35mm), *Farewell Lebanon / Adieu ô Liban / Wada'an ya Lubnan* (1967, 35mm).

LAHHAM, DUREID. Syrian filmmaker. After studying physics at Damascus University, graduating in 1958, he worked for 2 years as a schoolteacher before deciding to become an actor. He subsequently worked widely in theatre, television, and films. Together with Nouhad Kalahi he formed one of the Arab world's favorite comic teams, first on Syrian television, then in a series of 1960s Lebanese-Syrian co-productions: *The Pearl Necklace / Le collier de perles / Akd al-loulou* (1964, 35mm), *Meeting at Palmyra / Rencontre à Palmyre / Lika' fi tadmor* (1965, 35mm), *The Millionnaire / Le millionaire* (1965, 35mm), *I Am Antar / Je suis Antar / Ana Antar* (1967, 35mm), *One Plus One* (1971, 35mm), all directed by the Egyptian expatriate, Youssef Maalouf, together with a number made by Lebanese directors: *The Tramps / Les vagabonds / al-Charidan* (with Rida Myassar, 1966, 35mm), *Love in Istanbul / L'amour à Istamboul / Gharam fi Istambul* (with Tahsine Kawadri, 1966, 35mm), *Hotel of Dreams / Hôtel des rêves / Foundok al-ahlam* (1966, Albert Najib), *The Likeable Thief / Le voleur sympathique / al-Loss al-zarif* (1968, Youssef Issa). In Syria, he played the lead in Nabil al-Maleh's *Jealous James Bond / James Bond le jaloux / Ghawar James Bond* (1974) and, in the 1980s, began directing his own films. Feature films: *Borders / Les frontières / al-Hudud* (1984, 110', 35mm), *The Report / Le rapport / al-Taqrîr* (1986, 35mm), *The Attachment / al-mahabba* (1990), *Kafrun / Kafrun* (1991, 104', 35mm).

LAHOUD, ROMEO. Lebanese filmmaker. Feature film: *The Queen of Love / La reine de l'amour / Malikat al-hub* (1972, 35mm).

Lebanon Film Collective. In July 2006 a number of Lebanese filmmakers attending the Biennale des Cinémas Arabes in Paris were prevented from returning home by the outbreak of war. Their angry response resulted in some twenty short videos, thirteen of which were selected for screening by the Dubai International Film Festival under the title *Videos Under Siege.* The filmmakers involved included Akram Zaatari, Khalil Joreige, Joana Hadjithomas, Danielle Arbid, Tina Baz, Michel Kammoun, Samar Mogharbel, Gregory Buchakjian, Sabine El Chamaa, Ghassan Sahhab, Ahmad Ghsein, Rania Stephan, and Elie Yazbek.

LITTIN, MIGUEL.* Chilean director (of Palestinian descent) who directed one Palestinian feature, set in Palestine during and after World War I. Feature film: *The Last Moon / La ultima luna* (2004, 105', 35mm).

Lotfi, Lotfi. Syrian filmmaker. He worked in Syrian television from 1965 and made a number of documentaries: *Sad Melody / Triste mélodie / al-Lah'n-il h'azin* (1975), *The Child and the Sun / Le soleil et l'enfant, The Persian Hill / La colline des Perses, The Alley of Suffering / La ruelle des souffrances, In the Akba Prison / Dans la prison d'Akba, Souk Sarouja* (1989, 40').

Louis, Sarmad. Lebanese filmmaker. Born in 1972 in Lebanon, he studied filmmaking at IESAV and, simultaneously, photography in Beirut. He has worked as director of photography on a number of films of all kinds. He now teaches at IESAV. Short films: *Virtual Images / Images virtuelles* (1995), a series of commercials for a publicity campaign, *Baladi, baladati, baladyati* (1998), *Success Story* (1999), *The Blue Line / La ligne bleue* (2001), *The Purple Umbrella / Le parapluie mauve* (2004, 11', DV Cam).

Lutfi, Nabiha. Palestinian filmmaker. She was affiliated with the PLO in Beirut and made her film in the refugee camps in Lebanon. Documentary: *Because the Roots Will Not Die / Parce que les racines ne mourront pas / L'an al-judhur lan tamut* (1977).

Maakaron, Myrna. Lebanese filmmaker. Born in 1974, she has lived in Hamburg since 2002. She studied filmmaking at the Academy of Fine Arts in Beirut and drama at the Sorbonne in Paris. She has worked as an actress on stage since the age of 15 and has appeared in a number of Lebanese films: *Once upon a Time Beirut, The Civilised,* and *The Kite,* for example. Short films: *A Meeting / Une rencontre* (1995, 6', 16mm), *A Story for Adults / Conte d'adulte* (1997, 14', Beta SP), *Confusion* (1997, 10', Beta SP), *Little Sparrow / Kleiner Spatz* (2001, 5', Mini DV), *28* (2003, 1', Mini DV), and the documentary *BerlinBeirut* (2003, 23', Beta SP).

MAALOUF, YOUSSEF.* Egyptian director who followed a decade of Egyptian features with a number of Lebanese films, Lebanese-Syrian co-productions, and Syrian films. Those from 1964 to 1967 are Lebanese-Syrian co-productions starring the Syrian comic duo of Doured Lahham (later to direct Syrian films himself) and Nouhad Kalahi. Feature films: *The Broken Wings / Les ailes brisées / al-Ajniha al-mutakassira* (1962, 93', 35mm), *Abou Selim, Messenger of Love / Abou Sélim émissaire d'amour* (1963, 35mm), *The Pearl Necklace / Le collier de perles / Akd al-loulou* (1964, 35mm), *Meeting at Palmyra / Rencontre à Palmyre / Lika' fi tadmor* (1965, 35mm), *The Millionnaire / Le millionaire* (1965, 35mm), *I Am Antar / Je suis Antar / Ana Antar* (1967, 35mm), *The Outlaws / Les hors-la-loi* (1967, 35mm, in Syria). *One Plus One / 1 + 1* (1971, 35mm, in Syria), *Journey of Love / Voyage d'amour* (1972, 35mm, in Syria), *Love's Subterfuges / Les subterfuges d'amour* (1972, 35mm, in Syria).

MAASRI, MOUNIR. Lebanese filmmaker and actor. Feature film: *Fate / Le destin / al Kadar* (1972).

Madanat, Adnan. Jordanian filmmaker. He co-scripted Najdat Ismaïl Anzour's Jordanian feature, *Oriental Story* (1991). Short films: *A Report from Tel al-Za'tar / Khabaron min Tel al-Za'tar* (1976), *Palestinian Visions / Visions palestiniennes / Ro'a filastiniyyah* (1977).

Madi, Sandra. Jordanian filmmaker. Short documentary film: *Full Bloom / Qamar 14* (2006, 46', Beta SP).

Madian, Hany. Emirati filmmaker. He studied at the American University of Sharjah. Short films: *Unsubscribe Me* (with Nadeem A. Saleh, 2007, 1', Mini DV), *Epitaph* (with Raz, 2007, 5', Mini DV).

Madvo, Jacques. Lebanese filmmaker. Documentary: *Scattered by the Wind / Dispersés par le vent / Moubaatharoun fil hawa* (1970, 18').

Mahanna, Seoud. Palestinian filmmaker. Short documentary film: *Said / Sa'id* (2001, 11', Beta SP).

Mahmood, Mohamed Noori. Emirati filmmaker, Short documentary film: *Committees of Reconciliation* (2002, 20', Mini DV).

Mahmood, Talal. Emirati filmmaker. Born in Sharjah, where he worked as a writer and actor in theatre and film. Short films: *Exist* (2005, 7', Mini DV), *Summer Vacation* (2006, 17', Mini DV), *25 Cents* (2006, 10', DV Cam), *Rayhaan* (2008, 11', Mini DV).

Mahmoud, Catriona. Emirati filmmaker. Short fictional film: *Highschool Terror* (2007, 7', DVD).

Mahmoud, Khaled. Emirati filmmaker. Short fictional film: *Bent Alnokhatha* (2008, 17').

Makboul, Lina. Palestinian filmmaker. Based in Sweden. Documentary: *Leila Khaled: Hijacker* (2005, Jordan, 58').

MALAS, MOHAMED. Syrian filmmaker. Born in 1945 in Koneitra, he studied filmmaking at VGIK in Moscow. While in Moscow he shot three short films: *The Dream of a Small City / Hulm madinah saghira* (1972), *The Seventh Day / al-Youm as-sabe'eh* (1973), and his graduation film, *Everybody Is In His Place and Everything Is Under Control / Kullon fi makanihi wa koll shay' ala ma yuram sayyed*

al-dhabit (1974). After his return to Syria, he worked for Syrian television and also made further short films and documentaries: *Quneitra 74 / al-Konaytra 74* (1974, 20'), *Memory / La mémoire / al-Zakira* (1977, 25', 16mm) *Euphrates / Euphrate / Furât* (1975), *The Dream / Le songe / al-Manam* (1987, 45', 16mm), *On the Sand, Under the Sun / Taahta al-rami, fawqa al-shams* (with Hala Yakoub, 1998, 36', Beta SP), *Sabri Mudallal, Magrams for Pleasure / Sabri Mudallal, le semeur de voix* (1998, 52', Beta SP). He has won the top prize, the Tanit d'or, at the JCC in Tunis twice, in 1984 (*City Dreams*) and in 1992 (*The Night*). His first feature was co-scripted with Samir Zikra and his second with Oussama Mohammad. On video, he directed, with Omar Amiralay and Oussama Mohammad, two documentary portraits, *Shadows and Light / Nouron wa thilal* (1995, 52', Beta SP) about veteran filmmaker Nazih Shahbandar, and *Fateh al-Moudarress* (1995, 52', Beta SP). He has also published a novel, *Publicity for a City / Publicité pour une ville / I'alânat al madina*, a number of articles, scripts, and film diaries. Feature films: *City Dreams / Les rêves de la ville / Ahlam al-Madina* (1984, 120', 35mm), *The Night / La nuit / al-Layl* (1992, 115', 35mm), *Passion / Bab el-maqam* (2005, 98', 35mm).

Mamdouh, Mohammed. Emirati filmmaker. Born in Egypt but raised in the UAE, he studied at the American University of Sharjah. Short films: *Rise and Fall* (2006, 14', Mini DV), *An Emirati Dilemma* (2007, 7', Mini DV), *Hit and Run* (2007, 8', DVD), *The Fallen* (2008, 13', HDV).

Manea, Ali. Emirati filmmaker. Short animated film: *The Cat and the Smoke* (2008, 6', DVD).

Mansour, Aseel. Jordanian filmmaker and member of the Amman Filmmakers Cooperative. Born in 1977 in Baghdad, of Palestinian origin, he moved to Jordan in 1991. He later studied engineering at the University of Jordan and works as an IT consultant in Dubai. Short films—one a documentary: *Nightmares* *of Reality* (with Razan Khatib, 2003, 5', DV Cam), and three short fictional films: *Alert Guns* (2004, 11', Mini DV), *Little Feet* (2006, 8', Mini DV), *Pummelo* (with Yahya Abdullah, 2008, 29', DigiBeta).

Mansour, Carol. Lebanese filmmaker. Born in 1961 in Beirut, she worked for 10 years as editor, director, and producer in Lebanese television before founding her own media production company, Forward Productions. Documentaries: *100% Asphalt / 100% asphalte* (2002, 26', Beta SP), *Maid in Lebanon* (2005, 25', DV Cam), *A Summer Not to Forget* (2007, 27').

Mara'ana, Erbisam. Palestinian filmmaker. Documentary: *Paradise Lost* (2003, 56').

Marcos, Norma. Palestinian filmmaker. Born in 1951 in Nazareth, she has lived in Paris since 1977. She worked as assistant on a number of productions, co-directing a documentary *Bethlehem Under Surveillance / Bethléem sous surveillance* (1990) for Canal Plus. She has also worked as a film critic. Documentary films: *Veiled Hope / L'espoir voilé / al-'Amal al-ghamid* (1994, 55', 16mm), *Land Development* (1999, 15', video), *Waiting for Ben Gurion / En attendant Ben Gourion* (2006, 30', video).

Marie, Yasmine. Emirati filmmaker, Of Egyptian origin, but brought up in Dubai, she studied at the American University of Sharjah. Short fictional film: *5:08* (2006, 3', Mini DV).

MASHARAWI, RASHID. Palestinian filmmaker. Born in 1962, in the Shatila refugee camp in Gaza, he moved to Tel Aviv at the age of 12 to help support his family by taking on a succession of menial jobs. He began work in film at 18 and made his first shorts, *Partners* (1981), *Travel Document / Passeport / Jawaz dafar* (1986, 20'), and *The Shelter / L'abri / al-Malja'* (1989). He followed these with several documentaries: *Long Days in Gaza / Longues journées à Gaza / Lyaam tsawila fi Gaza* (1991, 30'), *House, Houses / Une maison, des maisons / Dar wa dûr* (1991, 52'), *The Magi-*

cian a.k.a. *Enchanting / Le magicien / as-Sahr* (1992). In 1993, he moved to the Netherlands for 3 years, returning to Ramallah to found a film production center there in 1996. Further documentaries: *Waiting / L'attente / Enewar* (1994, 90'), *Rebab* (1997, 20', video), *Stress / Tension / Tawattur* (1998, 26', video), *Against the Walls / Khalaf al-aswar* (1999), *The Land of Palestine / Filastin, ard al-miy'ad* (1999), *Out of Focus / Ghabash* (2000), *Upside Down / Makloubé / Maqluba* (2000, 6', Beta SP), *Live From Palestine / En direct de Palestine / Hona sawto filistin* (2001, 53', Beta SP), *Hummus for the Festival / Hummus al-eid* (2003, 12'), *Arafat, My Brother / Arafat, mon frère* (2005, 52', video), *Meters Away* (2005). He won the prize for first feature at the second Biennale des Cinémas Arabes in Paris in 1994. Feature films: *Curfew / Couvre-feu / Hatta isaar akhar* (1993, 75', 35mm), *Haifa / Haïfa / 'Haifa* (1996, 75', 35mm), *Season of Love / La saison de l'amour / Mawsim hubb* (2001), *A Ticket to Jerusalem / Un ticket pour Jérusalem / Tathkararaton ila al-Quds* (2002, 85', 35mm), *Waiting / Attente / Intizar* (2006, 90', 35mm), *Laila's Birthday / L'anniversaire de Laila / Eid milad Laila* (2008, 71', 35mm).

Mashareqa, Tayseer. Palestinian filmmaker. Short film: *Mariam's Dog / Kalb Maryam* (with George Khleifi, 2004).

Mashi, Mubarack. Emirati filmmaker. He studied at the Higher College of Technogy, Abu Dhabi Men's College. Sahort film: *The Mistake* (2007, 41').

MASRI, MAÏ. Palestinian filmmaker. Wife of the Lebanese documentarist Jean Chamoun. Born in 1959 in Amman in Jordan, she studied in the film department of San Francisco University. She has made a series of films with Jean Chamoun mostly situated in Lebanon: *Under the Debris / Sous les décombres / Tahatal ankad* (1983, 40', 16mm), *Wild Flowers: Women of South Lebanon / Fleurs d'ajonc: Femmes du Sud du Liban / Zahrat al-qandal* (1986, 71', 16mm), *War Generation—Beirut / Beyrouth, génération de la guerre / Jil al-harb* (1988, 50', 16mm), *Children of Fire / Les* *enfants du feu / Atfâl jabal al nâr* (1990, 50', 16mm), *Suspended Dreams / Rêves suspendus / Ahlam mu'allaqa* (1992, 50', 16mm), *Frontiers of Dreams and Fears / Frontières du rêve et de la peur / Ahlam al-manfa* (2001, 56', video), *Land of Women / Terre de femmes* (2004). Solo, she has made *Hanan Ashwari, a Woman of Her Time / Hana Ashwari: femme de son époque / Hanan Ashrawi . . . 'Imra'a fi zaman al-Tahaddi* (1995, 50', Beta SP), *Children of Shatila / Les enfants de Chatila / Atfl Shatila* (1998, 47', Beta SP), *Dreams of Exile / Rêves d'exil* (2001), *The Magic Lantern / La lanterne magique* (2004), *Comedy in the Line of Fire / Sourire en flammes* (2006), *Reviving Memory / La mémoire renaissante* (2006). Feature-length documentaries: *Beirut: Truth, Lies and Videos / Chroniques de Beyrouth: vérités, mensonges et videos* (2006, 76', DV Cam), *33 Days / 33 jours / 33 yaoum* (2007, 70', Beta SP).

Massad, Mahmoud. Jordanian filmmaker. Born in 1959 in Zarqa, to exiled Palestinian parents, he studied art and cinema at Yarmouk University in Jordan and travelled to Germany and the Netherlands. From 1988 he lived in Europe: Romania, Italy, Germany, and, from 1995, in the Netherlands. He returned to Jordan in 2003. Short films: *Human Landscape* (1998), *Block B / Le bloc B* (1998), *The Mercator Carter* (1999), *Hassan the Smart / Shater Hassan* (2001, 40', Beta SP), *Once upon a Time in the Middle East* (2004, 3', DV Cam). Feature-length documentary: *Recycle / Recyclage / Ea'adat khalk* (2007, 80', HDV transferred to 35mm).

MATALQA, AMIN. Jordanian filmmaker. Born in 1976 in Amman, he emigrated to the United States (where he still lives) at the age of 13. He lived in Columbus, Ohio, and studied at Ohio State University before moving to Los Angeles, where he made some twenty-five short films and studied at the American Film Institute. Feature film: *Captain Abu Raed / Le capitaine Abu Raed* (2007, 95', 35mm).

Matar, Mohammed. Emirati filmmaker. Short film: *Equality* (2006, 2', video).

Matloub, Reem. Emirati filmmaker. Grew up in Baghdad and studied at the American University of Sharjah. Short film: *A Blur of Perfection* (2006, 6', Mini DV).

MER-KHAMIS, JULIANO. Palestinian filmmaker. His first documentary is a study of the children who studied at the drama school run by his mother, the activist Arna Mer-Khamis. Feature-length documentary: *Arna's Children / Les enfants d'Arna / Atfal Arna* (2004, 84', Beta SP).

Mesalatie, Bassam. Emirati filmmaker. Studied at the University of Al-Ain, UAE. Short films: *Zionism Campaign* (with Samia al-Ghaferi, 2006, 22', HD), *For the Sake of Democracy* (with Samia al-Ghaferi, 2007, 5', HD), *For Release* (with Samia al-Ghaferi, 2007, 5', HD), *Small Terrorists* (with Samia al-Ghaferi, 2007, 7', HD).

Mesalatie, Osama. Emirati filmmaker. He studied at the University of Aleppo, Syria, and also took course in theatre directing and animation. He has also scripted several short films. Short films: *All Set to Go* (2007, 4', DVD), *Bush Here!* (2008, 5', DV Cam).

Meshmeshy, Ahmed. Emirati filmmaker. He studied at the American University of Sharjah. Short film: *Wide Awake* (2006, 6', Mini DV).

METNI, JAWAD. Lebanese filmmaker. Feature-length documentary: *Remnants of a War / Les restes d'une guerre* (2009, 77').

Midani, Hind. Syrian filmmaker. She studied filmmaking in Moscow and also made téléfilms for Syrian and Gulf television. Short documentary film: *A Distant Look / Regard à distance* (1986, 45').

Miqdadi, Hadeel. Emirati filmmaker. Born in 1986 in Abu Dhabi, of Palestinian origins. Studied at the American University of Sharjah. Short fictional film: *The Unexpected* (2006, 5', Mini DV).

Mitri, Reine. Lebanese filmmaker. Born in 1970 in Lebanon, she initially studied business management, but has since worked in documentary production and cinéclub organization. She studied at FEMIS in Paris, where she made her first documentary. Short films: *About the Pear / À propos de la poire* (2001), *Querido* (2003), *The Sound of Footsteps on the Pavement* (2004, 52', Mini DV).

MOBARAK, ABDEL HADI. Iraqi filmmaker. Feature film: *The Bride of the Euphrates / La mariée de l'Euphrate / Aros al-forat* (1961, 35mm).

Mogharbei, Samar. Lebanese filmmaker. Contributed *The War on Lebanon in the Eyes of the Kids* (3') to the collective project *Videos Under Siege* (DIFF 2008, 39', video).

Mohamed, Ahmed Fat'h al-Bab. Emirati filmmaker. Short films: *To Whom It May Concern* (2001, 18', Beta SP), *Marriage Fund* (2003, 14', Beta SP).

Mohamed, Fatima Saif. Emirati filmmaker. She studied at Abu Dhabi Women's College. Short film: *Rumour* (2005, 3', Mini DV).

MOHAMED, HATEM. Syrian filmmaker. Feature film: *The Long Night / La longue nuit* (2009).

Mohamed, Salah Eddine. Syrian filmmaker. He is also an architect and art critic. He has made a number of documentaries about Syrian art and culture, including the two-part *The Horizon of Civilizations / L'horizon de civilisations* (1992, 48' + 60').

MOHAMMAD, OUSSAMA. Syrian filmmaker. Born in 1954 at Lattakieh, he graduated from VGIK, the Moscow film school, in 1979. His graduation film was *Step by Step / Khutwa Khutwa* (1978, 22'). He made a number of short films and documentaries in Syria: *Today and Every Day / Aujourd'hui et tous les jours / al-Yawn wa kullu yawm* (1981 20'), *The Violets Are Dead / Les violettes sont mortes* (1982). He co-directed, with Mohamed Ma-

las and Omar Amiralay, two video portraits: *Shadows and Light / Nouron wa thilal* (1995, 52', Beta SP), on the pioneer filmmaker Nazir Shahbandar, and *Fateh al-Moudarress* (1995, 52', Beta SP). He also co-scripted Malas's *The Night*. Feature films: *Stars in Broad Daylight / Étoiles du jour / Nujum al-nahar* (1988, 105', 35mm), *The Cabinet of Life* a.k.a. *Peep Show / Le coffre de la vie* a.k.a. *Sacrifices / Sanduq al-dunia* (2001, 113', 35mm).

Mohammed, Fatima. Emirati filmmaker. Studied media production at the Dubai Woman's College and directed several television programes. She currently works for Dubai TV. Short films: *Dubai Women's Society* (2001, 5', DigiBeta), *Green Windows* (2001, 8', DigiBeta), *Al-Hazar El-Shadee* (2002, 60', Beta).

Mohammed, Hala. Syrian filmmaker. Born in Lattakiya, she is also a poet and journalist. She studied filmmaking at the Université de Paris VIII and has worked for the Hot Spot program of Al Jazeera. Documentaries: *Divorce and Marriage / Divorce et mariage, For a Little Piece of Cake / Pour un petit morceau de gâteau* (2005, 52', Beta SP).

Mohammed, Jassem. Emirati filmmaker. Short film: *Waste Management in Dubai* (2006, 9', DV Cam).

Mohammed, Mohammed Ibrahim. Bahraini filmmaker. Short film: *Burning Flowers* (2009, 23', HD Cam).

Mohammed, Salwa. Emirati filmmaker of Tunisian origin. Short film: *Always Happen in 16.9* (with Amina Ataya, 2007, 11', Mini DV, in Egypt).

Mohammed, Yasmin. Emirati filmmaker. She studied multimedia design. Short films: *Sever* (2005, 41', Mini DV), *Room 21* (2005, 6', Mini DV).

Mohd, Reem. Emirati filmmaker. She studied at the American University of Sharjah. Short experimental film: *Confiscated Footage* (with Mina Eltaieb, 2004, 10', Mini DV).

Moon, Farha. Emirati filmmaker. Short films: *Revolutionary Fools* (2007, 4', Mini DV), *Anti-Gendercide* (with Naima Abdelwahed, 2007, 1', Mini DV).

MORSI, AHMED KAMEL.* Egyptian filmmaker responsible for one of the first Iraqi feature films: *Leila in Iraq / Layla en Irak / Layla fi al Irak* (1948).

Mostafa, Ali F. Emirati filmmaker. He grew up in Dubai, with an English mother and UAE father, and studied from 2003 to 2005 at the London Film School, where he made six short films. Since his return, he has worked on commercials. Short films in UAE: *Scarred* (2002, Mini DV), *Under the Sun / Taht el Shams* (2005, 23', 16mm).

MOSTAFA, NIAZI.* Egyptian filmmaker responsible for one of the first Iraqi feature films: *Son of the East / Le fils de l'Orient / Ibn al-Chark* (1945).

Mouarkech, Pierre. Lebanese filmmaker. Short fictional film: *A Moonfish in the Waters of Lebanon / Un poisson lune dans les eaux du Liban* (2000, 12').

MOUAWAD, WAJDI. Lebanese filmmaker. He was born in 1968 in Beirut, where he spent his childhood. He left Lebanon for France during his adolescence and then moved to Quebec, where he now lives. He trained at the national theatre school of Canada, and he has worked as an actor and stage director. Feature film: *Littoral* (2004, 90', 35mm).

Mouchechawi, Ramez. Syrian filmmaker. Documentary: *The Waterpumps of Hama / Les norias de Hama* (1990, 40').

Mroue, Rabih. Lebanese filmmaker. Short fictional film: *Side A / Side B / Face A / Face B* (2002, 9').

Mrwesh, Saud. Emirati filmmaker. Short fictional film: *Roots and Seeds* (2006, 9', Mini DV).

Muadhdhen, Marwan. Syrian filmmaker. He made a documentary on Palestine. Documentary: *Joyous Celebrations / Joyeuse fête / Id sa'id* (1970).

MUHAMMAD, HASHIM. Kuwaiti filmmaker. Born in 1945, he worked in Kuwaiti television from 1973 and subsequently for the BBC. He made a number of documentaries, including *The Arts / Les arts / al-Funûn* (1974). Feature film: *The Silence / Le silence / al-Samt* (1979).

MUSALLAM, ISIDORE. Palestinian filmmaker. Born in Haifa, he studied at York University in Toronto, where he now lives. His first four features were made in Canada. Short films: *Foreign Nights / Layali al-ghurba* (1989), *Nothing to Lose / Rien à perdre* (1994), *Heaven Before I Die / al-Jinnaqalb mawti* (1997), *Adam and Eve / Adam et Eve / Adam wa Hawwa* (2003), *A Simple Story* (2008, animation, 32', 35mm). Feature film: *Today and Tomorrow / Aujourd'hui et demain / Keif al-hal* (2005, 35mm, in Saudi Arabia).

Musleh, Hanna. Palestinian filmmaker. Born in Beit Jala, Palestine. Studied at univerities in Leningrad and Manchester. Returned to teach at Bethlehem University in 1980. Short films: *Sahar's Wedding / La noce de Sahar / Urs Sahar* (1992, 42'), *Army of God / L'armée de Dieu / Jund allah* (1995, 54'), *I'm a Little Angel / Je suis un petit ange / Ana malik saqir* (2000, 40', Beta SP), *Living with Dignity / Vivre dignement / al-Aysh bi karama* (2002, 52', Beta SP), *Tear of Peace* (2003, 34'), *In the Spider's Web / Fi shibak al-'ankabut* (2005, 40'), *Memory of the Cactus: A Story of Three Palestinian Villages / Thakirat al-sabbar: Hikayat thalath qura Falasteenia* (2008, 42', DV Cam).

Mustafa, Ahmad. Emirati filmmaker. He studied at the American University of Sharjah. Short film: *The Pragmatist* (2005, 7', DV Cam).

Muthaffar, Enas. Palestinian filmmaker. Born in 1977 in Jerusalem, she studied at the Cairo Higher Film Institute and is based in London, where she studied at Goldsmith's

College. Short films: *Vision / Ru'ya* (1998), *Together We Were Raised / Sawa rben* (1999, 12', 35mm), *Oh, Grandmother / Ah ya sitty* (1999, 5', Beta SP), *The Path of Sidi Omar / La route de Sidi Omar / Sabil Sidi Omar* (2000, 14', 35mm), *For the Archives Only / Pour les archives seulement* (2001, 30', video), *East to West / De l'est à l'ouest* (2005). Contributed *A World Apart within 15 Minutes* (3' 12") to the collective film Summer 2006, Palestine (2006, 35', Beta SP).

Muwaddin, Mohamed. Syrian filmmaker. Alongside Mohamed Shahin and Nabil al-Maleh, he contributed one of three episodes, *Childbirth / L'accouchement / al-Makhad*, to the first feature produced by the National Organisation for Cinema: *Men Under the Sun / Des hommes sous le soleil / al-Sayyid al-taqaddumi* (1970, 108', 35mm).

MYASSAR, RIDA. Syrian-born Lebanese filmmaker. Many of his films were Lebanese-Syrian co-productions, and some made in Syria. Feature films: *The Rock of Love / Le rocher de l'amour / Sakhar al-hub* (1959, 35mm), *Loved by All / Aimée de tous / Habitat al-kol* (1964, 35mm), *Bitter Honey / Le miel amer / al-Assal al-morr* (1965, 35mm), *Body on Fire / Le corps en feu / Lahib al-jassad* (1965, 35mm), *Sultana / Sultana* (1966, 35mm), *The Arab Falcon / Le faucon des arabes / Sakr al-arab* (1966, 35mm), *The Tramps / Les vagabonds / al-Charidan* (1966, 35mm), *Do Not Touch My Wife / Ne touche pas à ma femme / Idak an mrati* (1967, 35mm), *The Palestinian in Revolt / Le palestinien révolté / al-Filastini al-thaer* (1969, 35mm), *Girls to Love / Des filles à aimer / Banat lil hob* (1972, 35mm), *The Shrews / Chipies / Banat akker zamane* (1972, 35mm), *The Gypsy in Love / La gitane amoureuse / al-Ghajaria al-achika* (1972, 35mm), *Fire Woman / Femme de feu / Imraa min nar* (1973, 35mm), *A Forced Marriage / Un mariage forcé* (1973, 35mm) *in Syria*, *Valuable Game / Gibier de valeur / al-Istiyad al-kabir* (1974, 35mm), *Voyage of Suffering / Voyage des souffrances* (1974, 35mm) *in Syria*, *A Nightingale in Lebanon / Un rossignol du Liban / Boulbol min Loubnan* (1982, 35mm), *Mothers' Suffering / La souffrance des mères / Azab al-oumahat* (1982,

35mm), *The South in Revolt / Le sud révolté* a.k.a. *Le sud insurgé / al-Janoub al-thaer* (1984, 35mm).

Naassani, Nasser. Syrian filmmaker. Short animated film: *Him and Her / Elle et lui* (1995, 4', 35mm).

Nabhan, Mohammed. Emirati filmmaker. Born in 1982 in Sharjah, of Palestinian origin, he studied at the American University of Sharjah. Short film: *Love vs. Death* (2004, 7', Mini DV).

Nabulsi, Yasmine Fawaz. Emirati filmmaker. Born in 1985 in Amman, Jordan, but raise in the UAE. She studied at the American University of Sharjah. Short fictional film: *"Perfect"* (2004, 4', Mini DV).

Naccache, Tina. Lebanese filmmaker. Short film: *Who Hangs the Laundry? Washing, War and Electricity in Beirut* (with Icelander Hrafnhildur Gunnarsdottir, 2002, 20', Beta SP).

Nacer, Jamil. Yemeni filmmaker. Documentary: *The New Yemen / Le nouveau Yémen* (1975).

NADDA, RUBA. Syrian filmmaker. Based in Canada. She made eleven internationally screened short fictional films in 1997–1999: *Interstate Love Story* (1997, 4', 16mm), *Wet Heat Drifts through the Afternoon* (1997, 8', 16mm), *Do Nothing* (1997, 4' 16mm), *So Far Gone* (1998, 1', 16mm), *The Wind Blows towards Me Particularly* (1998, 5' 16mm), *Damascus Nights* (1998, 17', 16mm), *Slut* (1999, 5', 16mm), *Laila* (1999, 5', 16mm), *I Would Suffer Cold Hands for You* (1999, 3', 16mm), *Blue Turning Grey Over You* (1999, 5', 16mm), *Black September* (1999, 5', 16mm). Other short film: *Aadan* (2004, 8', 35mm). Feature film (tracing the tensions of immigrant life in exile): *Sabah* (2004, 90', 35mm).

NAGUIB, ALBERT. Egyptian filmmaker who directed one Lebanese feature film: *Hotel of Dreams / Hôtel des rêves / Foundok al-ahlam* (1966, 35mm).

Nahas, Walid. Lebanese filmmaker. Short film: *Marriages and Childhood in Lebanon / Mariages et enfance au Liban* (2004, 24', Super8).

Naim, Oscar. Lebanese filmmaker. Documentary: *Grand Theater: A Tale of Beirut* (2000, 28', 16mm).

Najeeb, Mohamed. Emirati filmmaker. Fictional film: *A Place at Heart* (1996, 86', Beta SP).

NAJJAR, NAJWA. Palestinian filmmaker. Born in 1965 in Washington, D.C., to Palestinian parents, she studied politics and economics before taking training in filmmaking. She lives currently in Jerusalem. Short films: *Women in Development* (1995, 2 x 12', Beta SP), *Jerusalem: Dealmaker or Dealbreaker* (1995, 30', Beta SP), *Sesame Street* (1997, video clips), *Naim and Wadee'a / Naim et Wadee'a / Naim wa Wadee'a* (1999, 20', Beta SP), *A Boy Called Mohamed / Un garçon nommé Mohamed / Walad ismuhu Muhammad* (2001, 10', video), *Jewel of Oblivion* a.k.a. *Quintessence of Oblivion / Quintessence de l'oubli / Jawharat al-silwan* (2001, 45', Beta SP), *They Came from the East / Ils sont venus de l'est* (2004, 3'), *Yasmine's Song / La chanson de Yasmine / Yasmine tughani* (2006, 18', Beta SP). She also contributed one episode to the collectively made video documentary *One More Time (Five Stories about Human Rights in Palestine / Une fois encore (cinq histoires sur les droits de l'homme en Palestine)* (with Nada al-Yassir, Tawfik Abu Wael, Abdel Salam Shehada, Ismaïl Habash, 2002, 57', Beta SP). Feature film: *Pomegranates and Myrrh / La grenade et la myrrhe / Al-Mor wa al-rumman* (2008, 95', 35mm, in Lebanon).

Najjar, Razi. Palestinian filmmaker. Short film: *Pickled!* (2008, 16'). Contributed *To the Arabs of Haifa, a Special Message . . .* (1' 17") to the collective film *Summer 2006, Palestine* (2006, 35', Beta SP).

Najmi, Said. Jordanian filmmaker. Short fictional film: *The Other Side of My Neighbourhood* (2007, 12').

NAKKAS, OLGA. Lebanese filmmaker. Born in 1953 in Mersine (Turkey), she moved to Beirut at the age of 5 with her Turkish mother and Lebanese father. She took a master's degree in linguistics in the United States and a doctorate in English and Arabic literature in Paris. She then worked as a journalist and producer-director in London, Paris, and Beirut. Documentaries: *Saida, Portrait of a City / Saida, portrait d'une ville* (1986, 19', 35mm), *Ashoura / 'Ashura* (co-dir., 1987, 27', 35mm), *Halima* (2000, 40', 35mm). Feature-length documentary: *Lebanon: Bits and Pieces / Le Liban, fait de pièces et de morceaux* a.k.a. *Liban bout à bout / Lubnan min taraf ila taraf akhar* (1994, 60', Beta SP).

Naous, Nadine. Palestinian filmmaker. Documentary: *Everone His Own Palestine / Chacun sa Palestine* (with Léna Rouxel, 2006, 52', video).

Naser, Yaser. Bahraini filmmaker. Film and television actor and director. Short film: *The Way to Delmon* (2006, 16', Mini DV).

Nashashibi, Rosalind. Palestinian filmmaker. Born in 1973 in the United Kingdom to Irish and Palestinian parents. She is an award-winning experimental filmmaker. Short films: *The State of Things* (2000, 16mm), *Midwest* (2001, 16mm), *Humanjora* (2001), *District Post Office / Dahyat al-barid* (2002, 16mm), *Blood and Fire* (2003, 6', video), *Hreash House, Eyeballing* (2005).

Nasir, Tariq. Jordanian filmmaker. Based in the United States. Documentary: *Belonging* (2006, 68').

NASRI, SAMIR.* Egyptian-born filmmaker who directed two Lebanese 1960s feature films. Born in 1937 in Egypt, he worked first as a journalist. He worked as assistant to Youssef Chahine on several Egyptian features, including *A Man in My Life* (1961) and *Dawn of a New Day* (1964), as well as *The Seller of Rings* (1965), which was a Lebanese production. He moved to Beirut in the 1960s, where he worked for a time as film critic for two newspapers, before turning to film direction. He made a short documentary about the sufferings of the Southern Lebanese, *The South in the Claws of the Enemy / Le sud entre les griffes de l'ennemi / al-Janoub fi barâthen al-a'ada* (1970, 15'). He died in 1990. Feature films: *Youth in the Sun / Jeunesse au soleil / Chabab tahtal cham* (1966), *The Victory of the Vanquished / La victoire du vaincu / Intissar al-mounhazem* (1966).

NASSAR, ALI. Palestinian filmmaker. Born in 1954 in the village of Arrabeh in Galilee, he developed a passion for film at an early age. He received a scholarship to study at VGIK, the Moscow film school, where he graduated in 1981. He later worked as a journalist and photographer and directed an Arab theatre company in Haifa. Documentaries: *The City on the Coast / La ville sur la côte / Hilat madina 'ala al-shati'* (1985), *The Source of the Gift / La source intarissable / Naha'a alata al-da'im* (1992, 55', 16mm). Feature films: *The Wet Nurse / La nourrice / al-Mardha'ah* (1993), *The Milky Way / La voie lactée / Dar al-tabbanat* (1997, 105', 35mm), *In the Ninth Month / Au neuvième mois / Bahodesh hatshi'i* (2002, 106', 35mm).

NASSER, GEORGES. Lebanese filmmaker. Born in 1927 in Tripoli, he began by studying architecture at the University of Chicago but then turned to filmmaking, completing his diploma at UCLA. He continued making documentaries throughout his feature career: *IPC in Tripol* (1955), *Water Skiing Championship in Beirut / Championnat de ski nautique à Beyrouth* (1956), *Work in Progress* (1958), *This Ancient City of Byblos / Cette ancienne cité, Byblos* (1962), *Taming of the Iron* (1963), *Let the She-Goat Graze in Peace / Pour que la chèvre paisse en paix* (1968, Anti-Tank Attack / Assault anti-char* (1968), *Son, I am Proud / Mons fils, je suis fier / Waladi, anâ fakhûrun* (1968), *The Military School / L'école militaire* (1969), *Watch from the Sky / Vigie du ciel* (1970), *Handicraft in Lebanon / L'artisanat en Liban / Al-hiraf al-lubnâniya* (1972), *Holiday in Lebanon / Vacances en Liban* (1973). His

debut feature film was the first Lebanese film to be shown at Cannes (in 1957), but achieved little success at home. As a result, Nasser shot his second feature in French hoping, in vain, to attract an elite audience. His third and final film was a Syrian co-production. Feature films: *Towards the Unknown / Vers l'inconnu / Ila ayn* (1958, 90', 35mm), *The Little Stranger / Le petit étranger* (1961, 35mm), *A Man Is Needed / On demande un homme / Matlûb rajulun wahid* (1975, 35mm).

Nasser, Haifa. Emirati filmmaker. She studied at Dubai Women's College. Short film: *Color* (2006, 2', Mini DV).

Naysi, Majid. Emirati filmmaker. Born in Iran, but living in the UAE. Short documentary film: *My Friend, Mr. Bull* (2005, 21', Mini DV).

Nazari, Bahman. Emirati filmmaker. Born in 1977, he has worked in animation. Short animated film: *From Apple to Apple* (2004, 11', video).

Nazzal, Omar. Palestinian filmmaker. Short film: *The Cage* (2004).

Nicolas, Carine. Lebanese filmmaker. Short film: *Malaika* (2001, 16', video).

NIMR, SAMIR. Iraqi filmmaker. He was born in 1942 in Iraq, but most of his films deal with issues relating to Palestine and were made for Palestinian organizations. He began with documentaries before moving on to feature-length works. He subsequently moved to Tunisia, where he continued working as a documentarist. Short films and documentaries: *Zionist Terrorism / Le terrorisme sioniste / al-Irhâb al-subyûnî* (1973, 22', 16mm), *Palestinian Night / Nuit palestinienne / Layla filastîniya* (1973, 16mm), *The Four-Day War / La guerre de quatre jours / Harb al-ayyam al-arba'a* (1973, 35', 16mm), *The New Yemen / Le nouveau Yémen / al-Yeman al-jadid* (1974), *The Winds of Freedom / Les vents de la libération / Riâh al-tahrîr* (1974, 35', 16mm), *Who Is the*

Revolution For? / Pour qui la révolution? / Liman al-thaura? (1974, 20', 16mm), *Kafr Chuba / Kafr Shûba* (1975, 35'). Features: *Victory in His Eyes / La victoire dans ses yeux / Al nasr fi unyünihim* (1976), *The War in Lebanon / La guerre au Liban / Harb Lubnân* (1977, 75', 35mm), *The Children of Palestine / Les enfants de Palestine / Affâl Filasyîn* (1977), *Roots / Racines / al-Judhur* (1984), *Palestine on Fire / La Palestine en feu / Filastin fi al-lahb* (1988).

Noor, Ahmad. Emirati filmmaker. Born in 1984, he studied at the American University of Sharjah. Short films: *His Chance, My Chance, His Chance* (2004, 18', video), *The Steps* (2004, 9, DV Cam).

Noor, Hamdah Hassan. Emirati filmmaker. She studied at Dubai Women's College. Short film: *Predicting the Future* (2005, 2', Mini DV).

Noujaïm, Rym. Lebanese filmmaker. Studied at ALBA. Short fictional film: *Natasha* (2000, 10').

Noureddine, Wael. Lebanese filmmaker. Born in Lebanon, he studied filmmaking in Beirut and worked as a journalist. Short documentaries: *The Man with the Camera / L'homme à la caméra* (2000), *From Beyrouth with Love / Ça sera beau* (2005, 29', Beat SP), *July Trip* (2006, 35', Beta SP).

Numan, Mohamed. Bahraini filmmaker. Short fictional film: *Behind You* (2006, 7').

Obaid, Ahmed Abdulqader. Emirati filmmaker. He studied at Dubai Men's College. Short films: *Dodgy* (2002, 1', DV Cam), *Crashed-Up Cars* (2002, 1', DV Cam).

Odeh, Joud. Emirati filmmaker. He studied at the American University of Sharjah. Short film: *Choose Your Path* (with Kalid Mahmoud Abu Goumazah, 2007, 1', Mini DV).

Odeh, May. Palestinian filmmaker. Short documentary film: *When Walls Speak* (2008, 16'). Contributed *Called Off / Ferkesh* (1' 37") to the collective film *Summer 2006, Palestine* (2006, 35', Beta SP).

Ohisi, Ahmed Farouk. Syrian filmmaker, Documentary: *Petrol in the Battle / La pétrole dans la bataille / al-Bitrûl fi-l harb* (1974).

Omran, Salha. Emirati filmmaker. Studied media at UAE University, then worked as a reporter. Short films: *The Story of Piracy* (2005, 10', Beta SP), *The Prisoner* (2005, 1', DigiBeta), *Birthday* (2007, 6', Mini DV).

Oqabi, Hamid. Yemeni filmmaker. He studied cinema and theatre as well as radio and television (the latter in Baghdad). He worked at the College of Fine Art in Yemen. Short film: *Al-Ritaj* (2006, 34', Mini DV).

Oqaili, Jasim Ali. Saudi filmmaker. Short films: *A Dream: The Life* (2008, 7', Mini DV), *After the Ashes* (2008, 9', Mini DV).

Orsan, Ayman. Syrian filmmaker. Short fictional film: *Behind the Faces / Derrière les visages* (2005, 35').

Oubaïssi, Farouk. Syrian filmmaker. Documentary: *Ebla* (1978, 45').

Ousseimi, Maria. Lebanese filmmaker. Debut documentary: *Lost Childhood / Enfance perdue* (with Lamia Abu Haidar, 1992, 40', 16mm).

PACHACHI, MAYSOON. Iraqi filmmaker. Born in 1947 in Washington, D.C., where her father was a diplomat, she was educated in Iraq, the United States, and the United Kingdom, studying philosophy and film. She settled in the United Kingdom, where she worked in alternative theatre and as a film editor for television. In 2003, with Kassim Abid, she set up an Independent Film & TV College in Baghdad. After a short fictional film, *Strike 36* (1973, 35mm), she began her career as a documentary filmmaker in the late 1980s. Documentaries: *Voices of Gaza / Voix du Gaza* (1989), *Iraqi Women . . . Voices from Exile /*

Les Iraqiennes . . . une voix de l'exil (1993, 38', 35mm), *Smoke* (with Lucia Nogueira, 1996, 5'), *Living with the Past: People and Monuments in Medieval Cairo / Vivre avec le passé* (2001, 56'). Documentary feature films: *Iranian Journey / La femme-chauffeur, une traversée en bus de l'Iran* (1999, 60', video), *Bitter Water / Eau amère* (with Noura Sakkaf, 2003, 76', video), *Return to the Land of Wonders / Retour au pays des merveilles* (2004, 88', Beta SP), *Our Feelings Took the Pictures: Open Shutters Iraq / Nos sentiments ont pris les images: images de l'Irak* (2008, 102', DigiBeta).

Palestinian Filmmakers' Collective. Thirteen filmmakers, all living in Palestine, came together to each contribute a short film (3' or less) to make up a picture of Palestinian society: *Summer 2006, Palestine* (2006, 35', Beta SP). The contributors are: Akram al-Ashqar, Rowan al-Faqih, Amer Shomali, Ahmad Habash, Riyad Deis, Ismaïl Habash, Annemarie Jacir, Liana Bader, Mohanad Yaqubi, Razi Najjar, Naher Awwad.

Partamian, Antoine. Lebanese filmmaker. Studied at ALBA. Short film: *Explosion* (2000, 12').

Pidutti, Jordano. Lebanese pioneer filmmaker. Born in Italy, he arrived in Lebanon at the age of 24. He is the director of two pioneering short films: *The Adventures of Elias Mabrouk / Les aventures d'Elias Mabrouk / Moughamarat Elias Mabrouk* (1929, 90') and *The Adventures of Abou Abeid / Les aventures d'Abou Abeid / Moughamarat Abou Abeid* (1931, 35mm).

Politi, Edna. Palestinian filmmaker. Documentary: *Coming from Abroad: Women Immigrants / Venues d'ailleurs: femmes immigrées* (1983, 27').

Qader, Aseel. Jordanian filmmaker and member of the Amman Filmmakers Cooperative. Short film: *From Across the Oceans with Love* (2006).

Qadh, Tony. Palestinian filmmaker. Documentary: *Stolen Freedom . . . Occupied Palestine / La liberté volée . . . la Palestine occupée / al-Huriyya al-masluba . . . Filastin al-muhtalla* (1990).

Qaed, Abdul Halim Ahmed. Emirati filmmaker. Born in 1974 in Dubai, he studied at the Dubai Men's College and subsequently worked in advertising. Short films (several of them commercials): *A Sony Man Lost* (2000), *Professional Game* (2000), *The Art of Love* (2003, 1', Mini DV), *The Delivery* (2003, 8', Mini DV), *Watch, Listen Then Feel It* (2004, 2', Mini DV), *Cursed* (2004, 12', Mini DV), *One Moment for God* (2004, 1', Min DV), *Mirage* (2005, 20', Mini DV), *Fear* (2006, 14', DV Cam).

Qashoo, Oussama. Palestinian filmmaker. Documentaries: *My Dear Olive Tree* (2004), *Inside Outside* (2005), *No Choice Basis* (2006), *Soy palestino / Ana falastini* (2007, 65', DV Cam).

Qazi, Kristan. Palestinian filmmaker. Documentary: *A Death in Lebanon / Une mort au Liban / al-Mawt fi Lubnan* (1977).

Qumasha, Saif Ben. Emirati filmmaker. Born in 1986, he studied at the Dubai Men's College. Short film: *Brotherhood* (with Ahmed Juma Hassan, 2007, 2', DV Cam).

Quttaineh, Ammar. Jordanian filmmaker and member of the Amman Filmmakers Cooperative. Born in 1976 in Kuwait of Palestinian / Jordanian descent, he lives in Amman. He studied at the Applied Science University, Jordan, and works as a stock broker. Short films: *Power Blues* (2003), *Tough Luck*, (2004, 6', Mini DV), *Overdose* (2005, 14', Mini DV), *Sharar* (with Saleh Kasem and Hazim Bitar, 2006, 17', Mini DV).

Ra'ad, Riad Hani. Syrian filmmaker. He studied filmmaking and made several documentaries, including *Mosaic / Mosaïque* (1990, 21'), some fictional films, such as *The Boots / Les* *bottes*, and a thirty-episode scientific television series called *Scientific Horizons / Horizons scientifiques*.

Ra'ad, Walid. Lebanese filmmaker. Born in 1967 in Chibanieh, he has lived in Lebanon and the United States. He is an independent producer and teaches in the audio-visual department of Hampshire College in New York. Short films: *Up to the South / Vers le Sud-Liban* (with Jayce Salloum, 1993, 49', video), *Missing Lebanese Wars* (1996), *The Dead Weight of Suspended Quarrels / Le poids mort des querelles suspendues* (1999, 17', Beta SP), *Hostage: The Bachar Tapes (English Version) No. 17 & No. 31* (2001, 18', video).

RACHED, MARC ABI. Lebanese filmmaker. Feature film: *Help / Au secours* (2009, 77'.).

Rached, Tahani. Lebanese filmmaker. Based in Canada, Documentaries: *Angry Wireless / La phonie furieuse* (1982, 10', video), *Beirut Failing to Be Dead / Beyrouth à défaut d'être mort* (1983, 57', 16mm), *Hait Nous La Nous La* (1987, 28', video), *Au chic resto pop* (1990, 84', video), *Heart Doctors / Médecins de cœur* (1993, 110', video).

Rafeeq, Nesreen. Jordanian filmmaker and member of the Amman Filmmakers Cooperative. Studied at the Lebanese American University in Lebanon. Short film: *Model Blues* (2005).

RAFLA, HELMI.* Egyptian director of one Syrian feature film: *A Useful Man / Un homme convenable* (1970, 35mm).

Ragheb, Roula. Lebanese filmmaker. Born in 1972, in Beirut, she studied at IESAV in Beirut and at FEMIS in Paris, then worked in advertising. Short fictional film: *Through Them / À travers elles / Abrahunn* (1995, 10', 35mm).

RAHBANI, GHADI. Lebanese filmmaker. He scripted and produced various fictional films and co-directed his sole feature with his brother, Marwan Rahbani. Feature film: *At the End of Summer / À la fin de l'été / Akher as saif* (1980, 35mm).

RAHBANI, MARWAN. Lebanese filmmaker. He scripted and produced various films and co-directed his sole feature with his brother, Ghadi Rahbani. Feature film: *At the End of Summer / À la fin de l'été / Akher as saif* (1980, 35mm).

Raheb, Éliane. Lebanese filmmaker. Born in 1972 in Lebanon, she studied filmmaking at IESAV in Beirut, then worked as an editor and assistant director. She teaches filmmaking and is active in Beirut cultural organizations and the Beirut Film Festival. Short fims and documentaries: *The Crossing / La traversée* (1994), *The Last Screening / La dernière séance / al-Ardh al-akhir* (1995, 11', 16mm), *Encounter / Rencontre / Liqa'* (1996, 28', Beta SP), *So Near, Yet So Far / Si proche si loin / Qarib wa Ba'idi* (2001, 59', video), *Suicide / Intihar* (2003, 25', DV Cam), *I Desperately Need You* (2005, 2', DV Cam), *That's Lebanon / C'est ça le Liban / Haydha Lubnan* (2008, 58', video).

Rahi, Maryam. Emirati filmmaker. Born in 1985 in Dubai, of Iranian descent, she studied at the American University of Sharjah. Short fictional films: *Neglected Sight* (2007, 2', Mini DV), *Stick Notes* (2007, 5', Mini DV), *The Reflection* (2007, 3', Mini DV).

Rahman, Khalil Abdulwahed Abdul. Emirati filmmaker. Studied at Penn State University and Pennsylvania College of Technology. Short experimental and video art films: *Wadi* (2003, 3', DV Cam), *Desert* (2003, 4', DV Cam), *Driving* (2004, 3', DV Cam), *My Way* (2005, 7', Mini DV), *Bicycles* (2006, 5', video).

Ramadan, Wijan Mohammad. Emirati filmmaker. Born in Palestine, she was brought up in Dubai. She studied at the American University of Sharjah. Short fictional films: *Hope* (2004, 13', Mini DV), *Silence* (2004, 12', Mini DV).

Rashdan, Abdulla. Bahraini filmmaker. Short film: *Wooden Life* (2005, 21', Mini DV), *Al-Dawama* (2006, 21', Hi-8).

Rasheed, Hussein Abdul. Emirati filmmaker. Born in 1984 in Kuwait of Egyptian origin, he studied at the American University of Sharjah, Short fictional films: *Mish: Imbossible* (2004, 7', Mini DV), *September 12th* (with Theyab al-Tamimi and Hani Alireza, 2005, 11', Mini DV).

RASHEED, ODAY. Iraqi filmmaker. He made the first feature film to be shot in Iraq after the 2003 war. Short film: *An Entry to the Freedom Memorial / Une entrée au mémorial la Liberté* (1999, 27', 35mm). Feature film: *Underexposure / Sous-exposition / Ghair salih* (2004, 67', 35mm).

RASHID, MUSTAFA. Syrian filmmaker. Feature film: *The Lovers of the Demarcation Line of the Rain / Les amants de la ligne de démarcation de la pluie / Ushaq ala khat al-matar* (1993).

Rassam, Emmanuel. Iraqi filmmaker. Short fictional film on Palestine: *A Song / Une chanson / Ughniya* (1964).

Raz. Emirati filmmaker. Short film: *Epitaph* (with Hany Madian, 2007, 5', Mini DV).

REDA, HASSAN.* Egyptian director of one Syrian feature film: *The Quiet City / La ville tranquille* (1972, 35mm).

REMY, ANTOINE. Lebanese filmmaker. He studied at IDHEC and then at the Sorbonne in Paris. On his return to Lebanon in 1962, he worked in television, for which he made *Jerusalem Is in Our Thoughts / Jérusalem est dans nos esprits / al-Quds fil bal* (1967, 10'). Feature films (some of them Lebanese-Syrian co-productions): *Chouchou and the Million / Chouchou and the Million / Chouchou wal milion* (1963, 35mm), *For Women Only / Pour femmes seulement / Lil nisa'a fakat* (1966, 35mm), *Beirut 011 / Beyrouth 011 / Beyrouth*

sifr hdaache (1967, 35mm), *For You, Oh Palestine / Pour toi, ô Palestine / Fidaki ya Filestin* (1969, 35mm), *The Beach of Love / La plage de l'amour / Chaté al-hob* (1974, 35mm).

Richa, Menem. Lebanese filmmaker. Born in 1959 in Lebanon, she studied physics, then filmmaking at the École Nationale Supérieure Louis-Lumière in Paris. Short fictional film: *Mashi* (1995, 3', 35mm).

ROSEBIANI, JANO. Iraqi filmmaker. His sole feature film is the story of the building of an orphanage in the Kurdish city of Halabja. Feature film: *Jiyan* (2002).

Rum, Mohamed. Palestinian filmmaker. Documentary: *Jihad!* (co-dir., 2004).

Sa'adi, Muhmud Ibrahim. Palestinian filmmaker. Documentary: *Bleeding Memories / Thikrayaton damiya*.

Sa'ed, Alabbas. Jordanian filmmaker and member of the Amman Filmmakers Cooperative. He studied IT and works as teacher. Short film: *Free to Fly* (with Sajeda Abousaif, 2006, 6'), *I Love to Read* (2007).

SAAB, JOCELYNE. Lebanese filmmaker. Born in 1948 in Beirut. After studying economics at the Sorbonne in Paris, she worked as a journalist for Lebanese television. She then turned to making numerous documentaries, mostly in 16mm film, from a base in Paris. She has also worked as assistant director to Volker Schlöndorff (*Dr Fälscher / The Forger*). Documentaries: *Portrait of Qaddafi / Portrait de Khadafi* (1973, 52', 16mm), *The October Conflict / Guerre d'octobre* (1973, 15', 16mm), *Syria: A Grain of Sand / Syrie, le grain de sable* (1973, 26', 16mm), *Kurdistan / Irak: la guerre au Kurdistan* (1973, 35', 16mm), *Palestinians Keep On / Les Palestiniens continuent* (1973, 26', 16mm), *The Front of Refusal / Le front du refus* (1974, 10', 16mm), *Palestinian Women / Les femmes palestiniennes* (1974, 12', 16mm), *Portrait of a French Mercenary / Portrait d'un mercenaire français / Rasm shakhsî* *li-murtaziq faransî* (1975, 10', 16mm), *The Children of the War / Les enfants de la guerre / Atfâl al-harb* (1976, 10', 16 and 35mm), *Beirut, Never Again / Beyrouth jamais plus* (1976, 35', 16 and 35mm), *Southern Lebanon: The Story of a Village Under Seige / Sud-Liban, histoire d'un village assiégé* (1976, 13', 16mm), *For a Few Lives / Pour quelques vies / Min ajli b'adu al-hayât* (1976, 20', 16mm), *Egypt: The City of the Dead / Egypte, la cité des morts / Misr: madinatu al-mawtâ* (1977, 35', 16mm), *Letter from Beirut / Lettre de Beyrouth / Risâla min Bayrût* (1978, 50', 16mm), *Iran: Utopia on the March / Iran, l'utopie en marche* (1980, 50', 16mm), *Beirut My City / Beyrouth ma ville / Bayrût madînatî* (1982, 35', 16mm), *Balance Sheet of the War / Bilan de la guerre* (1982, 10', 16mm), *The Boat of Exile / Le bateau de l'exil / Safina al-manfa* (1982, 13', 16mm), *Egypt: The Architect of Luxor / Egypte, l'architecte de Louxor* (1986, 20', 16mm), *Egypt: The Ghosts of Alexandria / Egypte, les fantômes d'Alexandrie* (1986, 17', 16mm), *Egypt: The Cross of the Pharoah / Egypte, la croix des pharaons* (1986, 20', 16mm), *Egypt: The Love of God—Fundamentalism / Egypte, l'amour d'Allah—l'intégrisme* (1987, 17', 16mm), *The Lebanese, Hostages in Their Own City / Les libanais ôtages de leur ville* (1987, 10', 16mm), *The Female Killer / La tueuse* (1988, 6', 16mm), *The Belly Dancers / Les almées danseuses orientales* (1989, 26', 16mm), *Fertilisation in Video / Fécondation in vidéo* (1991, video), *The Lady from Saigon / La dame de Saïgon / Saida Saighon* (1997, 60', video). The Arabic title of her first fictional feature refers to a 1949 Egyptian film by Anwar Wagdi, *Gazal al-banât* (*Young Girls' Flirtations*). Features: *Lebanon in Torment / Le Liban dans la tourmente / Lubnân fi al-dawâma* (1975, 75', 16mm) (documentary), *The Sahara Is Not for Sale / Le Sahara n'est pas à vendre* (1977, 90', 35mm) (documentary), *A Suspended Life* a.k.a. *Teenage Flirtation / Une vie suspendue* a.k.a. *L'adolescente, sucre d'amour / Ghazal al-banât 2* (1985, 100', 35mm), *Once upon a Time, Beirut* a.k.a. *The Story of a Star / Il était une fois Beyrouth, histoire d'une star / Kan ya ma kan Beirut* a.k.a. *Qissah najmah* (1994, 104',

35mm), *Kiss Me Not on the Eyes / Dunia* (2005, 112', 35mm).

Saad, Ammar. Iraqi filmmaker. Documentary: *Damn Gun* (2005, 30').

Saadeh, Mazen. Palestinian filmmaker. Born in 1959 in Jordan, he now lives in Ramallah. He began his career as a journalist and has written novels and plays. He is also an actor and appeared in Hanna Elias's Palestinian feature *The Olive Harvest* (2002). After a first short fictional film, *Day and Night* (2002), he turned to documentary: *The Bitter Choice, My Friend, My Enemy / Mon ami, mon ennemi* (2004, 52', Beta SP), *The Guardian of Boredom* (2005).

Sabah, Omar. Emirati filmmaker. He has worked as editor on a number of short films. Short animated film: *My Grandfather* (with Mahmoud Yousouf al-Mashni, 2001, 4', Beta SP).

Sabbagh, Osama Khalid. Emirati filmmaker. Short documentary film: *Abu Dhabi: The Past and the Present* (2002, 5', DV Cam).

SAEED, JOUD. Syrian filmmaker. Feature film: *Once More / Encore une fois / Mara okhra* (2009).

Saeed, Rawia Abdullah. Emirati filmmaker. She studied at UAE University. Short films: *Bitter . . . Sweet* (2006, 3', DVC Pro), *Before I Grow Up* (2008, 17', Mini DV).

Saeed, Reem. Emirati filmmaker. She studied at Dubai Women's College. Short documentary film: *El Youleh* (2002, 7', Beta SP).

Saeed, Sameer. Emirati filmmaker. Short film: *Zayed: Dignity and Originality* (with Mohamed Ashoor, 2001, 36', Beta SP).

SAEEDI, EBRAHIM. Iraqi filmmaker. He worked as a cinematographer. Feature-length documentary: *All My Mothers / Toutes mes*

mères / *Hamey-e madrana-e man* (with Za-havi Sanjavi, 2009, 60').

Safadi, Akram. Palestinian filmmaker. Born in 1962 in Jerusalem, he studied art and social science at the University of Bir Zeit in Palestine and filmmaking in Italy. Professional work as a photographer and organizer of photographic events. Three experimental videos (1991–1994) including *Limits of a Dream* (1994, 4', DV). Documentary: *Song on a Narrow Path: Stories from Jerusalem / La chambre noire de Jérusalem / Qissas min al-Quds* (2001, 52', Beta SP).

Safadi, Sami. Emirati filmmaker. He studied at the American University of Sharjah. Short films: *The Robbery* (2004, 7', Mini DV), *The Torture* (2004, 3', DV Cam).

SAFIA, BASHIR. Syrian filmmaker. He studied filmmaking in Cairo and has worked largely for the Syrian General Organisation for Cinema. Short films: *Mari* (1972, 7'), *Palmyra / Palmyre* (1972, 9'), *Festival Love / Amour de festival*. He also shot one episode, *Slave / Escave / al-Abd*, of the collective film *Shame / La honte / al-'Ar* (1974), with Wadeih Yousef and Bilal al-Sabouni. Feature films: *The Celebration / La fête* (1974, 35mm), *The Jester's Love / L'amour du bouffon / Gharâm al-muharrij* (1976, 35mm). *The Manhunt / La chasse à l'homme / Saydu al-rijâl* (1976, 35mm), *Red, White and Black / Le rouge, le blanc et le noir / al-Ahmar wa al-abyad wa al-aswad* (1977, 35mm), *Love for Life / L'amour pour la vie / Hubbun lil-hayât* (1981), *Ghawar's Empire* (1982, 35mm).

Safwan, Ja'far. Jordanian filmmaker and member of the Amman Filmmakers Cooperative. He studies electrical engineering at Jordan University. Short films: *Out of Order* (2006, 5'), *Air Palestine* (2008).

Saghran, Hamad Abdulla. Emirati filmmaker. He studied at the Higher College of Technology, Ras Al-Khaimah Men's College. Short film: *Jet Stream* (2005, 16', Mini DV), *No for Speed* (2007, 1', Mini DV).

Said, Edward. Palestinian writer and intellectual, wrongly credited by some sources with directing the documentary *In Search of Palestine / En quête de Palestine* (1998, 52'). This in fact a BBC production, produced and directed by Charles Bruce, for which he worked only as presenter.

Said, Joud. Syrian filmmaker. Short film: *Monologue* (2007, 14'), *Farewell / Wada'an* (2008), 15').

Saimeh, Bassem. Emirati filmmaker. A Canadian citizen of Syrian origin and raised in Japan, he studied at the American University of Sharjah. Short film: *Due Assignment* (2005, 21', Mini DV).

SAIMON, WILLIAM. Iraqi filmmaker. Worked as a cinematographer. Feature film: *Basra 11 O'clock / Basrah 11 heures / Basrah saa da'ach* (1964, 35mm).

SAKKAF, NOURA. Iraqi filmmaker. Documentary feature film: *Bitter Water / Eau amère* (with Maysoon Pachachi, 2003, 76', video).

SALAH, MOHAMED. Syrian filmmaker. Feature film: *Three Operations in Palestine / Trois Opérations en Palestine / Thalath amali-yyatdâkhil Filistin* (with Abderrahman al-Khayali, 1969, 90', 35mm).

Salam, Lamis Yasir. Emirati filmmaker. She was born in 1985 in Abu Dhabi and studied at the American University of Sharjah. Short fictional films: *Latch* (2006, 7', Mini DV), *Within* (2007, 3', Mini DV).

Salameh, Marwan. Palestinian filmmaker. Documentary films: *Aida / 'Aayda* (1984, 22'), *The Olive Tree / L'olivier / Ahjarato-z-zaytoun* (1986, 20').

SALAMEH, SHIRIN. Palestinian filmmaker. Born in Cairo to Palestinian parents who moved to Australia when she was 3 years old. She worked as a journalist in Cairo and as a foreign correspondent for ABC. Feature-length documentary film: *A Wedding in Ramallah / Un mariage à Ramallah / Farah fi Ramallah* (2000, 90', Beta SP).

Salaris, Daniele. Lebanese filmmaker. Short documentary film: *The Beirut Apartment / L'appartement à Beyrouth* (2007, 50').

SALEEM, HINER. Iraqi filmmaker. Born in 1964 in Aqrah in Iraqi Kurdistan, he fled the regime of Saddam Hussein at the age of 16 and spent 20 years as a political refugee, first in Italy and then in France, where he now lives. He is also a novelist whose first novel, *My Father's Rifle: A Childhood in Kurdistan*, was published in French in 2005 and translated into twenty languages. His fourth feature was the first Iraqi film to be shown at Cannes in competition. Feature films: *Long Live the Bride . . . and the Liberation of Kurdistan / Vive la mariée . . . et la libération du Kurdistan* (1997), *Beyond Our Dreams / Passeurs de rêve* (1999), *Vodka Lemon / Vodka citron* (2003), *Kilometer Zero / Kilomètre zéro* (2005, 85', 35mm), *Beneath the Rooftops of Paris / Sous les toits de Paris* (2007), *Dol* (2007).

Saleh, Katia. Lebanese filmmaker. Born in 1972 in Beirut, she is now resisident in England. She has made a number of doumentaries produced Al Jazeera English: *Beirut: All Flights Cancelled 2006* (2006, 22'), *Ashura: Blood and Beauty* (2006, 20'), *The Singing Barber of Musul* (2006), *Organised Chaos* (2007, 23'), *Deadly Playground* (2007, 23').

Saleh, Kifaya. Iraqi fillmmaker. Studied at the Independent Film and Television Academy in Baghdad. Short documentary film: *Hiwar* (2005, 12').

Saleh, Liana. Palestinian filmmaker. Short film: *A Ball and a Coloring Box / Kura wa 'alba alwan* (2004).

Saleh, Nadeem A. Emirati filmmaker. He studied at the American University of Sharjah. Short film: *Unsubscribe Me* (with Hany Madian, 2007, 1', Mini DV),

Saleh, Omar. Jordanian filmmaker and member of the Amman Filmmakers Cooperative. He studied at the Yarmouk University and works as a telecom engineer. Short films: *Decision Man* (2005), *The Last Patch* (with Rifqi Assaf, 2006, 15'), *What a Job / Quel boulot* (with Mohamed Aboujarad and Hazim Bitar, 2006, 7', DV Cam), *I Am Ready* (2008, 12').

SALEH, TEWFIQ.* Egyptian director of one Syrian feature film, which won the top prize, the Tanit d'or, at the JCC in Tunis in 1972: *The Duped / Les dupes / al-Makhdhououn* (1972, 100', 35mm). Also one Iraqi film: *The Long Days / Les longues journées / al-Ayyam al-tawîla* (1980, 100', 35mm).

SALEM, ATEF.* Egyptian director of three Syrian feature films: Women's Tailor / Tailleur pour les dames (1969, 35mm), The Beautiful Shepherdess / La belle bergère (1972, 35mm), My Wife's a Hippy / Ma femme Youppie / Zawjati min hippies(1973, 35mm).

Salem, Jamal. Emirati filmmaker. Short fictional film: *People Are Their Values* (2002, 17', DV Cam).

Salem, Khalid. Emirati filmmaker. Short film: *Nightmare* (2001, 15', Beta SP).

Salem, Mamdouh. Saudi filmmaker. Documentary: *Full Moon Night* (2007, 32').

Salem, Nada. Emirati filmmaker. She studied at Dubai Women's College. Short documentary films: *Pirates of Karama* (2004, 8', Mini DV), *Adolescent Colors* (with Wafa Faisal, Maitha Ebrahim, Hana Abdullah Mohammed al-Mulla al-Muhairi, Heba al-Dhanhani, 2005, 28', DV Cam).

SALHAB, GHASSAN. Lebanese filmmaker. Born in 1958 in Dakar, he grew up in Senegal until his family moved to Lebanon in 1970. In 1975, he began his studies at the Academy of Fine Arts in Beirut and in France and now divides his time between Paris and Beirut. He has worked as an arts critic and made a number of short films, many of them experimental: *The Key / La clé* (1986), *The Other / L'autre* (1989), *After Death / Après la mort* (1991, 21', 35mm), *Phantom Africa / Afrique fantôme* (1993, 21', 35mm), *My Dead Body, My Living Body / Mon corps vivant, mon corps mort* (2000, 14', DV Cam), *Nobody's Rose / La rose de personne* (2000, 8', video), *Lost Narcissus / Narcisse perdu* (2004, 15', DV Cam), *(Posthumous) / (Posthume)* (2007, 28', DigiBeta). Feature films: *Beirut Phantoms / Beyrouth, ville fantôme / Ashbah Beirut* (1998, 105', 35mm), *Terra incognita / al-Ard al-majhoula* (2002, 120', 35mm), *The Last Man / Le dernier homme / Atlal* (2006, 101', 35mm), *1958* (2009, 66') (documentary).

Salibi, Maher. Syrian filmmaker. Short fictional video: *The Rain's Tale / Le conte de la pluie* (2005, 35', video).

SALIH, MASSOUD ARIF. Iraqi filmmaker. Born in 1973 in Duhok in Kurdish Iraq, he studied filmmaking at the Institut of Communication in Kurdistan. He acted in a dozen plays for Iraqi stage and television. His co-directed first feature was produced by a French-based company. Feature film: *Narcissus Blossom / Le temps des narcisses / U nergiz biskvin* (with Hussein Hasan Ali, 2005, 80', 35mm).

SALLOUM, JACQUELINE. Palestinian filmmaker. Born in Beit Jala, she is now based in New York. Documentaries: *Planet of the Arabs* (2003, 9', Beta SP), *Arabs a-Go-Go* (2003), *Who's the Terrorist? / Min irhabi?* (2003, 4', video). Feature-length documentary: *Slingshot Hip Hop* (2006, 89').

Salloum, Jayce. Lebanese filmmaker. Born in 1958 in Kelowna (Canada). Involved in cultural meetings in Europe and the United States. Short films: *Towards South Lebanon / Vers le Sud-Liban* (with Walid Ra'ad, 1993, 49', video), *This Is Not Beirut / Ce n'est pas Beyrouth* (1994, 49', Beta SP), *Untitled Part 1: Everything and Nothing* (2001 41', video), *Untitled Part 2: Beauty and the East* (2002, 11' video), *Untitled*

Part 3B: (as if) Beauty Never Ends (2003, 11', video).

Salloum, Pierre. Lebanese filmmaker. Documentary: *15 Millions and Counting* (1999, 30', video), *Leila's Pictures / Les photos de Leila* (2002, 20', video).

Salman, Eyas. Palestinian filmmaker. Short film: *Noor* (2008, 18').

Salman, Ibrahim. Iraqi filmmaker. He made a Kurdish feature film in exile in Greece. Feature film: *A Silent Traveller / Un voyageur silencieux* (1992).

SALMAN, SAAD. Iraqi documentary filmmaker. Born in 1950 in Baghdad, he studied at the School of Fine Arts in Baghdad, graduating in 1969. He worked initially for Iraqi television and then moved to Paris, where he lives and works as a film editor. He made a short film: *Once upon a Time There Was Beirut / Il était une fois Beyrouth* (1984, 16', 16mm), and a number of documentaries: *Rimbaud, the Moment of Flight / Rimbaud , l'heure du fuite* (1990, 52', video), *Tell Me About Shibam / Conte-moi Shibam* (1992, 41', Beta SP). Feature-length documentaries: *Because of Circumstances / En raison de circonstances* (1982, 82', 16mm), *Visa for Paradise / Visa pour paradis* (1996, 76', Beta SP), *Questioning Where Reality Begins and Ends, Baghdad On/Off* (2002, 86', Beta SP).

Salmeen, Saeed. Emirati filmmaker. Short film: *Bint Mariem* (2008, 25').

Salmy, Suzy. Palestinian filmmaker. Short films: *Palestine Is Waiting / La Palestine attend* (with Annemarie Jacir and Dahna Aburahme, 2003).

Salti, Ghassan. Jordanian filmmaker and member of the Amman Filmmakers Cooperative. Short film: *The 14th Parliament and Jordan First* (2003).

Salti, Ihab. Palestinian filmmaker. Short film: A Woman Like a Flower / Une femme comme une fleur / Tilk al-mara al-warda (2001).

Samar, Salmane. Lebanese filmmaker. Short film: *I Love This* (2001, 13', video).

Samara, Riham Mahmoud. Emirati filmmaker. Born in 1985 in Sharjah, of Palestinian origin, she studied at the American University of Sharjah. Short film: *One Day with Alzheimer* (2004, 4', Mini DV).

SAMIR. Iraqi filmmaker. Born in 1955 in Baghdad of an Iraqi father and Swiss mother. He has lived in Switzerland from the age of 6. He made a number of documentaries: *Semiology of a Homeland / Sémiologie d'une patrie* (1982), *A Silent Film / Un film muet* (1984), *Body Bent / Corps penché* (1985), *Cocoon / Cocon* (1985), *Glazer* (1985), *Morlov* (1986), *Martin Desler* (1987, *The Rogue / Le filou* (1988), *Always and Forever / Toujours et éternellement* (1991), *It Was Just a Job* (1992). Feature-length documentaries (both raising questions of identity): *Babylon II* (1993, 91', 35mm), *Forget Baghdad: Jews and Arabs—The Iraqi Connection / Oublie Bagdad: Juifs et Arabes—la connection irakienne* (2002, 112', 35mm).

Samman, Rima. Lebanese filmmaker. Born in 1966 in Tripoli, she undertook paramedical studies in orthopaedics in Marseilles and obtained a DEA in socio-linguistics in 1993. She turned to cinema in 1995, working as script-girl and production assistant. Trainee on Bruno Dumont's *L'humanité*. Short films: *Milk and Cream / Crème et crémaillère / Libna qishta* (1999, 11', 35mm), *Carla* (2002, 19', 35mm), *Yesterday Still / Hier encore* (2006, 47', 35mm).

SANJAVI, ZAHAVI. Iraqi filmmaker. He studied at the Moscow film school, VGIK. Feature-length documentary: *All My Mothers / Toutes mes mères / Hamey-e madrana-e man* (with Ebrahim Saeedi, 2009, 60').

Sansour, Larissa. Palestinian filmmaker. Born in Jerusalem in 1973, she lived in Beit Jala for 15 years before studying in London, New York, and Denmark, where she is now based. She is also a writer. Short films: *Bethlehem Bandolero* (2004, 5'), *Tank* (2005), *Happy Days* (2006, 3'), *Land Confiscation Order 06/24/T* (2006, 11', video), *Soup Over Bethlehem / Mloukhieh* (2006, 10'), *Sbara* (2008, 9', video), *A Space Exodus* (2008, 5', DigiBeta).

SANSOUR, LEILA. Palestinian filmmaker. Born in Bethlehem, she now lives in London, working as a journalist and producer. Short film: *Global Coverage* (2002, 6'). Feature-length documentary: *Jeremy Hardy vs. the Israeli Army* (2002, 75', Beta SP).

SARKISSIAN, HARRY. Iraqi filmmaker who has worked in Syria and Lebanon. Born in 1924 in Baghdad, he studied drama at the Fine Arts Institute in Baghdad and went to study filmmaking at a Hungarian film school. On completing his studies he began work for Syrian television. He made his only feature film, *The Street of Dreams*, in which he played a leading role, in Lebanon. It is the only Lebanese feature to use the Armenian language. Feature film: *The Street of Dreams / La rue des rêves / Târiq al-Ahlam* (1973).

Sayegh, Layla. Palestinian filmmaker. Short film: *The Trunk / al-Sanduq* (2004).

Seemba, Halima Saeed. Emirati filmmaker. She studied at Dubai Women's College. Short film: *The Dream* (2003, 3', Beta SP).

SEIFEDDINE, SOUBHI. Lebanese filmmaker. Feature films: *The Resistance Fighter / Le résistant / al-Rajol al-samed* (1975, 35mm), *Marriage of the Land / Les noces de la terre / Urs al-ard* (1978, 35mm), *Al-Mouzayafa* (1983, 35mm), *A Country Above Wounds / Un pays, les plaies, un déplacement / Watan fawq al-jirah* (1983, 35mm), *The Fifth Column / La cinquième colonne / al-Jiha al-khamisa* (1984, 35mm).

SELMANE, MOHAMED. Lebanese film-maker. Born in 1925, he began his artistic career as a singer and dancer in Egypt and appeared in several films there. On his return to Lebanon he turned to filmmaking, and unlike most of his contemporaries he was able to sustain his career as a filmmaker for a period of 25 years. During this time, he made over thirty commercial feature films, both musicals and melodramas, which achieved great success throughout the Arab world. Two of his later films were produced in Syria. Features: *The First Song / Le premier chant / al-Lahn al-awal* (1957, 35mm), *Rendezvous with Hope / Rendez-vous avec l'espoir / Moad maa al-amal* 1958, 35mm), *The Songs of My Love / Les chants de mon amour / Angham habibi* (1959, 35mm), *Hello, Love / Bonjour l'amour / Marhabane ayouhal hub* (1962, 35mm), *A Love Story / Histoire d'amour / Hikayat gharam* (1963, 35mm), *Lebanon at Night / Le Liban, la nuit / Loubnan fi leil* 1963, 35mm), *Praise for Love / Louange pour l'amour / Ya salam al-hub* (1963, 35mm), *Joys of Youth / Joies de la jeunesse / Afrah al-chabab* (1964, 35mm), *A Bedouin Girl in Paris / Une bédouine à Paris / Badawia fi Baris* (1964, 35mm), *The Idol of the Crowds / L'idole des foules / Fatinat al-jamahir* (1964, 35mm), *The Idol of the Desert / L'idole du désert / Fatinat al-sahra* (1965, 35mm), *In the Service of Love / Au service de l'amour / Bi amr al-hub* (1965, 35mm), *A Bedouin Girl in Rome / Une bédouine à Rome / Badawia fi Roma* (1965, 35mm), *The Bank / La banque / al-Bank* (1965, 35mm), *The Black Jaguar / La jaguar noire / al-Jaguar es sawda* (1965, 35mm), *Youth and Beauty / La jeunesse et la beauté / al-Siba wal jamal* (1965, 35mm), *Mawal / Mawal al-akdam al-zahabia* (1966, 35mm), *The Wheedler / L'enjôleuse / al-Daloua* (1966, 35mm), *Chouchou's Adventures / Les aventures de Chouchou / Moughamarat Chouchou* (1966, 35mm), *Canticles of Love / Cantiques d'amour / Alhane al-hub* (1967, 35mm), *Welcome to Love / Bienvenue à l'amour* (1968, 35mm), *Heroes and Women / Des héros et des femmes / Abtal wa nissa* (1969, 35mm), *Orchard of Love / Verger d'amour / Karm al-hawa* (1970, 35mm), *Waves / Vagues / Amwage* (1970, 35mm), *Bewilderment / L'égarement /* *al-Dayae* (1971, 35mm), *Paris and Love / Paris et l'amour / Baris al-hub* (1971, 35mm), *Passion on Fire / Passion en feu / Nar al-chawk* (1971, 35mm), *The Beautiful Girl and the Tiger / La beauté et le tigre / al-Hassna'wal nemr* (1972, 35mm), *Love's Guitar / La guitare de l'amour / Guitare al-hub* (1973, 35mm), *Words of Love / Des mots de l'amour / Kalam fi hub* (with Sayed Tantoui, 1973, 35mm), *Battle in the Desert / Combat dans le désert* (1974, 35mm) in Syria, *Professor Ayoub / Le professeur Ayoub / al-Oustaz Ayoub* (1975, 35mm), *The Horseman of Bani Abes / Le cavalier de Bani Abes* (1977, 35mm) in Syria, *Who Puts Out the Fire? / Qui éteint le feu? / Man youtfil al-nar* (1982, 35mm).

Selo, Jalal. Emirati filmmaker. Short fictional film: *Malibu* (2007, 4', Mini DV).

Sermini, Salah. Syrian filmmaker. Born in 1956 in Aleppo, he studied filmmaking at the Université de Paris III. Short films: *In the Margin of Real Events and of Others Imagined / En marge d'événements réeals et d'autres imaginés* (1981), *Ode to Death / Ode à la mort* (1985, 35'), *Memory and the Heart / La mémoire et le cœur / al-Zakira wal quab* (1988, 13', 16mm), *Illusions on the Threshold of a Legendary City / Illusions au seuil d'une ville légendaire* (1998, 24', video).

Sfair, Patrick. Lebanese filmmaker. Short animated film: *Hijo de la luna* (2004, 5').

Sfeir, Zeina. Lebanese filmmaker. Documentary: *In Spite of the War / Pied au nez à la guerre* (2001, 30').

SHA'ATH, GHALIB. Palestinian filmmaker. Born in 1935 in Jerusalem, he moved to Egypt, where he studied architecture at the University of Alexandria. After teaching for several years in Saudi Arabia, he decided to go to Europe to study filmmaking in Vienna. In 1967, he returned to Egypt, where he worked for television and made his only fictional feature film. He has since worked as a journalist and translator, settling in Beirut in 1974. Short films: *The Key / La clef / al-Muftâb* (1976, 25'), *Earth Day / La journée de la terre / Yawm al-Ard* (1978, 40'), *Olive Branch / Qusn al-Zaytun* (1978), *Don't Drop the Green Leaf / Ne laisse pas tomber la feuille verte / La toskiti-l-ghosna-l-akhdar* (1980). Feature film: *Shadows on the Other Bank / Des ombres sur l'autre rive / Dilâl alâ al-jânibi al-âkhar* (in Egypt, 1973).

Sha'ban, Qasim. Palestinian filmmaker. Documentary: *Nazareth '84 / al-Nasira '84* (1984).

Shabib, Sarah. Emirati filmmaker. Short film: *Yesterday Morning* (2004, 3', Mini DV).

Shafee, Shamma. Emirati student. She studied at the American University of Sharjah. Short film: *Don't Fear* (2003, 6', Mini DV).

Shahbandar, Nazih. Syrian pioneer filmmaker. Feature film: *Light and Darkness / Lumière et ténèbre / Nouron wa thilal* (1947).

Shahin, Khalifa. Bahraini filmmaker. Born in 1939, he studied filmmaking at Ealing Technical College in the United Kingdom during the early 1960s and went on to direct a number of short documentary films between 1967 and 1977, including *Pictures of an Island / Images d'une île*, *People on the Horizon / Des gens à l'horizon*, *The Black Wave / La vague noire*.

SHAHIN, MOHAMED. Syrian filmmaker. Began his artistic career in the theatre and television. Prolific filmmaker for both the state and the private sectors, with some twenty short films and documentaries and over a dozen fictional features. Short films: *Recollections of Damascus / Mémoires de Damas / Dhikrayâtun min Dimashq* (1965), *Water and Life / L'eau et la vie / al-Mâ wa al-hayât* (1968), *The Words of a Dry Tree / Les paroles d'un arbre sec* (1969), *Baraddâ / Baraddâ* (1969), *Youth and Students / Jeunesse et les étudiants / al-Shabiba al-talaba* (1975). He contributed one of three episodes to the first feature produced by the National Cinema Organisation: *Men Under the Sun / Des hommes sous le soleil / al-Sayyid al-taqaddumi* (with Nabil al-Maleh and Mohamed Muwad-

din, 1970, 108', 35mm). Feature films: *A City Rose / Une rose de la ville / Zahratun min al-madina* (1964, 35mm), *Another Facet of Love / Une autre facette de l'amour / Wahj akhar lil-hob* (1972, 35mm), *The Wounded Ballerina / La ballerine blessée / Râqisa alâ al-firâh* (1973, 35mm), *Cruel Woman / Femme cruelle* (1973, 35mm), *The Mameluke Jaber's Adventure / L'aventure du Mamelouk Jaber / Mughamarat al-Mamluk Jaber* (1974, 105', 35mm), *The Tents of Qaraqoz / Les tentes de Quaraqoz / Khaymatu Quaraqoz* (1974, 35mm), *The Agitators / Les fauteurs* (1975, 35mm), *Don't Say Goodbye to a Day That's Scarcely Gone / Ne dites pas adieu à un jour qui n'a guère passé / La taquli wadâ'an lil ams* (1977, 35mm), *The Jungle of Wolves / Le jungle des loups / Ghâbatu al-diâb* (1977, 35mm), *Farewell to the Past / Adieu au passé* (1978, 35mm), *A Murder Step by Step / Un meutre pas à pas / Qatlun . . . an tariq al-tasalsul* (1982, 35mm), *The Game of Love and Death / Le jeu de l'amour et de la mort / Lubatu al-hubb was al-gatl* (1983, 35mm), *The Drama of a Girl from the East / Le drame d'une fille de l'orient / Ma'asat fatât sharqiya* (1983, 35mm), *On a Rainy Day / Un jour pluvieux / ash-Shams fi yaum gha'im* (1985, 115', 35mm), *Cloud / Nuage / Sahâb* (1991, 35mm), *Oh Sea / Oh mer* (1993, 120', 35mm), *The Moneylender / L'usurier / al-Marabi* (1999, 35mm).

Shaker, Mounaf. Iraqi filmmaker. Studied at the Independent Film and Television Academy in Baghdad. His second documentary was made for Al Jazeera International. Short documentary films: *Omer Is My Friend* (2005, 15'), *Leaving* (2007, 16').

Shamma, Suad. Emirati filmmaker. Studied at the American University of Sharjah. Short film: *Angeldust* (2007, 4', Mini DV).

Shamounki, Nadine. Palestinian filmmaker. Short film: *Effaced* (2002).

Sharaf, Bashar. Jordanian filmmaker and member of the Amman Filmmakers Cooperative. Studied business administration. Short film: *To Speed or Not To Speed* (2003).

SHARGAWI, OMAR. Palestinian filmmaker. Based in Denmark. Fictional feature film: *Go with Peace Jamil / Ma salama Jamil* (2007, 90').

Sharidi, Nazim. Palestinian filmmaker. Documentaries: *Call of the Roots / Nida' al-judhur* (1984), *The Dehaysha Ghetto / Ghtu al-Dehayshiyya* (1988), *Between the Dream and the Memory / Ma bayn al-Hil wa al-dhakira* (1988), *The Surrounded City / La ville entourée / al-Madina al-muhasira* (1988), *Fertile Seasons / Des saisons fécondes / Mawasim al-khasab* (1988).

Sharief, Ahmed Mohammed. Emirati filmmaker. Born in 1978 in Dubai, he studied economics at UAE University. Short experimental films: *Sketches* (2003, 5', DV Cam), *Movie* (2004, 2', Mini DV).

Shawi, Burhan. Emirati filmmaker. Short fictional films: *Once upon a Night* (1999, 42', Beta SP), *Behind Closed Doors* (2000, 12', Beta SP).

SHAYYA, RIYAD. Syrian filmmaker. Born in 1951 at Souwayda, he studied filmmaking at VGIK in Moscow and made one short before completing his first feature. Feature film: *Al-Lajat / Al-Leja* (1995, 84', 35mm).

Shehada, Abdel Salam. Palestinian filmmaker. Now based in Ramallah. Documentary films: *Palestinian Diaries* (with Suheir Ismaïl and Nazih Darwaza, 1992, 52', Beta SP), *Innocence / al-Biy'a* (1994), *Women's Human Rights / Huquq al-mar'a al-ensaniyya* (1995, 25'), *Small Hands / al-'Aidai al-saquira* (1995, 26'), *Close to Death / Bi al-qrab min al-mawt* (1997, 26'), *Water, the True Challenge / al-Ma', al-tahadi al-haqiqi* (1998, 35'), *The Cane / al-Okkaz* (2000, 26'), *The Shadow / L'ombre / al-Zill* (2000, 43'), *Stone by Stone / Hajjar bi hajjar* (2000), *Mirage / al-Qasba* (2000), *Debris / Décombres / Radm* (2002, 19', Beta SP), *Rainbow / Qaws quzab* (2005, 40'), *Gaza, Another Kind of Tears* (2006, 53'), *To My Father / Ila aby* (2008, 52', DigiBeta). Also contributed one episode to the collectively made video documentary *One More Time (Five Stories about Human Rights in Palestine / Une fois encore (cinq histoires sur les droits de l'homme en Palestine)* (with Nada al-Yassir, Tawfik Abu Wael, Ismaïl Habash, Najwa Najjar, 2002, 57', Beta SP).

SHMEIT, GHASSAN. Syrian filmmaker. Born in 1956 in Quneitra, he studied at the Higher Film Institute in Kiev, graduating in 1982. Documentary and short films: *Bosra* (1983, 22'), *Friendship Stopovers* (1986, 20'), *Our Struggle in the Golan Heights* a.k.a. *Golan Diaries / La lutte des nôtres au Golan* (1987, 32'), *Together On the Road* (1989, 20'), *The Buds* (1990, 20'), *Roses and Thorns* (2003, 25'), *Glowing Beacons* (2004, 40'), *The Sun Castles* (2004, 20'). Feature films: *Something Is Burning / Quelque chose brûle / Shay'ma yahtariq* (1993), *Black Flour / La farine noire / Tahin al-Aswad* (2001, 120'), *I.D. / Vos papiers* (2007).

Shomali, Amer. Palestinian filmmaker. Contributed *Checkmate* (3' 06") to the collective film *Summer 2006, Palestine* (2006, 35', Beta SP).

Shoumali, Nabil Qusta. Jordanian filmmaker. Short fictional film: *The Dress / La robe* (5', 16mm).

Shuhaiber, Ramzy. Emirati filmmaker. Short film: *Sense of Detection* (with Jaidaa Adel, 2007, 8', Mini DV).

Sikias, Tatania. Lebanese filmmaker. Short fictional film: *Mawawil* (2002, 20'),

Sinnokrot, Nida. Palestinian filmmaker. Based in the United States. Short film: *Palestine Blues* (2006).

SIRHAN, IBRAHIM HASSAN. Palestinian-born filmmaker and pioneer of Jordanian cinema. Born in 1916 in Palestine, he began with a short documentary about a visit by King Saud: *The Visit of King Abd al-Aziz / Ziyara al-malak 'Abd al-'Aziz* (1935). He shot a number of other films, including *Dreams Realised / Ahlam tahaqqaqat* (1939), *Studio Palestine / Studio Filastin* (1945), *On the Night of* the Feast / Fi layla al-'ayd (1946), *Cinematic Introduction / Ahmed Hilmi Basha / 'Ahmad Hilmi Basha* (1946), before being driven into exile in what was then Trans-Jordan. There he produced two fictional films of unspecified length: *The Moon and the Sun / La lune et le soleil / al-Qamar wash-shams* (1957) and *The Struggle in Jarash / Combat à Djérash / Sira'a fi Jarash* (1958), which are the founding films of Jordanian cinema.

Siyyam, Ali. Jordanian filmmaker. Documentaries on Palestine: *The Flower of Cities / La fleur des cités / Zahrat al-madaen* (1968, 10'), *Exodus 67 / al-Khourouj* (1968, 17'), *A Book for You / Un livre pour toi / Kitab laka* (1968, 10'), *The Burnt Land / La terre brûlée / al-Ardh al-mahrouka* (1969, 12').

Skaff, Philippe. Lebanese filmmaker. Short fictional film: *Lesson No. 5 / La leçon No. 5* (2007).

Skaff, Raghida. Lebanese filmmaker. Short fictional film: *Images* (2000, 13').

Slim, Lokan. Lebanese filmmaker. Based in Germany. Documentary: *Massaker* (with Monika Borgmann and Hermann Theissen, 2005, 99', 35mm).

Smayra, Wissam. Lebanese filmmaker. Short fictional film: *Lebanese Non-footage / Non métrage libanais* (with Ghassan Kotait, 2003, 13', 16mm).

SOLFAN, MOHAMED. Syrian filmmaker. Feature film: *Sabiha, Seductress of the Desert / Sabiha la séductrice du désert* (1975, 35mm).

Soliman, Marwa Mohammed. Emirati filmmaker. She studied law and design. Short animated films: *Our POWs in Memory* (with Mohammed Mohamed Soliman, 2004, 8', video), *Emirates Knight* (with Mohammed Mohamed Soliman, 2005, 10', DVD).

Soliman, Mohammed Mohammed. Emirati filmmaker. Short animated films: *Our POWs in Memory* (with Marwa Mohamed Soliman, 2004, 8', video), *Emirates Knight* (with Marwa Mohamed Soliman, 2005, 10', DVD).

Sorrein, Cheirak. Iraqi filmmaker. Short fictional film about the Palestinian struggle: *The Game / Le jeu / al-Louba* (1973).

Soufan, Hamaza. Jordanian filmmaker and member of the Amman Filmmakers Cooperative. Short film: *Anxious Skies* (2005).

SOUWEID, MOHAMED. Lebanese filmmaker. Born in 1959 in Beirut, he worked as a film critic in the daily press from 1982 to 1994. His documentaries include: *Absence* (1991), *The Al-Fouad Cinema / Cinéma al-Fouad* (1993, 41', Umatic), *I Am in the Camelia / Je suis dans le camélia* (1994), *The House / La maison* (1994), *Hymn of Joy / Hymne de la joie* (1994), *Qatr el nada* (1994), *South / Sud* (1995, 37', Beta SP), *Roses of Passion / Roses de passion* (1996), *Fate / Destinée* (1997, 13', video. Feature films: *Tango of Yearning / Tango du désir* (1998, 70', 35mm), *Until the End of the Day* a.k.a. *Nightfall / Jusqu'au déclin du jour* (2000, 70', Beta SP) (documentary), *Civil War / Guerre civile* (2002), *My Heart Beats Only for Her / Mon cœur ne bat que pour elle / Ma hataftu li ghayriha* (2009, 86').

SROUR, HEINY. Lebanese filmmaker. Born in 1945 in Beirut, she studied sociology at the American University in Beirut and then completed a doctorate in social anthropology at the Sorbonne. She worked as a journalist in French, English, and Arabic in Paris and London and as a teacher at the London International Film School and at Goldsmiths's College in London. Her first film, *Bread of Our Mountains* (1968, 3', 16mm), about the liberation struggle in Oman, was lost during the Lebanese Civil War. Short films and documentaries: *The Singing Sheikh* (1991, 10', video), *The Eyes of the Heart / Les yeux du cœur* (1998, 52', video), *Women of Vietnam / Femmes du Vietnam /Nisa' Vietnam* (1998, 52', video), *Woman Global Strike 2000* (2000, video). Feature films: *The Hour of Liberation*

Has Struck / L'heure de la libération a sonné / Sâ'atu al-tahrîr daqqat yâ ist'immâr (1974, 62', 16mm), *Leila and the Wolves / Leila et les loups / Layla wa al-zi'ab* (1984, 90', 16mm).

SROUR, SHADI. Palestinian filmmaker. Born in Nazareth, she studied in San Francisco and Tel Aviv. She has written, directed, and acted in many plays. Short film: *Either Me . . . or Haifa / Ya ana . . . ya Haifa* (2007, 15', DV Cam). Feature film: *Sense of Need / L'épreuve du besoin* (2004, 90').

Stas, Khalil. Emirati filmmaker. Short documentaries: *Sharjah, A Civilised Place to Think and Work* (2001, 21', DigiBeta), *UAE: Growth, Development and Prosperity* (2001, 13', Digi-Beta).

Stephan, Rania. Lebanese filmmaker. Born in 1960 in Beirut, she studied filmmaking at the Université de Vincennes and went on to work in various technical roles in the United States and Australia. She worked as assistant director for the French documentarist, Simone Bitton. Several short films: *Ya layl ya ayn* (1985, 10', video), *The Wonder of Manekine / Le miracle de la Manekine* (1986, 24', video), *Murmur of the Breeze / Le Souffle de la brise* (1986, 5', video), *Adonis* (1991, 26', video), *Phèdre(s)* (1993, 3', hi 8), *The Tribe / La Tribu / al-Qabila* (1992, 9', Beta SP), *An Attempt at Jealousy / Tentative de jalousie* (1994, 4', Beta SP), *Baal and Death / Baal et la mort / Ba'l wa'l'mawt* (1996, 26', Beta SP), *Train, Trains / Train, trains, où est la voie / Wayn essekeh?* (1999, 33', Beta SP). Contributed *Bint jbeil* (2') and *Monday, August 14, Southern Suburb Bridge* (4') to the collective project *Videos Under Siege* (DIFF 2008, 39', video).

Subaihi, Khalid Hasan. Emirati filmmaker. He studied at the American University of Sharjah. Short films: *Searching for Subaira* (with Hasan Taryam Subaihi, 2004, 10', Mini DV), *Muweilleh: Unravelling Certain Truths* (2004, 13', Mini DV).

Subaihi, Taryam Hasan. Emirati filmmaker. He studied at the American University of Sharjah. Short films: *Searching for Subaira* (with Khalid Hasan Subaihi, 2004, 10', Mini DV), *My World, My Pitch* (2004, 10', DV Cam).

SULEIMAN, ELIA. Palestinian filmmaker. Born in 1960 in Nazareth and raised under Zionist occupation, he was driven into exile at the age of 17, spending a year in London and Paris. After a brief return to Nazareth, he left for the United States in 1981 as an illegal immigrant, where he was to live for the next 12 years. Documentaries: *Introduction to the End of an Argument / Introduction à la fin de l'histoire / Uqaddimah li-nihayat-jidal* (with the Canadian-Lebanese filmmaker Jayce Salloum, 1990, 45', video), *War and Peace in Vesoul* (with Israeli filmmaker Amos Gitaï, 1997, 70', 16mm), *The Arab Dream / Le rêve arabe / al-Hilm al-'arabi* (1998, 30', Beta SP), *Cyber-Palestine* (2000, 16', Beta SP). He also contributed one episode, *Homage by Assassination / Hommage par assassinat / Takrim bi al-qalt*, to the Tunisian-produced collective film *After the Gulf? / La guerre du Golfe . . . et après / Harbu al-khalîj wa ba'du?* (1992). Feature films: *Chronicle of a Disappearance / Chronique d'une disparition / Sijil 'ikhtifa'* (1996, 88', 35mm), *Divine Interventio / Intervention divine / Yadun 'Ilahiyya* (2002, 92', 35mm), *The Time That Remains / Le temps qu'il reste / al-Zaman al-baqi* (2009, 105', 35mm).

Sultan, Abdulwahab. Kuwaiti filmmaker. Born in 1940, he studied in the United States and made a number of documentaries between 1963 and 1975.

Sulukdjian Arzoumanian, Arine. Lebanese filmmaker. Born in 1972 in Beirut, she studied at IESAV and worked as trainee in Bruxelles, Paris and Beirut. She also worked as animator for Lebanese television. Short fictional film: *The Pigeon / Le pigeon / al-Hamama* (1994, 14', Beta SP).

Sursock, Sabine. Lebanese filmmaker. Born in 1977 in Beirut, she graduated from IESAV in Beirut in 2000 and went on to study scriptwriting at ECAL in Lausanne, Switzerland. She has worked in production and assistant director roles in television, then as producer. Now based in Paris. One short fictional film: *Who Has the Right? / A qui le droit* (2000), and two documentaries: *The Prompter / Le souffleur / al-Mulaqqin* (2000, co-dir., 26'), *To Whom It May Concern / A qui le droit / Ila man yaummuhu* (2001, 17', Beta SP).

Syriani, Fadi. Lebanese filmmaker. Short animated film: *Animated Fate / Destin animé* (2001, 5').

TABARI, ULA. Palestinian filmmaker. Born in 1970 in Nazareth, she has lived in Paris since 1998. During the 1990s, she was very active in various government initiatives involving education, theatre, and television. She is also a stage and screen actress, appearing most notably in two films by Elia Suleiman, *Chronicle of a Disappearance* and *Arab Dream*. Short film: *Diaspora* (2005, 17', 35mm). Feature-length video documentary: *Personal Inquiry* a.k.a. *Private Investigation / Enquête personnelle / 'Alaqna wa khalaqna* (2002, 90', Beta SP).

Tabet, Nadim. Lebanese filmmaker. Short fictional film: *Martine and Alia / Martiune et Alia* (2002, 27').

Tabet, Sylvio. Lebanese filmmaker. Born in 1970 in Beirut, he studied filmmaking at ESRA in Paris. Short film: *If the People One Day . . . / Si le peuple un jour . . .* (with Michèle Tyan, 25', Beta SP).

Taffal, Najah. Jordanian filmmaker and member of the Amman Filmmakers Cooperative. She studied secondary education for the deaf, and works as artist and instructor. Short film: *Najah's Puppets* (2003).

Tahrer, Shaker T. Iraqi filmmaker. Born in 1959 in Sumer, he studied filmmaking at Gothenburg in Sweden, where he worked in the audio-visual sector of a cultural center. Short films: *Atergang* (1995), *Min pappa grater inte* (2002), *A Footballer at Midnight / Un joueur de football à minuit* (2005).

Takash, Razan. Emirati filmmaker. Short films: *Discerning Memory* (with Youssef Jassim Buhamas, 2006, 10, Mini DV), *Kinetic Energy Ad* (2007, 1', DVD), *Infinite* (2007, 10', DVD).

TAKKOUCHE, IBRAHIM. Lebanese filmmaker. Feature films: *The Deadly Necklace / Le collier meutrier / al-Akd al-katel* (1960, 35mm), *I Am Not Guilty / Je ne suis pas coupable / Lastou mouzniba* (1960, 35mm).

Taleb, Dhafir. Iraqi filmmaker. Studied at the Independent Film and Television Academy in Baghdad. Short documentary film: *Let the Show Begin* (2005, 15').

Tamari, Vladimir. Lebanese filmmaker. Documentary: *Jerusalem / Jérusalem / al-Qods* (1968, 18').

TAMBA, HANY. Lebanese filmmaker. Born in 1961 in Beirut, he studied graphics in the United Kingdom (1977–1982) and became a freelance designer in London. He also worked on a number of commercials and animated films. Short films: *Beirut: This City's Barbers / Beyrouth: les barbiers de cette ville* (1997, 14'), *Mabrouk Again* (1999, 18', 35mm), *The Hair of the Beast / Du poil de la bête* (2002), *After Shave* (2004). Feature film: *Melodrama Habibi / Une chanson dans la tête* (2008, 94', 35mm).

Tan, Michéle. Lebanese filmmaker. Born in 1971 in Beirut, he studied at ESRA in Paris. Short film: *If the People One Day . . . / Si le peuple un jour . . .* (with Sylvio Tabet, 25', Beta SP).

Tanjour, Alfouz. Syrian filmmaker. Short film: *Little Sun* (2008, 17').

TANTAWI, SAYED. Egyptian filmmaker who made two Middle Eastern feature films, the first in Lebanon, the second in Syria. Feature films: *Words of Love / Des mots de l'amour / Kalam fi hub* (Lebanon, with Mohamed Selmane, 1973), *Meeting of Strangers / Rencontre des étrangères* (Syria, 1967, 35mm).

Tarazi, Gilles. Lebanese filmmaker. Documentary: *Tomorrow at 6.30 / Demain 6h30* (2007, 23', video).

Tariq, Sidra. Emirati filmmaker. Short film: *Grocery Shopping* (2007, 9', DVD).

Tarzan, Hamzah Ahmed Fakhri. Saudi filmmaker. Short fictional films *Living Backward* (2007, 16', DVD), *The Basement* (2008, 26', Mini DV).

Tawfik, Mohamed. Iraqi filmmaker. His early films deal with Palestine. Short films: *The Path of Surrender / Masira al-esteslam* (1981), *Umma Ali / Umm 'Ali* (1983), *The Child and the Game / al-Tif wa al-la'ba* (1985), *The Guard / al-Natur* (1988), *Poet of the Reed / Le poète du roseau* (1999, 55', Beta SP), *Tahaddiyat saai al-barid* (2002, 21', Beta SP), *Maria* (2006, documentary, 52', video).

Tawfik, Rania Mohammad. Iraqi filmmaker. She studied film in Copenhagen, where she currently lives. Short fictional films: *Nawal* (2001), *Khaled* (2002), *Home* (2002), *The Eternal Night / La nuit éternelle / Den Evige Nat* (with Katharina Raagaard, Lene Lavtsen, and Marie Andersen, in Denmark, 2005, 8', video), *The Spotlight Chaser* (in Denmark, 2004, 28', DV Cam).

Tawil, Helga. Palestinian filmmaker. Short films: *Not Going There, Don't Belong Here* (2002, 25', video), *Qalandia* (2003), *Isochronism: Twenty-Four Hours in Jabaa* (2004).

Terawi, Ghada. Palestinian filmmaker. Born in 1972 in Beirut to Palestinian militant parents, she was raised in Beirut, Tunis, and Cairo and graduated from the American University in Cairo in 1955. She has worked in documentary since 1998. Short documentary films: *Staying Alive / Nous voulons vivre / Bidna na'ish* (2001, 28', Beta SP), *What's Next? / Madha ba'd* (2004, 40'). *The Way Back Home* (2006, 33').

Thakur, Yusuf. Emirati filmmaker. Short films: *Endangered Dugongs* (2001, 14', Beta SP), *Jewel of the Mangrove*, 2001, 31', Beta SP).

Tokhmafshan, Fatima. Emirati filmmaker. Of Iranian origin, she studied at the American University of Sharjah. Short films: *Miracle* (1998), *Saeed in Name* (2003, 46', Beta SP).

Tossounian, Aznive. Emirati filmmaker. She has made one short documentary film: *Souvenirs of the Past* (2001, 15', DV Cam).

Toufic, Jalal. Lebanese filmmaker. Short film: *Saving Face / Sauver la face* (203, 9').

Toukhy, Amr. Jordanian filmmaker and member of the Amman Filmmakers Cooperative. He studied at the University of Jordan and works producing commercials. Short film: *Give Me One Good Reason Not To* (2003, 1', DV Cam).

Turk, Fadi Yeni. Lebanese filmmaker. Teaches at St Joseph University. Short experimental film: *Demo . . .* (2003, 6', Mini DV).

Vahedipour, Annie. Emirati filmmaker. She studied at the American University of Sharjah. Short fictional film: *The Mouse* (2004, 5', Mini DV).

VOTCHINITCH, BOSHKO* [also referred to as Poçko Poçkovic]. Yugoslav filmmaker, chosen by the Syrian government to train a new generation of young filmmakers. Feature film: *The Lorry Driver / Le cammioneur / Sa'iq ash-shahina* (1966, 90', 35mm).

Waked, Antoine. Lebanese filmmaker. Short film: *The Big Fall* (2005, 5', animation).

Wakim, Antone Wakim. Emirati filmmaker. Short film: *Rosy Dream* (2002, 6', DV Cam).

WAKIM, BECHARA. Lebanese filmmaker. Feature film: *Holiday in Lebanon / Les vacances au Liban* (1947, 35mm).

WALI, ABDL JABER. Iraqi filmmaker. Feature films: *Who Is Responsible? / Qui est responsable? / Man al-mas'oul?* (1956, 35mm), *Naima* (1962, 35mm).

Watfeh, Layal. Emirati filmmaker. Studied at Dubai Polytechnic and currently works in Dubai Media City. Short video advertisements: *The HigheR ThE LoweR* (2002, 2', DV Cam), *Flower* (2003, 1', DigiBeta).

Yacoub, Fajr. Syrian filmmaker of Palestinian origin. Born in 1963 in Damascus, he studied filmmaking in Sofia. Also translator and critic. Short films: *Solar Picture* (2003, 17', Beta SP), *Labyrinth* (2004, 3', Beta SP) *Romeo and Juliet* (2005, 10', Beta SP), *The Penguin / Le pingouin* (2005, 18', 35mm).

Yahmed, Cheker Bin. Bahraini filmmaker. Studied film in Morocco. Short fictional film: *One More Day* (2007, 8', DV Cam).

Yaqubi, Mohanad. Palestinian filmmaker. Short video films: *Fix* (2003), *Around* (2007, 3'), *Rico in the Night* (2007, 8'). Contributed *Trafic* (2' 51") to the collective film *Summer 2006, Palestine* (2006, 35', Beta SP).

Yassione, Dina. Lebanese filmmaker. Short fictional films: *Al-Aghair* (2000, 12'), *Demo* (2002, 8').

Yazbek, Elie. Lebanese filmmaker. Contributed *Before, After* (5') to the collective project *Videos Under Siege* (DIFF 2008, 39', video).

Yaziji, Haïdar. Syrian filmmaker. Documentary: *Message of Love for Syria Message d'amour pour la Syrie* (with Mahmoud Chabaane, 1992, 38').

YOUSEF, WADEIH. Syrian filmmaker. Short films and documentaries: *The Euphrates / L'Euphrate / Hawdu al-furât* (1970), *The Beginning / Le commencement / al-Bidaya* (1971), *The Great Dam on the Euphrates / La grande barrière sur l'Euphrate / Suddu al-furati al-adhîm* (1971), *Popular Ball / Bal populaire / Raq-*

sun shâ'bi (1971), *Busra / Busra* (1972), *The Resistance / La résistance / al-Sumûd* (1973), *The Killers / Les tueurs / al-Qatala* (1973), *Greetings from Quneitra / Salutations de Quneitra / Tahiyya min al-Qunaitra* (1974), *Violence / La violence / al-Ightisâb* (1974), *October Arrived / Octobre arriva / wa Ja'a uktûbar* (1974, 20'), *The Road to Qasiun / La route pour Qasiun / Al-tarîq ila Qasiun* (1978), *Syria in the Moscow Olympics / La Syrie aux jeux olympiques à Moscou / Sûriya fi Olimpiad Mosco* (1983), *The Commandant of the March / Le commandant de la marche / Qâid al-masîra* (1984), *The Birth / La naissance / al-Milâd* (1987). He also shot one episode, *Khero Alawaj*, of the collective film *Shame / La honte / al-'Ar* (1974), alongside Bilal al-Sabouni and Bashir Safia. Feature films: *And October Is Coming / Et l'octobre vient / Wa jâa tashrîn* (1973), *The Trap / Le piège / al-Masyada* (1979, 100', 35mm), *Al-tharwa al-samakia* (1975), *Smiling through the Tears / Le sourire à travers les larmes / Basima bayna al-dumû* (1985), *Vendetta of Love / Vendetta d'amour / al-Intiqam hubban* (1985).

Youssef, Karkis. Iraqi filmmaker. Short fictional film on Palestine: *Sad Oranges / Les oranges tristes / al-Burtugal el-h'azin* (1969).

Youssef, Mohamed. Emirati filmmaker. Born in 1984 in Al-Ain of Egyptian descent, he studied at the American University of Sharjah. Short documentary film: *Too Late Redemption* (2004, 9', Mini DV).

Youssef, Susan. Palestinian filmmaker. Based in the United States. Documentary: *Curfew* a.k.a. *Forbidden to Wander / Couvre-feu / Mamnu' al-tajawwul* (2003).

ZAATARI, AKRAM. Lebanese filmmaker. Born in 1966, he studied architecture at the American University of Beirut. Directed several short documentaries for television, in particular for Future Television in Beirut. Short films include both documentaries: *The Candidate / Le candidat* (1995), *Present / Cadeau* (1995, 4', Beta SP), and fictions: *Distant Shadows / Ombres lointaines* (with Rachad al-

Jisr, 1993, 11', Beta SP), *Countdown / Compte à rebours* (1995, 6', Beta SP), *Light / Lumière* (1995, 11', Beta SP), *Family Portrait / Portrait de famille* (1995, 10', Beta SP), *Teach Me / Apprends-moi* (1996, 6' Beta SP), *All's Well on the Border / Tout va bien à la frontière* (1997, 50', video), *Mad About You / Fou de toi* (1987), *Red Chewing Gum / Chewing Gum Rouge* (2000, 10', video), *Him and Her / Elle + lui* (2001, 32'), *Van Leo* (2001), *How Much I Love You / Que je t'aime Shou bhebbakj* (2001, 29', video), *The Hole / Le trou* (2005, 30', Beta SP). He has also created various video installations. Contributed two collaboratively made videos, *Airport 1* (40") and *Starry Night* (45"), to the collective project *Videos Under Siege* (DIFF 2008, 39', video). Feature-length documentary: *Today / Aujourd'hui* (2003, 86', Beta SP).

Zaccak, Hady. Lebanese filmmaker. Born in 1974 in Beirut, he studied at IESAV in Beirut, than at FEMIS in Paris. Author of *Le cinéma libanais: Itinéraire d'un cinéma vers l'inconnu (1929–1996)*. Documentaries and fictional shorts during and after his studies, including, *A Thousand and a Thousand Nights* (1999, 15', video), *Lebanon through Its Cinema / Le Liban à travers le cinéma* (2003, 15'), *Refugees for Life* (2006, 48').

Zadeh, Iman Tahsin. Emirati filmmaker. She has worked extensively as a film editor. Short film: *Are You Still Here?* (2006, 37', HD),

Zain, Ahmed. Emirati filmmaker. He studied at Abu Dhabi Men's College, Short films: *Mother* (2003, 28', DV Cam), *Marriage Fund* (2003, 14', Beta SP), *The Return to the Village* (2003, 46', Beta SP), *Bad End* (2004, 10, DV Cam), *Ghost of the Road* (2004, 7', DV Cam), *The Open Sea* (2005, 25', Mini DV), *Speed* (2005, 5' Mini DV), *Manoros* (2005, 7', Mini DV), *White Paper* (2006, 18', Mini DV), *Noor* (2006, 14', DigiBeta), *The Flag That United Us* (2006, 9', Mini DV), *Heartless / Bela qalb* (2007, 25', DV Cam), *Sea Shells* (2008, 16', HDV), *Al-Hamra Island in the Eyes of Emirati Filmmakers* (with Ahmed Arshi, 2009, 25', HD Cam), *Key* (2009, 16', HD Cam).

Zakaria, Moustafa. Emirati filmmaker. He studied at the American University of Sharjah. Short films: *The Red Button* (2005, 10', Mini DV), *It's All in My Head* (with Israa' Magdi Zayed, 2006, 3', Mini DV), *Cairo Dubai Cairo Dubai Cairo* (2006, 29', Mini DV), *Perceptions of Time* (2007, 1', HD), *A Film for All and None* (2007, 10', Mini DV), *The Beggar and Moustafa's Brain* (2008, 7', Mini DV).

Zakharia, Nasri. Palestinian filmmaker. Born to Irish and Palestinian parents, he studied at New York University's film school and lives in New York. Short film: *Tale of Three Mohameds* (2003).

Zaman, Hicham. Iraqi filmmaker. He is currently resident in Norway. Short fictional film: *Winterland* (2007, 52').

Zantut, Fu'ad. Lebanese filmmaker. His work concerns Palestine. Documentaries: *On the Path of the Palestinian Revolution / Sur le chemin de la révolution palestinienne / 'Ala tarik al-thaura al-filastinyyah* (1971), *Black Pages / Pages noires / Awraq sawda'* (1979), *Treason a.k.a. The Betrayal / Trahison / al-Khiyana* (1980).

Zaraket, Ali. Lebanese filmmaker. Short film: *Little Mornings—Beirut* (2008, 26').

Zayed, Israa' Magdi. Emirati filmmaker. She studied at the American University of Sharjah. Short fictional films: *It's All in My Head* (with Moustafa Zakaria, 2006, 3', Mini DV), *4.32pm* (2006, 9', Mini DV).

Zbib, Hassan. Lebanese filmmaker. Born in 1960 in Lebanon, he studied drama at the Faculty of Fine Art of the University of Beirut. He has lived in France since 1987. Short fictional film: *How Can I Explain It to You, Mother? / Comment t'expliquer, mère?* (1998, 18', 35mm).

Zéhil, Maryanne. Lebanese filmmaker. Born in 1969 in Beirut, she began as a journalist for the Lebanese Broadcasting Company. In 1997, she settled in Quebec and for 6 years worked for French-language television. She made her first short in 2004. French-language feature film: *From My Window, without a Home / De ma fenêtre, sans maison* (2006, 87', 35mm).

Zeidan, Samir. Iraqi filmmaker. Short fictional film: *The Mute / La muette* (1999, 25'. 35mm).

Zeine, Rawan. Jordanian filmmaker and member of the Amman Filmmakers Cooperative. She studied at Emerson College in the United States and works as a public relations consultant. Short experimental film: *Three Eyes* (with Hazim Bitar, 2007, 5').

ZENEDDINE, CHADI. Lebanese filmmaker. Born in 1979 in Libreville, he had professional training in filmmaking, video, and communication. He has worked in television, making dramas and documentaries, and directed short films. Based in Paris. Feature film: *Falling from Earth / Tomber de la terre / Wa-ala el-ard el-sama'a* (2007, 70', 35mm).

ZIKRA, SAMIR. Syrian filmmaker. Born in 1945 in Beirut but raised in Aleppo, he graduated from VGIK, the Moscow film school, in 1983. He collaborated on the scripts of Nabil al-Maleh's *Fragments of Images* (1979) and Mohamed Malas's *City Dreams* (1983). Short fictional and documentary films: *Never Let Us Forget / Nous n'oublierons jamais / Lan nansa abadan* (1974, 31'), *The Witnesses / Les témoins / al-Shuhûd* (1975, 32'), *The Sea Is Our Front Line / La mer est notre front / al-Bahr jabhatuna* (1975), *Women in Syria / La femme en Syrie / al-Mara'a fi Sûriya* (1978), *About Her / À propos d'elle / Anbâ* (1981 40'). Feature films: *The Half-Metre Incident / L'accident du demi-mètre*

/ *Hadithat al-nisf mitr* (1983, 117', 35mm), *Chronicle of the Coming Year / Chronique de l'année prochaine / Waqai al'am al-muqbil* (1986, 120', 35mm), *A Land for Strangers / La terre des étrangers / Turab al-ajaneb* (1998, 120', 35mm), *Public Relations / Relations publiques / Alaqat ammah* (2005, 140', 35mm).

Zoabi, Manar. Palestinian filmmaker. Short film: *In Between* (2005, 3').

Zoabi, Sameh. Palestinian filmmaker. Born in 1975 in Iksal, near to Nazareth, he graduated in film and English literature at Tel Aviv University in 1998. He subsequently received a bursary enabling him to spend 3 years studying for a master's in directing at Columbia University, New York. Short film: *Be Quiet / Reste tranquille* (2004, 19', Beta SP).

Zoabi, Taher. Palestinian filmmaker. Short film: *Satisfaction / al-Rida* (2004).

Zraiek, Hicham. Palestinian filmmaker. Documentary: *Sons of Eilaboun* (2008, 24').

Zureikat, Rabee. Jordanian filmmaker and member of the Amman Filmmakers Cooperative. He studied at the NDU in Lebanon and works as an advertising executive. Short films: *Ash* (2006, 5', DV Cam), *Not My Turn* (with Hazim Bitar, 2008, 6').

Zureikat, Sima. Jordanian filmmaker and member of the Amman Filmmakers Cooperative. Studied in the United States and works as writer and editor. Short films: *A Couple and a Silver Roof* (with Muna Asmar, 2003), *Dry* (2004).

Part Two

Feature-Film Chronologies

IRAQ

Size: 169,235 square miles
Population: 28,945,657
GDP: £25,293m
GDP per head: £887
Capital city: Baghdad (population:
  5,054,000)

FEATURE FILMS: 105

1940s	3
1950s	11
1960s	27
1970s	18
1980s	16
1990s	9
2000s	21

Iraqi Feature Filmmakers: 63

Faleh Abdel-Aziz, Layth Abdulamir, Kassim Abid, Mohamed al-Ansari, Kamel al-Azzawi, Dia' al-Bayati, Mohamed al-Daradji, Zuhair al-Dijaili, Borhan al-Din Jassem, Hussein Hasan Ali, Ja'far Ali, Safa Mohamed Ali, Borhan Jassem al-Imam, Sami al-Jader, Fawzi al-Janabi, Mohamed Youssef al-Janabi, Khairiya al-Mansour, Jawad al-Obali, Abdel Jabar al-Obeidi, Kamel al-Obeidi, Hyder al-Omer, Abdelhadi al-Rawi, Abdl Khaliq al-Samaraï, Hussen al-Samaraï, Abdel Karem al-Saraj, Amer Alwan, Mohamed al-Din al-Yasen, Mohamed Monir al-Yasen, Fayçal al-Yassiri, Faleh al-Zeïdi, Qays al-Zubaydi, Ravin Asaf, Khahil Chawqi, Hayder Mousa Daffar, Abbas Fahdel, Tahya Faïq, Mohamed Munir Fanari, Youssuf Gergis, Sahib Haddad, Karlo Hartyon, Kameran Hassani, Qassim Hawal, Ibrahim Jalal, Mohamed Choukri Jamil, Shawkat Amin Korki, Hikmet Labib, Abdel Hadi Mobarak, Samir

Nimr, Maysoon Pachachi, Oday Rasheed, Jano Rosebiani, Ebrahim Saeedi, William Saimon, Hiner Saleem, Massoud Arif Salih, Ibrahim Salman, Saad Salman, Samir, Zahavi Sanjavi, Harry Sarkissian, Abdl Jaber Wali.

Other Arab Feature Filmmakers Working in Iraq: 7

Salah Abou Seif, Fouad al-Tuhami, Ahmed Badrakhan, André Chotin, Ahmed Kamel Morsi, Niazi Mostafa, Tewfiq Saleh (marked with an asterisk [*] in the chronology).

Chronology

1945
Cairo-Baghdad / Le Caire-Bagdad / Al-Kahira-Bagdad (Ahmed Badrakhan*) (Egyptian co-production)
Son of the East / Le fils de l'Orient / Ibn al-Chark (Niazi Mostafa*) (Egyptian co-production)
1948
Alia and Issa / Alia et Issa / Alya wa Issa (André Chotin*)
1950
Fitna and Hassan / Fitna et Hassan / Fitna wa Hassan (Hyder al-Omer)
Leila in Iraq / Layla en Irak / Layla fi al Irak (Ahmed Kamel Morsi*) (Lebanese co-production)
1955
Regrets / Nadam (Abdl Khaliq al-Samari)
1956
Warda (Tahya Faïq)
Who Is Responsible? / Qui est responsable? / Man al-mas'oul? (Abdl Jaber Wali)
1957
Saïd Effendi (Kameran Hassani)

Tishwahen / Tiswahen (Hussen al-Samaraï)
1958
Doctor Hassan / Docteur Hassan / Doctor Hassan (Mohamed Monir al-Yasen)
Life's Lesson / La leçon de la vie / Ababathu al-hayat (Mohamed al-Ansari)
Take Pity on Me / Ayez pitié de moi / Irhamoini (Hyder al-Omer)
1959
The Will of the People / La volonté du peuple / Iradat al-chab (Borhan al-Din Jassem)
1960
I Am Iraq / Je suis l'Irak / Ana al-Irak (Mohamed al-Din al-Yasen)
1961
The Bride of the Euphrates / La mariée de l'Euphrate / Aros al-forat (Abdel Hadi Mobarak)
The Last Decision / La dernière décision / Hobat al-madlum (Safa Mohamed Ali)
1962
Abou Hella / Abu hila (Mohamed Choukri Jamil and Youssuf Gergis)
Chazhra the Bedouin / Chazhra la bédouine / Chazhra al-badawia (Borhan Jassem al-Imam)
For the Homeland / Pour la patrie / Min ajl al-watan (Fawzi al-Janabi)
Naima (Adbl Jaber Wali)
Nebuchadnezzar / Nabuchodonsor / Nabuocher nosser (Kamel al-Azzawi)
Sultana (Safa Mohamed Ali)
Wedding Proposal / Projet de mariage / Mashro zawadj (Kameran Hassani)
1963
Afra and Bader / Afra et Bader / Afra wa Bader (Faleh al-Zeïdi)
Autumn Leaves / Feuilles d'automne / Awrak al-kharif (Hikmet Labib)
Painful Nights / Les nuits de douleur / Layali al-adab (Jawad al-Obali)
Return to the Countryside / Retour à la campagne / Al-awda lil rif (Faleh Abdel-Aziz)
The Seven O'clock Train / Le train de sept heures / Qitar al-saa sabaa (Hikmet Labib)
1964
At Dawn / À l'aube / Maa al-fajr (Abdel Jabar al-Obeidi)
Basra 11 O'clock / Basrah 11 heures / Basrah saa da'ach (William Saimon)

Room No. 7 / Chambre No. 7 / Gorfa raqm sabaa (Kameran Hassani)
1965
The Hand of Fate / La main du destin / Yad al-qadar (Kamel al-Obeidi)
1966
The Path of Love / La voie de l'amour / Darb al-Hubb (Borhan al-Din Jassem)
1967
Farewell Lebanon / Adieu ô Liban / Wad'an ya Lubnan (Hikmat Labib)
Gazala (Safa Mohamed Ali)
The Path of Evil / La voie du mal / Trik al-char (Sami al-Jader)
1968
The Man / L'homme / al-Rajul (Fayçal al-Yassiri)
The Night Watchman / Le veilleur de nuit / al-Haris (Khahil Chawqi)
1969
The Bus Driver / Le contrôleur d'autobus / al-Jabi (Jaf'ar Ali)
The Good Omen / Le bon augure / Chaif Khir (Mohamed Choukri Jamil)
1970
The Al-Ahrar Bridge / Le pont d'al-Ahrar / Jisr al-ahrar (Dia' al-Bayati)
The Path of Darkness / La voie des ténèbres / Tariq al-dalam (Abdel Karem al-Saraj)
The Reward / La récompense / Al-jaza (Hussen al-Samaraï) (unreleased)
1972
The Thirsty Ones / Les assoiffés / al-Damiun (Mohamed Choukri Jamil)
1973
Love and Karaté / L'amour et karaté / Hubb wa karati (Fayçal al-Yassiri)
1974
Hamidou's Return / Le retour d'Hamidou / Awdat Hamidu (Fayçal al-Yassiri)
The Turning / Le tournant / al-Mun'ataf (Jaf'ar Ali)
A Very Particular Love / Un amour tout particulier / Gharâmiât khasa jidan (Fayçal al-Yassiri)
1975
Baghdad Nights / Les nuits de Bagdad / Layali Bagdad (Borhan al-Din Jassem)
1976
The Head / La tête / al-Ras (Fayçal al-Yasseri)

1977

The Attempt / L'essai / al-Tajruba (Fouad al-Tuhami*)

The Boat / La barque / al-Zawraq (collective)

The Houses in That Alley / Les maisons de cette ruelle / Bitut fi dhalika al-zuqaq (Qassim Hawal)

Lovers on the Road / Les amants en route / Ushâqalâ al-tariq (Fayçal al-Yassiri)

The River / Le fleuve / al-Nahr (Fayçal al-Yassiri)

1978

Another Day / Un autre jour / Yawm akhar (Sahib Haddad)

The Searchers / Les chercheurs / al-Bahithun (Mohamed Youssef al-Janabi)

1979

The Walls / Les murs a.k.a. *Les remparts / al-Aswar* (Mohamed Choukri Jamil)

1980

Hamad and Hammud / Hamad et Hammud / Hamad wa Hammud (Ibrahim Jalal)

The Long Days / Les longues journées / al-Ayyam al-tawîla (Tewfiq Saleh*)

The Sniper / Le canardeur / al-Qannes (Fayçal al-Yassiri)

1981

The Battle of Al-Qâdissiya / La bataille d'Al-Qâdissiya / al-Qâdissiya (Salah Abou Seif*)

Return to Haifa / Retour à Haifa / A'id ila Hayfa (Qassim Hawal)

1982

Mutawa and Bahia / Mutawa et Bahia / Mutawa wa Bahia (Sahib Haddad and Zuhair al-Dijaili)

The Princess and the River / La princesse et le fleuve / al-Amira wal-Nahr (Fayçal al-Yassiri) (animated feature)

1983

Clash of Loyalties a.k.a. *The Big Question / La grande question / al-Massala al-korba* (Mohamed Choukri Jamil)

1984

Palestine: A People's Record / La Palestine, chronique d'un peuple / Filstin, sjil sha' (Qays al-Zubaydi) (documentary)

1986

Borders in Flames / Frontières en flammes / Hudud al-mulahihah (Sahib Haddad)

Flat No. 13 / L'immeuble No. 13 / Imara rakm 13 (Sahib Haddad)

Love in Baghdad / L'amour à Bagdad / al-Hubb fi Baghdad (Abdelhadi al-Rawi)

The Lover / L'amant / al-'Ashiq (Mohamed Munir Fanari)

1988

20/20 Vision / Sitta 'ala sitta (Khairiya al-Mansour)

The House / La maison / al-Bayt (Abdelhadi al-Rawi)

A Little Strength / un peu de force / Chaï min al-quwwah (Karlo Hartyon)

1990

Iftarid nafsaka Sa'idan (Abdelhardi al-Rawi)

1992

100 Percent / Miya 'ala miya (Khairiya al-Mansour)

The Bride from Kurdistan / La mariée du Kurdistan / Arusat Kurdistan (Ja'far Ali)

Looking for Princess Leila / À la recherche de la princesse Layla / al-Baath . . . 'an Layla al-amiriyyah (Qassim Hawal)

A Silent Traveller / Un voyageur silencieux (Ibrahim Salman).

1993

Babylon II (Samir)

1997

Long Live the Bride . . . and the Liberation of Kurdistan / Vive la mariée . . . et la libération du Kurdistan (Hiner Saleem, 1997)

1999

Beyond Our Dreams / Passeurs de rêve (Hiner Saleem)

Iranian Journey / Une traversée en bus de l'Iran (Maysoon Pachachi) (documentary)

2002

Baghdad On/Off (Saad Salman)

Forget Baghdad: Jews and Arabs—The Iraqi Connection / Oublie Bagdad: Juifs et Arabes—la connection irakienne (Samir) (documentary)

Jiyan (Jano Rosebiani)

2003

Bitter Water / Eau amère (Maysoon Pachachi)

Vodka Lemon / Vodka citron (Hiner Saleem)

Zaman, the Reed Man / Zaman, l'homme aux roseaux (Amer Alwan) (documentary)

2004

Return to the Land of Wonders / Retour au pays des merveilles (Maysoon Pachachi) (documentary)

Underexposure / Sous-exposition / Ghair salih (Oday Rasheed)

2005

Dreams / Rêves / Ahlaam (Mohamed al-Daradji)

The Dreams of Sparrows / Rêves de moineaux (Hayder Mousa Daffar) (documentary)

Iraq: The Song of the Missing Men / Irak, le chant des absents (Layth Abdulamir) (documentary)

Kilometer Zero / Kilomètre zéro (Hiner Saleem)

Narcissus Blossom / Le temps des narcisses / U nergiz biskvin (Hussein Hasan Ali and Massoud Arif Salih)

2006

Crossing the Dust / À travers la poussière / Parinawa la ghobar (Shawkat Amin Korki)

2007

Dawn of the World / L'aube du monde (Abbas Fahdel)

2008

Life After the Fall / La vie après la chute / Hatay ma baad al-suqoot (Kassim Abid) (documentary)

Our Feelings Took the Pictures: Open Shutters Iraq / Nos sentiments ont pris les images images de l'Irak (Maysoon Pachachi) (documentary)

The Smell of Apples / Le parfum des pommes (Ravin Asaf)

2009

All My Mothers / Toutes mes mères / Hamey-e madrana-e man (Ebrahim Saeedi and Zahavi Sanjavi)

Son of Babylon / Fils de Babylone / Ibn Babil (Mohamed al-Daradji)

War, Love, God and Madness / Guerre, amour, dieu, et folie (Mohamed al-Daradji) (documentary)

Short Filmmakers (Fiction and Documentary): 36

Rtarek Abdelkrim, Layth Abdulamir, Kamel Akaf, Baz Shamoun al-Bazi, Saeed Aldaheeri, Hassanain al-Hani, Emad Ali, Kutaïba al-Janabi, Dhafir al-Khatib, Basheer al-Majid, Saad al-Massoudi, Ibrahim al-Sahen, Hussein Alwan, Bahram al-Zuhairi, Jamal Amin, Nizar Annadawi, Abbas Bani, Hiba Bassem, Alias Chlatt, Yassine El Bakri, Victor Haddad, Tariq Hashim, Cherif Abdel Hussein, Ahmed Jabbar, Ahmed Kamal, Emmanuel Rassam, Ammar Saad, Kifaya Saleh, Mounaf Shaker, Cheirak Sorrein, Shaker T. Tahrer, Dhafir Taleb, Mohamed Tawfik, Rania Mohamed Tawfik, Karkis Yousef, Hicham Zaman, Samir Zeidan.

IRAQ: REFERENCES

Al-Mafraji, Ahmed Fayadh. *The Cinema in Iraq.* Baghdad: Research and Studies Centre, General Establishment for Cinema and Theatre, Ministry of Culture and Information, n.d. [1978?].

Chebli, Hakki. "The Cinema and Theater in Iraq." In *Arab Cinema and Culture*, no. 3, pp. 28–34. Beirut: Arab Film and Television Centre, 1964.

———. "History of the Iraqi Cinema." In *The Cinema in the Arab Countries*, ed. Georges Sadoul, pp. 117–119. Beirut: Interarab Centre for Cinema and Television, 1966.

Haustrate, Gaston. "Irak: Mutation prometteuse du secteur cinéma." *Cinema 78* 233 (1978): 64–65.

Hawal, Kassem. "Regard sur le cinéma irakien." In *Septième Biennale des cinémas arabes*, pp. 99–113. Paris: Institut du Monde Arabe, 2004.

Hillhauer, Rebecca. "Iraq." In *Encyclopedia of Arab Women Filmmakers*, pp. 117–129. Cairo: American University in Cairo Press, 2005.

Ibrahim, Abbas Fadhil. "Le cinéma irakien: un accouchement de quarante ans." In *Les cinémas arabes*, ed. Mouny Berrah, Jacques Lévy, and Claude-Michel Cluny, pp. 76–83. Paris: Éditions du Cerf / Institut du Monde Arabe / *CinémAction* 43, 1987.

———. "The Iraqi Cinema in 1964." In *The Cinema in the Arab Countries*, ed. Georges Sadoul, pp. 185–186. Beirut: Interarab Centre of Cinema and Television, 1966.

Kennedy-Day, Kiki. "Cinema in Lebanon, Syria, Iraq and Kuwait." In *Companion*

Encyclopedia of Middle Eastern and North African Film, ed. Oliver Leaman, pp. 364–419. London: Routledge, 2001.

Khamarou, Samir. "Le cinéma documentaire en Irak de 1940 à 1980." In *La semaine du cinéma arabe,* pp. 55–60. Paris: Institut du Monde Arabe, 1987.

Mahajar, Jaffar. "The Transformation of the Act of Narration: Strategies of Adaptation of *Al-Qamar w'al-Aswar.*" *Alif: Journal of Comparative Politics* 28 (2008): 165–187.

Nouri, Shakir. *À la recherche du cinéma irakien, 1945–1985.* Paris: Éditions L'Harmattan, 1986.

Thoraval, Yves. "Irak: Des films ou une cinématographie nationale?" In *Les écrans du croissant fertile,* pp. 15–30. Paris: Atlantica / Séguier, 2002.

Tsoffar, Ruth. "Forget Baghdad: Jews and Arabs—The Iraqi Connection." In *The Cinema of North Africa and the Middle East,* ed. Gönül Dönmetz-Colin, pp. 256–265. London: Wallflower Press, 2007.

JORDAN

Size: 24,277 square miles
Population: 6,342,948
GDP: £7,201m
GDP per head: £1,300
Capital city: Amman (population: 1,060,000)

FEATURE FILMS: 10

1950s	2
1960s	3
1970s	—
1980s	—
1990s	1
2000s	4

Jordanian Feature Filmmakers: 7

Nassim Amrouche, Najdat Ismaïl Anzur, Abdel Wahab al-Hindi, Fadi Hindash, Mohamed Kaouach, Mahmoud Massad, Amin Matalqa.

Other Arab Feature Filmmaker Working in Jordan: 1

Ibrahim Hassan Sirhan (marked with an asterisk [*] in the chronology).

Chronology

1957
The Moon and the Sun / La lune et le soleil / al-Qamar wash-shams (Ibrahim Hassan Sirhan*)

1958
The Struggle in Jarash / Combat à Djérash / Sira'a fi Jarash (Ibrahim Hassan Sirhan*)
1964
My Beloved Homeland / Ma patrie bien aimée / Watani habibi (Mohamed Kaouach)
1969
The Road to Jerusalem / La route de Jérusalem / al-Tarikila al-Qods (Abdel Wahab al-Hindi)
Struggle till Liberation / Lutte jusqu'à la libération / Kifah hatta al-Tahrir (Abdel Wahab al-Hindi)
1991
An Oriental Story / Une histoire orientale / Hikâya sharqiyya (Najdat Ismaïl Anzur)
2007
Captain Abu Raed / Le capitaine Abu Raed (Amin Matalqa)
Recycle / Recyclage / Ea'adat khalk (Mahmoud Massad) (documentary)
2009
Goodbye Gary / Adieu Gary (Nassim Amrouche)
Not Quite the Taliban / Pas encore le Taliban (Fadi Hindash) (documentary)

Short Filmmakers (Fiction and Documentary): 54

Yahya Abdullah, Mohamed Aboujarad, Sajeda Abousaif, Mustafa Abu Ali, Nabil Issa al-Khatib, Dalia Alkury, Firas Abd al-Jahil al-Moderat, Adnan al-Rahmy, Amjad al-Rasheed,

Adnan al-Roumi, Muna Asmar, Rifqi Assaf, Muawia Attalah, Reem Bader, Hazim Bitar, Ala' Diab, Yazan Doughan, Merva Faddoul, Razan Ghalayini, Fadi G. Haddad, Hussam Hamarheh, Mais Hamarneh, Dima Hamdan, Samir Hassan, Khaled Hlailaat, Ahmad Humeid, Hussein Jafarawi, Mutaz Jankot, Saleh Kasem, Razan Khatib, Lina Khory, Amal Khoury, Adnan Madanat, Sandra Madi, Aseel Mansour, Said Najmi, Tariq Nasir, Aseel Qader, Ammar Quttaineh, Nesreen Rafeeq, Alabbas Sa'ed, Ja'far Safwan, Omar Saleh, Ghassan Salti, Bashar Sharaf, Nabil Qusta Shoumali, Ali Siyyam, Hamaza Soufan, Najah Taffal, Amr Touky, Rawan Zeine, Rabee Zureikat, Sima Zureikat. Plus the Amman Filmmakers Cooperative.

JORDAN: REFERENCES

Costandi, Nicholas. "The Cinema in Jordan." In *The Cinema in the Arab Countries,* ed. Georges Sadoul, pp. 182–184. Beirut: Interarab Centre of Cinema and Television, 1966.

Nicholas, Kostandi. "The Cinema and Television in the Hashemite Kingdom of Jordan." In *Arab Cinema and Culture,* vol. 3, pp. 22–25. Beirut: Arab Film and Television Centre, 1964.

See also: Amman Filmmakers Cooperative (AFC), http://JordanianFilms.com.

Jordan Short Film Festival (JSFF), http://JordanFilmFestival.com.

Many of the short films are available on YouTube/JordanianFilms.

LEBANON

Size: 4,036 square miles
Population: 4,017,095
GDP: £11,604m
GDP per head: £2,861
Capital city: Beirut (population: 1,846,000)

FEATURE FILMS: 245

1930s	1
1940s	3
1950s	12
1960s	71
1970s	43
1980s	51
1990s	24
2000s	40

Lebanese Feature Filmmakers: 75

Taysir Abboud, Nicolas Abou Samah, Philippe Akiki, Ali al-Ariss, Borhan Alawiyya, Samir al-Ghoussayni, Wiam al-Saidi, Philippe Aractingi, Danielle Arbid, Layla Assaf, Roger Assaf, Maroun Bagdadi, Alfred Bahri, Nigol Bezjian, Karam Boustany, Randa Chahal-Sabbagh, Georges Chamchoum, Jean Chamoun, Hassib Chams, Fouad Charafeddine, Youssef Charafeddine, Walid Charara, Jean-Claude Codsi, Christine Dabague, Julio De Luca, Ziad Doueiri, Sabine El Gemayel, Simon El Habre, Joseph Fahdi, Josef Farès, Dalia Fathallah, Assad Fouladkar, Gary Garabédian, André Gedeon, Georges Ghayad, Christian Ghazi, Joseph Ghorayeb, Samir Habchi, Zinardi Habis, Joana Hadjithomas, Rafic Hajjar, Michel Haroun, Bahij Hojeïj, Katia Jarjoura, Khalil Joreige, Fouad Joujou, Georges Kahi, Michel Kammoun, Tahsine Kawadri, Fares Khalil, Samir Khoury, Nadine Labaki, Romeo Lahoud, Mounir Maasri, Jawad Metni, Wajdi Mouawad, Rida Myassar, Olga Nakkash, Georges Nasser, Marc Abi Rached, Ghadi Rahbani, Marwan Rahbani, Antoine Remy, Jocelyne Saab, Ghassan Salhab, Soubhi Seifeddine, Mohamed Selmane, Mohamed Souweid, Heiny Srour, Ibrahim Takkouche, Hany Tamba, Bechara Wakim, Akram Zaatari, Chadi Zeneddine.

Other Arab Feature Filmmakers Working in Lebanon: 12

Samir Abdallah, Farouk Agrama, Ahmed al-Toukhi, Salah Badrakhan, Henri Barakat, Youssef Chahine, Youssef Issa, Youssef

Maalouf, Albert Naguib, Samir Nasri, Harry Sarkassian, Sayed Tantawi, (marked with an asterisk [*] in the chronology).

Chronology

1933

In the Ruins of Baalbeck / Dans les ruines de Baalbeck / Bayn hayakel Baalbeck (Julio De Luca and Karam Boustany)

1943

The Flower Seller / La vendeuse de fleurs / Bayyaat al-ward (Ali al-Ariss, unfinished)

1946

The Planet of the Desert Princess / Kawkab, princesse du désert / Kawkab amirat as-sahra (Ali al-Ariss)

Summer in Lebanon / L'été au Liban (Salah Badrakhan*)

1953

Remorse / Remords / Azab al-damir (Georges Kahi)

1957

The First Song / Le premier chant / al-Lahn al-awal (Mohamed Selmane)

Red Flowers / Fleurs rouges / Zouhour hamra (Michel Haroun)

1958

For Whom the Sun Rises / Pour qui se lève le soleil / Liman tachrok al-chams (Joseph Fahdi)

Memories / Souvenirs / Zikrayat (Georges Kahi)

Rendezvous with Hope / Rendez-vous avec l'espoir / Moad maa al-amal (Mohamed Selmane)

Towards the Unknown / Vers l'inconnu / Ila ayn (Georges Nasser)

1959

Days of My Life / Jours de ma vie / Ayyam min omri (Georges Kahi)

The Judgement of Fate / Jugement du destin / Hokm al-kadar (Joseph Ghorayeb)

The Rock of Love / Le rocher de l'amour / Sakhar al-hub (Rida Myassar)

The Songs of My Love / Les chants de mon amour / Angham habibi (Mohamed Selmane)

Two Hearts, One Body / Deux cœurs, un corps (Georges Kahi)

1960

Birth of the Prophet / Naissance du prophète / Mawled al-rassoul (Ahmed al-Toukhi*)

Burning Heart / Cœur brûlant / Fi kalbiha nar (Ahmed al-Toukhi*)

The Deadly Necklace / Le collier meurtrier / al-Akd al-katel (Ibrahim Takkouche)

I Am Not Guilty / Je ne suis pas coupable / Lastou mouzniba (Ibrahim Takkouche)

1961

The Little Stranger / Le petit étranger (Georges Nasser)

A Stranger in the House / Une étrangère à la maison / Fil dar ghariba (Joseph Fahdi)

The White Poison / Le poison blanc / al-Sam al-abiad (Georges Kahi)

1962

Abou Selim in the City / Abou Sélim en ville (Hassib Chams)

The Broken Wings / Les ailes brisées / al-Ajniha al-mutakassira (Youssef Maalouf*)

The Devil's Cart / La charrette du diable / Arabat al-chaitane (Georges Kahi)

Hello, Love / Bonjour l'amour / Marhabane ayouhal hub (Mohamed Selmane)

Years / Des années / Sinine (Georges Kahi)

1963

Abou Selim, Messenger of Love / Abou Sélim émissaire d'amour (Youssef Maalouf*)

Chouchou and the Million / Chouchou et le Million / Chouchou wal million (Antoine Remy)

Darbat al-wade' (Wiam al-Saidi)

Lebanon at Night / Le Liban, la nuit / Loubnan fi leil (Mohamed Selmane)

A Love Story / Histoire d'amour / Hikayat gharam (Mohamed Selmane)

Praise for Love / Louange pour l'amour / Ya salam al-hub (Mohamed Selmane)

Red on the Snow / Rouge sur neige / Dimaa al-talj (Wiam al-Saidi)

The Vigilant Eye / L'œil vigilant / al-Ayn al-sahira (Gary Garabédian)

1964

A Bedouin Girl in Paris / Une bédouine à Paris / Badawia fi Baris (Mohamed Selmane)

The Idol of the Crowds / L'idole des foules / Fatinat al-jamahir (Mohamed Selmane)

Joys of Youth / Joies de la jeunesse / Afrah al-chabab (Mohamed Selmane)

Loved by All / Aimée de tous / Habitat al-kol
  (Rida Myassar)

O Night / O nuit / Ya leil (Gary Garabédian)

The Pearl Necklace / Le collier de perles / Akd
  al-loulou (Youssef Maalouf*)

You Are My Life / Toi, ma vie / Anta omri
  (Georges Kahi)

1965

The Bank / La banque / al-Bank (Mohamed
  Selmane)

A Bedouin Girl in Rome / Une bédouine
  à Rome / Badawia fi Roma (Mohamed
  Selmane)

Bitter Honey / Le miel amer / al-Assal al-morr
  (Rida Myassar)

The Black Jaguar / Le jaguar noir / al-Jaguar
  al-sawda' (Mohamed Selmane)

Body on Fire / Le corps en feu / Lahib al-jassad
  (Rida Myassar)

Garo / Garo (Gary Garabédian)

The Idol of the Desert / L'idole du désert /
  Fatinat al-sahra (Mohamed Selmane)

In the Service of Love / Au service de l'amour /
  Bi amr al-hub (Mohamed Selmane)

Meeting at Palmyra / Rencontre à Palmyre /
  Lika' fi tadmor (Youssef Maalouf*)

The Millionnaire / Le millionaire (Youssef
  Maalouf*)

The Seller of Rings / Le vendeur de bagues /
  Biya al-khawatim (Youssef Chahine*)

Youth and Beauty / La jeunesse et la beauté /
  al-Siba wal jamal (Mohamed Selmane)

1966

Abou Selim in Africa / Abou Sélim en Afrique
  / Abou Sélim fi Afriquia (Gary Garabédian)

The Arab Falcon / Le faucon des arabes / Sakr
  al-arab (Rida Myassar)

Charbel (Nicolas Abou Samah)

Chouchou's Adventures / Les aventures de
  Chouchou / Moughamarat Chouchou
  (Mohamed Selmane)

The Conquerors / Les conquérants / al-Kahir-
  oun (Farouk Agrama*)

For Women Only / Pour femmes seulement /
  Lil nisa'a fakat (Antoine Remy)

Hotel of Dreams / Hôtel des rêves / Foundok
  al-ahlam (Albert Naguib*)

Love in Istanbul / L'amour à Istamboul /
  Gharam fi Istambul (Tahsine Kawadri)

Mawal / Mawal al-akdam al-zahabia
  (Mohamed Selmane)

Sultana / Sultana (Riad Myassar)

The Tramps / Les vagabonds / al-Charidan
  (Rida Myassar)

The Victory of the Vanquished / La victoire
  du vaincu / Intissar al-mounhazem (Samir
  Nasri)

The Wheedler / L'enjôleuse / al-Daloua
  (Mohamed Selmane)

Youth in the Sun / Jeunesse au soleil / Chabab
  tahtal cham (Samir Nasi)

1967

Beirut 011 / Beyrouth 011 / Beyrouth sifr
  hdaache (Antoine Remy)

Canticles of Love / Cantiques d'amour /
  Alhane al-hub (Mohamed Selmane)

Do Not Touch My Wife / Ne touche pas à ma
  femme / Idak an mrati (Rida Myassar)

Golden Sands / Sables d'or / Rimal min thaheb
  (Youssef Chahine*)

The Freedom Fighters / Les fédayins / al-
  Fidaiyyoun (Christian Ghazi)

I Am Antar / Je suis Antar / Ana Antar
  (Youssef Maalouf*)

The Mute Man and Love / Le muet et l'amour /
  al-Akhrass wal hub (Alfred Bahri)

The Realm of the Poor / Le royaume des pau-
  vres / Mamlakat al-foukara (Philippe Akiki)

Safar Barlek / Safar Barlek (Henri Barakat*)

1968

The Likeable Thief / Le voleur sympathique /
  al-Loss al-zarif (Youssef Issa*)

The Watchman's Daughter / La fille du gardien
  / Bint al-hares (Henri Barakat*)

Welcome to Love / Bienvenue à l'amour
  (Mohamed Selmane)

1969

The Bells of Return / Les cloches du retour /
  Ajrass al-awda (Taysir Abboud)

For You, Oh Palestine / Pour toi ô Palestine /
  Fidaki ya Phalestine (Antoine Remy)

Heroes and Women / Des héros et des femmes
  / Abtal wa nissa (Mohamed Selmane)

The Madness of Adolescent Girls / La folie
  des adolescentes / Jounoun al-mourahikat
  (Taysir Abboud)

The Palestinian in Revolt / Le palestinien ré-
  volté / al-Filastini al-thaer (Rida Myassar)

We Are All Freedom Fighters / Nous sommes

tous des fédayins / Koullouna fidaiyyoun
(Gary Garabédian)

1970

Orchard of Love / Verger d'amour / Karm al-hawa (Mohamed Selmane)

Waves / Vagues / Amwage (Mohamed Selmane)

1971

Bewilderment / L'égarement / al-Dayae (Mohamed Selmane)

The Lady with the Dark Glasses / La dame aux lunes noires / Saydat al-akmar as-sawda (Samir Khoury)

Paris and Love / Paris et l'amour / Baris al-hub (Mohamed Selmane)

Passion on Fire / Passion en feu / Nar al-chawk (Mohamed Selmane)

Salam After Death / Salam après la mort / Salam baad al-mawt (Georges Chamchoum)

1972

The Beautiful Girl and the Tiger / La beauté et le tigre / al-Hassna'wal nemr (Mohamed Selmane)

Fate / Le destin / al-Kadar (Mounir Maasri)

Girls to Love / Des filles à aimer / Banat lil hob (Rida Myassar)

The Gypsy in Love / La gitane amoureuse / al-Ghajaria al-achika (Rida Myassar)

A Hundred Faces for a Single Day / Cent visages pour un seul jour / Miat wajh li yom wahed (Christian Ghazi)

The Queen of Love / La reine de l'amour / Malikat al-hob (Romeo Lahoud)

The She-Cats of Hamra Street / Les chattes de la rue Hamra / Kotat charé al-Hamra (Samir al-Ghoussayni)

The Shrews / Chipies / Banat akker zamane (Rida Myassar)

The Visitor / La visiteuse (Henri Barakat*)

Wolves Do Not Eat Raw Meat / Les loups ne mangent pas la chair fraîche / Ziab la taakol al-lahm (Samir Khoury)

1973

The Best Days of My Life / Les plus beaux jours de ma vie (Henri Barakat*)

The Captive / La captive / al-Asira (Samir al-Ghoussayni)

Cherwale and Mini-Skirt / Cherwale et mini-jupe / Cherwale wa mini-jupe (Samir al-Ghoussayni)

Fire Woman / Femme de feu / Imraa min nar (Rida Myassar)

Love's Guitar / La guitare de l'amour / Guitare al-hub (Mohamed Selmane)

My Darling / Ma chérie (Henri Barakat*)

The Path of Dreams / Chemin des rêves / tariq al-ahlam (Harry Sarkassian*)

The Postman / Le facteur / Saii al-barid (Samir al-Ghoussayni)

Words of Love / Des mots de l'amour / Kalam fi hub (Mohamed Selmane, with Sayed Tantawi*)

1974

The Beach of Love / La plage de l'amour / Chaté al-hob (Antoine Remy)

Grand Prix / Grand prix / al-Jaiza al koubra (Samir al-Ghoussayni)

The Hour of Struggle Has Sounded—the Struggle in Oman / L'heure de la libération a sonné / Saat al-Tahrir dakkat ya Isti'mar (Heiny Srour)

Valuable Game / Gibier de valeur / al-Istiyad al-kabir (Rida Myassar)

Winter Women / Femmes d'hiver / Nisa'a lil chitaa (Samir al-Ghoussayni)

1975

Beirut Oh Beirut / Beyrouth ô Beyrouth / Beirut ya Beirut (Maroun Bagdadi)

Lebanon in Torment / Le Liban dans la tourmente / Lubnân fi al-dawâma (Jocelyne Saab) (documentary)

Life Is a Melody / La vie est une mélodie / al-Dounya nagham (Samir al-Ghoussayni)

A Man Is Needed / On demande un homme / al-Matloup rajol wahed (Georges Nasser)

Professor Ayoub / Le professeur Ayoub / al-Oustaz Ayoub (Mohamed Selmane)

The Resistance Fighter / Le résistant / al-Rajol al-samed (Soubhi Seifeddine)

1976

Does / Biches / Ghezlane (Samir al-Ghoussayni)

The Message a.k.a. *Mohammad, Messenger of God / Le message / al-Risalah* (Mustapha Akkad)

1977

Days in London / Des jours à Londres / Ayyam fi London (Samir al-Ghoussayni)

Fish Filet / Filet de poisson / Samak bila hassak (Samir al-Ghoussayni)

The Sahara Is Not for Sale / Le Sahara n'est pas à vendre (Jocelyne Saab) (documentary)
1978
It Is Not Enough for God to Be with the Poor / Il ne suffit pas que Dieu soit avec les pauvres / La yakfi an yakoun allah maal foukara (Borhan Alawiyya) (documentary)
Marriage of the Land / Les noces de la terre / Urs al-ard (Soubhi Seifeddine)
1980
At the End of Summer / À la fin de l'été / Akher as saif (Marwan and Ghadi Rahbani)
A Beauty and Some Giants / Une belle et des géants / Hassnaa wa amalika (Samir al-Ghoussayni)
The Shelter / L'abri / al-Malja' (Rafic Hajjar)
1981
Absence (Mohamed Souweid)
The Adventurers / Les aventuriers / al-Moughamiron (Samir al-Ghoussayni)
Beirut, the Encounter / Beyrouth, la rencontre / Beyrouth, al-liqa (Borhan Alawaya)
The Decision / La décision / al-Karar (Youssef Charafeddine)
Forgive Me, My Love / Pardonne-moi mon amour / Samehni habibi (Taysir Abboud)
The Island Devil / Le diable de l'île / Chaitane al-jazira (Samir al-Ghoussayni)
The Last Passage / Le dernier passage / al-Mamar al-akhir (Youssef Charafeddine)
1982
The Affair / L'affaire / al-Safaka (Samir al-Ghoussayni)
The Death Leap / Le saut de la mort / Kafzat al-mawt (Youssef Charafeddine)
The Explosion / L'explosion / al-Infijar (Rafic Hajjar)
The Last Night / La dernière nuit / al-Layl al-akhir (Youssef Charafeddine)
Lebanon in Spite of Everything / Le Liban, malgré tout / Loubnan roghma kulla shai' (André Gedeon)
Little Wars / Petites guerres / Houroub saghira (Maroun Bagdadi)
Mothers' Suffering / La souffrance des mères / Azab al-oumahat (Riad Myassar)
A Nightingale in Lebanon / Un rossignol du Liban / Boulbol min Loubnan (Rida Myassar)
Rendezvous with Love / Rendez-vous avec l'amour / Moad maa al-hub (Youssef Charafeddine)
Who Puts out the Fire? / Qui éteint le feu? / Man youtfii al-nar (Mohamed Selmane)
Women's Intrigue / La manigance des femmes / Loubat al-nisaa (Samir al-Ghoussayni)
1983
Al-Mouzayafa (Soubhi Seifeddine)
A Country above Wounds / Un pays, les plaies, un déplacement / Watan fawq al-jirah (Soubhi Seifeddine)
The Hero's Return / Le retour du héros / Awdat al-batal (Samir al-Ghoussayni)
Kidnapped / Le kidnappé / al-Makhtouf (Fouad Joujou)
Mr. Risk-Everything / Monsieur risque-tout / al-Moujazef (Youssef Charafeddine)
Our Little Kings / Nos petits rois / Mulûkundâ al-sighar (André Gedeon)
A Woman with a Monster / Une femme chez un monstre / Imraa fi bayt imlak (Zinardi Habis)
1984
Amani Under the Rainbow / Amani sous l'arc en ciel (Samir Khoury)
The Fifth Column / La cinquième colonne / al-Jiha al-khamisa (Soubhi Seifeddine)
Fragile Houses / Maisons fragiles / Bouyout min warak (Rafic Hajjar)
The Ghost from the Past / Le fantôme du passé / Chabah almadi (Georges Ghayad)
Leila and the Wolves / Layla et les loups / Layla wa al-zi'ab (Heiny Srour)
Maaraka / Maaraké (Roger Assaf)
My Eternal Love / Mon amour éternel / Hopubi lazi la yamout (Youssef Charafeddine)
The Siren / La sirène / Arouss al-bahr (Samir al-Ghoussayni)
The South in Revolt / Le sud révolté / al-Janoub al-thaer (Rida Myassar)
1985
Al-Marmoura (Wiam al-Saidi)
The Gipsy and the Heroes / La gitane et les héros / al-Ghajaria wal abtal (Samir al-Ghoussayni)
The Seductress and the Adventurer / La séductrice et l'aventurier / al-Fatina wal moughamer (Samir al-Ghoussayni)
A Suspended Life a.k.a. *Teenage Flirtation /*

Une vie suspendue a.k.a. *L'adolescente, sucre d'amour / Ghazal al-banât 2* (Jocelyne Saab)

The Vision / La vision / al-Rou'ya (Youssef Charafeddine)

1986

At the Mercy of the Winds / Au gré des vents / Fi mahab al-rih (Zinardi Habis)

At the Time of Pearls / Au temps des perles / Ayyam al-loulou (Wiam al-Saidi)

Me, the Radar / Moi, le radar / Ana al-radar (Wiam al-Saidi)

The Session Is Over / La séance est levée / Wa roufiat al-Jalsa (Georges Ghayad)

1987

Shame, Restoum / La honte, Restoum / Ayb ya Restoum (Wiam al-Saidi)

The Veiled Man / L'homme voilé / al-Rajul al-muhajjah (Maroun Bagdadi)

1989

Fadous and the Hitchhiker / Fadous et l'autostoppeuse (Samir al-Ghoussayni)

1990

Outside Life / Hors la vie / Kharif al-hayat (Maroun Bagdadi)

1991

The Cry / Le cri / al-Sarkha (Fouad Charafeddine)

For Whoever Sings of Love / Pour qui chante l'amour / Liman youghanni al-hub (Wiam al-Saidi)

Screens of Sand / Écrans de sable (Randa Chahal-Sabbag)

Uncle Vania and Co.'s Circus / Le cirque de l'oncle Vania et cie / Cirque al-ame Vania wa chourakah (Samir al-Ghoussayni)

The Woman Thief / La voleuse / al-Sarika (Youssef Charafeddine)

1992

The Girl from the Air / La fille de l'air (Maroun Bagdadi)

The Tornado / Le tourbillon / al-I'ssar (Samir Habchi)

1993

Mr. Gold / Monsieur Gold / Mr. Gold (Samir al-Ghoussayni)

1994

The Freedom Gang / Le gang de la liberté / al-Sheikha (Layla Assaf)

Karim Abou Chacra Does His Military Service / Karim Abou Chacra fait son service militaire / Karim Abdou Chacra fi khidmat al-alam (Fouad Joujou)

Lebanon: Bits and Pieces / Le Liban, fait de pièces et de morceaux / Lubnan qita, qita (Olga Nakkash)

Once upon a Time, Beirut a.k.a. *The Story of a Star / Il était une fois Beyrouth, histoire d'une star / Kan ya ma kan Beirut* a.k.a. *Qissah najmah* (Jocelyne Saab)

Operation: Golden Phoenix / Opération: golden phénix / Amaliat al-taer al-zahabi (Samir al-Ghoussayni)

The Story of a Return a.k.a. *A Time Has Come / Histoire d'un retour* a.k.a. *Il est temps / Ana al-awan* (Jean-Claude Codsi)

1995

Our Heedless Wars / Nos guerres imprudents / Hurubina al-ta'isha (Randa Chahal-Sabbag)

1997

The Infidels / Les infidèles (Randa Chahal-Sabbag)

Zeinab and the River / Zeinab et le fleuve / Zaynab wa-l-nahr (Christine Dabague)

1998

Beirut Phantoms / Beyrouth, ville fantôme / Ashbah Beirut (Ghassan Salhab)

Tango of Yearning / Tango du désir (Mohmcd Souweid)

We Shall Return One Day / Nous retour-nerons un jour (Samir Abdallah and Walid Charara) (documentary)

West Beyrouth / Beirut al-gharbiya (Ziad Doueiri)

1999

Around the Pink House / Autour de la maison rose / Al-bayt al-zahr (Joana Hadjithomas and Khalil Joreige)

The Civilised / Civilisées / al-Mutahadirat (Randa Chahal-Sabbag)

2000

Jalla! Jalla! (Josef Farès)

The Shadows of the City / L'ombre de la ville / Taif al-madina (Jean Chamoun)

Until the End of the Day a.k.a. *Nightfall / Jusqu'au déclin du jour* (Mohamed Souweid) (documentary)

2001

Meshwar (Samir Habchi)

When Maryam Spoke Out / Quand Maryam s'est dévoilée / Lamma hikt Maryam (Assad Fouladkar)

2002
Civil War / Guerre civile (Mohamed Souweid)
Terra incognita / al-Ardh al-majhoulah
 (Ghassan Salhab)
2003
Belt of Fire / Ceinture de feu / Zinnar al-nar
 (Bahij Hojeïj)
The Cops / Les flics (Josef Farès)
The Kite / Le cerf-volant / Yayyara min waraq
 (Randa Chahal-Sabbag)
*The Lady of the Palace / La dame du palais /
 Sayidat el-kasr* (Samir Habashi) (documen-
 tary)
Muron (Nigol Bezjian) (documentary)
Today / Aujourd'hui (Akram Zaatari) (docu-
 mentary)
2004
*Beirut between New York and Baghdad /
 Beyrouth entre New York et Bagdad* (Dalia
 Fathallah) (documentary)
*In the Battlefields / Dans les champs de ba-
 taille / Maarik hob* (Danielle Arbid)
Lila Says That / Lila dit ça (Ziad Doueiri)
Littoral (Wajdi Mouawad)
2005
Ayroum (Nigol Bezjian) (documentary)
The Bus / L'autobus / Bosta (Philippe
 Aractingi)
Dunia (Jocelyne Saab)
A Perfect Day / Un jour parfait / Yawm akhar
 (Joana Hadjithomas and Khalil Joreige)
Zozo (Josef Farès)
2006
Falafel (Michel Kammoun)
The Last Man / Le dernier homme / Atlal
 (Ghassan Salhab)
Terminator (Katia Jarjoura)
2007
Caramel (Nadine Labaki)
*Falling from Earth / Tomber de la terre / Wa-
 ala el-ard el-sama'a* (Chadi Zeneddine)
I Want to See / Je veux voir (Joan Hadjithomas
 and Khalil Joreige)
Khalass (Borhan Alawiya)
A Lost Man / Un homme perdu (Danielle
 Arbid)
*Under the Bombs / Sous les bombes / Taht el-
 qasef* (Philippe Aractingi)

2008
*After the War . . . / Après la guerre c'est tou-
 jours la guerre* (Samir Abdallah*) (docu-
 mentary)
Beirut Open City / Beyrouth ville ouverte
 (Samir Habchi)
Melodrama Habibi / Une chanson dans la tête
 (Hany Tamba)
Niloofar (Sabine El Gemayel)
*The One-Man Village / Le village d'un seul
 homme / Samaan bildayaa* (Simon El Habre)
 (documentary)
2009
1958 (Ghassan Salhab) (documentary)
Help / Au secours (Marc Abi Rached)
*My Heart Beats Only for Her / Mon cœur ne
 bat que pour elle / Ma hataftu li ghayriha*
 (Mohamed Souweid)
Remnants of a War / Les restes d'une guerre
 (Jawad Metni) (documentary)

**Short Filmmakers
(Fiction and Documentary): 142**

Anne-Marie Abboud, Serena Abi Aad, Jad Abi
Khalil, Maher Abi Samra, Hady Abi Wardeh,
Zeina Aboulhosn, Amani Abu Alwan, Lamia
Abu Haidar, Ajram Ajram, Myrna Akaron,
Rana Alamuddin, Fouad Alaywan, Rachad
al-Jisr, Dima al-Joundi, Jihan al-Tahri, Chadi
Aoun, Rania Attieh, Ruba Attieyeh, Abdel
Raheem Awjeh, Ray Barakat, Sheila Barakat,
Raymond Bassile, Tina Baz, Sofiane Belaid,
Hicham Bizri, Vatche Boulghourjian, Lucien
Bourjeily, Bass Brèche, Gregory Buchakjian,
Carlos Chahine, Elias Chahine, André Cham-
mas, Wissam Charaf, Jihane Chouaib, Cyn-
thia Choucair, Ely Dagher, Jacques Debs, Wael
Deed, Hagop Der-Ghougassian, Rolly Dib,
Amin Dora, De Gaulle Eid, Rana Eid, Rouba
El Asmar, Sabine El Chamaa, Dima El Horr,
Nadyne El Khoury, Tania El Khoury, Fouad El
Koury, Maounan El Rahabani, Nasser Fakih,
Dalia Fathallah, Zeina Fathallah, Bassem Fay-
ad, Daniel Garda, Jean Gebran, Lina Ghaibeh,
Amer Ghandour, Samer Ghorayeb, Nadine
Ghorra, Ahmad Ghsein, Samira Gloor-Fadel,
Mirella Habr, Maha Haddad, Merdad Hage,
Sara Haïdar, Moutia Halabi, Khalil Hanoun,

Amal Harb, Mounir Haydamous, Mahmoud Hojeij, Georges Homsey, Laila Hotait, Nadia Hotait, Lamia Joreige, Sayed Kaado, Leila Kanaan, Tarek Kandil, Raïf Karam, Fadi Kassem, Dimitri Khadr, Elie Khalifé, Elda Khanamirian, Yasmine Khlat, Talal Khoury, Rami Kodeih, Ghassan Kotait, Carmen Labaki, Sarmad Louis, Myrna Maakaron, Jacques Madvo, Carol Mansour, Reine Mitri, Samar Mogharbei, Pierre Mouarkech, Rabih Mroue, Tina Naccache, Walid Nahas, Oscar Naim, Carine Nicholas, Rym Noujaïm, Wael Noureddine, Maria Ousseimi, Antoine Partamian, Jordano Pidutti, Walid Ra'ad, Tahani Rached, Roula Ragheb, Eliane Raheb, Memem Richa, Daniele Salaris, Katia Saleh, Jayce Salloum, Pierre Salloum, Samar Salmane, Rima Samman, Patrick Sfeir, Zeina Sfeir, Tatania Sikias, Philippe Skaff, Raghida Skaff, Lokman Slim, Wissam Smayra, Rania Stephan, Arine Arzoumanian Sulukdjian, Sabine Sursock, Fadi Syriani, Nadim Tabet, Sylvio Tabet, Vladimir Tamari, Michèle Tan, Gilles Tarazi, Jalal Toufic, Fadi Yeni Turk, Antoine Waked, Dina Yassione, Helie Yazbek, Hady Zaccak, Fu'ad Zantut, Ali Zaraket, Hassan Zbib, Maryanne Zéhil.

LEBANON: REFERENCES

Al-Ariss, Ibrahim. "An Attempt at Reading the History of Cinema in Lebanon: From Cinema to Society and Vice Versa." In *Il cinema dei paesi arabi,* Quarta edizione / *Arab Film Festival,* 4th ed., pp. 34–70. Naples: Fondazione Labatorio Mediterraneo, 1997.

———. "Hommage à Maroun Bagdadi." In *Deuxième Biennale des cinémas arabes,* pp. 181–198. Paris: Institut du Monde Arabe, 1994.

Alawaya, Borhan. Interview with Anna Albertano. In *Il cinema dei paesi arabi,* Quarta edizione / *Arab Film Festival,* 4th ed., pp. 88–97. Naples: Fondazione Labatorio Mediterraneo, 1997.

———. "Sculpteur du temps" (interview). In *Cinéma et Méditerranée (Actes du 11e Festival International de Montpellier),* pp. 203–214. Montpellier: Festival de Montpellier / Climat, 1989.

Assaf, Roger. "Les images irrationelles" (interview with Djamal Boukella and Huber Corbin). In *Actes des 9e rencontres,* pp. 117–123. Montpellier: Festival de Montpellier, 1987.

Bagdadi, Maroun. *Hors la vie* (script). Paris: L'Avant-scène Cinéma, 1994.

———. "L'éternelle jeunesse du cinema" (interview with Thierry Lenouvel and Henri Talvat). In *Actes des 15e rencontres,* pp. 3–7. Montpellier: Festival de Montpellier, 1993.

Behna, Marie-Claude. "Gros plan sur le nouveau cinéma libanais." In *Troisième festival des cinémas arabes,* pp. 60–75. Paris: Institut du Monde Arabe, 1996.

Chamoun, Jean, and Maï Masri. "Contre la guerre-spectacle" (interview with Hubert Corbin and Michèle Driguez). In *Actes des 10e rencontres,* pp. 91–97. Montpellier: Festival de Montpellier, 1998.

Chmayt, Waid. "Images de la guerre du Liban." In *Les cinémas arabes,* ed. Mouny Berrah, Jacques Lévy, and Claude-Michel Cluny, pp. 84–89. Paris: Éditions du Cerf / Institut du Monde Arabe *CinémAction* 43, 1987.

Deeley, Mona. "Beyrouth al-Gharbiyya / West Beirut." In *The Cinema of North Africa and the Middle East,* ed. Gönül Dönmetz-Colin, pp. 190–198. London: Wallflower Press, 2007.

Hillhauer, Rebecca. "Lebanon." In *Encyclopedia of Arab Women Filmmakers,* pp. 130–195. Cairo: American University Press in Cairo, 2005.

Jabre, Farid. "The Industry in the Lebanon." In *The Cinema in the Arab Countries,* ed. Georges Sadoul, pp. 172–178. Beirut: Interarab Center for Cinema and Television, 1966.

Kennedy-Day, Kiki. "Cinema in Lebanon, Syria, Iraq and Kuwait." In *Companion Encyclopedia of Middle Eastern and North African Film,* ed. Oliver Leaman, pp. 364–419. London: Routledge, 2001.

Khatib, Lina. *"Kan ya ma kan Beirut /* Once upon a Time in Beirut." In *The Cinema*

of North Africa and the Middle East, ed.
Gönül Dönmetz-Colin, pp. 156–166.
London: Wallflower Press, 2007.
———. *Lebanese Cinema: Imagining the Civil
War and Beyond.* London: I. B. Tauris,
2008.
Khoury, Lucienne. "History of the Lebanese
Cinema." In *The Cinema in the Arab
Countries,* ed. Georges Sadoul, pp. 120–124.
Beirut: Interarab Center for Cinema and
Television, 1966.
Mohammad, Oussama. Interview with Henri
Talvat. In *Actes des 10e rencontres,* pp. 98–
100. Montpellier: Festival de Montpellier,
1998.
Srour, Heiny. "Femme, Arabe . . . et Cinéaste."
CinemArabe 4–5 (1976): 34–42.

Thoraval, Yves. "Liban de la dolce vita à la
maturité." In *Les écrans du croissant fertile,*
pp. 31–58. Paris: Atlantica / Séguier, 2002.
Wazen, Abdo. "War as Subject for Cinema."
*Arab Cinematics: Towards the New and the
Alternative,* ed. Ferial J Ghazoul (1995):
229–234.
Westmoreland, Mark. "Cinematic Dreaming:
On Phantom Poetics and the Longing for a
Lebanese National Cinema." *Text, Practice,
Performance* 4 (2002): 33–50.
Zaccak, Hady. *Le cinéma libanais: itinéraire
d'un cinéma vers l'inconnu (1929–1996).*
Beirut: Dar el-Machreq, 1997.

PALESTINE

**Size: 2,324 square miles (Israel: 8,522
square miles)**
Population: 3,761,646 (Israel: 7,243,600)
GDP: £2,769m (Israel: £71,729m)
GDP per head: £660 (Israel: £10,176)
**Capital city: Jerusalem (not fully recog-
nized) (population: 733,300)**

FEATURE FILMS: 50
1970s	3
1980s	5
1990s	10
2000s	32

Palestinian Feature Filmmakers: 25

Samir Abdallah, Hany Abu Assad, Tawfik
Abu Wael, Kamal al-Jafari, Osama al-Zain,
Mohamed Bakri, Cherien Dabis, Hanna Elias,
Nasri Hajjaj, Nizar Hassan, Annemarie Jacir,
Michel Khleifi, Rashid Masharawi, Maï Masri,
Juliano Mer-Khamis, Najwa Najjar, Ali Nas-
sar, Shirin Salameh, Jacqueline Salloum, Leila
Sansour, Ghalib Sha'ath, Omar Shargawi,
Shadi Srour, Elia Suleiman, Ula Tabari.

Other Arab Feature Filmmakers
Working in Palestine: 2

Miguel Littin, Samir Nimr (marked with an
asterisk [*] in the chronology).

Chronology

1976
*Victory in His Eyes / La victoire dans ses yeux
/ Al nasr fi unyünihim* (Samir Nimr*)
1977
*The Children of Palestine / Les enfants de
Palestine / Affâl Filasyîn* (Samir Nimr*)
*The War in Lebanon / La guerre au Liban /
Harb Lubnân* (Samir Nimr*)
1980
*Fertile Memory / La mémoire fertile / Al-
dhâkira al-khisba* (Michel Khleifi)
1984
Roots / Racines / al-Judhur (Samir Nimr*)
1987
*Wedding in Galilee / Noce en Galilée / Urs al-
jalil* (Michel Khleifi)
1988
*Palestine on Fire / La Palestine en feu /
Filastin fi al-lahb* (Samir Nimr*)

1989

Canticle of Stones / *Cantique de pierre* / *Nashid al-hajjar* (Michel Khleifi)

1993

Curfew / *Couvre-feu* / *Hatta isaar akhar* (Rashid Masharawi)

Order of the Day / *L'ordre du jour* (Michel Khleifi)

The Wet Nurse / *La nourrice* / *al-Marda'a* (Ali Nassar)

1996

Chronicle of a Disappearance / *Chronique d'une disparition* / *Sijil 'ikhtifa'* (Elia Suleiman)

Haifa / *Haïfa* / *'Haifa* (Rashid Masharawi)

Jasmine / *Yasmin* (Nizar Hassan)

The Milky Way / *La voie lactée* / *Darb al-tahanat* (Ali Nassar)

The Tale of the Three Jewels / *Conte des trois diamants* / *Hikayat al-jawaher al-thalatha* (Michel Khleifi)

1998

Myth a.k.a. *Ostura* / *Mythologies* / *Ustura* (Nizar Hassan)

2000

Cut / *Coupure* (Nizar Hassan)

A Wedding in Ramallah / *Farah fi Ramallah* (Shirin Salameh) (documentary)

2001

Season of Love / *La saison de l'amour* / *Mawsim hubb* (Rashid Masharawi)

2002

Divine Intervention / *Intervention divine* / *Yadun 'Ilahiyya* (Elia Suleiman)

Ford Transit (Hany Abu Assad) (documentary)

In the Ninth Month / *Au neuvième mois* / *Fishah al-tasi'* (Ali Nassar)

Jenin, Jenin / *Jénine, Jénine* (Mohamed Bakri)

Jeremy Hardy vs. the Israeli Army (Leila Sansour) (documentary)

The Olive Harvest / *La cueillette des olives* / *Mawsim al-zaytun* (Hanna Elias)

Personal Inquiry / *Enquête personnelle* (Ula Tabari) (documentary)

Rana's Wedding / *Le mariage de Rana* / *Urs Rana* (Hany Abu Assad)

A Ticket to Jerusalem / *Un ticket pour Jérusalem* / *Tathkararaton ila al-Quds* (Rashid Masharawi)

2003

Arna's Children / *Les enfants d'Arna* / *Atfal Arna* (Juliano Mer-Khamis) (documentary)

2004

The Last Moon / *La ultima luna* (Miguel Littin*)

Sense of Need / *L'épreuve du besoin* (Shadi Srour)

Thirst / *Soif* / *Atash* (Tawfik Abu Wael)

Writers on the Borders, a Journey to Palestine / *Écrivains des frontiers* (Samir Abdallah and Jose Reynes) (documentary)

2005

Palestine Post-9/11 / *La Palestine après le 11 septembre* (Osama al-Zain)

Paradise Now / *al-Jinna alaam* (Hany Abu Assad)

2006

Beirut: Truth, Lies and Videos / *Beyrouth: vérités, mensonges et vidéos* (Maï Masri) (documentary)

Since You Left / *Depuis que tu n'es plus là* / *Min youm ma ruhat* (Mohamed Bakri) (documentary)

Waiting / *Attente* / *Intizar* (Rashid Masharawi)

2007

33 Days / *33 jours* / *33 yaoum* (Maï Masri) (documentary)

2008

After the War . . . / *Après la guerre, c'est toujours la guerre* (Samir Abdullah) (documentary)

Laila's Birthday / *L'anniversaire de Laila* / *Eid milad Laila* (Rashid Masharawi)

Pomegranates and Myrrh / *La grenade et la myrrhe* / *Al-Mor wa al-rumman* (Najwa Najjar)

The Roof / *Le toit* / *al-Sateh* (Kamal al-Jafari) (documentary)

Salt of This Sea / *Le sel de la mer* / *Milh hadha al-bahr* (Annemarie Jacir)

Shadow of Absence / *L'ombre de l'absence* / *Dhil al-gheyab* (Nasri Hajjaj)

Slingshot Hip Hop (Jacqueline Salloum) (documentary)

2009

Amerrika / *Amreeka* (Cherien Dabis)

The Time That Remains / Le temps qu'il reste / al-Zaman al-baqi (Elia Suleiman)

Short Filmmakers
(Fiction and Documentary): 155

Hiam Abbas, Walid Abdelhadi, Firas Abdel-rahman, Samir Abdullah, Ahmad Abou-Zeid, Khadija Abu Ali, Mohamed Abu Dayyeh, Wael Abu Diqqa, Dima Abu Ghoush, Umayya Abu Hanna, Saed Abu Hmud, Darwish Abu Rish, Ahmad Abu Sa'da, François Abu Salem, Dahna Aburahme, Abdel Menem Adwan, Amir Ahmaro, Imad Ahmed, Akram al-Ashqar, Mohamed Alatar, Muayad Moussa Alayan, Darin Ali al-Baw, Ma'moun al-Buna, Hikmat al-Dawud, Yousef al-Deek, Ghasoub Aleddin, Rowan al-Faqih, Isma'il Alhabbash, Azza al-Hassan, Raed al-Helou, Kamal al-Jafari, Laith al-Juneidi, Basil al-Khatib, Nabil Issa al-Khatib, Izzidrin al-Masri, Omar al-Qattan, Mohamed al-Sawalmeh, Sama Alshaibi, Bakr al-Shirqawi, Nada al-Yassir, Sobhi al-Zobaïdi, Raed Andoni, Saed Andoni, Alia Arasoughli, Suha Arraf, Georgina Asfour, Hanna Selim Attallah, Gibril Awwad, Hahed Awwad, Mohamed Ayache, George Azar, Layaly Badr, Liana Badr, Salah al-Din Badr Khan, Yahya Barakat, Rima Barrak, Amahl Bishara, Walid Bitrawi, Lina Bokhary, Youssef Chabaane, Ismaïl Chamout, Fady Copty, Cherien Dabis, Rawen Damen, Nicolas Damuni, Hikmat Daoud, Iyad Daoud, Nazih Darwaza, Swasan Darwaza, Ziad Darwish, Salim Daw, Riyad Deis, Sahera Dirbas, Zeina Durra, Laila El Haddad, Majdi El Omari, Jamal El Yasin, Nada El Yasir, Rima Essa, Saeed Taji Farouky, Ali Fawzi, Mahdi Fleifel, Issa Freij, Maryse Gargour, Raneen Geries, Ahmad Habash, Ismaïl Habash, Mahmoud Halil, Anwar Hasen, Faycal BK Hassairi, Mona Hatoum, Riyad Ideis, Nabila Irshaid, Suheir Isma'el, Azz al-Din Isma'il, Hadi Jadallah, Ihab Jadallah, Sulafa Jadallah, Jennifer Jajeh, Hani Johariya, Mohamed Salah Kayali, Hichem Kayed, Jamal Khalaile, Mahmoud Khalil, Ibrahim Khill, George Khleifi, Buthina Canaan Khoury, Rina Khoury, Nabiha Lutfi, Seoud Mahanna, Lina Makboul, Aseel Mansour, Erbisam Mara'ana, Norma Marcos, Tayseer Mashareqa, Izidore

Musallim, Hanna Musleh, Enas Muthaffar, Razi Najjar, Nadine Naous, Rosalind Nashashibi, Omar Nazzal, May Odeh, Edna Politi, Tony Qadh, Oussama Qashoo, Kristan Qazi, Ra'ad Ra'ad, Mohamed Rum, Muhmud Ibrahim Sa'adi, Mazen Saadeh, Akram Safadi, Marwan Salameh, Liana Saleh, Suzy Salmy, Ihab Salti, Larissa Sansour, Layla Sayegh, Qasim Sha'ban, Nadine Shamounki, Nazim Sharidi, Abdel Salam Shehada, Amer Shomali, Nida Sinnokrot, Helga Tawil, Ghada Terawi, Mohanad Yaqubi, Susan Youssef, Nasri Zakharia, Manar Zoabi, Sameh Zoabi, Taher Zoabi, Hicham Zraiek.

PALESTINE: REFERENCES

Abdel-Malek, Kamal. *The Rhetoric of Violence: Arab-Jewish Encounters in Contemporary Palestinian Literature and Film.* New York: Palgrave Macmillan, 2005.
Bresheeth, Haim. "The Continuity of Trauma and Struggle: Recent Cinematic Representations of the Nakba." In *Nakba: Palestine, 1948, and the Claims of Memory,* ed. Ahmed H. Sa'di and Lila Abu-Lugod, pp. 161–187. New York: Columbia University Press, 2007.
———. "*Segell Ikhtifa* / Chronicle of a Disappearance." In *The Cinema of North Africa and the Middle East,* ed. Gönül Dönmetz-Colin, pp. 168–178. London: Wallflower Press, 2007.
Dabashi, Hamid, ed. *Dream of a Nation: On Palestinian Cinema.* London: Verso, 2006.
Di Giorgi, Sergio, and Joan Rundo. *Una Terra promessa dal cinema: Appunti sul nuovo cinema palestinese.* Palermo: Edizioni della Battaglia and La Luna nel Pozzo, 1998.
Gertz, Nurith, and George Khleifi. *Palestinian Cinema: Landscape, Trauma and Memory.* Edinburgh: Edinburgh University Press, 2008.
Hennebelle, Guy, and Janine Euvrard, eds. *Israel Palestine: Que peut le cinéma.* Paris: Société Africaine d'Édition / *L'Afrique Littéraire et Artistique* 47, 1978.
Hennebelle, Guy, and Khémais Khayati, eds. *La Palestine et le cinéma.* Paris: E.100, 1977.
Hillhauer, Rebecca. "Palestine." In

Encyclopedia of Arab Women Filmmakers, pp. 196–243. Cairo: American University in Cairo Press, 2005.

Karmy, Boulos. "Le cinéma palestinien: en attendant la fiction." In *Les cinémas arabes,* ed. Mouny Berrah, Jacques Lévy, and Claude-Michel Cluny, pp. 90–93. Paris: Éditions du Cerf / Institut du Monde Arabe / *CinémAction* 43, 1987.

Khayati, Khémais. "The Palestinian Cinema." In *Il cinema dei paesi arabi,* Quarta edizione / *Arab Film Festival,* 4th ed., pp. 71–79. Naples: Fondazione Labatorio Mediterraneo, 1997.

Khleifi, Michel. *Noce en Galilée* (script). Paris: L'Avant-scène Cinéma, 1988.

Krifat, Michel. "Gros Plan sur le cinéma palestinien." In *Sixième Biennale des cinémas arabes à Paris,* pp. 93–127. Paris: Institut du Monde Arabe, 2002.

Masri, Maï, and Jean Chamoun. "Contre la guerre-spectacle" (interview with Hubert Corbin and Michèle Driguez). In *Actes des 10e rencontres cinématographiques,* pp. 91–97. Montpellier: Festival de Montpellier, 1998.

Ramahi, Suyan. "Cinéma palestinien." In *La semaine du cinéma arabe,* pp. 61–66. Paris: Institut du Monde Arabe, 1987.

Thoraval, Yves. "Palestine: Images d'une nation errante." In *Les écrans du croissant fertile,* pp. 59–80. Paris: Atlantica / Séguier, 2002.

Thouard, Sylvie, ed. "Palestine-Israel—territoires cinématographiques." *La revue documentaire* 19–29 (2005): 5–124.

SYRIA

Size: 71,498 square miles
Population: 20,447,000
GDP: £17,061m
GDP per head: £879
Capital city: Damascus (population: 2,466,000)

FEATURE FILMS: 137

1930s	2
1940s	1
1950s	2
1960s	11
1970s	67
1980s	18
1990s	18
2000s	18

Syrian Feature Filmmakers: 48

Abdelatif Abdelhamid, Marouan Akkachi, Mustapha Akkad, Hala al-Abdallah Yakoub, Ammar al-Beik, Nidal al-Dibs, Marouan Al-kawey, Abderrahman al-Khayali, Khaldoun al-Mahled, Nabil al-Maleh, Waha al-Raheb, Bilal al-Sabouni, Zuhayr al-Shawwa, Omar Amiralay, Ismaïl Anzur, Ayyub Badri, Amin Bounni, Raymond Boutros, Salah Dehni, Mohamed Dhiaddine, Khatib El Bassel, Ahmed Erfan, Marwan Haddad, Haytham Hakki, Khaled Hamadeh, Maher Kaddo, Kanam Kanam, Souheil Kanaan, Sokheie Kawaan, Georges Khoury, Koshav, Dureid Lahham, Mohamed Malas, Hatem Mohamed, Oussama Mohammad, Mohamed Muwaddin, Ruba Nadda, Mustafa Rashid, Joud Saeed, Bashir Safia, Mohamed Salah, Nazih Shahbandar, Mohamed Shahin, Riyad Shayya, Ghassan Shmeit, Mohamed Solfan, Wadeih Yousef, Samir Zikra.

Other Arab Feature Filmmakers Working in Syria: 16

Borhan Alawiyya, Hassan al-Saïfi, Qays al-Zubaydi, Seif-Eddine Chawkat, Ahmed Fouad, Nagdi Hafez, Qassim Hawal, Youssef Maalouf, Rida Myassar, Helmi Rafla, Hassab Reda, Tewfiq Saleh, Atef Salem, Mohamed Selmane, Saed Tantawi, Boshko Votchinitch (marked with an asterisk [*] in the chronology).

Chronology

1931

Under the Skies of Damascus / Sous le ciel de Damas / Tahta sama' Dimask (Ismaïl Anzur)

1937

The Call of Duty / L'appel du devoir / Nada'al-wajih (Ayyub Badri)

1947

Light and Darkness / Lumière et ténèbre / Nouron wa thilal (Nazih Shahbandar)

1950

The Green Valley / La vallée verte / al-Wadi al-akhdar (Zuhayr al-Shawwa)

The Passer-By / Le passant / Abir sabil (Ahmed Erfan)

1963

Beyond the Borders / Au-delà des frontières / Wara al-hudud (Zuhayr al-Shawwa)

1964

A City Rose / Une rose de la ville / Zahratun min al-madina (Mohamed Shahin)

1966

The Lorry Driver / Le camioneur / Sa'iq ash-shahina (Boshko Votchinitch*)

Satan's Game / Le jeu de Satan / Laabart ash-shaytan (Zuhayr al-Shawwa)

1967

Love in Constantinople / Amour à Constantinople (Seif-Eddine Chawkat*)

Meeting of Strangers / Rencontre des étrangères (Sayed Tantawi*)

The Outlaws / Les hors-la-loi (Youssef Maalouf*)

Women Naked without Sin / Femmes nues sans péché (Koshav)

1969

Operations at 6 O'clock / Opérations à six heures / Amalyat al-saa 6 (Seif-Eddine Chawkat*)

Three Operations in Palestine / Trois Opérations en Palestine / Thalath amali-yyatdâkhil Filistin (Mohamed Salah and Abderrahman al-Khayali)

Women's Tailor / Tailleur pour les dames (Atef Salem*)

1970

The Hand / La main / al-Yad (Qassim Hawal*)

Men Under the Sun / Des hommes sous le soleil / Rijalun tahta ash-shams (Nabil al-Maleh, Mohamed Shahin and Mohamed Muwaddin)

The Two Friends / Les deux amis (Hassan al-Saïfi*)

A Useful Man / Un homme convenable (Helmi Rafla*)

1971

Bridge of the Wicked / Le Pont des méchants (Nagdi Hafez*)

One Plus One / 1 + 1 (Youssef Maalouf*)

A Woman Alone / Une femme seule (Nagdi Hafez*)

1972

Another Facet of Love / Une autre facette de l'amour / Wahj akhar lil-hob (Mohamed Shahin)

The Beautiful Shepherdess / La belle bergère (Atef Salem*)

The Crisis of the Young / La crise des jeunes (Nagdi Hafez*)

The Duped / Les dupes / al-Makhdhououn (Tewfiq Saleh*)

Journey of Love / Voyage d'amour (Youssef Maalouf*)

The Knife / Le couteau / al-Sikkin (Khaled Hamadeh)

The Leopard / Le léopard / al-Fahd (Nabil al-Maleh)

Love's Subterfuges / Les subterfuges d'amour (Youssef Maalouf*)

Mexico Trip / Des aventures comiques au Mexique (Seif-Eddine Chawkat*)

The Quiet City / La ville tranquille (Hassan Reda*)

The World in the Year 2000 / Le monde en l'an 2000 (Ahmed Fouad*)

1973

Cruel Woman / Femme cruelle (Mohamed Shahin)

Flat for Love / Appartement de l'amour (Nagdi Hafez*)

A Forced Marriage / Un mariage forcé (Rida Myassar*)

Memories of a Night of Love / Souvenirs d'une nuit d'amour (Seif-Eddine Chawkat*)

Muse and Amber / Muse et ambres (Mohamed Dhiaddine)

My Wife's a Hippy / Ma femme Youppie / Zawjati min hippies (Atef Salem*)

October Is Coming / L'octobre vient / Wa jâa tashrîn (Wadeih Yousef)

The Prostitutes of the Al Aram Avenue / Les prostituées de l'avenue Al Aram (Nagdi Hafez*)

The Wounded Ballerina / La ballerine blessée / Râqisa alâ al-firâh (Mohamed Shahin)

1974

Al-Yazirli (Qays al-Zubaydi*)

Battle in the Desert / Combat dans le désert (Mohamed Selmane*)

The Celebration / La fête (Bashir Safia)

The Crossing / La traversée / al-Ekhtiraq (Kanem Kanem)

Everday Life in a Syrian Village / La vie quotidien dans un village syrien / Al-hayat al-yawmiya fi qaria Suriya (Omar Amiralay) (documentary)

The Five Master Singers / Les cinq maîtres chanteurs (Nagdi Hafez*)

The Hero's Storm Cloud / La nuée du héros (Marouan Akkachi)

The Heroic Airforce Formations / Les héroiques formations aériennes / Kharq el-akhtâr (Marouan Alkawey)

The Horsemen of Liberation / Les cavaliers de la libération (Souheil Kanaan)

Jealous James Bond / James Bond, le jaloux / Ghawar James Bond (Nabil al-Maleh)

Kafr Kassem (Borhan Alawiya*)

The Mameluke Jaber's Adventure / L'aventure du Mamelouk Jaber / Mughamarat al-Mamluk Jaber (Mohamed Shahin)

The Progressive / Le Progressiste / al-Sayyid al-taqaddumi (Nabil al-Maleh)

Shame / La honte / al-'Ar (Bilal al-Sabouni, Bashir Safia, and Wadeih Yousef)

The Tents of Qaraqoz / Khaymatu Quaraqoz (Mohamed Shahin)

Voyage of Suffering / Voyage des souffrances (Rida Myassar*)

1975

The Agitators / Les fauteurs (Mohamed Shahin)

The Beauty and the Four Looks / La belle et les quatre regards (Seif-Eddine Chawkat*)

Conqueror of Space / Conquérant de l'espace (Sokheie Kawaan)

Good Night / Bonne nuit (Khaldoun al-Mahled)

If I Die Twice I Would Love You / Je meurs deux fois je t'aimerais (Georges Khoury)

Men's Nights / Nuits des hommes (Hassan al-Saïfi*)

Official Mission / Mission officielle (Seif-Eddine Chawkat*)

Sabiha, Seductress of the Desert / Sabiha la séductrice du désert (Mohamed Solfan)

The Wrong Way / Direction opposée / al-Ittijâh al-mu'âkis (Marwan Haddad)

1976

Al-Tharwa al-samakia (Wadeih Yousef)

The Jester's Love / L'amour du bouffon / Gharâm al-muharrij (Bashir Safia)

Manhunt / La chasse à l'homme / Saydu al-rijâl (Bashir Safia)

1977

Arrivals from the Sea / Les arrivants par la mer (Seif-Eddine Chawkat*)

Don't Say Goodbye to a Day That's Scarcely Gone / Ne dites pas adieu à un jour qui n'a guère passé / La taqIuli wadâ'an lil-ams (Mohamed Shahin)

Forbidden Love / L'amour interdit (Khaled Hamadeh)

Heroes Are Born Twice / Les héros naissent deux fois / al-Abtal yuadun marrayayn (Salah Dehni)

The Horseman of Bani Abes / Le cavalier de Bani Abes (Mohamed Selmane*)

The Jungle of Wolves / Le jungle des loups / Ghâbatu al-diâb (Mohamed Shahin)

Red, White and Black / Le rouge, le blanc et le noir / al-Ahmar wa al-abyadwa al-aswad (Bashir Safia)

1978

Farewell to the Past / Adieu au passé (Mohamed Shahin)

1979

The Fifth Arm of the Prison / La cinquième citadelle / al-Qal'a al-khâmisa (Bilal al-Sabouni)

The Report / Le rapport (Haytham Hakki)

Sweet Like a Berry, My Love / Doux comme un baie, mon amour / Habibati ya hab al-tout (Marwan Haddad)

The Trap / Le piège / al-Masyada (Wadeih Yousef)

1980

Fragments of Images / Fragments d'images / Baqaya suwar (Nabil al-Maleh)

Lion of the Desert / Le lion du désert / Omar al-Mukhtar (Mustapha Akkad)

1981

Love for Life / L'amour pour la vie / Hubbun lil-hayât (Bashir Safia)

1982

Ghawar's Empire (Bashir Safia)

A Murder Step by Step / Un meutre pas à pas / Qatlun . . . an tariq al-tasalsul (Mohamed Shahin)

1983

The Drama of a Girl from the East / Le drame d'une fille de l'orient / Ma'asat fatât sharqiya (Mohamed Shahin)

The Game of Love and Death / Le jeu de l'amour et de la mort / Lubatu al-hubb was al-gatl (Mohamed Shahin)

The Half-Metre Incident / L'accident du demi-mètre / Hadithat al-nisf mitr (Samir Zikra)

Story of a Dream / Histoire d'un rêve / Ta'rick hulm (Nabil al-Maleh)

1984

Borders / Les frontières / al-Hudud (Dureid Lahham)

City Dreams / Les rêves de la ville / Ahlam al-Madina (Mohamed Malas)

On a Rainy Day / Un jour pluvieux / Fi yawmin mumtir (Mohamed Shahin)

1985

Smiling through the Tears / Le sourire à travers les larmes / Basima baynaal-dumû (Wadeih Yousef),

Vendetta of Love / Vendetta d'amour / al-Intiqam hubban (Wadeih Yousef)

1986

Chronicle of the Coming Year / Chronique de l'année prochaine / Waqai al'am al-muqbil (Samir Zikra)

The Report / Le rapport / al-Taqrîr (Dureid Lahham)

1988

Stars in Broad Daylight / Étoiles du jour / Nujum al-nahar (Oussama Mohammad)

1989

The Nights of the Jackal / Les nuits du chacal / Layali ibn awa (Abdelatif Abdelhamid)

1990

The Attachment / L'attachement / al-Mahabba (Dureid Lahham)

1991

Cloud / Nuage / Sahâb (Mohamed Shahin)

The Greedy Ones / Les gourmands a.k.a. *Les algues d'eau douce / al-Tahalib* (Raymond Boutros)

Kafrun (Dureid Lahham)

Palestinian Memories / Mémoires palestiniennes (Amin Bounni) (documentary)

Verbal Messages / Messages verbaux / Rasa'il al Shafahyya (Abdellatif Abdelhamid)

1992

The Night / La nuit / al-Layl (Mohamed Malas)

1993

The Extras / Les figurants / al-Kombars (Nabil al-Maleh)

The Lovers of the Demarcation Line of the Rain / Les amants de la ligne de démarcation de la pluie / Ushaq ala khat al-matar (Mustafa Rashid)

Noises from All Sides / Le hénissement des directions / Sahil al-jibat (Maher Kaddo)

Oh Sea / Oh mer (Mohamed Shahin)

Something Is Burning / Quelque chose brûle / Shay'ma yahtariq (Ghassan Shmeit)

1995

Al-Lajat (Riyad Shayya)

1996

The Rising Rain / La montée de la pluie / Su'ud al-matar (Abdellatif Abdelhamid)

1997

The Displacement / Le déplacement / al-Terhal (Raymond Boutros)

1998

A Land for Strangers / La terre des étrangers / Turab al-ajaneb (Samir Zikra)

The Soul's Breath / Le souffle de l'âme / Nassim ar-ruh (Abdellatif Abdelhamid)

1999

The Moneylender / L'usurier / al-Marabi (Mohamed Shahin)

2000

The Last Message / Le dernier message (Khatib El Bassel)

2001

Black Flour / La farine noire / al-Tahin al-Aswad (Ghassan Shmeit)

Sacrifices / Sanduq al-dunia (Oussama
   Mohammad)
*Two Moons and an Olive Tree / Deux lunes
   et un olivier / Qamarn wa zayrunah*
   (Abdellatif Abdelhamid).
2003
*Dreamy Visions / Visions chimériques / Ra'a
   halima* (Waha al-Raheb)
2004
Sabah (Ruba Nadda)
2005
Passions / Bab el-maqam (Mohamed Malas)
*Public Relations / Relations publiques /
   'Alaqat 'ammah* (Samir Zikra)
Under the Ceiling / Sous le toit / Tahta al-saqf
   (Nidal al-Dibs)
2006
*I Am the One Who Brings Flowers to Her
   Grave / Je suis celle qui porte les fleurs vers
   sa tombe* (Hala al-Abdallah Yakoub and
   Ammar al-Beik) (documentary)
2007
I.D. / Vos papiers (Ghassan Shmeit)
*Out of Coverage / Hors réseau / Kahref al-
   taghtiya* (Abdellatif Abdelhamid)
2008
*Days of Boredom / Jours d'ennui / Ayyam al-
   dajar* (Abdellatif Abdelhamid)
Hasiba (Raymond Boutros)
*Hey! Don't Forget the Cumin / Hé! N'oublie
   pas le cumin* (Hala al-Abdallah Yacoub)
   (documentary)
2009
*Gate of Heaven / La porte au ciel / Bawabet
   al-janna* (Maher Kaddo)
Long Night, The / La longue nuit (Hatem
   Mohamed)
Once More / Encore une fois / Mara okhra
   (Joud Saeed)

Short Filmmakers
(Fiction and Documentary): 50

Ghassan Abdallah, Bashar Akad, Maamoun
al-Bunni, Tanjour Alfounz, Reem Ali, Khaldoun al-Mahled, Meyer al-Roumi, Mohamed
al-Roumi, Hicham al-Zouki, Ayham Arsan,
Ghassan Bayous, Ala-Eddine Cha'ar, Mahmoud Chabaane, Houssam Chahadat, Mohamed Youssef Dayoub, Ali Deyoub, Diana

El Jeiroudi, Abeer Esber, Youssef Fahdah,
Joude Gorani, Inas Hakki, Nadia Hamzeh,
Walid Hreib, Bassam Hussein, Oussama Hus-
seini, Mouneir Jahami, Karsan Jahry, Mounir
Jbawi, Soudade Kaadan, Sam Kadi, Saleh
Kasem, Mouaffak Kat, Mano Khalil, Kosaï
Khouly, Lotfi Lotfi. Hind Midani, Salah Ed-
dine Mohamed, Hala Mohammed, Ramez
Mouchechawi, Marwan Muadhdhen, Nasser
Naasani, Ahmed Farouk Ohisi, Ayman Orsan,
Farouk Oubaïssi, Riad Hani Ra'ad, Joud Said,
Maher Salibi, Salah Sermini, Alfouz Tanjour,
Fajr Yacoub, Haïdar Yaziji.

SYRIA: REFERENCES

Abdel Wahed, Mahmud. "Syrian Cinema:
   History and Evolution." In *Il cinema dei
   paesi arabi,* Quarta edizione / *Arab Film
   Festival,* 4th ed., pp. 127–182. Naples:
   Fondazione Labatorio Mediterraneo, 1997.
Abdelhamid, Abdellatif. "Comme un fil de
   soie dans les cœurs" (interview). In *Cinéma
   et Méditerranée* (*Actes du 11e Festival
   International de Montpellier*), pp. 195–202.
   Montpellier: Festival de Montpellier /
   Climat, 1989.
———. "La pluie est porteuse de fertilité"
   (interview with Henri Talvat). In *Actes
   du 18e Festival International,* pp. 55–56.
   Montpellier: Festival de Montpellier, 1996.
Al-Roumi, Mayyar [Meyar], and Dorothée
   Schmid. "Le cinéma syrien: du militan-
   tisme au mutisme." In *Cinéma et monde
   musulman, cultures et interdits. EuOrient*
   10 (2001): 4–25.
Chikhaoui, Tahar, ed. *Spécial: La nuit de
   Mohamed Malas.* Tunis: Édition Sahar /
   Cinécrits 9, 1995.
Cluny, Claude Michel. "Le cinéma syrien:
   une dizaine de bons films." In *Les cinémas
   arabes,* ed. Mouny Berrah, Jacques Lévy,
   and Claude-Michel Cluny, p. 75. Paris:
   Éditions du Cerf / Institut du Monde Arabe
   / *CinémAction* 43, 1987
———. "Syrie—un très proche orient."
   Cinéma 75 197 (1975): 100–101.
Corbin, Hubert, et al. "État du cinéma
   syrien." Roundtable discussion with
   Omar Amiralay, Mohamed Malas, and

Samir Zikra. In *Actes des 19e Rencontres Cinématographiques,* pp. 101–109. Montpellier: Festival de Montpellier, 1987.

Dehni, Salah. "History of the Syrian Cinema" and "The Syrian Cinema in 1963." In *The Cinema in the Arab Countries,* pp. 98–107, 179–181. Beirut: Interarab Centre of Cinema and Television, 1966.

———. "Une évolution difficile au service du cinéma arabe." *Cinéma 75* 197 (1975): 102–115.

———. "Quand cinéma et télévision se regardent en chiens de faïence." In *Les cinémas arabes,* ed. Mouny Berrah, Jacques Lévy, and Claude-Michel Cluny, pp. 72–75. Paris: Éditions du Cerf / Institut du Monde Arabe / *CinémAction* 43, 1987.

Hakki, Haytham. "Regard sur le documentaire syrien." In *Festival: Images du monde arabe,* pp. 80–111. Paris: Institut du Monde Arabe, 1993.

Hillhauer, Rebecca. "Syria." In *Encyclopedia of Arab Women Filmmakers,* pp. 244–255. Cairo: American University in Cairo Press, 2005.

Jabbour, Diana. "Syrian Cinema: Culture and Ideology." In *Screens of Life: Critical Film Writing from the Arab World,* ed Alia Arasoughli, pp. 40–62. Quebec: World Heritage Press, 1998.

Kennedy-Day, Kiki. "Cinema in Lebanon, Syria, Iraq and Kuwait." In *Companion Encyclopedia of Middle Eastern and North African Film,* ed. Oliver Leaman, pp. 364–419. London: Routledge, 2001.

Kilani, Dr. Ibrahim, and Salah Dehni. "The Cinema and Television in Syria, Their History and Future." In *Arab Cinema and Culture,* vol. 3, pp. 52–113. Beirut: Arab Film and Television Centre, 1964.

Malas, Mohamed. "*The Dream*: Extracts from a Film Diary." In *Arab Cinematics: Toward the New and the Alternative,* ed. Ferial J. Ghazoul, pp. 208–228. Cairo: American University in Cairo / *Alif* 15, 1999.

———. "Le cauchemar palestinien" (interview with Hubert Corbin). In *Actes des 9e Rencontres,* pp. 115–116. Montpellier: Festival de Montpellier, 1987.

Mohammad, Oussama. "Quand les gens sont sincères, ils se ressemblent" (interview with Henri Talvat). In *Actes des 10e Rencontres Cinématographiques,* pp. 98–100. Montpellier: Festival de Montpellier, 1998.

Mounir, Zamni. "Le cinéma syrien au passé et au présent." In *La semaine du cinéma arabe,* pp. 67–71. Paris: Institut du Monde Arabe, 1987.

Petiot, Benoîte, and Pierre Petiot. "Syrie, métaphores et réalités historiques." Roundtable discussion with Mohamed Malas and Nabil al-Maleh. In *Actes des 21e Rencontres,* pp. 30–34. Montpellier: Festival de Montpellier, 1999.

Salti, Rasha, ed. *Insights into Syrian Cinema: Essays and Conversations with Contemporary Filmmakers.* New York: Rattapallax Press / Arte East, 2006.

———. "Nujum al-Nahar / Stars in Broad Daylight." In *The Cinema of North Africa and the Middle East,* ed. Gönül Dönmetz-Colin, pp. 101–110. London: Wallflower Press, 2007.

Thoraval, Yves. "Syrie: Filmer malgré la censure." In *Les écrans du croissant fertile,* pp. 81–101. Paris: Atlantica / Séguier, 2002.

Zikra, Samir. "À force de mentir, on finit par se croire" (interview with Hubert Corbin). In *Actes des 9e Rencontres,* pp. 110–114. Montpellier: Festival de Montpellier, 1987.

THE GULF

The Six Members of the Gulf Cooperation Council, plus Yemen

OVERALL FEATURE FILMS: 23

Overall Feature Filmmakers: 18

Nujoon al-Ghanem (United Arab Emirates), Hassan al-Halibi (Bahrain), Maher al-Khaja (United Arab Emirates), Hkalia al-Meraikhy (Qatar), Abdullah al-Moheissen (Saudi Arabia), Hani al-Shaibani (United Arab Emirates), Khadija al-Salami (Yemen), Khalid al-Siddick (Kuwait), Bassam al-Thawadi (Bahrain), Mohamed al-Traifi (United Arab Emirates), Khalid al-Zadjali (Oman), Amer al-Zuhair (Kuwait), Bader Ben Hirsi (Yemen), Abdullah Boushahri (Kuwait), Saleh Karama (United Arab Emirates), Hashim Muhammad (Kuwait), Izzadore Mussalem (Saudi Arabia)

There are also 487 Gulf short filmmakers (fiction and documentary) (394 of these from the UAE and mostly students).

THE GULF: REFERENCES

Al-San'oussi, Muhammad. "The Cinema and Television in Kuwait." In *Arab Cinema and Culture*, vol. 3, pp. 26–27. Beirut: Arab Film and Television Centre, 1964.

"The Cinema in the Arabian Peninsula." In *The Cinema in the Arab Countries,* ed. Georges Sadoul, pp. 189–191. Beirut: Interarab Centre of Cinema and Television, 1966.

El Sanussi, Muhammad. "Cinema and TV in Kuwait." In *The Cinema in the Arab Countries,* ed. Georges Sadoul, pp. 187–188. Beirut: Interarab Centre of Cinema and Television, 1966.

Hillhauer, Rebecca. "Yemen" and "Other Countries." In *Encyclopedia of Arab Women Filmmakers,* pp. 256–262, 415–419. Cairo: American University in Cairo Press, 2005.

Kennedy-Day, Kiki. "Cinema in Lebanon, Syria, Iraq and Kuwait." In *Companion Encyclopedia of Middle Eastern and North African Film,* ed. Oliver Leaman, pp. 364–419. London: Routledge, 2001.

Naji, Andel Sattar. "Le cinéma et la télévision dans les pays du Golfe: Réalités et ambitions." In *Cinquième Biennale des cinémas arabes à Paris,* pp. 100–107. Paris: Institut du Monde Arabe, 2000.

See also the documentation relating to the *Dubai International Film Festival* (Dubai, from 2004), the *Middle East International Film Festival* (Dubai, from 2007), and the *Emirates Film Competition* (Abu Dhabi, from 2002).

BAHRAIN

Size: 278 square miles
Population: 1,046,814
GDP: £8,206m
GDP per head: 11,106
Capital city: Manama (population: 157,000)

Chronology

Feature films:
1988
The Obstacle / L'obstacle / Al-hajiz (Bassam al-Thawadi)

2003
Visitor / Visiteur (Bassam al-Thawadi)
2008
Bahraini Tale / Un conte de Bahrain / Hekaya Bahrainiya (Bassam al-Thawadi)
Four Girls / Quatre filles (Hassan al-Halibi)

Short Filmmakers (Fiction and Documentary): 26

Hussain Ghulom Abbas (Abu Jalal), Ali al-Ali, Abdulla Mohammad Jawad Albzzaz, Baqer Sadiq Zain Aldeen, Ebrahim Rashid al-Doseri, Gamal al-Gheilan, Hussain Abbas

al-Hulaybi, Majeed Radhi Ali, Jaafar al-Qad-
ami, Mohammad Noaman Alqasab, Hussein
al-Riffaei, Nidhal Bader, Riyadh Balwai, Mo-
hamed Rashed Bu-Ali, Jaffar Hamza, Anwar
Mohamed Hayat, Khalid Yousif Janabi, Nizar
Jawad, Mohamed Yousif Janabi, Nizar Jawad,
Majeed Kadhmi, Mohammed Ibrahim Mo-
hammed, Yaser Naser, Mohamed Numan,
Abdula Rashdan, Khalifa Shahin Cheker Bin
Yahmed.

KUWAIT

Size: 6,880 square miles
Population: 2,599,444
GDP: £52,510m
GDP per head: £20,201
Capital city: Kuwait City (population:
  2,063,000)

Chronology

Feature films:
1972
The Cruel Sea / Basya bahr (Khalid al-
  Siddick)
1976
*The Wedding of Zein / Les noces de Zein / Urs
  al-Zayn* (Khalid al-Siddick)
1979
The Silence / Le silence / al-Samt (Hashim
  Muhammad)

1985
Chahin / Shâhîn (Khalid al-Siddick)
2006
Losing Ahmad / En perdant Ahmad (Abdullah
  Boushahri)
2007
*When the People Spoke / Lorsque le peuple a
  parlé / Indama rtakalam al-sha'ab* (Amer
  al-Zuhair) (documentary)

Short Filmmakers
(Fiction and Documentary): 16

Ali Mohammad Afjjar, Meshari al-Arouj,
Walid al-Awadi, Faisal S. al-Duwaisan, Fathia
Alhaddad, Zeyed Alhusaini, Faisal Alibrahim,
Abdulrahman al-Khalifi, Meqdad al-Kout,
Nouri al-Saleh, Mohamed al-Sanousi, Tareq
al-Zamel, Dadeq Hussain Behbehani, Najm
Abdel Karim, Naser Kermani, Abdulwahab
Sultan.

OMAN

Size: 119,500 square miles
Population: 2,577,000
GDP: £18,290m
GDP per head: £7,183
Capital city: Muscat (population: 620,000)

Chronology

Feature film:
2006
The Dawn / L'aube / Al-Boom (Khalid al-
  Zadjali)

Short Filmmakers
(Fiction and Documentary): 10

Hamid al-Adwani, Jasim Albatashe, Abdullah Albatashi, Yusef Hassan al-Bloshi, Khalid Salem Alkalbani, Dawood al-Kiumi, Yasir
al-Kiyumi, Amer al-Rawas, Hamid bin Salem
Alshakaili, Mazin Habib.

QATAR

Size: 4,437 square miles
Population: 1,226,210
GDP: £26,941m
GDP per head: £32,802
Capital city: Doha (population: 370,656)

Chronology

Feature film:
2006
*Threads Beneath Sands / Des fils sous le sable /
Khyoot taht al-rimal* (Khalifa al-Meraikly)

Short Filmmakers
(Fiction and Documentary): 8

Abdulla Abdukaziz Abdulla, Abdulla Hafez
Ali, Hafiz Ali Ali, Mahdi Ali Ali, Meshaal Ali
Alkubaisi, Khalid Almahmoud, Mohammed
Alomany, Dawoud Hassan.

SAUDI ARABIA

Size: 864,869 square miles
Population: 24,242,578
GDP: £178,300m
GDP per head: £405
Capital city: Riyadh (population: 4,465,000)

Chronology

Feature films:
2006
*How Are Things? / Aujourd'hui et demain /
Keif al-hal* (Izzadore Mussalem*)
*Shadow of Silence / Les ombres du silence /
Dhalal al-samt* (Abdullah al-Moheissen)

Short Filmmakers
(Fiction and Documentary): 31

Akram Agha, Mahmoud Salem Ba Ajajah,
Hisham Mansour al-Abidi, Ali Hasan Mohamed Alameer, Mansour al-Badran, Mohamed al-Basha, Noor al-Dabbagh, Khalid
al-Dakheel, Nedhal K. al-Demashqi, Meshal
Mohamed al-Enzi, Abdullah al-Eyaf, Bader
Abdul Majeed al-Homoud, Haïfaa al-Mansour, Bashir Hassan al-Mohaishi, Rja Sair
al-Motri, Abdulaziz Nasser al-Nejaim, Mohammed Mahde al-Obaid, Abdullah Ibrahim Alomain, Faisal Shadid Alotaibi, Omer
Abdalaziz al-Robea, Moussa Jafer Altunayan,
Tawfik Alzeidi, Farah Ibrahim Arif, Samir
Ibrahim Arif, Abdullah Awad, Mohamed Bazaid, Mohammed Helal, Aseel Lababidi, Jasim
Ali Oqaili, Mamdouh Salem, Hamzeh Ahmed
Fakhri Tarzan.

UNITED ARAB EMIRATES

Size: 30,000 square miles
Population: 4,488,000
GDP: £93,056m
GDP per head: £21,903
Capital city: Abu Dhabi (population:
   1,493,000)

Chronology

Feature films:
2005
A Dream (Hani al-Shaibani)
2006
Haneen (Mohamed al-Traifi)
2007
Jumaa and the Sea / Jumaa wa al-Bahr (Hani
   al-Shaibani)
2008
Al Mureed (Nujoom al-Ghanem)
Henna (Saleh Karama)
2009
*The Fifth Chamber Ouija / La cinquième
   chambre d'Ouija* (Maher al-Khaja)

Short Filmmakers
(Fiction and Documentary): 395
(Mostly Students)

Mustafa Abbas, Marwa Abboud, Hussain Nabil Abdalla, Mona Abdallah, Naima Abdelwahab, Sara Tarek Abdou, Hani Abdul Azeem, Samantha Abdulaziz, Heba Abdulhalek, Heba Abdulkhalek, Suhail Matar Abdulla, Wedima Bilal Abdulla, Khalid Abdullah, Dawood Mohammed Hassan Abdulrahman, Adel Abed, Abdulrahman Aoubayda, Amjad Abu al-Ala, Khalid Mahmoud Abu Goumasaah, Shamma Abu Nawas, Nermeen Kamel Adam, Jaidaa Adel, Reema Adhami, Asma Ahmad, Nazima Ahmad, Abdul Rahman Abubaker Ahmed, Abdullah Hassan Ahmed, Ahmed Abdulla Ahmed, Asma Ahmed, Bader Ahmed, Roqia Murad Hohammed Ahmed, Yousef Hussain Ahmed, Ali al-Abdool, Khalid Ibrahim al-Abdooli, Khadher al-Aidarous, Alaa Mohammed al-Akawi, Masoud Amralla al-Ali, Saeeda al-Ameri, Reem al-Moodi, Sara al-Aqeeli, Zinab al-Ashoor, Lama al-Askari, Nadia Ahmed al-Awadi, Hamad Mansour Alawar, Maryam

al-Awar, Shoug al-Banna, Aballa Mohamed al-Bloushi, Shaikha Rashed al-Braikhi, Khadija Hussain al-Buloshi, Saeed Aldaheri, Salma Khaifa al-Darmaki, Hessa Abdulla Rashed al-Dhahery, Ahmed Saeed Ali al-Dhahiri, Hiba Ahmad al-Dhahri, Heba al-Dhanhani, Munira al-Doseri, Ahmed Abdullah al-Emadi, Rashid Harib al-Falahi, Dara al-Farqih, Khalid al-Fardan, Amen al-Farjani, Latifa Saeed al-Flasy, Yasser al-Gargawi, Samira al-Ghaferi, Bandar Alghamdi, Mohamed Fouad al-Haddad, Shmad Ali al-Haj, Saeed al-Hajri, Sultan al-Halami, Salama al-Hamad, Ali al-Hamadi. Reem al-Hamli, Aisha al-Hamly, Abdulla Ahmed al-Hammadi, Hamad al-Hammadi, Khadeeja Mohamed al-Hammadi, Khalid Ahmed al-Hammadi, Matiam Dawood al-Hammadi, Rana Mohamed al-Hammadi, Mohamed Abdallah al-Hammady, Ameer al-Hashemi, Buthaina al-Hashemi, Tariq al-Hashimi, Areej al-Hassan, Abeer Alhebsi, Dana Ali al-Hosani, Mohammad Alhuraiz, Khalid Ali, Sheefa Abdulla Ali, Hani Alireza, Adel al-Jabri, Hamad al-Jabri, Nawaf al-Janahi, Mohammad al-Jassim, Hiba Saleh al-Jermi, Abdullah Momen al-Junaibi, Afrah al-Junaibi, Abdulla Matar al-Kaabi, Saoud Alkaabi, Nadia Mohamed Alkarimi, Ali Hassan al-Katheeri, Howaidi Ali al-Katheery, Sabah al-Keisri, Fatima Seif Alketbi, Khahida al-Khaja, Nayla al-Khaja, Reef al-Khaja, Farid al-Khajah, Susan al-Kaldi, Sahar al-Khatib, Yasser al-Khayat, Khawla Zainal al-Khoori, Thuraya al-Khoori, Amani Ahmed al-Lawghani, Juma Hmaid al-Leem, Mohamed Allooh, Khalid al-Mahmoud, Khaled Saleem al-Mahrouqi, Bandar al-Mandeel, Asma al-Mansour, Mariam Abdulla al-Mansoori, Nayef al-Mansouri, Rashid al-Marri, Roudha al-Marri, Amena Abdul Aziz al-Marqouqi, Hind Mohammed Almarzouqi, Salah Mohamed al-Marzouqi, Samir Houssain al-Marzouqi, Mahmoud Yousouf al-Mashni, Asad Salem al-Mayahi, Ahmed Rashed al-Mazrooie, Afra al-Mazrouei, Ameena Abdulla al-Mazrouie, Sahar al-Medfa, Noura al-Mehairi, Zainab Almehdi, Badria Mohmmed al-Mehrizi, Reem al-Moodi, Amira al-Muathen, Aisha Mohamed Obaid al-Muhairi, Amna Ateeq al-Muhairi, Fadel Saeed al-Muhairi, Hamda Mohamed al-Muhairi,

Hana Abdullah Mohamed al-Mulla al-Muhairi, Fatma al-Mulla, Saoud Mohamed Ali al-Mulla, Saeed Salmeen al-Murry, Fatma Almushrraakh, Ahmed al-Mutara, Hafsa al-Mutawa, Khahil Sameer al-Naboulsi, Yaser Saeed Alneydi, Ali Khalifa al-Nizer, Mohammed al-Otaiba, Nasir Alowais, Hussain al-Qallaf, Aisha al-Qasimi, Maryam al-Qasimi, Maysoon al-Qassimi, Salem Faisal al-Qassimi, Bader Johar al-Qood, Mohamed Abdullah al-Qubaisi, Mohamed Najm al-Qubaisi, Saif Fadhel al-Rabeea. Nasser Jaber al-Rahman, Saleh al-Rahman, Maria Mohammad al-Rais, Khalid Alrayhi, Mohamed Jasim al-Redha, Hamad Saif al-Reyami, Omar al-Reyami, Salem Ghaleb al-Reyami, Yahya Bashier al-Rifai, Fatima Khalifa al-Romaithi, Rashed Mohamed al-Romaithi, Salama al-Romaithi, Shamma Mohamed al-Rumaithi, Rasha Ali al-Saadi, Miriam al-Sabah, Awra Alsabchi, Juma al-Sahli, Jassim Mohamed al-Salty, Mohamed al-Sanousi, Dareen al-Sarraj, Moza Ali al-Sayed, Fatema Salem al-Shabibi, Mohamed al-Shaibani, Hassan Abdulrahman al-Shaikh, Abdallah al-Shami, Abdallah Rashid al-Shamsi, Alia al-Shamsi, Shamsa al-Sharif, Hana al-Shateri, Ibtisam Ahmed al-Shayeb, Rashid Abdullah Abdu Aziz Alfahad Alshehhi, Walid al-Shehhi, Mustafa al-Sheikh, Jassim Ali al-Shemsi, Ahmed Mohammed al-Shirawi, Amena Saif al-Suboosi, Oshba Ahmad Alsuwaidi, Rehab Ibrahim al-Suwaidi, Saeed Mohamed al-Suwaidi, Salwa Hassan al-Suwaidi, Sumaya al-Suwaidi, Theyab al-Tamimi, Nasser al-Yakoubi, Naser al-Yaqobi, Khadija al-Yousuf, Fatima al-Zaabi, Essa Alzarooni, Azza al-Zarouni, Fatima al-Ziyoudi, Mamoun Alzoughbi, Noura Amiri, Massoud Amrallah, Hind Amro, Ahmed Arshi, Pranav Arya, Mohamed Ashoor, Montiana Bahgat Ashour, Abdullah Ataya, Amina Ataya, Rehab Omar Ateek, Hala Awadallah, Samya Ayish, Kaltham Bader, Waeed Masood Badri, Abdallah Bastaki, Salem Belyouha, Manal Ali Bin Amro, Maryam Bin Fahad, Nahla Bin Fahad, Moath Bin Hafez, Hussain Bin Haider, Maitha Mohammed Bin Owqad, Mohammed Abdulla Bin Sougat, Ahmed Abdul Majeed Bolooki, Yousef Bukhamas, Sahar Bustan, Drina Cabral, Souad Daou, Jasim Bou Dibs, Bara Fakhri Dweik, Maitha Ebrahim, Ibrahim El Sanjak, Carmen Elly, Mina Eltaieb, Ahmad Essam, Wafa Faisal, Ahmed Faour, Rana Farhat, Badr Fikree, Aymn Ibrahim Fuda, Lamya Hussein Gargash, Maha Gargash, Samar Ghanayem, Eiman Ahmed Ghanem, Lubnan Ghannam, Lekha Ghosh, Lubna Jasim Habash, Aida Butti Hadeed, Lara Osama Hafez, Mohamed Hafez, Mohamed Abdul Rahim Haji, Feruza Haleed, Orwa Hallak, Sarra Hamad, Yasmin Hamaideh, Aya Kassem Hammad, Ahmed Juma Hassan, Amira Mohammad Hassan, Reem Ahmad Hassan, Mohamed Khahil Hosa, Rami Hosni, Mohamed Abul Huda, Ahmed Juma Bu Humaid, Sherine Hesham Hussein, Hussain Ibrahim, Lamya Ibrahim, Mohamed Ibrahim, Muneer M Ibrahim, Omar Ibrahim, Reham Ibrahim, Sultan Abdulsalam Ibrahim, Vivian Mamdouh Ibrahim, Yousef Ibrahim, Hassan Ibrahim Hassan Ismail, Hiba Abdel Jaber, Jasim Jaber, Ahmad Jadallah, Ali Jamal, Taj Elsir Idris Jaroon, Mohammed Ahmed Ali Jassim, Ghazi Bugjah Ji, Abdullah Jingan, Mohammed Kabeel, Fadhil Abbas Mohammad Kaidy, Hala Abu Kansoul, Farah Kassem, Dima Arabi Katbi, Omar Kawan, Shadh Khaled, Jonathan Ali Khan, Asma Ahmed Khouri, Ahmed Kabeer Konath, Hany Madian, Mohamed Noori Mahmoud, Talal Mahmood, Catriona Mahmoud, Khaled Mahmoud, Mohamed Mamdouh, Ali Manea, Yasmine Marie, Mubarak Mashi, Mohammed Matar, Reem Matloub, Bassam Mesalatie, Osama Mesalatie, Ahmed Meshmeshy, Hadeel Miqdadi, Ahmed Fat'h al-Bab Mohamed, Fatima Sef Mohamed, Fatima Mohammad, Jassem Mohammed, Salwa Mohammed, Yasmin Mohammed, Reem Mohd, Farha Moon, Ali F. Mostafa, Saud Mrwesh, Ahmad Mustafa, Mohammed Nabhan, Yasmine Fawaz Nabulsi, Mohamed Najeeb, Haifa Nasser, Majid Naysi, Bahman Nazari, Ahmad Noor, Hamdah Hassan Noor, Ahmed Abdulqader Obaid, Joud Odeh, Salha Omran, Abdul Halim Ahmed Qaed, Saif Ben Qumasha, Maryam Rahi, Khalil Abdulwahed Abdul Rahman, Wijan Mohammad Ramadan, Hussein Abdul Rasheed, Raz, Omar Sabah, Osama Khalid Sabbagh, Rawia Abdullah Saeed, Reem Saeed, Sameer Saeed, Sami Safadi, Hamad Abdulla Saghran, Bassem Saimeh, Lamis Yasir

Salam, Nadeem A Saleh, Jamal Salem, Khalid Salem, Nada Salem, Saeed Salmeen, Riham Mahmoud Samara, Halima Saeed Seemba, Jalal Selo, Sarah Shabib, Shamma Shafee, Suad Shamma, Ahmed Mohanned Sharief, Burhan Shawi, Ramzy Shuhaiber, Marwa Mohammed Soliman, Mohammed Mohammed Soliman, Khalil Stas, Khalid Hasan Subaihi, Taryam Hasan Subaihi, Razan Takash, Sidra Tariq, Yusuf Thakur, Fatima Tokmafshan, Aznive Tossounian, Annie Vahedipour, Antone Wakim Wakim, Layal Watfeh, Mohamed Youssef, Iman Tahsin Zadeh, Ahmed Zain, Moustafa Zakaria, Israa' Magdi Zayed.

YEMEN

Size: 207,286 square miles
Population: 23,066,000
GDP: £9,732m
GDP per head: £448
Capital city: Sana'a (population: 2,008,000)

Chronology

Feature films:
2000
The English Sheikh and the Yemeni Gentleman / Le cheikh anglais et le gentleman yéménite (Bader Ben Hirsi) (documentary)

2005
A New Day in Old Sana'a / Un jour nouveau dans le vieux Sana'a (Bader Ben Hirsi)
2006
Amina (Khadija al-Salami) (documentary)

Short Filmmakers (Fiction and Documentary): 4

Saad Hassan al-Zubaidi, Naima Bachiri, Jamil Nacer, Hamid Oqabi.

Part Three

Index of Feature-Film Titles

1 + 1 / One Plus One (Youssef Maalouf, 1971, Syria)

100 Percent / Miya 'ala miya (Khairiya al-Mansour, 1992, Iraq)

1948 (Mohamed Bakri, 1998, Palestine) documentary)

1958 (Ghassan Salhab, 2009, Lebanon) (documentary)

20/20 Vision / Sitta 'ala sitta (Khairiya al-Mansour, 1988, Iraq)

33 Days / 33 jours / 33 yaoum (Maï Masri, 2007, Palestine)

33 jours / 33 Days / 33 yaoum (Maï Masri, 2007, Palestine)

À l'aube / At Dawn / Maa al-fajr (Abdel Jabar al-Obeidi, 1964, Iraq)

À la fin de l'été / At the End of Summer / Akher as saif (Marwan and Ghadi Rahbani, 1980, Lebanon)

À la recherche de la princesse Layla / Looking for Princess Leila / al-Baath . . . 'an Layla al-amiriyyah (Qassim Hawal, 1992, Iraq)

À travers la poussière / Crossing the Dust / Parinawa la ghobar (Shawkat Amin Korki, 2006, Iraq)

Abou Hella / Abu hila (Mohamed Choukri Jamil and Youssuf Gergis, 1962, Iraq)

Abou Sélim émissaire d'amour / Abou Selim, Messenger of Love (Youssef Maalouf, 1963, Lebanon)

Abou Sélim en Afrique / Abou Selim in Africa / Abou Sélim fi Afriquia (Gary Garabédian, 1966, Lebanon)

Abou Sélim en ville / Abou Selim in the City (Hassib Chams, 1962, Lebanon)

Abou Selim in Africa / Abou Sélim en Afrique / Abou Sélim fi Afriquia (Gary Garabédian, 1966, Lebanon)

Abou Selim in the City / Abou Sélim en ville (Hassib Chams, 1962, Lebanon)

Abou Selim, Messenger of Love / Abou Sélim émissaire d'amour (Youssef Maalouf, 1963, Lebanon)

Absence (Mohamed Souweid, 1981, Lebanon)

Adieu au passé / Farewell to the Past (Mohamed Shahin, 1978, Syria)

Adieu Gary / Goodbye Gary (Nassim Amrouche, 2009, Jordan)

Adieu ô Liban / Farewell O Lebanon / (Kikmat Labib, 1967, Iraq)

Adventurers, The / Les aventuriers / al-Moughamiron (Samir al-Ghoussayni, 1981, Lebanon)

Affair, The / L'affaire / al-Safaka (Samir al-Ghoussayni, 1982, Lebanon)

Afra and Bader / Afra et Bader / Afra wa Bader (Faleh al-Zeïdi, 1963, Iraq)

Afra et Bader / Afra and Bader / Afra wa Bader (Faleh al-Zeïdi, 1963, Iraq)

After the War . . . / Après la guerre c'est toujours la guerre (Samir Abdallah, 2008, Lebanon) (documentary)

Agitators, The / Les fauteurs (Mohamed Shahin, 1975, Syria)

Aimée de tous / Loved by All / Habitat al-kol (Rida Myassar, 1964, Lebanon)

Al-Ahrar Bridge, The / Le pont d'al-Ahrar / Jisr al-ahrar (Dia' al-Bayati, 1970, Iraq)

Alia and Issa / Alia et Issa / Alya wa Issa (André Chotin, 1948, Iraq)

Alia et Issa / Alia and Issa / Alya wa Issa (André Chotin, 1948, Iraq)

Al-Lajat (Riyad Shayya, 1995, Syria)

All My Mothers / Toutes mes mères / Hamey-e madrana-e man (Ebrahim Saeedi and Zahavi Sanjavi, 2009, Iraq) (documentary)

Al-Mahabba (Dureid Lahham, 1990, Syria)

Al-Marmoura (Wiam al-Saidi, 1985, Lebanon)

Al-Mouzayafa (Soubhi Seifeddine, 1983, Lebanon)

Al-Mureed (Nujoom al-Ghanem, 2008, United Arab Emirates)

Al-Tharwa al-samakia (Wadeih Yousef, 1976, Syria)

Al-Yazirli (Qays al-Zubaydi, 1974, Syria)

Amani sous l'arc en ciel / Amani Under the Rainbow (Samir Khoury, 1984, Lebanon)

Amani Under the Rainbow / Amani sous l'arc en ciel (Samir Khoury, 1984, Lebanon)

Amerrika / Amreeka (Cherien Dabis, 2009, Palestine)

Amina (Khadija al-Salami, 2006, Yemen) (documentary)

Amour à Constantinople / Love in Constantinople (Seif-Eddine Chawkat, 1967, Syria)

Amour d'enfants / Childish Love (Fares Khalil, 2008, Lebanon)

Another Day / Un autre jour / Yawm akhar (Sahib Haddad, 1978, Iraq)

Another Facet of Love / Une autre facette de l'amour / Wahj akhar lil-hob (Mohamed Shahin, 1972, Syria)

Appartement de l'amour / Flat for Love (Nagdi Hafez, 1973, Syria)

Après la guerre c'est toujours la guerre / After the War . . . (Samir Abdallah, 2008, Lebanon) (documentary)

Arab Falcon, The / Le faucon des arabes / Sakr al-arab (Rida Myassar, 1966, Lebanon)

Arna's Children / Les enfants d'Arna / Atfal Arna (Juliano Mer-Khamis, 2003, Palestine) (documentary)

Around the Pink House / Autour de la maison rose / al Beitt al-zahr (Joana Hadjithomas and Khalil Joreige, 1999, Lebanon)

Arrivals from the Sea / Les arrivants par la mer (Seif-Eddine Chawkat, 1977, Syria)

At Dawn / À l'aube / Maa al-fajr (Abdel Jabar al-Obeidi, 1964, Iraq)

At Our Listeners' Request / Au plaisir des auditeurs / Ma yatlubuhu al-mustami'un (Abdellatif Abdelhamid, 2003, Iraq)

At the End of Summer / À la fin de l'été / Akher as saif (Marwan and Ghadi Rahbani, 1980, Lebanon)

At the Mercy of the Winds / Au gré des vents / Fi mahab al-rih (Zinardi Habis, 1986, Lebanon)

At the Time of Pearls / Au temps des perles / Ayyam al-loulou (Wiam al-Saidi, 1986, Lebanon)

Attachment, The / L'attachement / Al-mahabba (Doureid Lahham, 1990, Syria)

Attempt, The / L'essai a.k.a. *L'expérience / al-Tajruba* (Fouad al-Tuhami, 1977, Iraq)

Attente / Waiting / Intizar (Rashid Masharawi, 2006, Palestine)

Au gré des vents / At the Mercy of the Winds / Fi mahab al-rih (Zinardi Habis, 1986, Lebanon)

Au neuvième mois / In the Ninth Month / Fi-shah al-tasi' (Ali Nasser, 2002, Palestine)

Au plaisir des auditeurs / At Our Listeners' Request / Ma yatlubuhu al-mustami'un (Abdellatif Abdelhamid, 2003, Iraq)

Au secours / Help (Marc Abi Rached, 2009, Lebanon)

Au service de l'amour / In the Service of Love / Bi amr al-hub (Mohamed Selmane, 1965, Lebanon)

Au temps des perles / At the time of Pearls / Ayyam al-loulou (Wiam al-Saidi, 1986, Lebanon)

Au-delà des frontières / Beyond the Borders / Wara al-hudud (Zuhayr al-Shawwa, 1963, Syria)

Aujourd'hui / Today (Akram Zaatari, 2003, Lebanon)

Autour de la maison rose / Around the Pink House / al Beit al-zahr (Joana Hadjithomas and Khalil Joreige, 1999, Lebanon)

Autumn Leaves / Feuilles d'automne / Awrak al-kharif (Hikmet Labib, 1963, Iraq)

Ayez pitié de moi / Take Pity on Me / Irhamoini (Hyder al-Omer, 1958, Iraq)

Ayroum (Nigol Bezjian, 2005, Lebanon)

Babylon II (Samir, 1983, Iraq)

Baghdad Nights / Les nuits de Bagdad / Layali Bagdad (Borhan al-Din Jassem, 1975, Iraq)

Baghdad On/Off (Saad Salman, 2002, Iraq)

Bahraini Tale / Un conte de Bahrain / Hekaya Bahrainiya (Bassam al-Thawadi, 2008, Bahrain)

Boat, The / La barque / al-Zawraq (collective, 1977, Iraq)

Body on Fire / Le corps en feu / Lahib al-jassad (Rida Myassar, 1965, Lebanon)

Bonjour l'amour / Hello, Love / Marhabane ayouhal hub (Mohamed Selmane, 1962, Lebanon)

Bonne nuit / Good Night (Khaldoun al-Mahled, 1975, Syria)

Borders / Les frontières / al-Hudud (Dureid Lahham, 1984, Syria)

Borders in Flames / Frontières en flammes / Hudud al-mulahihah (Sahib Haddad, 1986, Iraq)

Breeze of the Soul / Le souffle de l'âme / Nassim ar-ruh (Abdellatif Abdelhamid, 1999, Syria)

Bride from Kurdistan, The / La mariée du Kurdistan / Arusat Kurdistan (Ja'far Ali, 1992, Iraq)

Bride of the Euphrates, The / La mariée de l'Euphrate / Aros al-forat (Abdel Hadi Mobarak, 1961, Iraq)

Bridge of the Wicked / Le Pont des méchants (Nagdi Hafez, 1971, Syria)

Broken Wings, The / Les ailes brisées / al-Ajniha al-mutakassira (Youssef Maalouf, 1964, Lebanon)

Burning Heart / Cœur brûlant / Fi kalbiha nar (Ahmed al-Toukhi, 1960, Lebanon)

Bus, The / L'autobus / Bosta (Philippe Aractingi, 2005, Lebanon)

Bus Driver, The / Le contrôleur d'autobus / al-Jabi (Jaf'ar Ali, 1969, Iraq)

Cairo-Baghdad / Le Caire-Bagdad / Al-Kahira-Bagdad (Ahmed Badrakhan, 1945, Iraq)

Call of Duty, The / L'appel du devoir / Nada'al-wajih (Ayyub Badry, 1937, Syria)

Canticle of Stones / Cantique de pierre / Nashid al-hajjar (Michel Khleifi, 1989, Palestine)

Canticles of Love / Cantiques d'amour / Alhane al-hub (Mohamed Selmane, 1967, Lebanon)

Cantique de pierre / Canticle of Stones / Nashid al-hajjar (Michel Khleifi, 1989, Palestine)

Cantiques d'amour / Canticles of Love / Alhane al-hub (Mohamed Selmane, 1967, Lebanon)

Captain Abu Raed / Le capitaine Abu Raed (Amin Matalqa, 2007, Jordan)

Captive, The / La captive / al-Asira (Samir al-Ghoussayni, 1973, Lebanon)

Ceinture de feu / Circle of Fire / Zinnar al-nar (Bahij Hojeïj, 2003, Lebanon)

Celebration, The / La fête (Bashir Safia, 1974, Syria)

Cent visages pour un seul jour / A Hundred Faces for a Single Day / Miat wajh li yom wahed (Christian Ghazi, 1972, Lebanon)

Chahin / Shâhîn (Khalid al-Siddick, 1985, Kuwait)

Chambre No. 7 / Room No. 7 / Gorfa raqm sabaa (Kameran Hassani, 1964, Iraq)

Charbel (Nicolas Abou Samah, 1966, Lebanon)

Chazhra la bédouine / Chazhra the Bedouin / Chazhra al-badawia (Borhan Jassem al-Imam, 1962, Iraq)

Chazhra the Bedouin / Chazhra la bédouine / Chazhra al-badawia (Borhan Jassem al-Imam, 1962, Iraq)

Chemin des rêves / The Path of Dreams / Rariq al-ahlam (Harry Sarkassian, 1973, Lebanon)

Cherwale and Mini-Skirt / Cherwale et mini-jupe / Cherwale wa mini-jupe (Samir al-Ghoussayni, 1973, Lebanon)

Cherwale et mini-jupe / Cherwale and Mini-Skirt / Cherwale wa mini-jupe (Samir al-Ghoussayni, 1973, Lebanon)

Childish Love / Amour d'enfants (Fares Khalil, 2008, Lebanon)

Children of Palestine, The / Les enfants de Palestine / Affâl Filasyîn (Samir Nasr, 1977, Palestine)

Chipies / The Shrews / Banat akker zamane (Rida Myassar, 1972, Lebanon)

Chouchou and the Million / Chouchou et le Million / Chouchou wal milion (Antoine Remy, 1963, Lebanon)

Chouchou et le Million / Chouchou and the Million / Chouchou wal milion (Antoine Remy, 1963, Lebanon)

Chouchou's Adventures / Les aventures de Chouchou / Moughamarat Chouchou (Mohamed Selmane, 1966, Lebanon)

Chronicle of a Disappearance / Chronique d'une disparition / Sijil 'ikhtifa' (Elia Suleiman, 1996, Palestine)

Des aventures comiques au Mexique / Mexico Trip (Seif-Eddine Chawkat, 1972, Syria)

Des filles à aimer / Girls to Love / Banat lil hob (Rida Myassar, 1972, Lebanon)

Des fils sous le sable / Threads Beneath the Sands / Khyoot taht al rimal (Khalifa al-Meraikly, 2006, Qatar)

Des héros et des femmes / Heroes and Women / Abtal wa nissa (Mohamed Selmane, 1969, Lebanon)

Des hommes sous le soleil / Men Under the Sun / Rijalun tahta ash-shams (Nabil al-Maleh, Mohamed Shahin and Mohamed Muwaddin, 1970, Syria)

Des jours à Londres / Days in London / Ayyam fi London (Samir al-Ghoussayni, 1977, Lebanon)

Des mots de l'amour / Words of Love / Kalam fi hub (Mohamed Selmane, with Sayed Tantawi, 1973, Lebanon)

Des ombres sur l'autre rive / Shadows on the Other Bank / Dilâl alâ al-jânibi al-âkhar (Ghalib Shaath, 1973, Palestine)

Deux cœurs, un corps / Two Hearts, One Body (Georges Kahi, 1959, Lebanon)

Deux lunes et un olivier / Two Moons and an Olive Tree / Qamarn wa zayrunah (Abdellatif Abdelhamid, 2001, Syria).

Devil's Cart, The / La charrette du diable / Arabat al-chaitane (Georges Kahi, 1962, Lebanon)

Direction opposée / The Wrong Way / al-Ittijâh al-mu'âkis (Marwan Haddad, 1975, Syria)

Displacement, The / Le déplacement / al-Terhal (Raymond Boutros, 1997, Syria)

Divine Intervention / Intervention divine / Yadun 'Ilahiyya (Elia Suleiman, 2002, Palestine)

Do Not Touch My Wife / Ne touche pas à ma femme / Idak an mrati (Rida Myassar, 1967, Lebanon)

Docteur Hassan / Doctor Hassan / Doctor Hassan (Mohamed Monir al-Yasen, 1958, Iraq)

Doctor Hassan / Docteur Hassan / Doctor Hassan (Mohamed Monir al-Yasen, 1958, Iraq)

Does / Biches / Ghezlane (Samir al-Ghoussayni, 1976, Lebanon)

Don't Say Goodbye to a Day That's Scarcely Gone / Ne dites pas adieu à un jour qui n'a guère passé / La taqIuli wadâ'an lil ams (Mohamed Shahin, 1977, Syria)

Doux comme un baie, mon amour / Sweet Like a Berry, My Love / Habibati ya hab al-tout (Marwan Haddad, 1979, Syria)

Drama of a Girl from the East, The / Le drame d'une fille de l'orient / Ma'asat fatât sharqiya (Mohamed Shahin, 1983, Syria)

Dream, A (Hani Shaibani, 2005, United Arab Emirates)

Dreams / Rêves / Ahlaam (Mohamed al-Daradji, 2005, Iraq)

Dreams of Sparrows, The / Rêves de moineaux (Hayder Mousa Daffar, 2005, Iraq) (documentary)

Dreamy Visions / Visions chimériques / Ra'a halima (Waha al-Raheb, 2003, Syria)

Dunia (Jocelyne Saab, 2005, Lebanon)

Duped, The / Les dupes / al-Makhdhououn (Tewfiq Saleh, 1972, Syria)

Eau amère / Bitter Water (Maysoon Pachachi, 2003, Iraq) (documentary)

Écrans de sable / Screens of Sand (Randa Chahal-Sabbag, 1991, Lebanon)

Écrivains des frontières / Writers on the Borders, a Journey to Palestine (Samir Abdalah and Jose Reynes, 2004, Palestine) (documentary)

En perdant Ahmad / Losing Ahmad (Abdullah Boushahri, 2006, Kuwait) (documentary)

En raison de circonstances / Because of Circumstances (Saad Salman, 1982, Iraq) (documentary)

Encore une fois / Once More / Mara okhra (Joud Saeed, 2009, Syria)

English Sheikh and the Yemeni Gentleman, The / Le cheikh anglais et le gentleman yéménite (Bader Ben Hirsi, 2000, Yemen) (documentary)

Enquête personnelle / Personal Inquiry (Ula Tabari, 2002, Palestine)

Étoiles du jour / Stars in Broad Daylight / Nujum al-nahar (Oussama Mohammad, 1988, Syria)

Everyday Life in a Syrian Village / La vie quotidien dans un village syrien / Al-hayat

Four Girls / Quatre filles (Hassan al-Halibi, 2008, Bahrain)

Fourteenth Chick, The / Le quatorzième poussin / Het veertiende kippetje (Hany Abu Assad, 1998, Palestine)

Fragile Houses / Maisons fragiles / Bouyout min warak (Rafic Hajjar, 1984, Lebanon)

Fragments d'images / Fragments of Images / Baqaya suwar (Nabil al-Maleh, 1980, Syria)

Fragments of Images / Fragments d'images / Baqaya suwar (Nabil al-Maleh, 1980, Syria)

Freedom Fighters, The / Les fédayins / al-Fidaiyyoun (Christian Ghazi, 1967, Lebanon)

Freedom Gang, The / Le gang de la liberté / al-Sheikha (Layla Assaf, 1994 Lebanon)

Frontières en flammes / Borders in Flames / Hudud al-mulahihah (Sahib Haddad, 1986, Iraq)

Game of Love and Death, The / Le jeu de l'amour et de la mort / Lubatu al-hubb was al-gatl (Mohamed Shahin, 1983, Syria)

Garo / Garo (Gary Garabédian, 1965, Lebanon)

Gate of Heaven / La porte au ciel / Bawabet al-janna (Maher Kaddo, 2009, Syria)

Gazala (Safa Mohamed Ali, 1967, Iraq)

Ghawar's Empire (Bashir Safia, 1982, Syria)

Ghost from the Past, The / Le fantôme du passé / Chabah almadi (Georges Ghayad, 1984, Lebanon)

Gibier de valeur / Valuable Game / al-Istiyad al-kabir (Rida Myassar, 1974, Lebanon)

Gipsy and the Heroes, The / La gitane et les héros / al-Ghajaria wal abtal (Samir al-Ghoussayni, 1985, Lebanon)

Girl from the Air, The / La fille de l'air (Maroun Bagdadi, 1992, Lebanon)

Girls to Love / Des filles à aimer / Banat lil hob (Rida Myassar, 1972, Lebanon)

Golden Sands / Sables d'or / Rimal min thaheb (Youssef Chahine, 1967, Lebanon)

Good Night / Bonne nuit (Khaldoun al-Mahled, 1975, Syria)

Good Omen, The / Le bon augure / Chaif Khir (Mohamed Choukri Jamil, 1969, Iraq)

Goodbye Gary / Adieu Gary (Nassim Amrouche, 2009, Jordan)

Grand Prix / Grand prix / al-Jaiza al koubra (Samir al-Ghoussayni, 1974, Lebanon)

Grand prix / Grand Prix / al-Jaiza al koubra (Samir al-Ghoussayni, 1974, Lebanon)

Greedy Ones, The / Les gourmands a.k.a. *Les algues d'eau douce / al-Tahalib* (Raymond Boutros, 1991, Syria)

Green Valley, The / La vallée verte / al-Wadi al-akhdar (Zuharyr al-Shawwa, 1950, Syria)

Guerre, amour, dieu, et folie / War, Love, God and Madness (Mohamed al-Daradji, 2009, Iraq) (documentary)

Guerre civile / Civil War (Mohamed Souweid, 2002, Lebanon)

Gypsy in Love, The / La gitane amoureuse / al-Ghajaria al-achika (Rida Myassar, 1972, Lebanon)

Haifa / 'Haifa (Rashid Masharawi, 1996, Palestine)

Half-Metre Incident, The / L'accident du demi-mètre / Hadithat al-nisf mitr (Samir Zikra, 1983, Syria)

Hamad and Hammud / Hamad et Hammud / Hamad wa Hammud (Ibrahim Jalal, 1980, Iraq)

Hamad et Hammud / Hamad and Hammud / Hamad wa Hammud (Ibrahim Jalal, 1980, Iraq)

Hamidou's Return / Le retour d'Hamidou / Awdat Hamidu (Fayçal al-Yassiri, 1974, Iraq)

Hand of Fate, The / La main du destin / Yad al-qadar (Kamel al-Obeidi, 1965, Iraq)

Hand, The / La main / al-Yad (Qassim Hawal, 1970, Syria)

Haneen (Mohamed al-Traifi, 2006, Emirati)

Hasiba (Raymond Boutros, 2008, Syria)

Hé! N'oublie pas le cumin / Hey! Don't Forget the Cumin (Hala al-Abdulla Yacoub, 2008, Syria) (documentary)

Head, The / La tête / al-Ras (Fayçal al-Yasseri, 1976, Iraq)

Hello, Love / Bonjour l'amour / Marhabane ayouhal hub (Mohamed Selmane, 1962, Lebanon)

In the Ruins of Baalbeck / Dans les ruines de Baalbeck / Bayn hayakel Baalbeck (Julio De Luca and Karam Boustany, 1933, Lebanon)

In the Service of Love / Au service de l'amour / Bi amr al-hub (Mohamed Selmane, 1965, Lebanon)

Infidels, The / Les infidèles (Randa Chahal Sabbag, 1997, Lebanon)

Intervention divine / Divine Intervention / Yadun 'Ilahiyya (Elia Suleiman, 2002, Palestine)

Irak, le chant des absents / Iraq: The Song of the Missing Men (Layth Abdulamir, 2005, Iraq)

Iranian Journey / La femme-chauffeur, une traversée en bus de l'Iran (Maysoon Pachachi, 1999, Iraq) (documentary)

Iraq: The Song of the Missing Men / Irak, le chant des absents (Layth Abdulamir, 2005, Iraq)

Island Devil, The / Le diable de l'île / Chaitane al-jazira (Samir al-Ghoussayni, 1981, Lebanon)

It Is Not Enough for God to Be with the Poor / Il ne suffit pas que Dieu soit avec les pauvres / La yakfi an yakoun allah maal foukara (Borhan Alawiyya, 1978, Lebanon) (documentary)

Jalla! Jalla! (Josef Farès, 2000, Lebanon)

James Bond, le jaloux / Jealous James Bond / Ghawar James Bond (Nabil al-Maleh, 1974, Syria)

Jasmine / Yasmin (Nizar Hassan, 1998, Palestine) (video)

Je meurs deux fois je t'aimerais / If I Die Twice I Would Love You (Georges Khoury, 1975, Syria)

Je ne suis pas coupable / I Am Not Guilty / Lastou mouzniba (Ibrahim Takkouche, 1960, Lebanon)

Je suis Antar / I Am Antar / Ana Antar (Youssef Maalouf, 1967, Lebanon)

Je suis celle qui porte les fleurs vers sa tombe / I Am the One Who Brings Flowers to Her Grave (Hala al-Abdallah Yakoub and Ammar al-Beik, 2006, 110', Syria) (documentary)

Je suis l'Irak / I Am Iraq / Ana al-Irak (Mohamed al-Din al-Yasen, 1960, Iraq)

Je veux voir / I Want to See (Joan Hadjithomas and Khalil Joreige, 2007, Lebanon)

Jealous James Bond / James Bond, le jaloux / Ghawar James Bond (Nabil al-Maleh, 1974, Syria)

Jenin, Jenin / Jénine, Jénine (Mohamed Bakri, 2002, Palestine) (documentary)

Jénine, Jénine / Jenin, Jenin (Mohamed Bakri, 2002, Palestine) (documentary)

Jeremy Hardy vs. the Israeli Army (Leila Sansour, 2002, Palestine) (documentary)

Jester's Love, The / L'amour du bouffon / Gharâm al-muharrij (Bashir Safia, 1976, Syria).

Jeunesse au soleil / Youth in the Sun / Chabab tahtal cham (Samir Nasi, 1966, Lebanon)

Jiyan (Jano Rosebiani, 2002, Iraq)

Joies de la jeunesse / Joys of Youth / Afrah al-chabab (Mohamed Selmane, 1964, Lebanon)

Journey of Love / Voyage d'amour (Youssef Maalouf, 1972, Syria)

Jours de ma vie / Days of My Life / Ayyam min omri (Georges Kahi, 1959, Lebanon)

Jours d'ennui / Days of Boredom / Ayyam al-dajar (Abdellatif Abdelhamid, 2008, Syria)

Joys of Youth / Joies de la jeunesse / Afrah al-chabab (Mohamed Selmane, 1964, Lebanon)

Judgement of Fate, The / Jugement du destin / Hokm al-kadar (Joseph Ghorayeb, 1959, Lebanon)

Jugement du destin / The Judgement of Fate / Hokm al-kadar (Joseph Ghorayeb, 1959, Lebanon)

Jumaa and the Sea / Jumaa et la mer / Jumaa wa al-bahr (Hani al-Shaibani, 2007, United Arab Emirates)

Jumaa et la mer / Jumaa and the Sea / Jumaa wa al-bahr (Hani al-Shaibani, 2007, United Arab Emirates)

Jungle of Wolves, The / Le jungle des loups / Ghâbatu al-diâb (Mohamed Shahin, 1977, Syria)

Jusqu'au déclin du jour / Until the End of the Day a.k.a. *Nightfall* (Mohamed Souweid, 2000, Lebanon) (documentary).

L'œil vigilant / *The Vigilant Eye* / *al-Ayn al-sahira* (Gary Garabédian, 1963, Lebanon)

L'ombre de l'absence / *Shadow of Absence* / *Dhil al-gheyab* (Nasri Hajjaj, 2008, Palestine) (documentary)

L'ombre de la ville / *The Shadows of the City* (Jean Chamoun, 2000, Lebanon)

L'ordre du jour / *Order of the Day* (Michel Khleifi, 1993, Palestine)

L'usurier / *The Moneylender* / *al-Marabi* (Mohamed Shahin, 1999, Syria)

La ballerine blessée / *The Wounded Ballerina* / *Râqisa alâ al-firâh* (Mohamed Shahin, 1973, Syria)

La banque / *The Bank* / *al-Bank* (Mohamed Selmane, 1965, Lebanon)

La barque / *The Boat* / *al-Zawraq* (collective, 1977, Iraq)

La bataille d'Al-Qâdissiya / *The Battle of Al-Qâdissiya* / *al-Qâdissiya* (Salah Abou Seif, 1981, Iraq)

La beauté et le tigre / *The Beautiful Girl and the Tiger* / *al-Hassna'wal nemr* (Mohamed Selmane, 1972, Lebanon)

La belle bergère / *The Beautiful Shepherdess* (Atef Salem, 1972, Syria)

La belle et les quatre regards / *The Beauty and the Four Looks* (Seif-Eddine Chawkat, 1975, Syria)

La captive / *The Captive* / *al-Asira* (Samir al-Ghoussayni, 1973, Lebanon)

La charrette du diable / *The Devil's Cart* / *Arabat al-chaitane* (Georges Kahi, 1962, Lebanon)

La chasse à l'homme / *Manhunt* / *Saydu al-rijâl* (Bashir Safia, 1976, Syria)

La cinquième chambre d'Ouija / *The Fifth Chamber Ouija* (Maher al-Khaja, 2009, United Arab Emirates)

La cinquième citadelle / *The Fifth Arm of the Prison* / *al-Qal'a al-khâmisa* (Bilal al-Sabouni, 1979, Syria)

La cinquième colonne / *The Fifth Column* / *al-Jiha al-khamisa* (Soubhi Seifeddine, 1984, Lebanon)

La crise des jeunes / *The Crisis of the Young* (Nagdi Hafez, 1972, Syria)

La cueillette des olives / *The Olive Harvest* / *Mawsim al-zaytoon* (Hanna Elias, 2002, Palestine)

La dame aux lunes noires / *The Lady with the Dark Glasses* / *Saydat al-akmar as-sawda* (Samir Khoury, 1971, Lebanon)

La dame du palais / *The Lady of the Palace* / *Sayidat el-kasr* (Samir Habchi, 2003, Lebanon) (documentary)

La décision / *The Decision* / *al-Karar* (Youssef Charafeddine, 1981, Lebanon)

La dernière décision / *The Last Decision* / *Hobat al-madlum* (Safa Mohamed Ali, 1961, Iraq)

La dernière nuit / *The Last Night* / *al-Layl al-akhir* (Youssef Charafeddine, 1982, Lebanon)

La farine noire / *Black Flour* / *al-Tahin al-aswad* (Ghassan Shmeit, 2001, Syria)

La fête / *The Celebration* (Bashir Safia, 1974, Syria)

La fille de l'air / *The Girl from the Air* (Maroun Bagdadi, 1992, Lebanon)

La fille du gardien / *The Watchman's Daughter* / *Bint al-hares* (Henri Barakat, 1968, Lebanon)

La folie des adolescentes / *The Madness of Adolescent Girls* / *Jounoun al- mourahikat* (Taysir Abboud, 1969, Lebanon)

La gitane amoureuse / *The Gypsy in Love* / *al-Ghajaria al-achika* (Rida Myassar, 1972, Lebanon)

La gitane et les héros / *The Gipsy and the Heroes* / *al-Ghajaria wal abtal* (Samir al-Ghoussayni, 1985, Lebanon)

La grande question / *Clash of Loyalties* a.k.a. *The Big Question* / *al-Massala al-korba* (Mohamed Choukri Jamil, 1983, Iraq)

La grenade et la myrrhe / *Pomegranates and Myrrh* / *Al-Mor wa al-rumman* (Najwa Najjar, 2008, Lebanon)

La guerre au Liban / *The War in Lebanon* / *Harb Lubnân* (Samir Nasr, 1977, Palestine)

La guitare de l'amour / *Love's Guitar* / *Guitare al-hub* (Mohamed Selmane, 1973, Lebanon)

La honte / *Shame* / *al-'Ar* (Bilal al-Sabouni, Bashir Safia, and Wadeih Yousef, 1974, Syria)

La honte, Restoum / *Shame, Restoum* / *Ayb ya Restoum* (Wiam al-Saidi, 1987, Lebanon)

La vie après la chute / *Life After the Fall* / *Hatay ma baad al-suqoot* (Kassim Abid, 2008, Iraq) (documentary)

La vie est une mélodie / *Life Is a Melody* / *al-Dounya nagham* (Samir al-Ghoussayni, 1975, Lebanon)

La vie quotidien dans un village syrien / *Everyday Life in a Syrian Village* / *Al-hayat al-yawmiya fi qaria Suriya* (Omar Amiralay, 1974, Syria) (documentary)

La ville tranquille / *The Quiet City* (Hassan Ridha, 1972, Syria)

La vision / *The Vision* / *al-Rou'ya* (Youssef Charafeddine, 1985, Lebanon)

La visiteuse / *The Visitor* (Henri Barakat, 1972, Lebanon)

La voie de l'amour / *The Path of Love* / *Darb al-Hob* (Borhan al-Din Jassem, 1966, Iraq)

La voie des ténèbres / *The Path of Darkness* / *Tariq al-dalam* (Abdel Karem al-Saraj, 1970, Iraq)

La voie du mal / *The Path of Evil* / *Trik al-char* (Sami al-Jader, 1967, Iraq)

La voie lactée / *The Milky Way* / *Darb al-tahanat* (Ali Nasser, 1996, Palestine)

La voleuse / *The Woman Thief* / *al-Sarika* (Youssef Charafeddine, 1991, Lebanon)

La volonté du peuple / *The Will of the People* / *Iradat al-chab* (Borhan al-Din Jassem, 1959, Iraq)

Lady of the Palace, The / *La dame du palais* / *Sayidat el-kasr* (Samir Habchi, 2003, Lebanon) (documentary)

Lady with the Dark Glasses, The / *La dame aux lunes noires* / *Saydat al-akmar al-sawda* (Samir Khoury, 1971, Lebanon)

Laila's Birthday / *L'anniversaire de Laila* (Rashid Mashawari, 2008, Palestine)

Land for Strangers, A / *La terre des étrangers* / *Turab al-ajaneb* (Samir Zikra, 1998, Syria)

Laila's Birthday / *L'anniversaire de Laila* (Rashid Mashawari, 2008, Palestine)

Last Decision, The / *La dernière décision* / *Hobat al-madlum* (Safa Mohamed Ali, 1961, Iraq)

Last Man, The / *Le dernier homme* / *Atlal* (Ghassan Salhab, 2006, Lebanon)

Last Message, The / *Le dernier message* (Khatib El Bassel, 2000, Syria)

Last Moon, The / *La ultima luna* (Miguel Littin, Palestine, 2004)

Last Night, The / *La dernière nuit* / *al-Layl al-akhir* (Youssef Charafeddine, 1982, Lebanon)

Last Passage, The / *Le dernier passage* / *al-Mamar al-akhir* (Youssef Charafeddine, 1981, Lebanon)

Layla en Irak / *Leila in Iraq* / *Layla fi al Irak* (Ahmed Kamel Morsi, 1950, Iraq)

Layla et les loups / *Leila and the Wolves* / *Layla wa al-zi'ab* (Heiny Srour, 1984, Lebanon)

Le bon augure / *The Good Omen* / *Chaif Khir* (Mohamed Choukri Jamil, 1969, Iraq)

Le Caire-Bagdad / *Cairo-Baghdad* / *Al-Kahira-Bagdad* (Ahmed Badrakhan, 1945, Iraq)

Le camioneur / *The Lorry Driver* / *Sa'iq ash-shahina* (Boshko Votchinitch, 1966, Syria)

Le canardeur / *The Sniper* / *al-Qannes* (Fayçal al-Yassiri, 1980, Iraq)

Le capitaine Abu Raed / *Captain Abu Raed* (Amin Matalqa, 2007, Jordan)

Le cavalier de Bani Abes / *The Horseman of Bani Abes* (Mohamed Selmane, 1977, Syria)

Le cerf-volant / *The Kite* (Randa Chahal-Sabbag, 2003, Lebanon)

Le cheikh anglais et le gentleman yéménite / *The English Sheikh and the Yemeni Gentleman* (Bader Ben Hirsi, 2000, Yemen) (documentary)

Le cirque de l'oncle Vania et cie / *Uncle Vania and Co.'s Circus* / *Cirque al-ame Vania wa chourakah* (Samir al-Ghoussayni, 1991, Lebanon)

Le collier de perles / *The Pearl Necklace* / *Akd al-loulou* (Youssef Maalouf, 1964, Lebanon)

Le collier meutrier / *The Deadly Necklace* / *al-Akd al-katel* (Ibrahim Takkouche, 1960, Lebanon)

Le contrôleur d'autobus / *The Bus Driver* / *al-Jabi* (Jaf'ar Ali, 1969, Iraq)

Le corps en feu / *Body on Fire* / *Lahib al-jassad* (Rida Myassar, 1965, Lebanon)

Le couteau / *The Knife* / *al-Sikkin* (Khaled Hamada, 1972, Syria)

Le cri / *The Cry* / *al-Sarkha* (Fouad Charafeddine, 1991, Lebanon)

Le progressiste / *The Progressive* / *al-Sayyid al-taqaddumi* (Nabil al-Maleh, 1974, Syria)

Le quatorzième poussin / *The Fourteenth Chick* / *Het veertiende kippetje* (Hany Abu Assad 1998, Palestine)

Le rapport / *The Report* (Haytham Hakki, 1979, Syria)

Le rapport / *The Report* / *al-Taqrîr* (Dureid Lahham, 1986, Syria)

Le résistant / *The Resistance Fighter* / *al-Rajol al-samed* (Soubhi Seifeddine, 1975, Lebanon)

Le retour à Haifa / *Return to Haifa* / *A'id ila Hayfa* (Qassim Hawal, 1981, Iraq)

Le retour d'Hamidou / *Hamidou's Return* / *Awdat Hamidu* (Fayçal al-Yassiri, 1974, Iraq)

Le retour du héros / *The Hero's Return* / *Awdat al-batal* (Samir al-Ghoussayni, 1983, Lebanon)

Le rocher de l'amour / *The Rock of Love* / *Sakhar al-hub* (Rida Myassar, 1959, Lebanon)

Le rouge, le blanc et le noir / *Red, White and Black* / *al-Ahmar wa al-abyad wa al-aswad* (Bashir Safia, 1977, Syria)

Le royaume des pauvres / *The Realm of the Poor* / *Mamlakat al-foukara* (Philippe Akiki, 1967, Lebanon)

Le Sahara n'est pas à vendre / *The Sahara Is Not for Sale* (Jocelyne Saab, 1977, Lebanon) (documentary)

Le saut de la mort / *The Death Leap* / *Kafzat al-mawt* (Youssef Charafeddine, 1982, Lebanon)

Le sel de la mer / *Salt of This Sea* / *Milh hadha al-bahr* (Annemarie Jacir, 2008, Palestine)

Le silence / *al-Samt* / *The Silence* / (Hashim Muhammad, 1979, Kuwait)

Le souffle de l'âme / *Breeze of the Soul* / *Nassim ar-ruh* (Abdellatif Abdelhamid, 1999, Syria)

Le sourire à travers les larmes / *Smiling through the Tears* / *Basima bayna al-dumû* (Wadeih Yousef, 1985, Syria)

Le sud révolté / *The South in Revolt* / *al-Janoub al-thaer* (Rida Myassar, 1984, Lebanon)

Le temps des narcisses / *Narcissus Blossom* / *U nergiz biskvin* (Hussein Hasan Ali and Massoud Arif Salih, 2005, Iraq)

Le temps qu'il reste / *The Time That Remains* / *al-Zaman al-baqi* (Elia Suleiman, 2009, Palestine)

Le toit / *The Roof* / *al-Sateh* (Kamal al-Jafari, 2008, Palestine) (documentary)

Le tourbillon / *The Tornado* / *al-I'sar* (Samir Habchi, 1992, Lebanon)

Le tournant / *The Turning* / *al-Mun'ataf* (Jaf'ar Ali, 1974, Iraq)

Le train de sept heures / *The Seven O'clock Train* / *Qitar al-saa sabaa* (Hikmet Labib, 1963, Iraq)

Le veilleur de nuit / *The Night Watchman* / *al-Haris* (Khahil Chawqi, 1968, Iraq)

Le vendeur de bagues / *The Seller of Rings* / *Biya al-khawatim* (Youssef Chahine, 1965, Lebanon)

Le village d'un seul homme / *The One-Man Village* / *Samaan bildayaa* (Simon El Habre, 2008, Lebanon) (documentary)

Le voleur sympathique / *The Likeable Thief* / *al-Loss al-zarif* (Youssef Issa, 1968, Lebanon)

Lebanon: Bits and Pieces / *Le Liban, fait de pièces et de morceaux* / *Lubnan qita, qita* (Olga Nakkash, 1994, Lebanon)

Lebanon at Night / *Le Liban, la nuit* / *Loubnan fi leil* (Mohamed Selmane, 1963, Lebanon)

Lebanon in Torment / *Le Liban dans la tourmente* / *Lubnan fi al-dawâma* (Jocelyne Saab, 1975, Lebanon) (documentary)

Lebanon in Spite of Everything / *Le Liban, malgré tout* / *Loubnan roghmakulla shai'* (André Gedeon, 1982, Lebanon)

Leila and the Wolves / *Layla et les loups* / *Layla wa al-zi'ab* (Heiny Srour, 1984, Lebanon)

Leila in Iraq / *Layla en Irak* / *Layla fi al Irak* (Ahmed Kamel Morsi, 1950, Iraq)

Leopard, The / *Le léopard* / *al-Fahd* (Nabil al-Maleh, 1972, Syria)

L'épreuve du besoin / *Sense of Need* (Shadi Srour, 2004, Palestine)

Les ailes brisées / *The Broken Wings* / *al-Ajni-ha al-mutakassira* (Youssef Maalouf, 1964, Lebanon)

Les rêves de la ville / *City Dreams* / *Ahlam al-Madina* (Mohamed Malas, 1984, Syria)

Les restes d'une guerre / *Remnants of a War* (Jawad Metni, 2009, Lebanon) (documentary)

Les subterfuges d'amour / *Love's Subterfuges* (Youssef Maalouf, 1972, Syria)

Les tentes de Qaraqoz / *The Tents of Qaraqoz* / *Khaymatu Quaraqoz* (Mohamed Shahin, 1974, Syria)

Les vagabonds / *The Tramps* / *al-Charidan* (Rida Myassar, 1966, Lebanon)

Life After the Fall / *La vie après la chute* / *Hatay ma baad al-suqoot* (Kassim Abid, 2008, Iraq) (documentary)

Life Is a Melody / *La vie est une mélodie* / *al-Dounya nagham* (Samir al-Ghoussayni, 1975, Lebanon)

Life's Lesson / *La leçon de la vie* / *Ababathu al-hayat* (Mohamed al-Ansari, 1958, Iraq)

Light and Darkness / *Lumière et ténèbre* / *Nouron wa thilal* (Nazih Shahbandar, 1947, Syria)

Likeable Thief, The / *Le voleur sympathique* / *al-Loss al-zarif* (Youssef Issa, 1968, Lebanon)

Lila dit ça / *Lila Says That* (Ziad Doueiri, 2004, Lebanon)

Lila Says That / *Lila dit ça* (Ziad Doueiri, 2004, Lebanon)

Lion of the Desert / *Le lion du désert* / *Omar al-Mukhtar* (Mustapha Akkad, 1980, Syria)

Little Stranger, The / *Le petit étranger* (Georges Nasser, 1961, Lebanon)

Little Strength, A / *Un peu de force* / *Chaï min al-quwwah* (Karlo Hartyon, 1988, Iraq)

Little Wars / *Petites guerres* / *Houroub saghira* (Maroun Bagdadi, 1982, Lebanon)

Littoral (Wajdi Mouawad, 2004, Lebanon)

Long Days, The / *Les longues journées* / *al-Ayyam al-tawîla* (Tewfiq Saleh, 1980, Iraq)

Long Live the Bride . . . and the Liberation of Kurdistan / *Vive la mariée . . . et la libération du Kurdistan* (Hiner Saleem, 1997, Iraq)

Long Night, The / *La longue nuit* (Hatem Mohamed, 2009, Syria)

Looking for Princess Leila / *À la recherche de la princesse Layla* / *al-Baath . . . 'an Layla al-amiriyyah* (Qassim Hawal, 1992, Iraq)

Lorry Driver, The / *Le camioneur* / *Sa'iq ash-shahina* (Boshko Votchinitch, 1966, Syria)

Lorsque le peuple a parlé / *When the People Spoke* / *Indama rtakalam al-sha'ab* (Amer al-Zuhair, 2007, Kuwait) (documentary)

Losing Ahmad / *En perdant Ahmad* (Abdullah Boushahri, 2006, Kuwait) (documentary)

Lost Man, A / *Un homme perdu* (Danielle Arbid, 2007, Lebanon)

Louange pour l'amour / *Praise for Love* / *Ya salam al-hub* (Mohamed Selmane, 1963, Lebanon)

Love and Karaté / *L'amour et karaté* / *Hubb wa karati* (Fayçal al-Yassiri, 1973, Iraq)

Love for Life / *L'amour pour la vie* / *Hubbun lil-hayât* (Bashir Safia, 1981, Syria)

Love in Baghdad / *L'amour à Bagdad* / *al-Hubb fi Baghdad* (Abdelhadi al-Rawi, 1986, Iraq)

Love in Constantinople / *Amour à Constantinople* (Seif-Eddine Chawkat, 1967, Syria)

Love in Istanbul / *L'amour à Istamboul* / *Gharam fi Istambul* (Tahsine Kawadri, 1966, Lebanon)

Love Story, A / *Histoire d'amour* / *Hikayat gharam* (Mohamed Selmane, 1963, Lebanon)

Love's Guitar / *La guitare de l'amour* / *Guitare al-hub* (Mohamed Selmane, 1973, Lebanon)

Love's Subterfuges / *Les subterfuges d'amour* (Youssef Maalouf, 1972, Syria)

Loved by All / *Aimée de tous* / *Habitat al-kol* (Rida Myassar, 1964, Lebanon)

Lover, The / *L'amant* / *al-'Ashiq* (Mohamed Munir Fanari, 1986, Iraq)

Lovers of the Demarcation Line of the Rain, The / *Les amants de la ligne de démarcation de la pluie* / *Ushaq ala khat al-matar* (Mustafa Rasid, 1993, Syria).

Lovers on the Road / *Les amants en route* / *Ushâqalâ al-tariq* (Fayçal al-Yassiri, 1977, Iraq)

Lumière et ténèbre / *Light and Darkness* / *Nouron wa thilal* (Nazih Shahbandar, 1947, Syria)

Lutte jusqu'à la libération / *Struggle till Liberation* / *Kifah hatta al-Tahrir* (Abdel Wahab al-Hindi, 1969, Jordan)

Murder Step by Step, A / Un meutre pas à pas / Qatlun . . . an tariq al-tasalsul (Mohamed Shahin, 1982, Syria)

Muse and Amber / Muse et ambres (Mohamed Dhiaddine, 1973, Syria)

Muse et ambres / Muse and Amber (Mohamed Dhiaddine, 1973, Syria)

Mutawa and Bahia / Mutawa et Bahia / Mutawa wa Bahia (Sahib Hadad and Zuhair al-Dijaili, 1982, Iraq)

Mutawa et Bahia / Mutawa and Bahia / Mutawa wa Bahia (Sahib Hadad and Zuhair al-Dijaili, 1982, Iraq)

Mute Man and Love, The / Le muet et l'amour / al-Akhrass wal hub (Alfred Bahri, 1967, Lebanon)

My Beloved Homeland / Ma patrie bien aimée / Watani habibi (Mohamed Kaouach, 1964, Jordan)

My Darling / Ma chérie (Henri Barakat, 1973, Lebanon)

My Eternal Love / Mon amour éternel / Hopubi lazi la yamout (Youssef Charafeddine, 1984, Lebanon)

My Heart Beats Only for Her / Mon cœur ne bat que pour elle / Ma hataftu li ghayriha (Mohamed Souweid, 2009, Lebanon)

My Wife's a Hippy / Ma femme Youppie / Zawjati min al-hippies (Atef Salem, 1973, Syria)

Myth a.k.a. Ostura / Mythologies / Ustura (Nizar Hassan, 1996, Palestine)

Mythologies / Myth a.k.a. Ostura / Ustura (Nizar Hassan, 1996, Palestine)

Nabuchodonsor / Nebuchadnezzar / Nabuocher nosser (Kamel al-Azzawi, 1962, Iraq)

Naima (Adbl Jaber Wali, 1962, Iraq)

Naissance du prophète / Birth of the Prophet / Mawled al-rassoul (Ahmed al-Toukhi, 1960, Lebanon)

Narcissus Blossom / Le temps des narcisses / U nergiz biskvin (Hussein Hasan Ali and Massoud Arif Salih, 2005, Iraq)

Ne dites pas adieu à un jour qui n'a guère passé / Don't Say Goodbye to a Day That's Scarcely Gone / La taqIuli wadâ'an lil ams (Mohamed Shahin, 1977, Syria)

Ne touche pas à ma femme / Do Not Touch My Wife / Idak an mrati (Rida Myassar, 1967, Lebanon)

Nebuchadnezzar / Nabuchodonsor / Nabuocher nosser (Kamel al-Azzawi, 1962, Iraq)

New Day in Old Sana'a, A / Un jour nouveau dans le vieux Sana'a (Bader Ben Hirsi, 2005, Yemen)

Night, The / La nuit / al-Layl (Mohamed Malas, 1992, Syria)

Night Watchman, The / Le veilleur de nuit / al-Haris (Khahil Chawqi, 1968, Iraq)

Nightfall a.k.a. Until the End of the Day / Jusqu'au déclin du jour (Mohamed Souweid, 2000, Lebanon) (documentary).

Nightingale in Lebanon, A / Un rossignol du Liban / Boulbol min Loubnan(Riad Myassar, 1982, Lebanon)

Nights of the Jackal, The / Les nuits du chacal / Layali ibn awa (Abdelatif Abdelhamid, 1989, Syria)

Niloofar (Sabine El Gemayel, 2008, Lebanon)

Noce en Galilée / Wedding in Galilee / Urs al-jalil (Michel Khleifi, 1987, Palestine)

Noises from All Sides / Le hénissement des directions / Sahil al-jibat (Maher Kaddo, 1993, Syria).

Nos guerres imprudents / Our Heedless Wars / Hurubina al-ta'isha (Randa Chahal Sabbagh, 1995, Lebanon)

Nos petits rois / Our Little Kings / Mulûkundâ al-sighar (André Gedeon, 1984. Lebanon)

Nos sentiments ont pris les images images de l'Irak / Our Feelings Took the Pictures: Open Shutters Iraq (Maysoon Pachachi, 2008, Iraq) (documentary)

Not Quite the Taliban / Pas encore le Taliban (Fadi Hindash, 2009, Jordan) (documentary)

Nous retournerons un jour / We Shall Return One Day (Samir Abdallah and Walid Charara, 1998, Lebanon) (documentary)

Nous sommes tous des fédayins / We Are All Freedom Fighters / Koullouna fidaiyyoun (Gary Garabédian, 1969, Lebanon)

Nuage / Cloud / Sahâb (Mohamed Shahin, 1991, Syria)

Nuits des hommes / Men's Nights (Hassan al-Saïfi, 1975, Syria).

Ô nuit / Oh Night / Ya leil (Gary Garabédian, 1964, Lebanon)

Obstacle, The / L'obstacle / Al-hajiz (Bassam al-Thawadi, 1990, Bahrain)

Pas encore le Taliban / Not Quite the Taliban (Fadi Hindash, 2009, Jordan) (documentary)

Passer-By, The / Le passant / Abir sabil (Ahmed Erfan, 1950, Syria)

Passeurs de rêve / Beyond Our Dreams (Hiner Saleem, 1999, Iraq)

Passion en feu / Passion on Fire / Nar al-chawk (Mohamed Selmane, 1971, Lebanon)

Passion on Fire / Passion en feu / Nar al-chawk (Mohamed Selmane, 1971, Lebanon)

Passions / Bab el-maqam (Mohamed Malas, 2005, Syria)

Path of Darkness, The / La voie des ténèbres / Tariq al-dalam (Abdel Karem al-Saraj, 1970, Iraq)

Path of Dreams, The / Chemin des rêves / Rariq al-ahlam (Harry Sarkassian, 1973, Lebanon)

Path of Evil, The / La voie du mal / Trik al-char (Sami al-Jader, 1967, Iraq)

Path of Love, The / La voie de l'amour / Darb al-Hob (Borhan al-Din Jassem, 1966, Iraq)

Pearl Necklace, The / Le collier de perles / Akd al-loulou (Youssef Maalouf, 1964, Lebanon)

Perfect Day, A / Un jour parfait / Yawm akhar (Joana Hadjithomas and Khalil Joreige, 2005, Lebanon)

Personal Inquiry / Enquête personnelle (Ula Tabari)

Petites guerres / Little Wars / Houroub saghira (Maroun Bagdadi, 1982, Lebanon)

Planet of the Desert Princess, The / Kawkab, princesse du désert / Kawkab amirat as-sahra (Ali al-Ariss, 1946, Lebanon)

Pomegranates and Myrrh / La grenade et la myrrhe / Al-Mor wa al-rumman (Najwa Najjar, 2008, Lebanon)

Postman, The / Le facteur / Saii al-barid (Samir al-Ghoussayni, 1973, Lebanon)

Pour femmes seulement / For Women Only / Lil nisa'a fakat (Antoine Remy, 1966, Lebanon)

Pour la patrie / For the Homeland / Min ajl al-watan (Fawzi al-Janabi, 1962, Iraq)

Pour qui chante l'amour / For Whoever Sings of Love / Liman youghanni al-hub (Wiam al-Saidi, 1991, Lebanon)

Pour qui se lève le soleil / For Whom the Sun Rises / Liman tachrok al-chams (Joseph Fahdi, 1958, Lebanon)

Pour toi ô Palestine / For You, Oh Palestine / Fidaki ya Phalestine (Antoine Remy, 1969, Lebanon)

Praise for Love / Louange pour l'amour / Ya salam al-hub (Mohamed Selmane, 1963, Lebanon)

Princess and the River, The / La princesse et le fleuve / al-Amira wal-Nahr (Fayçal al-Yassiri, 1982, Iraq) (animated feature)

Professor Ayoub / Le professeur Ayoub / al-Oustaz Ayoub (Mohamed Selmane, 1975, Lebanon)

Progressive, The / Le progressiste / al-Sayyid al-taqaddumi (Nabil al-Maleh, 1974, Syria)

Projet de mariage / Wedding Proposal / Mashro zawadj (Kameran Hassani, 1962, Iraq)

Prostitutes of the Al Aram Avenue, The / Les prostituées de l'avenue Al Aram (Nagdi Hafez, 1973, Syria)

Public Relations / Relations Publiques / Alaqat ammah (Samir Zikra, 2005, Syria)

Quand Maryam s'est dévoilée / When Maryam Spoke Out / Lamma hikyit Maryam (Assad Fouladkar, 2001, Lebanon)

Quatre filles / Four Girls (Hassan al-Halibi, 2008, Bahrain)

Queen of Love, The / La reine de l'amour / Malikat al-hob (Romeo Lahoud, 1972, Lebanon)

Quelque chose brûle / Something Is Burning / Shay'ma yahtariq (Ghassan Shmeit, 1993, Syria).

Qui est responsable? / Who Is Responsible? / Man al-mas'oul? (Abdl Jaber Wali, 1956, Iraq)

Qui éteint le feu? / Who Puts Out the Fire? / Man youtfii al-nar (Mohamed Selmane, 1982, Lebanon)

Quiet City, The / La ville tranquille (Hassan Ridha, 1972, Syria)

Racines / Roots / al-Judhur (Samir Nimr, 1984, Palestine) (documentary)

Rana's Wedding / Le mariage de Rana / Urs Rana (Hany Abu Assad, 2002, Palestine)

*Sabiha la séductrice du désert / Sabiha, Seduc-
tress of the Desert* (Mohamed Solfan, 1975,
Syria)

Sables d'or / Golden Sands / Rimal min thaheb
(Youssef Chahine, 1967, Lebanon)

Sacrifices / Sanduq al-dunia (Oussama Mohamed, 2001, Syria)

Safar Barlek / Safar Barlek (Henri Barakat,
1967, Lebanon)

*Sahara Is Not for Sale, The / Le Sahara n'est
pas à vendre* (Jocelyne Saab, 1977, Lebanon) (documentary)

Saïd Effendi (Kameran Hassani, 1956, Iraq)

*Salam After Death / Salam après la mort /
Salam baad al-mawt* (Georges Chamchoum, 1971, Lebanon)

*Salam après la mort / Salam After Death /
Salam baad al-mawt* (Georges Chamchoum, 1971, Lebanon)

*Salt of This Sea / Le sel de la mer / Milh hadha
al-bahr* (Annemarie Jacir, 2008, Palestine)

*Satan's Game / Le jeu de Satan / Laabart ash-
shaytan* (Zuhayr al-Shawwa, 1966, Syria)

Screens of Sand / Écrans de sable (Randa
Chahal-Sabbag, 1991, Lebanon)

Searchers, The / Les chercheurs / al-Bahithun
(Mohamed Youssef al-Janabi, 1978, Iraq)

*Season of Love / La saison de l'amour /
Mawsim hubb* (Rashid Masharawi, 2001,
Palestine)

*Seductress and the Adventurer, The / La
séductrice et l'aventurier / al-Fatinawal
moughamer* (Samir al-Ghoussayni, 1985,
Lebanon)

*Seller of Rings, The / Le vendeur de bagues /
Biya al-khawatim* (Youssef Chahine, 1965,
Lebanon)

Sense of Need / L'épreuve du besoin (Shadi
Srour, 2004, Palestine)

*Session Is Over, The / La séance est levée / Wa
roufiat al-Jalsa* (Georges Ghayad, 1986,
Lebanon)

*Seven O'clock Train, The / Le train de sept
heures / Qitar al-saa sabaa* (Hikmet Labib,
1963, Iraq)

*Shadow of Absence / L'ombre de l'absence /
Dhil al-gheyab* (Nasri Hajjaj, 2008, Palestine) (documentary)

*Shadows of Silence / Les ombres du silence /
Dhalal al-samt* (Abdullah al-Moheissen,
2006, Saudi Arabia)

Shadows of the City, The / L'ombre de la ville
(Jean Chamoun, 2000, Lebanon)

*Shadows on the Other Bank / Des ombres sur
l'autre rive / Dilâl alâ al-jânibi al-âkhar*
(Ghalib Shaath, 1973, Palestine)

Shame / La honte / al-'Ar (Bilal al-Sabouni,
Bashir Safia, and Wadeih Yousef, 1974,
Syria)

*Shame, Restoum / La honte, Restoum / Ayb ya
Restoum* (Wiam al-Saidi, 1987, Lebanon)

*She-Cats of Hamra Street, The / Les chattes
de la rue Hamra / Kotat charé al-Hamra*
(Samir al-Ghoussayni, 1972, Lebanon)

Shelter, The / L'abri / al-Malja' (Rafic Hajjar,
1980, Lebanon)

Shrews, The / Chipies / Banat akker zamane
(Rida Myassar, 1972, Lebanon)

Silence, The / Le silence / al-Samt (Hashim
Muhammad, 1979, Kuwait)

Silent Traveller, A / Un voyageur silencieux
(Ibrahim Salman, 1992, Iraq)

*Since You Left / Depuis que tu n'es plus là /
Min youm ma ruhat* (Mohamed Bakri,
2006, Palestine) (documentary)

Siren, The / La sirène / Arouss al-bahr (Samir
al-Ghoussayni, 1984, Lebanon)

Slingshot Hip Hop (Jacqueline Salloum, 2008,
Palestine) (documentary)

Smell of Apples, The / Le parfum des pommes
(Ravin Asaf, 2008, Iraq)

*Smiling through the Tears / Le sourire à travers
les larmes / Basima bayna al-dumû* (Wadeih Yousef, 1985, Syria)

Sniper, The / Le canardeur / al-Qannes (Fayçal
al-Yassiri, 1980, Iraq)

Soif / Thirst / Atash (Tawfik Abu Wael, 2004,
Palestine)

*Something Is Burning / Quelque chose brûle /
Shay'ma yahtariq* (Ghassan Shmeit, 1993,
Syria).

Son of Babylon / Fils de Babylone / Ibn Babil
(Mohamed al-Daradji, 2009, Iraq)

*Son of the East / Le fils de l'Orient / Ibn al-
Chark* (Niazi Mostafa, 1945, Iraq)

Tiswahen (Hussen al-Samaraï, 1956, Iraq)

Today / Aujourd'hui (Akram Zaatari, 2003, Lebanon) (documentary)

Toi, ma vie / You Are My Life / Anta omri (Georges Kahi, 1964, Lebanon)

Tomber de la terre / Falling from Earth / Wa-ala el-ard el-sama'a (Chadi Zeneddine, 2007, Lebanon)

Tornado, The / Le tourbillon / al-I'sar (Samir Habchi, 1992, Lebanon)

Toutes mes mères / All My Mothers / Hamey-e madrana-e man (Ebrahim Saeedi and Zahavi Sanjavi, 2009, Iraq) (documentary)

Towards the Unknown / Vers l'inconnu / Ila ayn (Georges Nasser, 1958, Lebanon)

Tramps, The / Les vagabonds / al-Charidan (Rida Myassar, 1966, Lebanon)

Trap, The / Le piège / al-Masyada (Wadeih Yousef, 1979, Syria)

Trois Opérations en Palestine / Three Operations in Palestine / Thalath amaliyyatdâkhil Filistin (Mohamed Salah and Abderrahman al-Khayali, 1969, Syria)

Turning, The / Le tournant / al-Mun'ataf (Jaf'ar Ali, 1974, Iraq)

Two Friends, The / Les deux amis (Hassan al-Saïfi, 1970, Syria),

Two Hearts, One Body / Deux cœurs, un corps (Georges Kahi, 1959, Lebanon)

Two Moons and an Olive Tree / Deux lunes et un olivier / Qamarn wa zayrunah (Abdellatif Abdelhamid, 2001, Syria).

Un amour tout particulier / A Very Particular Love / Gharâmiât khasa jidan (Fayçal al-Yassiri, 1974, Iraq)

Un autre jour / Another Day / Yawm akhar (Sahib Haddad, 1978, Iraq)

Un conte de Bahrain / Bahraini Tale / Hekaya Bahrainiya (Bassam al-Thawadi, 2008, Bahrain)

Un homme convenable / A Useful Man (Helmi Rafla, 1970, Syria)

Un homme perdu / A Lost Man (Danielle Arbid, 2007, Lebanon)

Un jour nouveau dans le vieux Sana'a / A New Day in Old Sana'a (Bader Ben Hirsi, 2005, Yemen)

Un jour parfait / A Perfect Day / Yawm akhar (Joana Hadjithomas and Khalil Joreige, 2005, Lebanon)

Un jour pluvieux / On a Rainy Day / Fi yawmin mumtir (Mohamed Shahin, 1984, Syria)

Un mariage forcé / A Forced Marriage (Rida Myassar, 1973, Syria)

Un meutre pas à pas / A Murder Step by Step / Qatlun . . . an tariq al-tasalsul (Mohamed Shahin, 1982, Syria)

Un pays, les plaies, un déplacement / A Country above Wounds / Watan fawq al-jirah (Soubhi Seifeddine, 1983, Lebanon)

Un peu de force / The House / Chaï min al-quwwah (Karlo Hartyon, 1988, Iraq)

Un rossignol du Liban / A Nightingale in Lebanon / Boulbol min Loubnan (Rida Myassar, 1982, Lebanon)

Un ticket pour Jérusalem / A Ticket to Jerusalem / Tathkararaton ila al-Quds (Rashid Masharawi, 2002, Palestine)

Un voyageur silencieux / A Silent Traveller (Ibrahim Salman, 1992, Iraq).

Uncle Vania and Co.'s Circus / Le cirque de l'oncle Vania et cie / Cirque al-ame Vania wa chourakah (Samir al-Ghoussayni, 1991, Lebanon)

Under the Bombs / Sous les bombes / Taht el-qasef (Philippe Aractingi, 2007, Lebanon)

Under the Ceiling / Sous le toit / Tahta al-safr (Nidal al-Dibs, 2005, Syria)

Under the Skies of Damascus / Sous le ciel de Damas / Tahta sama' Dimask (Ismaïl Anzur, 1931, Syria)

Underexposure / Sous-exposition / Ghair salih (Oday Rasheed, 2004, Iraq)

Une autre facette de l'amour / Another Facet of Love / Wahj akhar lil-hob (Mohamed Shahin, 1972, Syria)

Une bédouine à Paris / A Bedouin Girl in Paris / Badawia fi Baris (Mohamed Selmane, 1964, Lebanon)

Une bédouine à Rome / A Bedouin Girl in Rome / Badawia fi Roma (Mohamed Selmane, 1965, Lebanon)

Une belle et des géants / A Beauty and Some Giants / Hassnaa wa amalika (Samir al-Ghoussayni, 1980, Lebanon)

Warda (Tahya Faïq, 1956, Iraq)

Watchman's Daughter, The / La fille du gardien / Bint al-hares (Henri Barakat, 1968, Lebanon)

Waves / Vagues / Amwage (Mohamed Selmane, 1970, Lebanon)

We Are All Freedom Fighters / Nous sommes tous des fédayins / Koullouna fidaiyyoun (Gary Garabedian, 1969, Lebanon)

We Shall Return One Day / Nous retournerons un jour (Samir Abdallah and Walid Charara, 1998, Lebanon) (documentary)

Wedding in Galilee / Noce en Galilée / Urs al-jalil (Michel Khleifi, 1987, Palestine)

Wedding in Ramallah, A / Farah fi Ramallah (Shirin Salameh, 2000, Palestine) (documentary)

Wedding of Zein, The / Les noces de Zein / Urs al-Zayn (Khalid al-Siddick, 1976, Kuwait)

Wedding Proposal / Projet de mariage / Mashro zawadj (Kameran Hassani, 1962, Iraq)

Welcome to Love / Bienvenue à l'amour (Mohamed Selmane, 1968, Lebanon)

West Beyrouth / Beyrouth al-gharbiya (Ziad Doueiri, 1998, Lebanon)

Wet Nurse, The / La nourrice / al-Marda'a (Ali Nasser, 1993, Palestine)

Wheedler, The / L'enjôleuse / al-Daloua (Mohamed Selmane, 1966, Lebanon)

When Maryam Spoke Out / Quand Maryam s'est dévoilée / Lamma hikyit Maryam (Assad Fouladkar, 2001, Lebanon)

When the People Spoke / Lorsque le peuple a parlé / Indama rtakalam al-sha'ab (Amer al-Zuhair, 2007, Kuwait) (documentary)

White Poison, The / Le poison blanc / al-Sam al-abiad (Georges Kahi, 1961, Lebanon)

Who Is Responsible? / Qui est responsable? / Man al-mas'oul? (Abdl Jaber Wali, 1956, Iraq)

Who Puts Out the Fire? / Qui éteint le feu? / Man youtfii al-nar (Mohamed Selmane, 1982, Lebanon)

Will of the People, The / La volonté du peuple / Iradat al-chab (Borhan al-Din Jassem, 1959, Iraq)

Winter Women / Femmes d'hiver / Nisa'a lil chitaa (Samir al-Ghoussayni, 1974, Lebanon)

Wolves Do Not Eat Raw Meat / Les loups ne mangent pas la chair fraîche / Ziab la taakol al-lahm (Samir Khoury, 1972, Lebanon)

Woman Alone, A / Une femme seule (Nagdi Hafez, 1971, Syria)

Woman Thief, The / La voleuse / al-Sarika (Youssef Charafeddine, 1991, Lebanon)

Woman with a Monster, A / Une femme chez un monstre / Imraa fi bayt imlak (Zinardi Habis, 1983, Lebanon)

Women Naked without Sin / Femmes nues sans péché (Koshav, 1967, Syria)

Women's Intrigue / La manigance des femmes / Loubat al-nisaa (Samir al-Ghoussayni, 1982, Lebanon)

Women's Tailor / Tailleur pour les dames (Atef Salem, 1969, Syria),

Words of Love / Des mots de l'amour / Kalam fi hub (Mohamed Selmane and Sayed Tantawi, 1973, Lebanon)

World in the Year 2000, The / Le monde en l'an 2000 (Ahmed Fouad, 1972, Syria).

Wounded Ballerina, The / La ballerine blessée / Râqisa alâ al-firâh (Mohamed Shahin, 1973, Syria)

Writers on the Borders, a Journey to Palestine / Écrivains des frontières (Samir Abdalah and Jose Reynes, 2004, Palestine) (documentary)

Wrong Way, The / Direction opposée / al-Ittijâh al-mu'âkis (Marwan Haddad, 1975, Syria)

Yasmin / Jasmine (Nizar Hassan, 1998, Palestine)

Years / Des années / Sinine (Georges Kahi, 1962, Lebanon)

You Are My Life / Toi, ma vie / Anta omri (Georges Kahi, 1964, Lebanon)

Youth and Beauty / La jeunesse et la beauté / al-Siba wal jamal (Mohamed Selmane, 1965, Lebanon)

Youth in the Sun / Jeunesse au soleil / Chabab tahtal cham (Samir Nasi, 1966, Lebanon)

BIBLIOGRAPHY

GENERAL STUDIES OF ARAB MIDDLE EASTERN CINEMAS

Abdel-Malek, Kamal. *The Rhetoric of Violence: Arab-Jewish Encounters in Contemporary Palestinian Literature and Film.* New York: Palgrave Macmillan, 2005.

Al-Mafraji, Ahmed Fayadh. *The Cinema in Iraq.* Baghdad: Research and Studies Centre, General Establishment for Cinema and Theatre, Ministry of Culture and Information, n.d. [1978?].

Arab Cinema and Culture (three roundtable conferences). Beirut: Arab Film and Television Centre, 1962, 1963, 1964.

Arasoughli, Alia, ed. *Screens of Life: Critical Film Writing from the Arab World.* Quebec: World Heritage Press, 1998.

Armes, Roy. "Cinema." In *The Oxford Encyclopedia of the Modern Islamic World,* ed. John Esposito, pp. 286–290. New York: Oxford University Press, 1995.

———. *Third World Filmmaking and the West.* Berkeley: University of California Press, 1987.

Baghdadi, Maroun. *Hors la vie* (script). Paris: L'Avant-scène Cinéma, 1994.

Beaugé, Gilbert, and Jean-François Clément, eds. *L'image dans le monde arabe.* Paris: CNRS Éditions, 1995.

Berrah, Mouny, Jacques Lévy, and Claude-Michel Cluny, eds. *Les cinémas arabes.* Paris: CinémAction 43 / Cerf / Institut du Monde Arabe, 1987.

Cluny, Claude Michel. *Dictionnaire des nouveaux cinémas arabes.* Paris: Sindbad, 1978.

Dabashi, Hamid, ed. *Dreams of a Nation: On Palestinian Cinema.* London: Verso, 2006.

De Arabische Film. Amsterdam: Cinemathema, 1979.

Di Giorgi, Sergio, and Joan Rundo. *Una Terra promessa dal cinema: Appunti sul nuovo cinema palestinese.* Palermo: Edizioni della Battaglia and La Luna nel Pozzo, 1998.

Di Martino, Anna. "The Representation of Woman in Contemporary Arab Cinema." In *Il cinema dei paesi arabi,* Quarta edizione / Arab Film Festival. 4th ed., pp. 80–87. Naples: Fondazione Labatorio Mediterraneo, 1997.

Farid, Samir. *Arab Film Guide.* Cairo: Samir Farid, 1979.

Gertz, Nurith, and George Khleifi. *Palestinian Cinema: Landscape, Trauma and Memory.* Edinburgh: Edinburgh University Press, 2008.

Ghazoul, Ferial J., ed. *Arab Cinematics: Toward the New and the Alternative.* Cairo: American University in Cairo / *Alif* 15, 1995.

Hennebelle, Guy, and Janine Euvrard, eds. *Israel Palestine: Que peut le cinéma?* Paris: Société Africaine d'Édition / *L'Afrique Littéraire et Artistique* 47, 1978.

Hennebelle, Guy, and Khémais Khayati, eds. *La Palestine et le cinéma.* Paris: E.100, 1977.

Hillauer, Rebecca. *Freiräume--Lebensträume, Arabische Filmemacherinnen.* Unkel am Rhein: Arte-Édition, 2001. English translation: *Encyclopedia of Arab Women Filmmakers.* Cairo: American University in Cairo Press, 2005.

Kennedy-Day, Kiki. "Cinema in Lebanon, Syria, Iraq and Kuwait." In *Companion Encyclopedia of Middle Eastern and North African Film,* ed. Oliver Leaman, pp. 364–419. London: Routledge, 2001.

Khatib, Lina. *Filming the Modern Middle East: Politics in the Cinemas of Hollywood and the Arab World.* London: I. B. Tauris, 2006.

———. *Lebanese Cinema: Imagining the Civil War and Beyond.* London: I. B. Tauris, 2008.

Khayati, Khémais. *Cinémas arabes, topographie d'une image éclatée.* Paris: Éditions L'Harmattan, 1996.

Khelil, Hédi. *Résistances et utopies, essais sur le cinéma arabe et africain.* Tunis: Édition Sahar, 1994.

Khleifi, Michel. *Noce en Galilée* (script). Paris: L'Avant-scène Cinéma, 1988.

Landau, Jacob M. *Studies in the Arab Theater*

and Cinema. Philadelphia: University of Pennsylvania Press, 1958. French translation: *Études sur le théâtre et le cinéma arabes.* Paris: G. P. Maisonneuve et Larose, 1965.

Léon, Marys, and Magda Wassef, eds. "L'image de la femme dans le cinéma arabe." Paris: *CinémArabe* no. 10–11 (1978): 55–73.

Malkmus, Lizbeth, and Roy Armes. *Arab and African Film Making.* London: Zed Books, 1991.

Mandelbaum, Jacques. "Au Moyen-Orient, tous les cinéastes sont des Palestiniens." In *Au sud du cinéma,* ed. Jean-Michel Frodon, pp. 60–73. Paris: Cahiers du Cinéma / ARTE Éditions, 2004.

Millet, Raphaël. *Cinémas de la Méditerranée: Cinémas de la mélancholie.* Paris: Éditions L'Harmattan, 2002.

Morini, Andrea, Erfan Rashid, Anna Di Morini, and Adriano Aprà. *Il cinema dei paesi arabi.* Venice: Marsilio Editori, 1993.

Naficy, Hamid. *An Accented Cinema: Exilic and Diasporic Filmmaking.* Princeton, N.J.: Princeton University Press, 2001.

———, ed. *Home, Exile, Homeland: Film, Media, and the Politics of Place.* New York: Routledge, 1999.

Naji, Andel Sattar. "Le cinéma et la télévision dans les pays du Golfe, réalités et ambitions." In *Cinquième Biennale des cinémas arabes à Paris,* pp. 100–107. Paris: Institut du Monde Arabe, 2000.

Nouri, Shakir. *À la recherche du cinéma irakien, 1945–1985.* Paris: Éditions L'Harmattan, 1986.

Sadoul, Georges, ed. *The Cinema in the Arab Countries.* Beirut: Interarab Centre for Cinema and Television, 1966. French translation: *Les cinémas des pays arabes.* Beyrouth: Centre Interarabe du Cinéma et de la Télévision, 1966.

Sakr, Naomi, ed. *Women and Media in the Middle East: Power through Self-Expression.* London: I. B. Tauris, 2004.

Salti, Rasha, ed. *Insights into Syrian Cinema: Essays and Conversations with Contemporary Filmmakers.* New York: Rattapallax Press / Arte East, 2006.

Shafik, Viola. *Der arabische Film: Geschichte und kulturelle Identität.* Bielefeld: Aisthesis Verlag, 1996. English translation: *Arab Cinema: History and Cultural Identity.* Cairo: American University in Cairo Press, 1998.

Thorval, Yves. *Les écrans du croissant fertile.* Paris: Atlantica / Séguier, 2002.

Tryster, Hillel. *Israel Before Israel: Silent Film in the Holy Land.* Jerusalem: Steven Spielberg Jewish Film Archive, 1995.

Zaccak, Hady. *Le cinéma libanais, itinéraire d'un cinéma vers l'inconnu (1929–1996).* Beirut: Dar el-Machreq, 1997.

FILM REVIEWS, CATALOGUES, ETC.

Adhoua: lumières du cinéma. Palaiseau, 1980–1981, four issues.

Arab Film Festival. Los Angeles, annually from 1997.

Biennale des cinémas arabes. Paris: Institut du Monde Arabe, 1992, 1994, 1996, 1998, 2000, 2002, 2004, 2006.

CinémArabe. Paris, 1976–1979, 12 issues.

Damascus International Film Festival. Damascus, biennially from 1979.

Deuxième festival du film arabe. Paris: L'Association pour le film arabe, 1984.

Dubai International Film Festival. UAE, from 2004.

Emirates Film Competition. UAE, annually from 2001.

Festival: Images du monde arabe. Paris: Institut du Monde Arabe, 1993.

Festival du film arabe: jeunesse du cinéma arabe. Paris: L'Association pour le film arabe, 1983.

Il cinema dei paesi arabi, Quarta edizione / *Arab Film Festival,* 4th ed. Naples: Fondazione Labatorio Mediterraneo, 1997.

Images Nord-Sud. Paris: Éditions ATM, from 1988, 76 issues.

International Film Guide. London, annually 1964–2006, 2008.

Journées cinématographiques de Carthage. Tunis, biennially from 1966.

La semaine du cinéma arabe. Paris: Institut du Monde Arabe, 1987.

London Palestine Film Festival. London: Palestine Film Foundation, 2005, 2006, 2008.

Middle East International Film Festival. Abu Dhabi, annually from 2007.

Troisième festival du film arabe. Paris: L'Association pour le film arabe, 1985.

HISTORICAL BACKGROUND: SELECT BIBLIOGRAPHY

Ajami, Fouad. *The Arab Predicament: Arab Political Thought and Practice Since 1967.* Cambridge: Cambridge University Press, 1982.
———. *The Dream Palace of the Arabs: A Generation's Odyssey.* New York: Pantheon Books, 1998.
Al-Rasheed, Madawi. *A History of Saudi Arabia.* Cambridge: Cambridge University Press, 2002.
Alsharekh, Alanoud, ed. *The Gulf Family: Kinship, Politics and Modernity.* London: Saqi Books and SOAS, 2000.
Alsharekh, Alanoud, and Robert Springborg, eds. *Popular Culture and Political Identity in the Arab Gulf States.* London: Saqi and Middle East Institute SOAS, 2008.
Anderson, Benedict. *Imagined Communities: Reflections on the Origin and Spread of Nationalism,* 2nd ed. London: Verso, 1991.
Ashcar, Gilbert, and Michael Warschawski. *The 33-Day War: Israel's War on Hezbollah in Lebanon and Its Aftermath.* London: Saqi, 2007.
Dresh, Paul. *A History of Modern Yemen.* Cambridge: Cambridge University Press, 2000.
Finkelstein, Norman G. *Image and Reality of the Israel-Palestine Conflict,* 2nd ed. London: Verso, 2003.
Fisk, Robert. *Pity the Nation: Lebanon at War.* Oxford: Oxford University Press, 2001.
Goldberg, David J. *To the Promised Land: A History of Zionist Thought.* Harmondsworth, England: Penguin Book, 1996.
Gregg, Gary S. *The Middle East: A Cultural Psychology.* Oxford: Oxford University Press, 2005.
Halliday, Fred. *100 Myths about the Middle East.* London: Saqi, 2005.
———. *Arabia without Sultans.* Harmondsworth, England: Penguin Books, 1974.
———. *Islam and the Myth of Confrontation.* London: I. B. Tauris, 2003 [1996].
Hiro, Dilip. *Iraq: A Report from the Inside.* London: Granta Publications, 2003.
Hopwood, Derek. *Syria 1945–1986: Politics and Society.* London: Routledge, 1989.
Hourani, Albert, Philip S. Khoury, and Mary C. Wilson, eds. *The Modern Middle East.* London: I. B. Tauris, 1993.
Karmi, Ghada. *Married to Another Man: Israel's Dilemma in Palestine.* London: Pluto Press, 2007.

Lewis, Bernard. *The Multiple Identities of the Middle East.* London: Weidenfeld and Nicolson, 1998.
Lockman, Zachary, and Joel Beinin, eds. *Intifada: The Palestinan Uprising against Israeli Occupation.* London: I. B. Tauris, 1990.
Mackey, Sandra. *Mirror of the Arab World: Lebanon in Conflict.* New York: W. W. Norton, 2008.
Mackintosh-Smith, Tim. *Yemen: Travels in Dictionary Land.* London: John Murray, 1997.
Mansfield, Peter. *The Arabs.* Harmondsworth, England: Penguin Books, 1980.
———. *A History of the Middle East,* 2nd ed. Harmondsworth, England: Penguin Books, 2003.
Marr, Phebe. *A Modern History of Iraq.* Boulder, Colo.: Westview Press, 2004.
McCarthy, Justin. *The Ottoman Peoples and the End of Empire.* London: Arnold, 2001.
Morris, Benny. *1948: The First Arab-Israeli War.* New Haven, Conn.: Yale University Press, 2008.
———. *One State, Two States.* New Haven, Conn.: Yale University Press, 2009.
Nasr, Vali. *The Shia Revival.* New York: W. W. Norton, 2006.
Owen, Roger. *State, Power and Politics in the Making of the Modern Middle East.* London: Routledge, 1992.
Pappe, Ilan. *A History of Modern Palestine: One Land Two Peoples.* Cambridge: Cambridge University Press, 2006.
Polk, William R. *Understanding Iraq.* London: I. B. Tauris, 2006.
Pryce-Jones, David. *The Closed Circle: An Interpretation of the Arabs.* London: Paladin, 1990.
Robins, Philip. *A History of Jordan.* Cambridge: Cambridge University Press, 2004.
Roded, Ruth, ed. *Women in Islam and the Middle East: A Reader.* London: I. B. Tauris, 1999.
Ross, Stewart. *The Middle East Since 1945.* London: Hodder Education, 2006.
Roy, Olivier. *The Politics of Chaos in the Middle East.* London: Hurst and Co., 2007.
Rubin, Barry. *The Tragedy of the Middle East.* Cambridge: Cambridge University Press, 2002.
———. *The Truth about Syria.* New York: Palgrave Macmillan, 2007.
Sa'di, Ahmad H., and Lila Abu-Lughod, eds. *Nakba: Palestine, 1948, and the Claims of Memory.* New York: Columbia University Press, 2007.

Said, Edward. *From Oslo to Iraq and the Roadmap.*
  London: Bloomsbury, 2004.
———. *The Question of Palestine.* London:
  Routledge and Kegan Paul, 1980.
———. *Reflections on Exile.* London: Granta
  Books, 2001.
Seale, Patrick. *Asad: The Struggle for Power in the
  Middle East.* London: I. B. Tauris, 1988.
Shepherd, Naomi. *Ploughing Sand: British Rule
  in Palestine 1917–1948.* New Brunswick, N.J.:
  Rutgers University Press, 2000.

Shindler, Colin. *A History of Modern Israel.*
  Cambridge: Cambridge University Press, 2008.
Shlaim, Avi. *The Iron Wall: Israel and the Arab
  World.* London: Penguin Books, 2000.
———. *Palestine and Israel.* London: Verso, 2009.
Tripp, Charles. *A History of Iraq.* Cambridge:
  Cambridge University Press, 2007.
Whitaker, Bryan. *What's Really Wrong with the
  Middle East.* London: Saqi, 2009.
Wynbrandt, James. *A Brief History of Saudi
  Arabia.* New York: Facts on File, 2004.

ROY ARMES is Professor Emeritus of Film at Middlesex University. He has published widely on world cinema for the past 40 or so years, and this is his twentieth book. His most recent publications are *Postcolonial Images: Studies in North African Film* (2005), *African Filmmaking: North and South of the Sahara* (2006), and *Dictionary of African Filmmakers* (2008), all published by Indiana University Press.